Praise for *A*

'*All Rise* is fascinating on many levels. Moseneke's industry and energy in producing it are welcome. The book makes a serious and positive contribution to South Africans' knowledge and insight into many interesting issues. *All Rise* shines an important light on key aspects of governance in South Africa in the first decades of the existence of the Constitutional Court. And the shining of that light is a marker, as Justice Moseneke would have it, of the hygiene of South Africa's democratic project.'
– ANTON KATZ, *Daily Maverick*

'As a member of the team that drafted the interim Constitution, Moseneke's insights into the Constitutional Court's structure, the values it embodies and the cases that were brought to it make for fascinating reading.'
– ORIELLE BERRY, *Cape Argus*

'*All Rise* is as much about Moseneke's 15-year judicial career as it is a biography of South Africa's post-apartheid jurisprudence and a civic education manual on how the judiciary, particularly the Constitutional Court, works. It also casts a spotlight on the laborious process of judging and the rancour that accompany the role, especially in an era chaperoned by a self-serving political elite whose misdeeds threaten the very survival of the democratic project.'
– MUKONI RATSHITANGA, *Citizen*

'Moseneke writes thoughtfully, with flashes of humour and vivid characterisation. As a result, these memories spring from the page and engage the reader in the challenges of legal reasoning, giving telling insights into the birth pangs of the new South Africa.'
– PATRICIA MCCRACKEN, *Farmer's Weekly*

All Rise

A Judicial Memoir

Dikgang Moseneke

PICADOR AFRICA

First published in 2020 by Picador Africa

This edition published in 2021 by Picador Africa
an imprint of Pan Macmillan South Africa
Private Bag x19, Northlands
Johannesburg, 2116

www.panmacmillan.co.za

ISBN 978 1 77010 733 5
EBOOK ISBN 978 1 77010 734 2

© 2020, 2021 Dikgang Moseneke

All rights reserved. No part of this publication may be reproduced, stored in or introduced into a retrieval system, or transmitted, in any form, or by any means (electronic, mechanical, photocopying, recording or otherwise), without the prior written permission of the publisher. Any person who does any unauthorised act in relation to this publication may be liable to criminal prosecution and civil claims for damages.

While every effort has been made to ensure the accuracy of the details, facts, names and places mentioned, as an autobiography this book is partly based on memory. The publisher and author welcome feedback, comments and/or corrections that could further enrich the book.

Editing by Alison Lowry
Proofreading by Russell Martin
Indexing by Christopher Merrett
Design and typesetting by Triple M Design, Johannesburg
Cover design by publicide
Cover photograph by Gallo Images/The Times/Daniel Born

Printed and bound by Bidvest Data, Capet Town.

*This judicial memoir would not have been possible
if I had not been privileged by my country to serve
its people as a servant of the public.
Perforce, I dedicate this memoir to all the people of our land and
of Africa who deserve respect, freedom and social justice, absent which, I
pray, they will know and will revolt so that they All Rise.*

Contents

FOREWORD BY EDWIN CAMERON ix
PROLOGUE xiii

EARLY CAREER
1 Choosing law 3
2 The right to robe 9
3 Detour to the bench 17
4 A permanent appointment 29
5 A formidable workload 34
6 Free and fair 45
7 Constitutional Court: Genesis and nomination 55

CHASKALSON COURT
8 Who will guard the guardians? 61
9 The class of '95 69
10 Reporting for duty 77
11 New ways of doing things 83
12 A clean slate 91
13 Judicial architecture reformed 103
14 A common purpose 116
15 Tenure and intellectual bonding 126

LANGA COURT
16 Second-generation leaders 137
17 Clouds gathering, storm brewing 141
18 The Hlophe matter 151
19 Jurisprudence – a full repertoire 180
20 'You see, Sboshwa ...' 194

NGCOBO COURT
21 A new political elite 203

MOGOENG COURT
22 Banishing the elephant 219
23 Harmony and turbulence 229
24 Challenging the courts 240
25 Jurisprudence amid executive hostilities 251
26 Final sitting 266

AFTER THE CONSTITUTIONAL COURT
27 The Life Esidimeni Commission of Inquiry 273
28 'Retirement' 285

ACKNOWLEDGEMENTS 297
APPENDIX: FAREWELL ADDRESS 299
NOTES 307
INDEX 349

Foreword

When Dikgang Moseneke served out the last day of his fifteen-year term limit as a justice of the Constitutional Court in 2016, a momentous period – perhaps, even, an epoch – had come to an end.

One of the last significant links to the Chaskalson Court, those eleven first justices President Nelson Mandela appointed in 1994, had been lost. The court felt shaken, a little uncertain, like a family losing a wise, generous big brother.

I was privileged to share the court's bench with Dikgang for nearly eight years. In combination of intellect, personality, jurisprudential force and physical presence, he was the golden heart of the court. In keenly divided decisions, when Dikgang cast his vote, you knew that the force of his reasoning and personality would often draw two or three colleagues with him. He and I differed, sometimes profoundly, occasionally fractiously. But our differences were rare. For the most part, I was honoured to be his ally, his sparring partner and, in some momentous interventions, his co-author.

Dikgang led the forces in the court who sought fair-minded development of the common law, generous-spirited application of constitutional principles, and unflinching insistence on constitutional observance by the legislature and the executive.

His illustrious presence in the court was as large and forceful as his impact outside it. His was a persistently generous, warm-hearted, forward-looking, richly-giving spirit.

In this splendid memoir, a fitting sequel to his first volume, *My Own Liberator*, Dikgang recounts in abundance the court's bloody battles, monumental achievements and sweet moments. He does so congenially, encompassingly and invitingly, taking readers on a gracious and considerate journey into South Africa's legal history, the roots of the Constitution, the mind of a judge, and the workings of the court.

There are self-knowing asides. There are light touches and, very occasionally, crests of humour; but, for the most part, Dikgang's pen exudes his life's purpose: to bring social justice, good governance, and enlightened conditions of autonomy to the people of our country.

What an extraordinary person. Imprisoned on Robben Island at fifteen by a pitiless apartheid judge, he gained his school-leaving and first law qualification while in prison. He then surmounted the rigidly tiered echelons of the legal world, facing off bigotry and winning acclaim for the sheer force of his mind, lawyerliness and personality.

His memoir shares with the reader moments of acute poignancy. In the midst of a masterly overview of the Constitutional Court's main achievements while he was part of it, Dikgang entrusts the reader with painfully personal moments – when he was passed over for the post to which his every virtue and capacity entitled him, the chief justiceship.

In a speech at the court's dazzling farewell dinner for Dikgang, I compared him to Oliver Deneys Schreiner, the great anti-apartheid appellate judge in the 1950s, whom the apartheid government passed over repeatedly for chief justice.

The similarity lies not only in the due recognition of high office that each was unjustly denied. It consists also in the force and lasting importance of their large-spirited impact on South Africa's legal heritage. In the high moral and constitutional crisis of *Collins v Minister of the Interior* in 1957, Schreiner's dissent showed that South African legal principle afforded enough, just enough, to repel some of apartheid's most shameful enactments.

Dikgang's jurisprudence helped nurture that promise into full constitutional florescence.

But there was one telling difference. When the apartheid government deliberately flooded the court with five new appointments to dilute its determined resistance to cancelling the coloured vote, Schreiner and his colleagues refused to play bowls (yes, bowls) with the new arrivals, and refrained from socialising with them.

Not Dikgang. These pages are near-unceasingly generous. They depict the intricate relationship Dikgang formed with Chief Justice Mogoeng Mogoeng, after he was passed over for the third and final time. With Mogoeng, Dikgang worked in close collaboration, association and alliance during the critical years of the Jacob Zuma presidency, as the forces of malignancy and corruption sought to thieve from us our constitutional prize and deprive our people of the rule of law and of the means it offers to a just and even society.

Dikgang's pen is not without some occasional acerbity. Memorably, but laconically, he invites Minister Jeff Radebe, who as President Zuma's minister of justice carried out much of the unseemly grubby work of his political master, to account for it. It is a call Radebe may choose to evade, but its resonance will echo in our history.

More significantly, even, Dikgang sets out in remorseless detail the most shameful episode in our democracy's judicial history: the events surrounding the visits to the court in the first half of 2008, while important litigation by Zuma was pending for decision, by Cape Judge President John Hlophe. As the clouds of fierce controversy continue to swirl around Hlophe's head, what exactly happened during those two visits has never been decisively determined. Why? Because of a dozen years of points-taking, obstruction, delays, evasions and filibustering.

Dikgang's memoir soberly gives readers the incontestable facts. He then invites the readers to make their own assessment.

This is an important and memorable book.

Written with dignity and grace, it puts on candid display a deeply complex, deeply rich, deeply integrated human being of enormous capacities:

one who continues in everything he does to point our country forward to its destination of justice under law.

EDWIN CAMERON
Inspecting Judge of Correctional Services
Chancellor: Stellenbosch University
March 2020

Prologue

My life's journey – so far, at least – has been characterised by a number of unscheduled detours, both in a personal sense and a professional and political one.

So it was that, on 16 August 2019, just over three years after I had retired as deputy chief justice of the Republic of South Africa, I made an unscheduled stopover in a small village called Mazimbu, near the town of Morogoro, in the United Republic of Tanzania.

I was in that country to present a report to the SADC heads of state on the facilitation work I had been doing on constitutional and other governance reforms in the Kingdom of Lesotho, as requested by President Cyril Ramaphosa. When I heard that the president might visit Morogoro, I impulsively asked him if I could hitch a ride, without realising that our mode of transport was to be a very small seven-seater aircraft and the journey rather turbulent; not to mention the airstrip at the other end, which was about as narrow as a goat track, and gave us a somewhat bumpy landing. But then, if I was used to anything, it was turbulence and barely discernible pathways.

My reason for hoping to cadge a lift was to undertake a pilgrimage of a kind, and emotionally layered. It presented an opportunity to see, for myself, the famous Solomon Mahlangu Freedom College in Mazimbu.

We presented ourselves at the plush, brand-new Julius Nyerere International Airport, where our pilots were two young South African Air Force colonels. They greeted us deferentially in the Setswana language.

'Mr President, are we good?' I asked nervously just before take-off. After all, we had on board the first couple of our Republic, the president being suitably chaperoned by his gentle and polite partner, Tshepo Motsepe. Also on board were a senior minister of state of Tanzania, the president's heart physician, a lady who spoke in soft, muffled tones, two aides and me.

'Yes, Dikgang, we are good,' the president smiled. 'This craft is as hardy as a beast of burden.'

If this wasn't quite enough to reassure me, I consoled myself with the thought that many people would surely have done their homework so as not to imperil the first couple. I buckled myself in.

We landed safely in Mazimbu, provoking a massive cloud of dust, which did nothing to spoil the red carpet treatment and the full protocol provided. All was superbly executed. Our return flight to Dar es Salaam was just as professional. On the descent the pilots allowed us a leisurely sweep over the beautiful azure-blue bay and we landed elegantly and perfectly on time. The president and I took pictures with the two fresh-faced pilots as a mark of our gratitude and, for me, a memento of this unanticipated short trip.

The visit to the college, named after a liberation hero who had fled South Africa after 1976, joined MK and returned to continue the struggle, only to be arrested, sentenced to death and, ultimately, hanged, brought to the surface of my mind much painful remembrance. Alongside it, however, was the jubilation of human triumph.

Morogoro is one of the primal shrines of our liberation effort. As soon as I was in Tanzania I developed an instant but deep desire to go and pay my respect to those women and men, from Tanzania and from our country, who gave up so much so that we might live. Their sacrifices should not ever have been in vain. They gave their hearts, their minds and their bodies so that young pilots might soar with us up to 13 000 metres above sea level with guts and gusto. So that I might be privileged to serve our judiciary for fifteen years, hopefully with as much guts and gusto. So that we might rescue

PROLOGUE

ourselves from the margins of a disgusting society and be brought to the centre of a just and inclusive democracy.

And so that we might be free to find our full humanity.

In 2019 our liberation project was facing life-threatening obstacles. I felt that I needed *umrhabulo*. I needed, under a traditional blanket, to inhale fresh inspiration up my nostrils.

In the liberation legend, Morogoro is remembered as the site for the historic conference of the exiled African National Congress which did so much to create cohesion in a troubled movement. The broader Tanzania is also remembered with gratitude for hosting the cadres of other liberation movements such as the Pan Africanist Congress of Azania and the Black Consciousness Movement of Azania.

In 1978, the exiled African National Congress established the college at Mazimbu as an educational institution on land of 600-odd hectares in extent donated by the Tanzanian government. Oliver Reginald Tambo was not only a steadfast leader of the liberation movement in exile but also a veteran teacher at home and abroad. He was concerned that the many young activists who had fled South Africa after the 1976 Soweto uprising and the children of cadres already in exile had to be afforded a primary and secondary education.

Not only that, but it had to be an education superior to Bantu Education and which would prepare the young cadres for the start of our democratic rule. SOMAFCO would provide both an academic and vocational education. The farmlands would supply food to the institution and the college would include a hospital. The furniture and other effects were to be made by the students. The college was built mainly with stones gathered from the nearby mountain and it was officially opened by Oliver Tambo in 1985. The collection of most impressive edifices now serves as a university campus.

Exiled cadres who had succumbed lie buried in a nearby graveyard close to a small stone-walled chapel. Each grave lies beneath a stone casing and a meticulously carved headstone on which the name of the deceased is engraved. There is no epitaph.

PROLOGUE

The pilgrimage to Morogoro was a deeply moving experience for me. It imposed on me afresh and in retrospect the difficult question of whether I had honoured our collective sacrifices of the past by playing my part in the reconstruction of our land.

Had I helped to support our collective journey from a miserable and warring past to a peaceful, inclusive, refashioned and prosperous society that is tolerant of all of us in our vast assortment?

And what of my life on the bench? Had I been a good judge?

I hope to address these questions in the pages that follow.

EARLY CAREER

CHAPTER 1

Choosing law

Did I always want to be a judge? I think not! In my earlier memoir, *My Own Liberator*, I tell the tale of how, when I was no more than five years old, I replied to a question posed by my aunt, Rrakgadi Mashikwane *(Robala ka Kagiso, Mokwena!)*, that I wanted to be a speed-cop. My aunt laughed this off – she thought it was hilarious – but added an emphatic, 'No, no, Dikgang!' My fledgling imagination must have been fired by the traffic officer who directed afternoon traffic across a tiny intersection in the small town of Bela-Bela with notable poise and authority. He would have cut an impressive figure to a small boy, this tall man in his smart uniform, with knee-high brown leather boots polished so they shone and pants that bulged sideways around the knees. Immaculate cream-white leather gloves ran up to his elbows; and beneath his peaked cap he sported a pair of wide sunglasses, behind which, I was certain, were stern, all-knowing eyes.

By the time I was in high school my sparkling mathematics and physical science grades made me hope for a career in medicine. At that time, in the early 1960s, an African medical practitioner was the near-perfect exit from the rigours of class and racial oppression. This was not to be, however. My long political captivity on Robben Island put paid to that ambition. In the Island prison there were no laboratories or operating rooms or frozen corpses to cut up and explore. So I resorted to studying law through distance tuition.

My first meeting with a judge, which took place in 1963, was less than amicable and was in fact inimical. It was in the Pretoria High Court and the judge was Judge Petrus Cillié. He sat high up behind a wooden bench, distant from the accused stand. With his full crop of flaxen hair – which would have been the envy of most judges of yesterday; judicial wigs are a poor cousin of that distinguished look – he looked the part. The severe expression preferred by judges above random smiling was set on his face. His trial courthouse was the Old Synagogue on Paul Kruger Street, which former place of worship would become famous for the many political trials that were held there.[1]

On that day in 1963, together with fellow high school students and comrades from the Pan Africanist Congress of Azania, I was indicted for a joint attempt – or, in elevated language, a conspiracy – to overthrow the apartheid regime by force. At the end of the mass trial of sixteen mainly student accused, the judge imposed direct sentences ranging from five years to life imprisonment with hard labour. He gave these sentences without batting an eyelid, then adjourned the court and, as judges do, disappeared into the rear room known as the judge's chambers.

My penalty was ten years' imprisonment.

I was fifteen years old.

That moment was perhaps the most important, even if ironic, spur towards my formation as a judge of the very same high court where I was condemned. When I was sentenced to this long term of imprisonment I had no idea that I would be favoured with a judicial career of fifteen successive years stretching from the high court to the highest court of our land, the Constitutional Court. Standing in the accused box, how could I have possibly prophesied rising to the rank of deputy chief justice of the Republic of South Africa?

Yes, my early and unkind meeting with a court of law was an unlikely incentive towards judicial office, but that was not the only, or sufficient, catalyst. If it were so, that would have made for a linear cause-and-effect story robbed of difficult and intriguing contours. The human condition rarely permits us the luxury of an easy passage. Testing journeys are our measure. As we are reminded: 'Struggle is the meaning of life; defeat or victory is in the hands of God. But struggle itself is man's duty (and – I add – woman's duty) and should be his (or her) joy.'[2]

While hard-labouring as a political prisoner on Robben Island, it would have been fanciful to think I might become a judge. But, I thought, I could possibly become a practising attorney or advocate despite my incarceration. For that to happen, I swiftly understood, I had to matriculate. I did. Next, I acquired a university bachelor's degree in English literature and political science, followed by a law degree with the school of law of the University of South Africa, an open distance university of high repute. In this way, imprisonment became a bearable and fruitful outing.

As early as first year, I could sense that the course offering was stridently Eurocentric. The starting point for an entry into the LLB – Bachelor of Laws – degree was a compulsory pass in first-year courses in Afrikaans-Nederlands, Latin and English. The neon lights went up and started flashing in my young brain. Only those skilled in the chosen foreign languages were to be admitted to law qualifications. The triple language requirement alone was a considerable barrier to entry. I suppose the barricade was deliberate and was thought to make sense. The legal system was imported and so, too, were the languages one needed to access the study of law. Nevertheless I engaged my youthful energy and passed all three languages. Then I moved on to confront the content courses.

These were derived in part from ancient Roman law edicts and in another part from annotations and other writings of Roman-Dutch law scholars in the fifteenth and sixteenth centuries.[3] Yet another part was drawn from English law in areas not already populated by Roman-Dutch law. The two main streams of European law found their way into South Africa during the different waves of colonial incursion by the Dutch and the English between 1652 and 1902 at the end of the Second Anglo-Boer War, which I prefer to call the Tweede Vryheidsoorlog.[4] The free-spirited Voortrekkers trekked from the Cape to avoid British domination and, when the British followed them into the interior, the Voortrekkers, rightly, resisted further British hegemony. But once they thought they were done with their British tormentors, the Voortrekkers chose, wrongly, to repress their generous indigenous neighbours and dispossess them of their land and cattle.

The fusion of imported law was called the South African common law. It was said to be unwritten law that was common to all inhabitants and thus was meant to run across the length and breadth of the country. It was deemed to be binding on everyone who found themselves on the fused land which from 1910 was called the Union of South Africa. I need to add that the Union stipulated that although only people of European descent would be citizens, its laws were also to bind the voteless indigenous and other powerless citizens. Thus was the common law put in place. All other laws and customs became subservient to the statutes of a sovereign parliament and the common law. The principles of the common law were to be taught in law schools and they were policed by judges. This explains why in ordinary idiom the common law was also called 'the judges' law'. It was the judges who were required to rule whether any part of the common law was good or bad law; whether it was still alive or extinct; and whether it was a legitimate target for change or development. Provided judges did not threaten or undermine laws made by parliament, they had a free hand in how to manage the common law. When the common law and a law made by parliament appeared to differ, the two had to be read harmoniously in order not to offend the resolve of the sovereign parliament.

That was how the colonial conquest cookie crumbled. In that setting, indigenous law and any other system of law counted for nothing. Perhaps the most adverse and inhumane impact of the supremacy of the common law was in family law. Marriages of black people were not regarded as marriages unless they were settled according to the marriage laws that gave effect to the common law. The law attached no value or results to otherwise valid marriages. Marriages, for example, concluded in accordance with African indigenous law, the Muslim religion or under Hindu custom, and any other customary or faith-based marriages, were invalid in the eyes of the common law. The results were devastating and degrading. Parties, and in particular women and children, were left without dignity or the legal protection that was due to married couples and their offspring. In a dispute or at the end of the relationship no enforcement through the courts was permitted. The children of these marriages were deemed illegitimate. On separation or death, the property of the parties was unregulated. In short, then, the common law caused inequality, pain, indignity and alienation.

The common law was the main stream of the law I had to master if I wanted to pass. The courses of study were smaller streams of norms intended to regulate distinct human conduct in marked areas under the coercion of the state. Other courses focused on the external relationship of the sovereign state or its subjects with other states or foreign subjects.

In theory, all domestic laws, alone or together, are intended to protect the legal interest of the individual and to pursue public good. The scheme of the rules of law is intended to achieve or restore equilibrium between and among people living in the country. The law is also supposed to preserve good governance between the state and its inhabitants by supervising that unequal relationship. In sum, the law is taught as an instrument to procure private and public well-being; to promote a just society.

But the theoretical public good, I could not help but notice as I worked through my courses, imprisoned on the Island, was trumped by the harsh reality imposed by colonial and apartheid prejudice, exclusion and repression.

The teaching of the law was catalogued into 24 courses over four years of study after a bachelor's degree. A further hurdle was the requirement that all final-year LLB courses – private law, mercantile law, constitutional law and criminal law – had to be passed together at the same year-end examination.

As an innocent bystander, the turf battles were obvious to me. The Afrikaner ruling elite, and in particular law academics and judges, urged the supremacy of Roman-Dutch law and they went to great lengths, in their literature and court judgments, to oust any leftovers of the English colonial imposition. English law was tolerated only in commercial law, where the common law was seen as inadequate.

The law schools and the courts were blind, however, to what, to me, was glaringly obvious. They never gave a thought to the fact, nor did they care, that the common law was a colonial imposition on indigenous and other people of the country. They never openly admitted that the common law was not home-bred, but the truth is, it wasn't. It was a direct result and an incident of the colonial project. Young as I was then, this historical truth did not escape me.

However, the task at hand on Robben Island was simple and so I applied my mind. I studied the law as it was presented in the study guides and I passed all the prescribed courses. My resolute and immediate task in prison was to gain good grades and pass the LLB degree. It might have been a case of get into the tent to live in order to fight another day, but first I needed to get into the tent.

CHAPTER 2

The right to robe

My term of imprisonment ended. By then I had firmed up my objectives. I would take all the steps necessary in order to practise law.

Becoming a candidate attorney required the navigation of many bumps in the road and not a few hurdles – these are described in some detail in *My Own Liberator* – but through my focused desire and the goodness of others, I achieved this first goal. I got my degree, with excellent grades. At the end of my internship, not only did I crack the attorneys' admission examinations but I did so at the top of my class. Supported by my principal, I litigated ferociously to be admitted as an attorney despite my past political conviction. I got that right too.[1]

Later I was called to the Bar. Again, I served pupillage and passed the admission examinations with flying colours. The next obstacle facing me was the racist admission practices of the Pretoria Bar. I took this on with vigour and the colour bar fell away. I became a practising and resident member of the same Bar for many years, and was even elected by its members to the governing Bar Council. I like to think that those who resisted my membership of the Bar were persuaded that I was a worthy and able member of the advocates' profession, that my racial extraction was not the measure of my pedigree. This little shift and early racial mixing of the Bar unfolded at odds with the repressive and divisive apartheid arrangements in the broader society.

Ten years later I acquired the status of senior counsel. When this happens one is issued with letters patent. This is an official document signed by the president of the country which certifies that you have become a senior counsel or, as the saying goes, you have acquired silk status. The language of silk derives from the United Kingdom where only senior barristers don silk gowns. These were the work attire of QCs – Queen's Counsel; they wore silk gowns and were known as silks. This pompous colonial artifice of silk gowns had its own sway even in the former British colonies. I confess that despite my radical anti-colonial position, as soon as I had received my letters patent I rushed off to Ede & Ravenscroft on 93 Chancery Lane in Westminster, London, to buy, at great cost, my silk gown, collar wings, studs and cufflinks. I thought I had earned the right to look the part of a silk and for some reason acquiring these outer trappings of the status gave me a self-satisfied feeling. I don't really know why; I'm not able to explain the not so unwitting attraction towards the finery of our colonisers. Did I secretly envy the swagger of their attire and the manner in which they practised law? What was it? I wonder. Thank goodness I did not have to buy a wig, which to this day many counsel in former colonies still don. Perhaps I owe gratitude to the Afrikaner legal elite for this small mercy; they had flung the wigs far away when they gained independence from the Queen of England. Their narrow nationalism also prompted them rather to call their silks SCs – Senior Counsel – instead of Queen's Counsel. Even so, the Afrikaners kept most of the legal artifices of their erstwhile oppressors.

A silk is appointed by a head of state on the advice of the Bar Council. The head of state issues letters patent, certifying the senior status and the order of precedence of the advocate concerned in the national Bar system. Before so recommending, the Bar Council needs to satisfy itself that the advocate is of 'silk material'. Silk status is intended to be rare. It is meant to convey to colleagues and the public that the advocate concerned is well versed, experienced and competent in the art and science of advocacy. The status confers seniority in the courts and in dealings with junior counsel. The cases a silk appears in or works on usually present significant legal complexity. For this reason, a silk is paid considerably more than the juniors who, traditionally, support their leader in presenting the case at hand for a set fraction of a silk's fees. Silks are expected to present their client's case in a manner which assists the court in arriving at a just decision. They are to display the highest fidelity to the law and to professional ethics because they are potential judges and often act as judges.

My letters patent were signed by President FW de Klerk before the end of official apartheid in 1994. The irony was palpable and putrid. I was a decorated officer of the court and of the law, dressed in the finest silk gown but, along with my people, I was an outcast. I had no right to vote and the law denied me equal protection and human worth.

Even so, it was not all irony and doom. My journey as an attorney and later as an advocate meant that I came in the presence of a judge again, only this time in circumstances that were a little more benign. This time I was an officer of the court and of the law. Forget the twists and turns. I had earned the right to robe and rise for others from the well of the courtroom, to do this for my clients in defence of their vital interests, which might have been in harm's way. I rose to address a judge not from the accused dock, as I had done during my trial at the Old Synagogue, but as counsel, as an advocate of the high court and of the Supreme Court of South Africa. I stood up in court as of right and not at the whim of a judge. The judge was obliged to hear me out. If he did not, that would be a gross irregularity – and a welcome ground to set the judge's decision aside on appeal and to the benefit of my client. Later in my career I would rise in the well of the Constitutional Court – by then as a silk who was held in high regard; yes, a silk in full voice and with a tenacious mastery of the craft of advocacy.

My practice at the Bar was a matter of enormous pride to me, my family and friends. This was not because the system of law under apartheid was just in any sense of the word. I was not proud because I thought I might reform the system from inside. If anything, I always sought to destroy apartheid and all its vestiges, that 'crime against humanity' masked as a place of the rule of law when it was no more than oppression by the law. Apartheid was a living example of how the law may be harnessed to entrench colonial power relations and in the process do evil; and produce poverty, inequality and injustice. For me it went beyond personal validation. I practised law to advance the struggle for freedom, equality and justice in another form. I sought to show how, as a matter of law and justice, colonialism and apartheid were irrational, selfish, inhumane and undemocratic, and bound to crumble. They were the opposite of a just society.

At a personal level, I confess to a certain smugness that I had got the better of the system of repression and exclusion. As a matter of collective agency, I knew that my small point of entry would let in a host of other champions of a new and just social order – and this did indeed happen. Immediately after me, many spirited young black lawyers and competent ones of all ages joined the Bar in Pretoria and Johannesburg. But even more importantly, I sat with the deep conviction that the racist minority regime would tumble and that good women and men of all classes, genders and races in the law would be required to help heal the sick society.

However, I would be less than candid if I were not to admit to the professional and technical satisfaction, and joy, of preparing and presenting cases within the narrow strictures of the law, even though the law was tainted by the colonial project. It challenged me and I am a person who relishes challenge. I had constantly to search for the soft belly of the normative beast in order to bring temporary relief and redress to the vulnerable litigants for whom I stood up. I was blessed with a rampant and abundant practice which translated into several reported decisions.[2] My practice at the Bar was both a blighted and a blissful forerunner of my later life on the bench.

Simply put, the Bar is a society of advocates, and in those days it was a truly elitist affair. There was a clear divide between officers of superior and of inferior courts of justice – a relic and echo of the British divide between the upper and lower classes. Barristers or advocates had an exclusive right to appear in the superior courts while solicitors or attorneys appeared only in the lower courts. In contrast, advocates had an automatic right to appear in inferior courts, and when they did they were not obliged to robe or put on their gown before a magistrate. When appearing before a superior court they were always obliged to robe. The robes or gowns of attorneys and advocates were markedly different. Advocates wore with their gowns a white fluffy bib or collar wings, while an attorney could appear in court in any colour shirt; a regular business tie would suffice. The form of address for the judicial officer in the magistrate's court was, and still is, 'Your Worship', and in the superior courts it is a deferential 'My Lady' or 'My Lord'. The Constitutional Court took a different view when it came to forms of address and hierarchies, which I will explain later.

Under rules of the Bar, advocates acted only on instructions or on a brief from an attorney; they could not take instructions directly from a member of the public. Barristers were thus spared the bother of finding clients or customers from the street who might need the services of an advocate, or the hassle or nuisance of extracting fees or monetary cover from clients. Advocates were shielded from the risk associated with the recovery of their professional fees. They did not have to look any further than the instructing attorney for the payment of their fees, which had to be settled within a short and uniform time as set by the Bar rules. Depending on their seniority or the number of years they had been practising, advocates were required to charge a fee within a given range; the fees were also set by the Bar. Failure to do so was deemed to be unethical conduct and punishable.

When I was at the Bar, attorneys had to pay fees due to an advocate within three months of completing the case or face being 'blacklisted'. This meant that every advocate who was owed fees for more than three months was obliged to report the instructing attorney to the Bar Council. The Council would then list the attorney as not allowed to instruct any other advocate until all outstanding fees due to their advocates had been settled in full. To my mind the blacklisting rule was manifestly unfair, inflexible and harsh to attorneys. In effect the attorney was obliged to act as surety for the payment of fees by clients whatever the reason for non-payment by the client. Also, once blacklisted, an attorney could not take instructions or work which required the use of an advocate in the superior courts, where at this time only advocates appeared.

During the years of many political trials – between 1983 and 1990 – as an advocate I knew that nearly all of my instructing attorneys had no cover of fees. Among their clients were combatants of Umkhonto we Sizwe (MK), the Azanian People's Liberation Army (APLA), internal activists of the Black Consciousness Movement and the United Democratic Front (UDF), working-class leaders and followers in police detention who did not have the facility to place their attorney in funds. The last thing I wanted to do was blacklist attorneys who briefed me in political trials. They were a vital cog in the resistance of the people. At the point of accepting the brief I knew, and the attorney knew, that he or she had no funds for the work at hand. And yet neither the attorney nor I as advocate could possibly decline the duty to appear for activists only because they had no money to pay us.

I developed a neat practice, devised never to trigger the blacklisting rule. Simply put, my fees never became due and payable. I sent off my brief and fee note only if and when the attorney had made a welcome call to me to say that he had received funds. Funds generally came from a few sources: the Southern African Catholic Bishops' Conference;[3] the South African Council of Churches;[4] the International Defence and Aid Fund in London;[5] a firm of solicitors in London called Carruthers and Co;[6] or Gay J McDougall's Southern Africa Project of the Lawyers' Committee for Civil Rights under Law, of Washington.[7] To these progressive entities we owe a big debt of gratitude for their domestic and international solidarity with our struggle. We can never thank them enough. They often, although not always, found donations to support accused people who stood up to the regime.

My instructing attorneys who participated in political defences were therefore never blacklisted and, technically, I was not breaching the Bar blacklisting rule, for which I cared not in any event.

Another emphatic class disparity between attorneys and advocates was that only silks or senior counsel could be appointed judges of superior courts. Naturally this ensured that judges were exclusively white and male and well embedded in the expedient ethos of never having seen or heard of colonial and apartheid inequity, exclusion and repression.

The Bar of my time was cursed with the ills of the broader apartheid society it served. It was unashamedly lacking in diversity of gender, race and class. Most of the elite at the Bar pretended that all was well and regarded themselves as members of the 'honourable' profession. And yet these same members happily went along with the racial exclusion of black advocates. I can think of many examples of the latter: Adv Ismail Mahomed SC,[8] Adv Duma Nokwe,[9] and Adv 'Sgoob' Mabiletsa, at the Johannesburg Bar, and later Adv Thembile Lewis Skweyiya SC,[10] and Adv Zak Yacoob SC[11] in Durban. These fine advocates could not occupy working space or chambers in the same building as their white counterparts.

Most of the societies of advocates of the time had constitutions that brazenly carried clauses that barred black people from becoming members. Despite this, many members of the Bar pretended that the Bar was wonderful and that their practices generated just outcomes under the rule of law. In most areas of the law, this simply was not so. It was rule by unjust laws, which they helped enforce. Most advocates were allies of the apartheid regime. This, indeed, was what allowed them to manage their full and rich practices. Even those who prided themselves on having commercial practices were frontline beneficiaries and allies of the system, which fed them well. The Bar was the nursery of successive all-white male judges who shored up the ways of the callous regime. Exceptions there were – there were those who raised their voices against the injustice of apartheid and accepted briefs that attracted the displeasure of the ruling elite, but this was not the norm. Notable names among the white advocates who made their voices heard were Issy Maisels QC; Sydney Kentridge QC; Arthur Chaskalson SC; Vernon Berrangé QC; Jules Browde SC; Jack Unterhalter SC; Johann Kriegler SC; George Bizos SC; Andrew Wilson SC; Denis Kuny SC; Jeremy Gauntlett QC SC; Edwin Cameron SC; and Ian Farlam SC.

For the few of us who were outsiders and outliers within it, the Bar nevertheless offered tutelage, professional growth and ethical guidance sufficient for the beckoning judicial role that would be demanded of us by the certain political transition to democracy and social renewal.

Much of what I have described about the attorneys' and advocates' professions in my time has, and happily so, been moderated, but still only in part.

CHAPTER 3

Detour to the bench

As certain as the sun will rise, so will the sun set for a wicked social order. Bad political regimes never flourish for long. The seeds of their ruin lie in the belly of their misrule. It's only a matter of time before the people rise and flush out an unjust or inept government. In contrast, caring and sharing societies are rewarded with peace, prosperity and long life. Ordinarily, a just society is fertile ground for human growth and wellness.

Formal apartheid ended in 1994 and governance changes were many and urgent. Unsurprisingly, the judiciary was an early and prime target for renewal. Judges wielded huge public power. The benches of the courts, and of the superior courts in particular, mirrored the racialised masculinity of apartheid. The judges were white men. Exceptions were a few white women. A notable exception to white males was Judge Ismail Mahomed, who opted to accept an appointment even before the formal democratic transition of 1994. Another notable exception was Justice Tholi Madala,[1] who served on the bench of the 'independent' Transkei state. There may have been a few less notable exceptions on the benches of the high courts of Bophuthatswana and the Ciskei.

As a senior counsel I was eligible to be called up for an acting judge appointment. Silks were a ready reservoir of acting judges. For budgetary and other reasons, there were always fewer permanent judges than the workload in the high courts required. The convention was well settled that a silk might not decline the judge president's invitation to act as a judge.

When one morning at my chambers the phone rang and I heard Judge President Frikkie Eloff's[2] voice on the line, I knew what was coming. After 1994 my reason for refusing to act as a judge had fallen away. I accepted the invitation. I acted as a judge of the Tshwane High Court for one term in September 1994, which worked out to nearly three months. When I joined judges before whom I had regularly appeared as an advocate, but now as my colleagues and equals, in the tea room and elsewhere in the courthouse, the irony and symbolism of my presence did not escape me. Nor did it escape judicial colleagues and the advocates who appeared in my courtroom.

The Palace of Justice is located on Church Square, the historic centre of Pretoria. It is a magnificent building, designed in the 1890s by the Dutch architect Sytze Wopkes Wierda in the Italian Renaissance style. If the façade is beautiful, inside the building is imposing. It has high white ceilings of pressed steel and a floor composed of petite black and white ceramic tiles. The courtrooms are panelled with polished solid wood and the benches, too, stand solid, very tall and ornately carved. In each of the main courtrooms hang huge, grand and bright chandeliers.

Of course it was not the first time I had seen the building close to Paul Kruger's statue in Church Square.[3] As a child growing up in Pretoria I had seen it many times from outside and then, in 1963 – and still a child – I saw it from the inside. That was when I entered the building as a political accused. Many years later, once I was admitted to the Bar and was practising as an advocate, I would appear in the same courthouse on multiple occasions.

This time it was different, however. I sat up on the high bench, my head not too far from those glittering chandeliers, robed as a judge. I felt a little like an intruder in a palace, this magnificent citadel of our seedy past, but in September 1994 I was a legitimate intruder. We had had our first-ever democratic election in April that year and, officially, we were a democracy. Not only was it springtime in South Africa, it was also our political springtime. Fresh optimism had sprung. Vulnerable green buds were raring to burst into full bloom. It was a season of new possibilities, our moment of heady hope, our hour of magnificent potential for renewal. They may have been baby steps, perhaps unsteady ones, but we were taking our first steps towards a just society.

Judge President Frikkie Eloff allocated me a full share of the judicial load. He assured and reassured me, continually, that I was acquitting myself well. Then, in my last week, he invited me for coffee in his generous chambers and urged me to stay on, to accept a permanent appointment. His anxiety that I might not stay on was well founded. Barring me and Judge Ismail Mahomed, who had left for an acting appointment at the Supreme Court of Appeal in Bloemfontein, the Gauteng bench in 1994 was made up of only white male judges – this at the start of an era which demanded that the bench reflect the diversity of our population.

Nevertheless I chose not to accept a permanent appointment. I recognised that I would have to do judicial service sometime in the future, but not then. I was 46 years of age. Selfishly, my thinking was that I was too young for a permanent assignment. After all, I reasoned, judicial temperament does not come easily to the young. Also, I could be trapped within judicial service for potentially three decades, to the age of 75 years. I was not ready to make this commitment.

The hope that I should be conscripted for immediate judicial service did not die there, however. After April 1994, Chief Justice Corbett called for nominations for the appointment of the first judges of the newly founded Constitutional Court. A busybody whose name I cannot now remember had nominated me and, foolishly, I had accepted the nomination. Almost as soon as I had done so, I developed cold feet. The night before the interviews I found the fax number of the office of Chief Justice Corbett and transmitted my withdrawal of the acceptance of the nomination.

A posting on the bench, in my mid-40s, was not my idea of how to celebrate and enjoy our newly won freedom. Outside the judicial ivory tower, in a new democratic setting the world could be my oyster. The possibilities of a fuller life seemed as seductive as they were endless.

It was not long afterwards that the minister of posts, telecommunications and broadcasting, Pallo Jordan, phoned me. 'Would you consider serving as the chairperson of Telkom SA (Ltd), with a newly convened board of directors?' he asked. He followed up with a long erudite statement on the seamless interface between information technology and communication. Pallo was persuasive. Our fledgling developmental state, he pointed out, would need a powerful innovative telecommunications sector. And he assured me that President Mandela and Deputy President Mbeki were aware of his approach to me and they both supported my appointment.

I was in deep doubt and anxiety, but I opted for the riskier new path. I left my law practice at the Bar for a role in business. I served seven years as chairman of Telkom SA with considerable satisfaction and success. In 1996 Jay Naidoo became the new minister of telecommunications. In time, subsequent to my stint as chairperson and acting chief executive, Sizwe Nxasana came on board as the chief executive. Together we tackled life-enhancing projects at many levels of information technology and communications. We spread voice and data access across the country, particularly in rural and working-class neighbourhoods. We co-founded and funded Vodacom, with Vodafone as a strategic partner, and in so doing made mobile telephony and data access widespread and affordable. We procured domestic and global connectivity through satellite and underwater cabling. We concluded a strategic partnership with two foreign telecommunications enterprises to secure further capital funding and modern technology. One outcome of these corporate renewals was that Telkom became a highly profitable state-owned enterprise (SOE), which paid regular and large dividends to the state and had no sovereign debt burden.

Those were heady days. They held promise for economic rebirth and expansion led by black entrepreneurs. In tandem with my non-executive role at Telkom, I became a shareholder and executive director at New Africa Investment Limited (Nail), a listed black-controlled enterprise founded by Dr Nthato Motlana (*Robala Ka Kagiso Kgabo, Mokgatla*) and Jonty Sandler. The executive team inspired much hope. It included Matamela Cyril Ramaphosa, who is now president of the Republic of South Africa, and Zwelakhe Sisulu

(*Lala Ngoxolo, Mfokabawo*). Let it suffice to record that at the best of times Nail's market capitalisation soared to R17 billion and Nail made the Top 40 Index of the Johannesburg Stock Exchange.

I have many other tales about my post-democracy career in business but, gainful as that period in my life's journey may have been, those stories are not for these pages. You might call this detour a clearing of the overgrowth ahead of the story of my return to my core skills and perhaps my true calling – the judicial bench.

*

During the first quarter of 2001 I relented. I agreed to be nominated for a position as a permanent judge of the high court in Tshwane. I could no longer push back the constant badgering by many well-meaning women and men who thought it was time for me to make myself available for judicial work. Foremost among these voices was that of my beloved father, Samuel John Sedise Moseneke (*Robala ka kagiso Mokwena o mo tonna*). My father was disparaging about my being in business, always maintaining that I was better suited to the judicial role. After he passed on in October 1999, I did not act instantly on my father's censure but his words stayed with me.

President Thabo Mbeki was another person who was less than approving of my continued stay in business and he found a number of occasions to nudge me towards the judiciary. By the time he became head of state, the need for more and speedier change on the bench which the country had inherited was self-evident. Chief Justice Arthur Chaskalson, with whom I had served on the technical committee that had drafted the interim Constitution, was equally intolerant of my delay in assuming a judicial role.[4] He was motivated by the purest sentiments in favour of our baby democracy; he was looking for dutiful women and men who would serve as he did. Arthur sometimes resorted to borderline means to reach and rebuke me and he used a specific occasion to accost me.

After my beloved father had succumbed in 1999, the Master of the high court declined to have his deceased estate administered through his office. This was because the old-order legislation required the Master to wind up estates of only white deceased people. The law was a vintage apartheid relic, designed to segregate people by race in life and in death. I did not think that my father, who did so much to battle unfair exclusion, should suffer the indignity even after he had passed on. In fact I would have none of it. I lodged an unfair discrimination claim against the Master, which resulted in my attending the hearing, as an applicant, in the Constitutional Court.

My counsel in the claim against the Master was a young and fresh-faced Adv Vincent Maleka, now an accomplished senior counsel. He argued well before an animated bench presided over by Justice Chaskalson, who was president of the Constitutional Court at the time. It shocked all concerned that the new government had not cleaned up this apartheid irritation. The law still stood in the statute books and civil servants had to abide by its horrific prescripts.

I sat in the well of the court as a litigant, not as counsel. It felt a little awkward. I had been counsel for the state and on my feet, arguing in the same courtroom. In my own case I had chosen counsel well and I had no cause for any anxiety. By the time the hearing ended the outcome appeared reasonably predictable. (In time the court struck down the offending legislation as unconstitutional and invalid.[5])

Immediately after the adjournment, Justice Chaskalson's law clerk came hurrying towards me. 'The president wants to see you in his chambers,' he said. 'Now.' Without waiting for my reaction he turned and led the way. As I strode after him I wondered what this could be about. It could not be about my case – judicial ethics wouldn't allow the president to talk about a case he had just heard in the absence of the respondent. But, as I would quickly discover, this was nothing to do with my case. After exchanging one or two pleasantries with me, Justice Chaskalson went straight to his issue. 'We need people of your kind to come onto the bench,' he said bluntly. 'Stop this business nonsense.'

I was taken aback by his emphatic and forthright manner, but I told him

I would think about it. A week or two later, Mr Mandela, our retired president, who was a close associate of Arthur, called me. He was even more forthright than Chaskalson. 'Dikgang,' he said, 'you must become a judge. Your people need you.' Now that such distinguished citizens as these had joined the refrain of people like Justice Ismail Mahomed, Judge President Bernard Ngoepe, Adv Marumo Moerane SC and Adv Mojanku Gumbi, who had been after me for years, I could no longer ignore the chorus.

My partner and wife, Kabonina, who always has a balanced mind on these matters, cautioned me. 'This is about your life,' she said. 'The choice is not theirs, but yours. Do it only if you want to be a judge.'

*

At the beginning of the first term of 2001, Judge President Bernard Makgabo Ngoepe invited me to act as a judge in the Tshwane High Court. He never confessed to me why he asked me. His invitation called to mind the invitation Judge President Eloff of the same division had extended to me seven years earlier. The difference on this occasion, however, was that I had to burn my canoe on a no-return trip. In our system, judges on full-time service may not occupy any other office of reward or profit and must avoid any real or potential conflict of interest.

I resigned from my post as chairman of Telkom and executive director of Nail and from all other boards of subsidiaries of Nail. This meant that I was heading for a radical change in my career path and a harsh reduction in my private sector income.

In July 2001 I reported at the Tshwane High Court as an acting judge. This time around, there were far fewer surprises or ironies than had been the case during my first acting stint in 1994. I already had a long professional liaison with this judge president. We had graduated with the LLB degree at Unisa on the same day at the same ceremony. We had entered articles as candidate attorneys during the same period in separate but mainly Afrikaans law firms. He went to Hofmeyr Van der Merwe attorneys in Johannesburg and I went to Dyason, Douglas, Muller & Meyer attorneys in Pretoria. After articles of clerkship, we had set up our own law firms, at more or less the same time. He set up his in Polokwane as Ngoepe, Machaka & Nkadimeng and I mine in Tshwane as Maluleke, Seriti & Moseneke. We joined the Pretoria Bar at much the same time, where, for a long time, we were the only two black members. Ngoepe took silk just after I did, and in 1993 we served together on the technical committee that drafted the interim Constitution.

Our paths parted with the advent of democracy. In 1995, Ngoepe accepted a permanent judicial appointment and I did not. In 1998, President Mandela nominated Judge Ngoepe for appointment as the judge president of the Gauteng provincial division amidst clamour by some of the senior judges that the deputy judge president, Judge Piet van der Walt, should be appointed. In order to keep the peace at the Tshwane High Court, Ngoepe suggested to Adv Mojanku Gumbi[6] that Van der Walt be appointed judge president ahead of him; he said he was happy to serve as deputy judge president until Van der Walt retired. In effect, Ngoepe was positing the conformist view that seniority on the bench ought to trump the need for transformation.

Mojanku, however, would have none of it. She solicited my support and she, Ngoepe and I went to lunch. She made it quite clear that Deputy President Mbeki was firm about bringing speedy diversity to the leadership of the judiciary. Judge Ngoepe girded his loins and emerged from the lunch resolute. He subsequently took up the leadership of the court and became a long-serving and excellent judge president. His bust stands proudly side by side with that of Judge President Frikkie Eloff in the entrance hall of the Palace of Justice in Tshwane. And the rest, as the saying goes, is history.

As I came to start my acting stint at the high court, I was proud and pleased to work under Judge President Ngoepe. He was a friend and colleague now turned my judicial superior. I was relaxed about this and ready to take orders. He had opted for judicial office ahead of me and it was proper that he led the way. He looked and played the part of a leader of the court – he was far less jovial than he'd been in our past.

The composition of the bench had changed, but only marginally. A small number of women and black judges were added on. I remember fondly a good few of those female judges who braved appointment to the high courts shortly after democratic rule in 1994, and they have all served our country with great distinction. Among these were Judge Lucy Mailula, who in 1995 was the first black woman appointed to the high court, and Judge Navanethem (Navi) Pillay, who later rose to become the United Nations High Commissioner for Human Rights, from 2008 to 2014. In December 1998, Judge Thokozile Masipa was one of the early female appointments to the high court and later became known for presiding over the Oscar Pistorius murder trial. Another was Judge Leona Theron who, in 1999, aged 33 years, was the first black female to be appointed to the KwaZulu-Natal provincial division; later she was elevated to the Supreme Court of Appeal and she now serves at the Constitutional Court.

Judge Bess Nkabinde was appointed to the high court, Mafikeng, in November 1999. From then she steadily rose through the ranks to act at the Labour Appeal Court and the Supreme Court of Appeal; later she served on the Constitutional Court, where she remained until her retirement in 2018. Judge Mandisa Maya served at the Mthatha High Court from 2000 and in time rose up the ranks to become, in 2017, the first female to serve as president of the Supreme Court of Appeal. To this illustrious group one must add Judge Sisi Khampepe, who accepted to serve on the high court bench in 2000; she has served at the Constitutional Court since 2009. One should also note Judge Nonkosi Mhlantla. She was appointed to the Eastern Cape High Court in 2002 and worked her way to the Supreme Court of Appeal. She was appointed to the Constitutional Court in 2015, and currently still serves that court. So, too, one should mention Kathy Satchwell, who was appointed a high court judge in 1996.

A notable appointment to the high court was that of Judge Johann van der Westhuizen. He was appointed to the high court in Tshwane by President Mandela in 1999 after a stellar academic career at the University of Pretoria. This included being the founding director of the Centre for Human Rights (CHR), where he served from 1986 to 1998. The centre assumed a progressive and pro-human rights stance in an environment and on a university campus that were significantly right-wing.

The practice of appointing judges from the ranks of senior counsel only fell into disuse under the new Constitution, but the cohort of older and conservative judges remained trapped in the old convention. They were as prejudiced and intolerant of academics as they were of women who became judges under the new order. Clearly, they were misguided. The new order required a judge to be any person who was properly qualified and a fit and proper person to be a judge. Certain legal academics – and Johann van der Westhuizen was one of them – more than satisfied the appointment requirements. Van der Westhuizen was also an associate member of the Bar and had regularly appeared in the courts.

The 'old boys' club' of judges felt significantly threatened by the new order. I have already talked about their displeasure over new appointments, which they perceived to be of a lesser quality than themselves. They were stuck in what I choose to call the 'in-my-time syndrome'. Every appointment after them was bound to be inferior. Whatever followed could not match their golden era. Black people, women and academic lawyers were suspect categories. In their reasoning it followed that change and diversity within the bench meant a lowering of 'high' judicial standards. Had one called the older judges on this, no doubt they would have denied it, and unanimously stated that they were ready for change. But in truth they were saying that unless you were a white male and had been an advocate trained at the Bar as they had been, you would not make a good judge.

Some older judges, many of whom I had known from the Bar for a long time, would seek continually to reassure me that I had come through the 'correct pipeline of silks', meaning that I would not lower judicial standards. What they never confronted was that, for horrible reasons of the past, virtually all senior counsel were drawn from the white communities and were male. This was the first blind spot. If this remained the only pool for the selection of judges, the bench would remain male, white, elitist and unchanged. And for that matter, I might immediately add: given their past practices and the new Constitution, with its progressive tenets, not every senior counsel was fit and proper to be a judge.

The second blind spot on the part of sitting judges was that many senior attorneys and senior academics were accomplished lawyers who would bring enormous value to the quality of the bench.

Our new democratic order was wise to require a judiciary that was representative of the demography of the country and drawn from all who satisfied the measure of being suitably qualified and fit and proper to be a judge. Barring a few instances, the new appointment criteria have served the country well, given the robust judiciary we have today, and its jurisprudence. Virtually all of the old-order judges have retired and the judicial heavens have not caved in.

The old-order judges insisted on the maintenance of many unwritten rules of the bench. One of these was retaining the formal address of 'My Lord' and 'My Lady' in court proceedings. Another was the seniority system. A more senior judge led his juniors in every way: the names of the judges on the court roster appeared in the order of seniority; the allocation of cases to be heard by judges was done on the seniority principle; the allocation of specific courtrooms in a courthouse was done in the order of seniority; and the order of entering and leaving the courtroom and the sitting of a panel of judges was always according to seniority. Ordinarily, the most senior judge led the exchanges with counsel first. Only thereafter would junior judges be permitted to join the debate. The most senior judge decided which member of the panel would write the judgment. The pecking order extended to the allocation to judges of their chambers, their parking spaces and where they sat in the tea room. The senior judges clustered around the same (reserved) coffee tables and spoke first in judges' meetings.

Being an acting judge, I was considered a rank junior to every permanent judge in every way of the bench. This did not irk me. I had made a conscious and self-serving detour in order to go to the bench later and, to my mind, it was right that I join the queue from the back. I had expected that the workload would be considerable and this proved to be so. I already knew that I would have to perform a wide variety of judicial functions, preceded by extensive reading and preparation, particularly in relation to the motion court, appeals and divorces.

I was ready, willing and able.

CHAPTER 4

A permanent appointment

It is useful, I hope, to understand how judges have been appointed since the start of our constitutional democracy. It is very different from the process that held under apartheid.

In the past only a senior counsel, or silk, was eligible for appointment to the high court but this was about to change. Although no law specified that only silks may be judges, the practice was entrenched by convention. Ordinarily, the judge president would invite silks to act as judges. This gave him an opportunity to assess the readiness of the silk for judicial appointment. When a vacancy occurred in a division of the high court, the minister of justice would consult with the judge president and decide singularly on who to appoint. Usually, although not exclusively, the choice would be from the silks who had acted as judges. In sum, the appointment was a political matter in the exclusive discretion of the minister of justice, once he had been consulted by the judge president.

By 1994 we knew that, historically, this type of appointment system had produced a racialised and masculine bench with a predictable ideological bent. The appointments were not adequately shielded from political preference and influence. After 1994 we had to devise a selection process more suited to the democratic project.

In the new order, judges are appointed in a different manner, set by the Constitution and legislation.[1] The formal requirements for picking candidates to the bench are, foremost, proper qualifications and fitness to hold judicial office. The first requirement is objective and speaks simply to whether the aspirant has acquired academic training in the field of law. Ordinarily, the minimum qualification would be a university law degree. Fitness to hold judicial office poses a collection of questions on whether the person will be a good judge. These relate to background; practical experience; fidelity to the Constitution and the law; judicial temperament; and ethics. The selection process is open to the public and must be informed by the need for diversity and demographic fairness.

Judges are appointed by the president of the country on the recommendation of the Judicial Service Commission (JSC) – the body specially set up by the Constitution to appoint judges and regulate other affairs of judges.[2] The JSC is a diverse and inclusive body. It is chaired by the chief justice – or, in his absence, by the deputy chief justice – and is made up of the minister of justice, judges, practising lawyers, academic lawyers, members of parliament and appointees of the president.

The JSC conducts the interviews, in public, of candidates who aspire to become judges. Any member of the public may nominate a candidate or object to the candidacy of any aspirant judge. A candidate must disclose prescribed information to the commission and any other information which, in the knowledge of the candidate, may stand in the way of their appointment. Failure to disclose information adverse to one's candidacy is considered a severe breach of the full and frank disclosure requirement that ordinarily will disqualify an aspirant judge.

The Constitution requires the JSC to appoint only a candidate who holds proper qualifications and who is fit to become a judge. Its appointments must mirror, broadly, the racial and gender composition of the country. Judges may only be appointed on the advice of the commission; there is no alternative option. The president of the country may not bypass or ignore the commission. He may not appoint as a judge someone he might, for whatever reason, prefer. This is an important safeguard of judicial competence and independence. Just as important is the knowledge of the aspirant judge that no political party, nor the president, can favour or help them become a judge. This appointment process is a near-foolproof safeguard against a patronage system or cadre deployment.

When it comes to the appointments of the chief justice and deputy chief justice of the Constitutional Court, and the president and deputy president of the Supreme Court of Appeal, the procedure is different. Here it is the president who starts the selection process and ultimately makes the appointment. This happens after consultation with the JSC and, in the cases of the chief justice and the deputy chief justice, also after consultations with leaders of political parties in the National Assembly.[3] Unlike in the appointment of all other judges, the president has the prerogative to choose the chief justice and deputy chief justice and also the president and deputy president of the Supreme Court of Appeal, subject to a limited consultation requirement.

The Constitution does not prescribe the attributes of the person the president may appoint to these four powerful judicial posts, but the JSC has developed a convention on the consultation. The president's choice must submit to an open interview by the commission, which must satisfy itself that the person is properly qualified and fit and proper to occupy the position and to assume the high office. This is a very important safeguard. The president may choose the candidate for the high office but the commission is obliged to certify him or her to be fit for purpose. We are yet to confront the difficulty where the JSC has refused to endorse a presidential selection, but if that were to happen a constitutional crisis of sorts would arise. A chief justice or deputy chief justice or a president or deputy president of the Supreme Court of Appeal who were to ascend to the position without the JSC's approval would suffer from lack of significant public and professional credibility – an impression a judicial posting must avoid at all cost.

*

In September 2001, the Black Lawyers Association (BLA)[4] nominated me for a permanent post at the high court and I accepted the nomination. I had made peace with following a judicial path to the end of my working life.

I came before the JSC at its sitting of October 2001. The session was chaired, as was custom, by the chief justice, Arthur Chaskalson.

My interview was not threatening nor overly probing. I had already received rounds of support from many JSC members, among these Phineas Mojapelo, who rose up the judicial ladder to serve as a distinguished deputy judge president of the South Gauteng division of the High Court. Both Marumo Moerane SC and Kgomotso Moroka SC declared our past acquaintances and supported my appointment. With both I had in the past fought many cases as co-counsel; we were members of the BLA and they were both dear friends of mine. Also on the panel was Milton Seligson SC, who chaired and represented the General Council of the Bar under which I had served as an advocate and senior counsel. It was pleasant to see Professor Johann Neethling on the panel; at the time he was dean of the Law faculty at my alma mater, the University of South Africa. In fact I had studied competition law in my final-year LLB degree under him. He, too, made the disclosure of past dealings he and I had had; he also posed a few penetrating questions about the judicial function.

I was not aware that any other aspirant judge contested my appointment. There was no objection from any member of the public, nor did any professional body raise any flaws concerning my candidacy. Duty-bound as I was, I disclosed my previous political conviction, how and why I was convicted, and my stay in prison for a decade. I drew attention to the decisions of two courts which had examined the circumstances of my conviction and found that I was properly qualified and fit and proper to be admitted as an attorney and later an advocate. Also, in time, I acquired silk status.

The JSC was aware that I came before it as an acting judge of the Gauteng provincial division and that my nomination was supported by Judge President Ngoepe, the head of the court at which I wanted to serve. I had to assure the commission that I had resigned from all my board appointments in the corporate world and that I would not earn any other remuneration or other financial reward. I also had to reassure them that I was not a member of any political formation or party. At the time of their appointment, a judge may not be a member of a political party.

CHAPTER 5

A formidable workload

A few excited colleagues couldn't contain themselves. They told me that the JSC had recommended that I be appointed to the high court bench in Tshwane. They spoke out of turn, of course, but were seemingly overwhelmed by the urge to disclose what they thought was good news.

Being settled in as a newly appointed high court judge is something of a militaristic affair. There are a good few logistics to get out of the way before one starts functioning as a judge. On a morning in November 2001 Judge President Ngoepe called me to his office. He handed me my letter of appointment as a permanent judge 'headquartered' in Tshwane. It was signed by President Mbeki. Then the judge president asked me to stand up while he swore me in:

> I, Dikgang Moseneke, swear that, as a judge of the high court, I will be faithful to the Republic of South Africa, will uphold and protect the Constitution and the human rights entrenched in it, and will administer justice to all persons alike without fear, favour or prejudice, in accordance with the Constitution and the law. So help me God.[1]

Other than the judge president, nobody else was within hearing, and yet every word dropped off my lips like lead. I had no idea what the next fifteen years of judicial life would throw at me, but at that moment, the moment

I took the oath, the solemnity of what I was committing to struck me profoundly.

Then and there the judge president assigned me permanent chambers, a courtroom and a parking space. And he urged me immediately to appoint a law clerk and registrar. I had to buy red-black-and-grey judge's robes for criminal hearings and order an official car. The registrar of the court got me to complete a multitude of forms for entry into public service and the remuneration platform.

A senior colleague, Judge Chris Botha, made time to tell me that my official photograph at appointment had to be taken by Martin Gibbs, the court's official photographers.

Martin Gibbs is a very 'Pretoria' institution. They have been taking studio pictures forever. The name took me back to one particular Saturday morning when I was about eight years old, with my father hurrying us to wash and dress up for a family photo at Martin Gibbs. I remember the camera box mounted on a tall tripod stand and the photographer sternly telling my father, my mother, my siblings and me how to sit and pose. A little smile from him would have helped. When he covered his head with a thick maroon cloth, I thought he looked like a magician. Then *flash*! the bulb went off and it was done. My dad had to wait a few days before collecting the black-and-white photo, which was mounted on hardboard, and came along with a few negatives in a small envelope. I thought the picture was wonderful – in fact it survived 60 years and made it into *My Own Liberator*.

Over the years, Chris Botha, now retired, managed the archiving process meticulously. To this day the photographs of the judges who have served at the court for more than a hundred years hang on one or other interior wall of the courthouse. They are arranged in lines that suggest seniority and passage of time. Each photograph has a discreet silver nameplate with the name of the judge, their date of appointment and of retirement or promotion to a higher court. My picture joined the many and to this day it hangs on the Tshwane High Court wall.

The gallery of black-and-white pictures of dead judges gave me the eerie feeling of human transience. Judges, like all human beings, serve, grow old and die. A new photo just hung, as mine was not long afterwards, affirms renewal and continuity of life. My turn had arrived to play my part as a judge and in time I, too, would bow out.

The chamber, or office, I was allocated was on one of the upper floors of the new courthouse which stood a street behind the Palace of Justice. Its last occupant had been a senior judge who had since passed on and the office had obviously not been used for a good few years. The chamber needed thorough cleaning so early one evening I asked Kabonina for 'technical support' to give the place a good scrub before I settled in. Kabo turned the desk upside down and pulled out all the drawers. The top drawer on the right had a smaller, concealed inner drawer. Wanting to clean every dusty crevice, Kabo pulled out the secret drawer and in it she found six or so yellow carbon copies, the handwriting on them somewhat faded. She took a closer look and then threw the papers at me. 'Read what you judges were up to in the past,' she said sharply. They were carbon copies of warrants of death sentences, each one bearing the judge's signature. They were the old type of death warrants, the ones that read: 'You are sentenced to death to hang by your neck until you are dead'. I had known the judge before his demise and I had also appeared before him in court. Why did he keep copies of the warrants? I wondered. Did the death sentences weigh so heavily on him that it was difficult for him to discard them? And why had he kept them in that secret drawer? His motivation preyed on my mind for quite a long time. I remain grateful that, by courtesy of our Constitutional Court,[2] I would not have to impose the death penalty on anyone, however horrific the crime.

The full heft of the work of a high court judge is often undervalued. For one thing, seats of the high court in large urban centres have an inadequate number of posts for their workload. The proof is the large number of acting judges, without whom most big divisions would grind to a halt. In the past the apartheid government created a parallel and diversionary court system for black citizens only. This meant that the high courts, in the main, served the white minority population and the corporate class. With the start of democracy, race-based civil courts were dismantled and segregation in the courts ceased. With high courts now having the power to hear all the disputes, without regard to the skin colour of the parties to them, their caseloads spiked almost immediately. Not only did new posts for judges not keep pace with the increased volume of court cases, but an expanding economy and population growth kept up the pressure.

As I expected, my stint at the Tshwane High Court turned out to be a very absorbing affair and came with a formidable workload. A sense of one's workload for a particular quarter of the year is gathered from the roster. This complex schedule, which is issued by the head of court, runs into tens of pages of print. It tells every judge of a division the work they are to take on for the quarter. The roster is delivered to each judge's chambers and is also posted up on the public notice-board. Everyone who cared would know who the judge or judges of their dispute were going to be.

When I was in practice as an advocate I always insisted on knowing 'my' judge well beforehand. Without sacrificing the core contentions, I would prepare my written and present my oral argument to the taste and fancy of 'my' judge. The judge is, after all, the target of my capture and persuasion. To verbose judges, I gave many words. To judges who thrived on the strict letter of the statute, I gave black-letter law arguments. The philosopher judges I fed with legal philosophy and sometimes floating notions of justice. To judges in constant search for a knock-out point to end the dispute, I would find one, if not two or maybe even three, 'bullseye' points. Through many years of practice, I came to recognise that it always helps to know your case and your judge. And the starting point is the quarterly roster.

In turn, the roster tells a judge and their law clerks which cases have been allocated to their specific chamber and alerts them to the preparatory reading they will have to do ahead of the day of hearing. It is not uncommon ahead of the hearing for pleadings or appeal records that judges have to read hundreds, if not thousands, of pages. The roster prompts a good judge, like a good Scout, to be prepared.

For my first week in the high court the roster told me that my posting was in the motion court. I had appointed Bongani Khoza, who was then studying law, to clerk for me and I was ready to get stuck in.

A motion court judge decides the fate of disputes brought, as the word implies, by way of application or on paper. The claimant or their lawyer writes down the relief or remedy they're asking for. Lawyers call this a notice of motion. The notice is supported by an affidavit in which the claimant advances facts to support the claim. These two documents are served, or delivered, on the respondent or the person or entity against whom the claim is made. The respondent may admit the claim or dispute it on paper by delivering a sworn opposing statement and ask that the court dismiss the application. The roll of court is divided into opposed and unopposed applications.

A motion court judge decides the unopposed applications first. They may grant the order asked for, even though not opposed, but only if it is in accordance with the law. This means that the judge must read and study every file to satisfy themselves that the claim is valid in law. A motion court judge will spend all of the weekend working through a variety of unopposed claims by money-lenders for repayment of money, such as summary judgment, provisional sentence and orders of execution of mortgaged property, and provisional or final sequestrations or liquidations. The sums claimed often run into many millions of rands per claim. The judge has to ensure that unopposed claims for sequestration, liquidation, business surrender or administration are good. Many motions ask for the appointment of a wide variety of office-bearers like curators, liquidators, trustees, executors or even arbitrators. Many other motions seek to compel the opposing litigant in the main claim to follow or act in the manner that the rules of court for conducting cases require.

The duty of a judge to act impartially and with complete fidelity to the law is tested most in the unopposed motion court. The mere absence of opposition in motion or any other proceedings does not mean the claimant is entitled to the order they seek. The order asked for must be permissible under law and, above all, it must be a just order. A diligent motion court judge will know that it is only by peering through the claims on paper that they will know whether the orders the claimants seek are in accordance with the law and are just.

As if all this was not enough in one week of one's judicial life, I also had to decide, as all judges are obliged to do, urgent applications in the motion court. Ordinarily, the law aims to prevent harm which cannot be later repaired. A person who has an urgent claim is entitled to approach an urgent court judge at any time for relief. Throughout the 24 hours in a day there is a judge assigned to be on call for urgent matters.

A claim is urgent when irreparable harm will occur if the relief asked for is not granted. Over the years courts have set different categories of urgency and have allowed non-compliance with the procedural rules in order to prevent harm that cannot be remedied later. In short, a litigant is allowed to jump the queue of cases waiting to be heard. This would be the case when one parent unlawfully wants to leave the country with a minor child of the parties; or where the one party seeks an order against domestic violence; where one seeks to prevent the unlawful sale of property at an auction or execution; where the claimant seeks to be released from unlawful custody; or where there is a reasonable fear that a mobile asset such as a ship or aircraft, which is the subject of a dispute, may leave the port beyond the reach and power of the court. In the days of the death penalty, the classic urgent application was for the stay of its execution pending an appeal or possible executive reprieve.

Grounds for urgency of a claim are many and varied. As a new urgent duty judge, I was surprised at the number of urgent matters that came to my court during the day and to my chambers or home during the evening in one week. It wasn't unusual for Mr Botha, the deputy registrar of the court, to arrange to bring counsel to my residence at night. The more senior judges warned me that some attorneys and advocates would try to take advantage of a new judge who might be lenient on urgency, and claim urgency unduly. These salted colleagues had me remember that the first enquiry in an urgent application is whether the relief sought is truly urgent. If it is not, the claimant is probably trying to jump the queue and elbow his way ahead of the many other claims waiting to be heard. The censure for lack of urgency is severe: an immediate dismissal of the claim, with costs.

In bigger court divisions, the motion court judges hear opposed applications later in the same week. Parties appear in person or with counsel to argue whether the claim should be granted. The first enquiry is whether the claim can be properly decided without oral evidence. If the judge cannot decide the disputes of fact on the affidavits, they may dismiss the application or refer it to an oral hearing. After every opposed hearing the judge must give reasons, however brief, for granting or dismissing the application. In the heat of a truly full week, judges tend to reserve judgment, which means that the judge takes time out to think about the proper outcome and to write down the reasons for the decision. In other words, the judge pens the judgment.

In the weeks during which I was in the opposed motion court, there would be 15 to 20 opposed applications to hear. I tended to deliver nearly half to 60 per cent of the judgments *ex tempore*: meaning that as the argument ended I would immediately make my decision known and provide the reasons forthwith. The instant judgment of this kind was recorded; later I would edit the transcript, if necessary – for language, not substance. The remaining 40 per cent of the reserved judgments I would write overnight during the same week and deliver them the following week before regular court sitting started. In sum, during motion court week, a high court judge works very hard day and night, preceded by half a week of reading and preparation in the evenings and over weekends.

Not long ago a number of high court judges were reported by litigants or their head of court to the JSC's Judicial Conduct Committee (JCC) for failing to produce judgments in good time.[3] Apart from appointing judges, the JSC is also the disciplinary body for the misconduct of judges. The delays in producing judgments varied from six months to a few years. Most of the delayed judgments are picked up during motion court week. Once a task like judgment writing is deferred, it is likely to be deferred again and again as the facts get hazier and the arguments on each side become ever foggier.

On the other hand, litigants are entitled to know the outcome of their dispute. Judges are judges because they are bound to judge. Their core task is to decide a dispute between litigants in accordance with the law and make known the outcome and the reasons for that decision.

Beyond motion court duty, I served in other courts. Perhaps the most uneventful and boring was the unopposed divorce court. On a Friday morning I would walk into a courtroom filled with plaintiffs who sought to be parted from their erstwhile loved ones and partners. By far, most of the claimants were women. Often the men would walk away and leave it to the women to submit to the ritual of ending the marriage. It all boils down to five minutes during which the woman repeats variations on the mantra: that she was married to him, all love is lost, he has left the common home for another lover, the marriage relationship has irretrievably broken down. In most divorces the parties would already have agreed on a draft order that settled their material possessions and, in light of a family advocate's report, the custody of the minor children. If there was no agreement on the important aspects of the break-up, the case would be removed from the roll and sent to the opposed trial roll.

By the time the day ended, I would have listlessly said, at least 60 times: 'A decree of divorce is granted.'

I found the divorce court an unhappy place. Some claimants took the witness stand dressed very smartly, looking as if they were ready to celebrate the formal end of their marriage. Others were unkempt and looked downright miserable at the fact that the real end was about to happen. Many of the grounds for the breaking down of marriage were predictable but disturbing none the less. The grounds were suggestive of the ancient wisdom that there is only a faint line between love and hatred; between bliss and wrath.

One of my joys at the high court was the early morning automatic reviews of convictions by magistrates' courts.[4] The criminal procedure law requires that a judge in chambers should review a sentence of imprisonment or a fine above a certain threshold imposed by a magistrate on an undefended accused person.[5] This was a progressive pre-democracy criminal justice measure. A judge is the additional line of protection for an undefended accused person. The judge is required to study the record of the proceedings and the reasons for the conviction in order to decide whether the conviction is in accordance with the law. The reviews are said to be automatic because the law imposes the process without the knowledge or request of the convicted accused person. At its cost, the state transcribes the reviewable proceedings and sends them to the high court for review. If the accused files an appeal, the automatic review falls away. In a few instances a magistrate may, after imposing a sentence, develop doubt about the legal correctness of the conviction or sentence. If this happens, the case is sent to the high court with the request that a judge certify the lawfulness of the proceedings.

In my time, I received around five court files with automatic reviews every morning. They were, so to speak, my breakfast snack. Before my court day started, I read the record and certified the correctness of the conviction and sentence. In some instances I would write an enquiry to the magistrate who had presided, asking for their explanation of an aspect of the case. If I intended to upset the conviction or sentence imposed, I would invite the magistrate to say why I should not do so.

If I had concluded that the conviction should be set aside, I would authorise a warrant for the release of the prisoner immediately, even before I had formulated reasons for my decision. This hasty release of a person who is found not to be guilty is prompted by a precious principle of law in a democracy. The freedom of any person is a sacrosanct right. Once the denial of freedom is not in accordance with the law, it becomes urgent that the prisoner concerned be released forthwith. In other words, the liberty of an unlawfully detained person is always an urgent matter and may not be unduly delayed. A crop of judgments I wrote while on the high court on criminal justice arose from automatic judicial reviews. The judgments were my early morning offerings of justice to vulnerable women and men who were exposed to the less-than-perfect judicial process.

My stay on the high court was otherwise uneventful. The roster moved me around like all judges to do criminal or civil appeals from the magistrates' courts. The criminal appeals tended to be substantial because the criminal jurisdiction of the regional court had been increased up to life imprisonment. Many convicted accused appealed through attorneys or the centres of Legal Aid South Africa. In many instances my interference with sentences of the regional court was at the level of the harshness of the sentences rather than the cogency of the reasoning supporting the conviction.

One court sitting I always found evocative, despite doing it a good few times, was the admission of attorneys and advocates as officers of the high court. The admissions were still made in the same courtroom – the A Court in the Palace of Justice – in which I had been admitted as an attorney, so perhaps my emotion was a throwback to the past, when I had had to fight my way into the profession in that very same court. I felt more ready to find as a judge that the candidate had complied with all the admission requirements than the other judge I sat with. I was the junior judge and I was happy to be led without demurring. Happily, no candidate for admission was ever refused admission while I was part of the bench of two judges.

On the day of admission as an attorney or advocate, one's loved ones and friends attend in support. If something goes wrong with the admission, as had happened to me on my first attempt, the sense of regret and rejection is huge. Admission candidates have to make sure that they have ticked every box. Judges hate to decline admission for technical non-compliance or negligence in preparing admission papers.

I also did several civil trials, which I enjoyed. So, too, appeals from a single judge of the high court to a full bench of three judges of the same division. I wrote several judgments and started to enjoy the writing, sitting up most evenings to draft them. At the start, it was rather confusing knowing which judgments might be reportable. Not every judgment written by a judge carries interest beyond the parties to a particular dispute. However, when a judgment might be of interest or of future value and guidance to other judges or the legal community, it is said to be reportable. This usually happens when the judgment sets a new principle of law or restates an existing principle or a collection of precedents usefully or with greater clarity. If this is so, then the judgment ought to appear in a regular collection of judgments – law reports.

On the front page of every final version of a draft judgment is a stamp inviting the judge concerned to mark the judgment as reportable or not, but their opinion is not decisive. The decision sits out of the reach of the judge and somewhere between the resident editor of the law reports and the publishing company.

This reminds me of an anecdote when I was an acting judge in 1994. I knocked at the door of a very senior and reputable judge of yesteryear, Kees van Dijkhorst, whose chamber was near mine, to ask his opinion about a draft judgment. Like me, he was an early bird in chambers and his mind seemed to work best before the sun rose. I had entered his chambers before, seeking his guidance on automatic reviews. He received me pleasantly but his manner was headmaster-like. He was an impressive and thorough lawyer but of the near-mechanistic ilk. He was a fierce positivist. Once he believed he had found what the law was, that was the law and he applied it. He did not have many kind words for the new Constitution. He thought it was vague and open-ended in great part and would be difficult to implement. (I did not agree but I did not have to say so.) Even so, he accepted that it was the supreme law. This was because he placed a judge's fidelity to the law uppermost.

So on this particular morning, with the draft judgment in my hand, my question was whether I should mark my judgment reportable. He lifted his head, his expression somewhat surprised. 'No, you should not!' he fired. Before I could ask why not, he continued, 'You see, it will take a good few years before you write something reportable.' He meant no malice; he was simply making the point that as a baby junior judge, it would take a long time before senior judges and lawyers would care to read what I wrote. Of course my ego was booted down to where it belonged – at my ankles. I none the less continued writing and a number of my high court judgments are reported. And, hopefully, they are also readable.[6]

CHAPTER 6

Free and fair

Barring the heavy load of court work, my stay at the Tshwane High Court was uneventful. President Mbeki had been elected to office on 14 June 1999. This was after Nelson Rolihlahla Mandela had served a single term of presidential office, ending around June 1999. The full import of Nelson Mandela giving up presidential power freely when more was within his grasp is yet to sink in on our continent and elsewhere. Most in that position – we know who they are – want their term extended beyond the constitutional limit, usually in order to do more public harm than good, although this, for now, is an aside to my present narration.

As he assumed power, President Mbeki brought new urgency to the vision of the rebirth or renaissance of the African continent. His resolve was as explicit as it was admirable. The early years of his presidency were coloured by an unmistakable push for continental renewal. He was in the forefront of a re-energised Pan-Africanist vision supported by new continental institutions. Within less than three months of the start of his presidency, on 9 September 1999 the heads of state and government of the Organisation of African Unity (OAU) issued a declaration – the Sirte Declaration – calling for the creation of an African Union.[1] Rightly so, the Declaration acknowledged the role of the OAU in ridding the continent of the remnants of the colonial project and apartheid and in growing unity and solidarity among African states. In particular, the Declaration recognised the role of the OAU's Liberation Committee in supporting liberation movements in the fight against apartheid.

What was clear, though, was that the OAU had come to the end of its runway. It would be replaced by a new organisation, the African Union (AU). The thrust of the new formation was futuristic and visionary. Its primary goal was to secure the political and economic integration of African economies. With this united thrust it was hoped that the collective African economies would find a meaningful stake within a global economy – all this in order to remedy the social, economic and political challenges made worse by negative aspects of globalisation. African leaders hoped for sustainable economic development that would raise the living standards of their people. Although predictable, the AU added to the economic integration theme the task to sponsor peace, security and stability. It committed to democratic principles and institutions, popular participation and good governance which must observe and respect human and people's rights in accordance with the African Charter on Human and Peoples' Rights and other applicable human rights instruments.[2]

The formation of the AU was a matter of swift and trenchant steps. President Mbeki, who had just been sworn in as president, was the foremost intellectual leader and promoter of the AU. In July 1999, the OAU Assembly resolved to take formal steps to form the African Union. Four summits were convened, culminating in the Durban summit of 2002.[3] So South Africa served as the midwife state, as the AU was launched and the first Assembly of the heads of states was convened.

The brand new African Union set up impressive organs. The Assembly of heads of state was to be the supreme decision-making body. Ministers of each member state served as the executive council answerable to the Assembly. The decisions of the Assembly or of executive council were to be implemented by a commission led by a chairperson, a deputy and eight commissioners, each responsible for a designated portfolio. The AU set up a number of special-purpose organs enabling of continental governance. One such body was the Peace and Security Council. Peace was an obvious precondition for continental political and economic integration. Another important organ was the Pan-African Parliament. This was intended to be an organ that afforded citizens of different countries participation in governance, development and economic integration. Also set up was the Economic, Social and Cultural Council, an advisory organ composed of different social and professional groups of the member states. The plan included setting up a continental Court of Justice.

The New Partnership for Africa's Development (NEPAD) was the strategic framework for Africa's renewal. Its founding document owed its origin to a mandate given by the OAU to the five initiating heads of state – Algeria, Egypt, Nigeria, Senegal and South Africa – to develop an integrated socio-economic development framework for Africa.[4] The framework outlined early priorities. All represented overdue responses to obvious continental maladies. The framework identified prevention of conflict and the creation of enduring peace. These would be best achieved in a democratic order observing good political, economic and corporate governance as well as human rights. Africa had to eradicate poverty, achieve its development goals – in particular, human development – and increase its levels of domestic savings and investments. The continent was obliged to build capacity for policy development, regional integration, sustainable economic growth and negotiation in international trade and markets. Africa was required to create genuine partnerships with developed countries based on mutual respect and accountability.

At an implementation level, the African Peer Review Mechanism was in effect an openness and accountability tool devised to have member countries submit to reporting to and an examination by peers over the execution of developmental goals like short-term regional infrastructure programmes.

Zimbabwe was due to hold a national general election in 2002. By all media accounts the election was likely to be a highly contested affair with the rise and seeming electoral popularity of the Movement for Democratic Change (MDC), led by Morgan Tsvangirai. Other media suggested that the ruling party – the Zimbabwe African National Union-Patriotic Front

(ZANU-PF) – would not tolerate an electoral challenge to their grip on political power, which they had enjoyed since 18 April 1980 – a period of 22 consecutive years.

Within the prevailing air of continental optimism and a renewed sense of regional integration President Mbeki conceived of a judicial observer mission to witness Zimbabwe's election, separate from the 50-person-strong multi-party SA Observer Mission he appointed at the invitation of the then president of Zimbabwe, Robert Mugabe. Mbeki was one of the protagonists of NEPAD, if not the central protagonist. He was also the chief emissary of the AU in brokering peace in Zimbabwe.

A judicial mission of this kind and its usefulness had no earlier example, however, and when the presidency approached Judge President Ngoepe, my immediate boss, requesting that I and Judge Sisi Khampepe comprise the judicial observer mission, he was surprised – but he relented. Chief Justice Chaskalson called me to express a muted unhappiness with an observer mission, which ordinarily should not be undertaken by judges, but he did not make his objection public. Instead he agreed to the mission and on 12 February 2002 Justice Khampepe and I were officially appointed. We were released from our regular high court duties (in Joburg and Pretoria respectively) in order to perform this unusual service. It remains unclear to me why President Mbeki appointed only two judges or on what basis he selected the two of us. The SA Observer Mission was also appointed, under the leadership of Ambassador Samuel Motsuenyane.

The terms of reference of the judicial observer mission were to observe and report to the president of South Africa on whether, in the period before, during and shortly after the election, the Constitution, electoral and any other laws of Zimbabwe were able to ensure credible or substantially free and fair elections and, if so, whether the election had been held in substantial compliance with the legislative framework.

Judge Khampepe and I set up office at the SA embassy in Harare and prepared to fulfil our mandate. We studied and broadly reviewed the electoral framework, including the laws we listed in our final report. We held discussions on the scope and proper interpretation of the legislative framework with the chief justice of Zimbabwe, Godfrey Chidyausiku, the judge president, P Gware, as well as other judges of the high court. We also sought an understanding of the electoral framework from the minister of justice, legal and parliamentary affairs, Patrick Chinamasa, the attorney general, Andrew Ranganayi Chigovera, who in terms of the Constitution was the principal legal adviser to the government, and the registrar-general of elections, Mr Tobaiwa Mudede, who was the most senior state official entrusted with the conduct and management of the election. We also met with the president and vice-president of the Law Society of Zimbabwe representing both advocates and attorneys. We studied the consolidated daily occurrence reports of the SA Observer Mission, which were filed by its observers deployed in various provinces of Zimbabwe; and we read reports of the SA Observer Mission on electoral concerns from Zimbabwean non-governmental organisations (NGOs), civic and religious bodies, human rights formations and election support groups, as well as the representatives of the two key political parties, ZANU-PF and the MDC. We visited the offices of a few provincial registrars-general; and attended a briefing and information session on the planned conduct of the election addressed by the Electoral Supervisory Commission,[5] the chief electoral officer and his staff.

Judge Khampepe and I held discussions with high-ranking officers of the Zimbabwe Republic Police in some of the provinces. We went out to election rallies and gatherings held by presidential candidates Robert Mugabe and Morgan Tsvangirai. On actual voting day, we observed the casting of votes at many polling stations and later we observed the counting of votes at counting centres in Harare.

The election in Zimbabwe, more than anything else, was marked by a high level of polarity between two of the five presidential candidates, Robert Mugabe and Morgan Tsvangirai, and between members of their respective political parties. The origin of their respective political parties, their political outlook, election manifestos, slogans and culture diverged.

Judge Khampepe and I compiled a report to President Mbeki on the election. In it we recorded our primary findings. I repeat only a few of them here in order to make the point about the place of the Zimbabwe electoral project in the early days of my career as a judicial officer.

We recorded that intimidation and violence in certain geographical areas of Zimbabwe were the hallmark of the pre-election period. Between the periods March 2000 and March 2002, at least 107 people, whose names, places of residence and dates of death had been published, were reported killed in politically related attacks. Although the police were reluctant to provide any statistics, by far the majority of those victims were said to be members or supporters of the MDC. Some supporters of ZANU-PF were said to have been victims of assault and intimidation by members or supporters of the MDC. It was uncontested that ZANU-PF had established a militarily trained youth group, also known at the time as a youth militia. Reports by our and other observer missions showed that this youth militia had been the primary perpetrator of violence and intimidation against members and supporters of the MDC, or sections of the population which appeared not to support ZANU-PF.

In varying degrees, the election-related violence and threats of violence, arson and hostage-taking curtailed freedom of movement, freedom of speech, freedom of assembly and freedom of association of voters. As would be expected, the violence and intimidation must have engendered fear in connection with the electoral process. In certain areas, freedom of choice must have been undermined.

In the lead-up to the election the electoral laws of Zimbabwe were drastically amended and manipulated by executive decrees. The president had the remarkable power to amend laws of parliament by executive instruments. This resulted in the main and supplementary voters' rolls not being accessible to the public and to opposition party agents. The compilation of the voters' roll lacked the transparency the law required. This meant that there were significant obstacles to citizens having their names added to the voters' roll. Also, there was uncertainty over applicable voter qualifications. As a result, a material number of persons who were previously on the voters' roll belatedly lost their right to vote. Core to the legal uncertainty was the decree that gave wide powers to the registrar-general and constituency registrars. They altered the voters' roll and removed voters from the roll. Also, they registered voters beyond legally permissible cut-off dates without permitting and announcing general access by the public to such extended voter registration. The provision of voter education by any body or group other than groups designated or approved by the Electoral Supervisory Commission was prohibited. Election supervisors and monitors were drawn only from the ranks of public servants to the exclusion of the broad citizenry. Final voters' rolls and information at polling stations were not available timeously. There was no equal or equitable access to publicly owned and funded media.

The executive government disregarded the rule of law by either failing to give effect to decisions of both the high court and the Supreme Court or by introducing statutory instruments or regulations which altered, reversed or undermined court decisions. The treatment of supporters of each of the two main candidates by the police appeared to be partial. The number of polling stations in urban constituencies, and particularly in Harare and Chitungwiza, was substantially reduced. This reduction severely curtailed the access of voters to polling stations. On the third day of polling, not all voters who wished to cast their vote had a reasonable opportunity to do so. The number of voters who were prevented from voting could not be ascertained.

It should, however, be recorded that in all other constituencies, polling stations were easily accessible to the electorate. The secrecy of the ballot was generally observed. Requirements such as the effective design of ballot papers, ballot boxes, impartial assistance to voters if necessary, transporting of election materials and protection of polling stations were adequately accomplished. Consequently, in our view, save for the districts of Harare and Chitungwiza, on polling days the conduct of elections was accomplished in a satisfactory manner.

We observed no material counting irregularities. If any existed, they were not drawn to our attention or reported on. It was principally the pre-polling, legal and other environments which informed our assessment of the conduct of elections. We recognised that opposition parties fully participated in the electoral process up to the end. We acknowledged that on polling days no significant irregularities, save in Harare and Chitungwiza, occurred. The counting of votes was completed regularly and timeously. Notably, the actual polling occurred peacefully.

In the final paragraph of the report, the Judicial Observer Mission stated:

> However, having regard to all the circumstances, and in particular the cumulative and substantial departures from international standards of free and fair elections found in Zimbabwe during the pre-election period, the elections, in our view, cannot be considered to be free and fair.

Judge Khampepe and I submitted the report to the presidency and returned to our judicial postings at the high court.

Journalists and media houses asked many times for a copy of the report on the election. We refused to furnish a copy to the media. It was in the hands of the authority that had commissioned it, the presidency, and the presidency was at liberty to reveal our findings to the public. In the event the presidency chose not to make the report public, despite several requests from the media. One of the media houses then instituted formal court proceedings in the high court against the presidency for the disclosure of the report. The high court ordered the presidency to disclose the report.[6] The presidency appealed the decision to the Supreme Court of Appeal and that court, too, ordered the disclosure of the report.[7] On appeal the Constitutional Court, in two staggered judgments, ordered disclosure of the report.[8]

Let it suffice to make two points. The first is that the African rebirth project of the African Union imagined from 1999 was premised on democratic rule. It was inducted for the people and, hopefully, with the people of Africa. A vital condition for democratic rule, good governance and public good is electoral hygiene. This is self-evident because public power must be acquired legitimately and lawfully, not by stealth, threats of violence or violence, or fraudulence. It goes without saying that the political and economic integration of Africa cannot possibly take root in a climate of electoral manipulation, coercion and fraud. Mere political power without ethical and legal legitimacy cannot be a credible platform for trust, development and integration of the African continent.

At the outset it seemed plain to me that the Zimbabwean electoral process had to be lawful and legitimate. As a bare minimum, the election had to match, in substance, the yardstick the laws of Zimbabwe had laid down. Rightly so, the terms of reference of our judicial mission asked of us to say whether the elections were conducted lawfully and were free and fair. We found that they were not in accordance with Zimbabwe's Constitution and the law of that country.

The argument that a search for peace and stability ought to trump justice and lawfulness is disingenuous and often self-serving. Firstly, I do not understand how void elections could advance or restore peace and stability to any country, let alone a divided one. If anything, the opposite is true. Secondly, electoral fraud rewards the bad guys. It keeps rulers in power against the will of the people. Thirdly, repeated electoral impropriety robs the people of a country of the fresh leadership legs necessary for renewal. Long-serving rulers develop impunity, false formalism and resistance to accountability and transparency. Leaders of that ilk often act selfishly and stand in the way of economic and social innovation. In short, if Africa is to rise, it needs regular and credible elections that stand for the honest and preferably informed wishes of the people.

As a matter of hindsight, I am grateful that so early in my judicial career I had the presence of mind to approach my task with careful impartiality. I am satisfied that I, together with my esteemed colleague, Judge Khampepe, had the courage to arrive at a decision that was bound to be politically unpopular at home and among the political elite of Zimbabwe, even though it was correctly made.

ZANU-PF had been a long-standing ally of the oppressed people of southern Africa and their liberation movements in the struggle against colonialism and apartheid. In those quarters, the Movement for Democratic

Change and its leader, Morgan Tsvangirai, were viewed with considerable suspicion and as a fly in the ointment of post-colonial political power and dividend. I focused on the legal inquiry at hand and screened out my personal or historical likings and linkages. So, the Zimbabwe 2002 presidential election was an unlikely but useful training ground for the judicial career lying ahead of me.

The election of 2002 stood as if it was valid and Robert Mugabe was sworn in as president. He was declared winner of later presidential elections in 2008 and 2013 amid accusations of intimidation of and violence against opposition parties and electoral fraud.

On 21 November 2017, President Robert Mugabe resigned after he had served as head of state and president of Zimbabwe for 37 years. The great nation of Zimbabwe had become considerably emaciated and in desperate need. Its most able citizens had fled their home and become hewers of wood and drawers of water in other lands. His resignation appears to have been at the demand of the army, which had left its barracks and barricaded the streets of Harare and the people who, as a result, swelled the streets in protest as they demanded that Mugabe retire.

A rising Africa, at peace with itself and tending the vital social and economic needs of its people, remains a vital tenet of the Pan-Africanist vision. However, the starting point of that ideal of a united continent, at peace with itself, asserting its innate right to self-determination and obsessed with the mission that its people must rise and find their full potential, must be electoral hygiene.

Africa needs competent, transparent, independent and corruption-free processes of giving valid power to its leaders. We may not thwart the genuine democratic expression of the people and pretend to abide fraudulent elections because that is the price they have to pay for peace. When we do that we entrench bad leaders. Their impunity locks Africa into stubborn social stagnation. In that setting, despite many flowery continental declarations and protocols, poverty of the people is predictable and Africa will hardly rise.

CHAPTER 7

Constitutional Court: Genesis and nomination

Around June 2002, I returned from the Zimbabwe judicial observer mission to the daily chores of a high court judge. I was somewhat relieved and pleased to go back to the more predictable and familiar world of judging. Like most fulfilling jobs, being a judge grows on you. My extended absence from the bench had built up a craving to return to the addiction of judicial clout.

Judges are not unaware of the authority they enjoy and the deference most lawyers and citizens give them on and off the bench. For a judge, it is earned trust and respect, more than anything else, that is their highest reward. No one becomes a judge for the money; money is made elsewhere. And no one becomes a judge for popularity or fame; popularity one has to search for elsewhere too. Every decision a judge makes earns them the scorn and disapproval of the losing party and its fans. It is much like every penalty a soccer referee awards. It earns the referee the wild wrath of the lovers of the punished team. It is certain that the unhappy enthusiasts will hurl unkind words at the referee – or even water bottles and oranges. Judicial office is indeed not a home for fame or fortune.

My first year on the high court was to end in November 2002. Well before then, the Black Lawyers Association nominated me for elevation to the Constitutional Court. The vacancy on that court occurred when the term of Justice Johann Kriegler ended.

Before accepting the BLA nomination, I observed the customary courtesy of asking my judge president, Bernard Ngoepe, and the chief justice, Arthur Chaskalson, whether they supported my nomination. On a matter like that, I chose rather to swim with the tide than against it. Both said they did; Arthur being the more emphatic one. He wanted me to serve at his court immediately and about that he did not mince his words. When I hinted that I might want to route my career through the Supreme Court of Appeal, he curtly retorted: 'No, Dikgang, it is not necessary.' I remain grateful to Arthur's clear view, even early in my judicial career, that I would make a good addition to his court.

I duly accepted the nomination by the BLA. It was extremely heart-warming to be validated by my peers and progressive lawyers in the push against injustice and to know that they trusted that I would serve them and the people well at the summit of the judicial function.

I was not the first nor the last candidate that the BLA tendered for judicial appointment. From the start of democracy they offered a steady flow of nominations. They, more than anyone else, were focused on securing a credible and competent judiciary that mirrored our population and they went on the trot – knocking at the doors of senior practitioners, urging them to abandon their lucrative private practices for the judiciary. Many heeded the call to join a deliberate makeover of the judicial bench. Their nominees, perhaps barring one, have become a dependable, diverse and independent judiciary for most of the 25 years since the advent of our democratic project.

It had been only a year since I had come before the JSC for a post in the high court and now I was to do so again. My interview was set for October 2002 in Cape Town. In quick succession members were asked to weigh my fitness to hold judicial office in a higher forum.

The interview was less than memorable. It was chaired by a chief justice who had confessed to me, and disclosed within the commission, that he supported my enlistment to his court. Indeed several of the members were open about their support for my appointment to the Constitutional Court. The first to voice it after the chief justice was the minister of justice of the

CONSTITUTIONAL COURT: GENESIS AND NOMINATION

time, Penuell Maduna; he was followed by the veteran advocate and activist George Bizos SC, with whom I had appeared as counsel in many cases against the apartheid state.[1]

It may rightly be said that the interview was a sweetheart affair. As I had been practising law for a long time by then, the majority of panellists knew me, I knew them and we had a shared past of one kind or another in the law field. The tempering feature was that the commission was not made up of people from the law profession only. There were parliamentarians drawn from the ruling and opposition political parties as well as members of the JSC appointed by the president as head of the executive arm. There was no valid fear that any of the upstanding panellists would abandon the duty the law had imposed on them. Their task was to probe whether I had the required qualifications and experience in the field of law and whether I was a person fit and proper to hold judicial office.

By the time I left the interview I felt that I had done well and stood a fair chance of moving on to the Constitutional Court. I was thrilled about the mere possibility of serving on the apex court. But why? What was the genesis of the Constitutional Court? Why would my elevation to it be meaningful to me and my country? Back then I did not know the answer, but I knew that given the opportunity I would do my best, whatever the task at hand.

It was perhaps an echo of my days as a Scout under the tutorship of my decorated scoutmaster, Mr CTD Marivate, in my urban village of Atteridgeville. He insisted that each Scout be dressed in a khaki shirt and shorts with a green-and-gold scarf twirled around his tiny neck. Then, after a brief drill, we would swear the oath. It ran: 'On my word of honour; I promise to do my best, my duty to God and my Queen and my country, so help me God.'

The colonial terms and the reference to the Queen reflected the status of South Africa of the time. We were still a dominion within the British Commonwealth. It was what it was. But here is the important bit. I might have been a little boy when I first said those words, but what stayed with me was this: that one takes an oath on one's 'word of honour' and nothing else.

CHASKALSON COURT

CHAPTER 8

Who will guard the guardians?

Once it became obvious that the apartheid state was to be brought to a halt, the leading questions among most participants at the negotiations at the Convention for a Democratic South Africa (CODESA),[1] and certainly many lawyers like me, were: Which institutions would police the democratic project? Who would guard the guardians? Who would ensure that the duties imposed by the freshly ground Constitution were fulfilled?

There were two layers to the enquiry. The first pointed to the history and the legal culture of the courts. The second asked what the name, location and character of the new arbiter would be.

The first question was whether, in the transition, the old-order courts would be suited to play midwives of the brave new just society. Would they enforce a daring supreme law inspired by the ethos of our liberation struggle and shored up by explicit values of justice that were quite different from those of the colonial and apartheid state? The new Constitution was a post-conflict compromise. It was meant to be a covenant of all the people of our land – 'we the people' – despite a contested history mired in centuries of land dispossession, racial and class conflict, and outward difference and diversity. Its centrepieces were the democratic will of the people, human dignity, the achievement of equality, the rule of law and a supreme constitution. All these features were foreign to the colonial power structure.

Each of these foundational values was profound and each was intended to be a clean break from our horrific past. Apartheid law was a subset of colonialism. It was avowedly Eurocentric.[2] It served a racist, minority ruling elite. It cared not for the will or well-being of the majority of its citizens. In fact it suppressed popular will and punished anyone who stood for an inclusive democratic rule. The grossest feature of apartheid law was the manner in which it trampled on human dignity. The majority of its citizens were deemed worthless and dispensable.

Our past was founded on inequality not only of race and gender but also of class and many other facets of life. The majority were in the main dispossessed of their land, unskilled and poor working people. Inequality of citizens and of other inhabitants was the cornerstone of the political and social arrangement. Moreover, the law was harnessed to maintain 'order', which was a synonym for state tyranny. More importantly, the law was to secure the vital economic interest of the ruling class. In essence, the system was rule *by* law and not rule *of* law. The law was harnessed to produce an unequal and unjust social order.

The new design was that the Constitution was to become the supreme law and no law or conduct may breach or dishonour it. Everyone, including the president and his government, the speaker of parliament and the chief justice and his courts, was to be bound by the supreme law. All armed forces and security agencies, all institutions of state and all public servants were to obey the command of the Constitution. It naturally followed that all inhabitants of the Republic were to obey all laws, the Constitution being in the front row.

The new order was intended to differ in look and substance from the rule of the apartheid state. In the minority regime parliament was supreme. Its laws, good or bad, had to be obeyed. Judges and courts could not test the laws of parliament for substantive validity. Maybe their courts could tell parliament that it had omitted a formal or procedural requirement in making the law but they could never say a law was in essence unjust or unconstitutional. Theirs was to enforce the will and design of the ruling party in parliament. Even when the intention of parliament was unclear, the courts had to give the statute concerned a meaning that was 'clear'. But the courts were not free to refuse to apply the law or to tell parliament that its law was bad or that it needed to be written with more clarity.

Courts enforced even patently unjust laws made by parliament. Their jurisprudence was inspired by positivism – a theory of law that teaches that law is valid because parliament says so and it is always binding on the courts; courts are obliged not to second-guess or remake the law, but only to interpret and apply the law. In that way apartheid judges – not unlike Pontius Pilate, the Roman governor of Judaea, who was known for having presided over the trial and crucifixion of Jesus – washed their hands of the unfairness of the outcomes they ordered.

So the fear that judges of yesteryear would not be suited to the new task was widely held and well grounded. They might struggle or fail to give effect to or unwittingly frustrate the democratic state which hoped to birth a new society.

The level of suspicion and antipathy towards sitting judicial officers was palpable. Before 1994, some people demanded that judges should not retain their posts at the start of the new court system. This would have entailed them vacating their posts, undergoing a fresh appointment process and taking new vows pledging loyalty to the new Constitution.

That posture during the negotiations, I thought, was consistent with the newly found drive for renewal. A fresh oath of office would have been emblematic of the birth of the new and just society hoped for. In theory, it would have signalled the end of a settler-colonial paradigm in favour of a fresh start of reconstruction.

It was not to be, however. There was not going to be a judicial clean break. The negotiation compromise fell on the side of judicial continuity and the least disruption during the transition to democracy. All judicial officers who were in posts at the start of the new Constitution were deemed to have been lawfully appointed under it.

The negotiators chose the path of the least disruption to governance during the transition. The choice was not wholly without merit and this is why:

aside from the historical mistrust of the old-order judiciary, the new state did not have ready substitutes for the sitting magistrates and judges. It could not possibly wave a magic wand and instantly produce a judiciary suited to the new task.

One way to cure a historically tainted judicial culture was to introduce constitutional supremacy that would make past laws and the related reasoning of old-order judges lame ducks and vulnerable, and thus at the mercy of the new legal order. All law and conduct which on the day the Constitution took root were not in keeping with it was invalid. This meant that over time parliament and the courts would weed out bad law. Another way was to procure a new hierarchy of courts with the highest court above all existing courts. Yet another way was to change the manner in which judges were appointed.

The selection process had to be free, to the extent possible, from political or executive whim or control. Unlike in the past, appointments had to reflect the population or demography of the country. And, importantly, new judges and so, too, incumbent judges had to swear to uphold the Constitution and all other law.

So when the democratic whistle blew in 1994 the judicial institutions and their culture were supposed to transform forthwith, but with the recognition that many of the old judicial habits would die hard. In fact, in time there was a considerable pushback from some quarters of the judiciary who sought to pretend that they did not need to heed the new legal order. About this I say more when I look at the evolving work of the Constitutional Court under Chief Justice Chaskalson.

The second debate was about the name and character of the new court. We chose to name it the Constitutional Court. It would be headed by a president and would be located in Braamfontein, Johannesburg. This was a break from the common law tradition of calling the highest court a supreme court. This was done for at least two important reasons. The name underscored the centrality of democracy and constitutionalism on the one end, and the core function of the Constitutional Court on the other. At the beginning, it was to be the highest court on constitutional matters only. The previous highest court of the apartheid state, the Supreme Court, was retained, with its judges on board, but was renamed the Supreme Court of Appeal; headed by a chief justice, it remained located in Bloemfontein. It continued to be the highest court in non-constitutional issues. What the compromise at the negotiations yielded, in effect, was two apex courts. This quickly proved to be a monster with two heads, set up to compete for territory and supremacy.

In practice the two heads proved to be a massive headache. Who was the true head of the judiciary – the president or the chief justice? It was unclear. Which cases were non-constitutional matters in a state where the Constitution was pervasive and was supreme law? Would the country develop two streams of law and judicial precedents, both equally binding? In a case of conflict between the decisions of the two courts on a similar matter, which one would be final? In short, would there be one law or two laws in one country – the common law and constitutional law? And where would indigenous or customary law find space as the two systems jostled for power? Would indigenous law remain, as it was historically, a mere footnote to or poor cousin of the common law?

The two-headed monster reared its heads again in an important state ceremony – the first swearing-in of President-elect Mbeki in 1999. Both Chief Justice Ismail Mahomed of the Supreme Court of Appeal and President Arthur Chaskalson of the Constitutional Court mounted the swearing-in podium. The tiff about who properly ought to conduct the swearing-in of the country's new president was hushed but hot. Probably only keen watchers of the courts would have noticed the jostling. The compromise was that they would share the swearing-in function.

Happily, a constitutional amendment[3] placed it beyond doubt that the Constitutional Court is the highest court on constitutional matters and any other dispute that deserves its attention or that it has granted leave or permission to hear. Also it became clear that the seat of the chief justice, deputy chief justice and nine other justices was at the Constitutional Court as the highest point in the judicial hierarchy.

The new court structure would have four tiers in place of the three levels of the past. The magistrate's court would remain the cornerstone court with a national footprint divided into districts.[4] Easily 80 per cent by volume of civil disputes and criminal prosecutions are heard in the magistrates' courts. They are grassroots courts. They are very busy courts without which the judicial system of our country would grind to a halt. We all owe a big debt of gratitude to those dedicated judicial officers in every district and region who work with inadequate resources and remarkably high case-loads. This means that the encounter with the law by most communities and people is at the magistracy. The magistracy is the ordinary face of justice or perhaps, in some cases, the first and last stop of injustice. Only a tiny portion of convicted people or other litigants gain access to appellate justice.

Within the magistracy system there are regional courts which enjoy the power to hear cases over a collection of related districts and have a higher criminal and civil jurisdiction than the district courts. Over the years the criminal jurisdiction of the regional court has been steadily increased to hear very serious crimes, including murder. That court is entitled to impose sentences up to life imprisonment. Regional courts have also acquired the power to hear civil cases as the workload of the district courts and, I may add, of the high courts has spiked.[5]

The second tier of courts is the high court, whose divisions tended to mirror the provinces of the country; each seat of a division tends to be located in the capital of the province. More recently, new seats of the high court were established in provinces that came into being after the alteration of provincial geography at the start of the new Constitution.[6] In large and busy provinces there would also be a local division, as one finds in Johannesburg and Durban.[7]

The high court has original jurisdiction in virtually any civil cause or dispute of any size or any criminal prosecution. In other words the high court is open to any or all inhabitants seeking to have their disputes resolved by application of the law. This is a vital protection to litigants. They are assured of access to justice by approaching the high court particularly against a perceived injustice in a lower court, or repression of one kind or another, or in cases of great hurry or urgency. Perhaps the most compelling example would be seeking a writ ordering a prisoner to be brought before a judge, commonly known as a habeas corpus order. The writ would be appropriate when a prisoner's place of detention is unknown or is unlawful or where a prisoner may have disappeared in detention or where the detainee has not been produced in court in the time prescribed by law. Indeed the high court hears all kinds of cases across the full spectrum of legal disputes, save for a small sliver of cases reserved for specialised courts.[8]

However, ordinarily the high court discourages parties from rushing to it in a case in which the magistracy has jurisdiction and can provide the same relief. This the high court does by granting the successful party costs at the far lower scale of the magistrate's court. Having burned their fingers on costs, litigant parties learn quickly to choose the court best suited to resolve their dispute cost-effectively.

From 1910, the appellate division of the Supreme Court had its seat in Mangaung (then known as Bloemfontein). Until 1994 it was known as the judicial capital of the country because the appellate division was the highest court of the land on all matters.[9] It was renamed the Supreme Court of Appeal, headed by a president and deputy president. In the main it hears appeals from the high court with leave of the high court or of its own leave. The Supreme Court of Appeal hears appeals on all cases, including constitutional matters, and its decisions stand until reversed on appeal by the Constitutional Court.

The Constitutional Court is the highest court in our land. Its primary task is to police and enforce the commands of the Constitution. It decides what is a constitutional matter or not and it makes final and binding decisions on constitutional matters and all other matters that, in its discretion, deserve to be heard by it. Those schooled in parliamentary supremacy always looked askance at courts that had the power to set aside laws made by parliament. The war cry was that judges were unelected officials whose voices had to give way to the voice of the people through their representatives in parliament.

On this argument elected officials had to have the final word over unelected judges. To this perennial concern I will return later when I deal with the review powers of the Constitutional Court and incessant complaints by the politicians of judicial trespass.

In the 40 years of my legal career I had the singular privilege and agony of appearing as an attorney or advocate in all the courts I have described and many other labour and administrative tribunals I do not have the space to describe now. The Constitution chose the judiciary as the guardian of the guardians. It conferred on the courts full powers to police the democratic project and the transformation of our land. The courts had to observe the constitutional limits of their own powers and yet they were duty-bound to ensure that the state in its fullness and all its inhabitants observed the dictates of the Constitution and all other valid law.

CHAPTER 9

The class of '95

Tuesday, 10 May 1994 was no ordinary sunny winter's morning in South Africa. More than 50 000 citizens thronged the lower end of the magnificent gardens of the Union Buildings. High above them, overlooking the capital of the nation, Tshwane, was the office of the past president and it was just about to become the office of the new president, the leader who had been chosen by most of our people. They gathered in jubilation and full voice. They seemed to dance ceaselessly. The people hoped to catch a glimpse of the inauguration of Nelson Rolihlahla Mandela as the first president of our democratic republic, but they would perhaps have to be content to imagine and hear rather than see this glorious ritual as the gardens were much lower than the swearing-in podium on the raised stone arena of the Union Buildings.

Heads of states from just about every nation of the world had descended on our capital city. As we waited with wild expectation a voice boomed: 'Ladies and gentlemen, please welcome Robert Mugabe, the president of Zimbabwe; please welcome Fidel Castro, the president of Cuba; please welcome Sam Nujoma, the president of Namibia; please welcome Muammar Gaddafi – Brother Leader of Libya; please welcome Al Gore, the vice president of the United States of America; please welcome Boutros Boutros-Ghali, secretary general of the United Nations; please welcome the first lady of the United States of America, Hillary Clinton; and ladies and gentlemen, please welcome

Yasser Arafat, the chairman of the Palestine Liberation Organisation.' On and on the loudhailer boomed as exotic names of the good and not so good political leaders of the world were announced. All who were present that day would want to be able say, 'I was there when Nelson Rolihlahla Mandela was sworn in as president.' And indeed it was a wondrous event, the full historical import of which escaped most of us. The momentary joy overcame thoughts of what might or might not come out of all this.

*

It has been a quarter of a century since that momentous day, and the swearing-in of Nelson Mandela as South Africa's first democratically elected president.

There are activists today who argue that what ought to have been a meaningful change of guard was in reality no more than a bogus victory. In the event it did nothing, they say, for the cheering, clapping, singing and dancing crowds who celebrated joyously that day, with hope in their hearts. In fact that hope was a mere shimmer which in time disappeared like a faraway mirage or a distant delusion. The fact of the matter was that most of the tools of oppression and exclusion remain unaltered.

Taking stock at the 25-or-so-year point, what does South Africa have to show for democracy, they say, and one cannot dismiss the bleakness of the picture that is painted on the canvas for all to see.

Economic growth is at best flat or small. Jobs are few and hard to find in an ever-renewing digital age. The norm is disruption and not consolidation. It is less about what you have learned and know and more about what you are likely to innovate or make anew. Newness trumps orthodoxy as the skilled and privileged accumulate more and the unskilled remain on the edge. This difficult social order also deepens fault lines such as gender, race, class or socio-economic status, mental and physical disability, sexual orientation and migrant status. As though that were not enough, the poor are disproportionally high victims of crime on the one end and of the erratic ravages of climate change on the other.

A large majority of citizens are dispossessed of land and are still landless and homeless. Social disparity has deepened rather than decreased. More and more people live on the fringes of social wellness; they survive from hand to mouth and look to the safety net of the state. The means of creating goods and services continue to be the preserve of the few resourced and skilled people and entities. Patriarchy and the resultant social inequality and oppression of women and girls remain entrenched. On all showings, violence against and ill-treatment of women and girls have been rising.

And yet ... none of these setbacks can ever justify erasing the seminal moment of change that Mandela symbolised and stood for. He ushered in the space, however limited and imperfect, and we, the foot soldiers, failed him. We failed in great part to grasp the nettle. We lacked the courage to change our world irreversibly, and particularly of those in need. Instead we gorged ourselves on our newly acquired power over the people; we fed ourselves sick. We paid little devotion to the goals of our long, glorious struggle. Wide-eyed, we made the way of George Orwell's *Animal Farm* a self-fulfilling prophecy. One might be forgiven for asking the question: is it cast in stone that leaders of a revolution will betray their followers?

*

Past the ceremonies, Nelson Mandela knew that from the outset the country deserved good initial judges whose ability and history would be beyond reproach. The new Constitutional Court would not be the whole judiciary but it was to be the leader in giving content and value to the vast promises of our democratic freedom.

In June 1994, within a month of becoming president, Nelson Mandela appointed Arthur Chaskalson SC as president of the Constitutional Court – this after consultation with the cabinet and the chief justice of the time, Justice Michael Corbett. The interim Constitution required that after certain set discussions the president appoint four judges from the ranks of sitting judges from the Supreme Court, as it was then called. The four were Justices Ismail Mahomed, Tholi Madala, Laurie Ackermann and Richard Goldstone.[1] Shortly thereafter, during October 1994 the president chose the remaining six justices from a shortlist of ten sent to him by the JSC after they had interviewed no fewer than 25 aspirants who had been drawn from a bulky longlist of other hopefuls.

The six were Justice Johann Kriegler, Justice John Didcott, Adv Pius Langa SC, Prof Kate O'Regan, Prof Yvonne Mokgoro and Prof Albie Sachs. Each was to serve a non-renewable term of seven years; this was later extended to a period of between twelve and fifteen years, depending on when the judge was first appointed and whether they had prior years of service on the bench.[2]

The racial mix of the anointed ones raised certain eyebrows. We had just emerged from a society where race was everything. Many could not help wondering why Nelson Mandela preferred seven of the eleven justices to be white people. As past beneficiaries of apartheid, how could they possibly shut the door firmly on our horrific and uneven past? The fact obscure to the critics was that Nelson Mandela did not have a free hand. The pre-agreed selection processes were negotiated and written up in the interim Constitution. The four Supreme Court judges Mandela had to choose were likely to be white South Africans because there were virtually no black judges then to choose from – Justices Madala and Mahomed were all he had. Also, at that time people other than judges who might be suited for judicial roles were more likely to be white than black. But even so, Nelson Mandela's choice of the new judges stood and was accepted. Remember, he could do no wrong and mercifully the new Constitutional Court took off with so much excellence and integrity that the discomfort about racial bulk soon fell away.

On the morning of 14 February 1995 President Mandela officially opened the Constitutional Court, with Arthur Chaskalson as the president and Ismail Mahomed as deputy president. All eleven judges took the oath of office wearing green robes. (I never did like those green robes but back then I didn't have to; my turn to wear that colour was still to come.) In attendance was Dullah Omar, the minister of justice.

Once properly constituted, the new court got down to work. The very next day, being 15 February 1995, the eleven justices took their seats to hear the first case – *State v Makwanyane*[3] – on whether the new Constitution permitted the death penalty. Each of the eleven judges led by President Chaskalson wrote a judgment in support of the unanimous conclusion that capital punishment was inconsistent with the ground rules of our constitutional ethos.

Chief Justice Corbett retired in 1996 and Justice Ismail Mahomed was elevated to the position of the chief justice at the Supreme Court of Appeal in Bloemfontein, a position he held until his untimely death in 2000.[4] Justice Pius Langa filled the vacancy of deputy president at the Constitutional Court.

The bench of the Constitutional Court was colourful in many admirable senses. No fewer than six of the eleven were veteran judges who had served in courts before the democratic regime but all had earned wide respect by setting themselves apart from the apartheid legal ethos. They brought their competence and big reputations to the new job and they knew it. Counsel after counsel related how difficult it often was to put in a word or argue before the court uninterrupted. In the early days, the judges often displayed open intellectual jostling.

I remember well my appearance as a senior counsel before the same court in 1995. I was counsel for the minister of home affairs, Prince Mangosuthu Buthelezi, and the government of South Africa, who sought me to defend the constitutional validity of certain provisions in legislation which regulated publication. Certain provisions in the law banned or disallowed free expression of 'lewd' and 'indecent' materials – which was the jargon of lawyers for pornography.[5] For once in my career I was appearing for the government and had to defend apartheid-era legislation that was meant to suppress free expression.

I did not think the legislation was constitutionally compliant but Umntwana, Prince Buthelezi, the minister concerned, thought otherwise, even in the face of the right to free expression in the new Constitution. My difficulty at the hearing was that I could not get a word in as the learned justices debated stridently among themselves. This they did by posing questions to each other through me. Before I could fully grapple with a question another justice would ask, 'This is simple, Mr Moseneke, is the answer to the question not so and so?' Yet another judge would interject and ask, 'Even better, Mr Moseneke, is the answer not so and so?' These were extremely clever judges who knew the answers to most of the questions the other judges asked and that they themselves asked. Not long thereafter the learned judges found each other's measure and the hearings went more calmly as the Constitutional Court settled into a fine cauldron of debate and writing.

Chaskalson and Langa kept a relatively quiet stance during the hearings. They were very good listeners. Good judges listen even to views they find meritless. This allows one to keep what we call an open mind. One's own initial view may well be wrong and may be corrected or altered only when one listens to the other view.

Arthur and Pius could have been judges earlier but neither opted for the judicial role before 1994. Up to then, both chose lawyering of the radical genre. Arthur was a quintessential public interest litigator and Pius did much the same as an advocate at the Bar outside a public interest law firm. In time he became the leader and president of the National Association of Democratic Lawyers, an activist and non-statutory formation of lawyers that opposed the apartheid legal system.

Arthur and later Pius led the Constitutional Court without any sense of self-diminution. Arthur was gifted with an incredibly bright mind which cut through the rubble to the core issues with remarkable ease and precision. Along with that legal expertise was his developed sense of right and wrong or, if you will, the nous for what is just and what is not. On the other hand, Pius's near silence betrayed his profound understanding of the issues before court. He wrote far better judgments than he spoke. In a tribute to him after he had retired as chief justice, I talked about Pius exuding quiet wisdom and ever-present compassion.[6]

As we have seen, six members of the eleven on the new court were sitting judges; two were senior counsel. The remaining three judges were law professors, each with a solid academic showing. They were frontier kids. They slayed stereotypes of the past. First, justices Yvonne Mokgoro and Kate O'Regan were the first women to be appointed judges after the start of democracy. Second, before then no professor of law had been appointed straight onto the bench without serving a sizeable time at the Bar. They were solid agents for change suited to the looming constitutionalism. They brought from the academy to the bench a useful taxonomy – that is, systematic legal thinking which tends to understand the scheme and connectedness of the law and not just the rules that call for case-by-case decision-making, which is how conventional judges often work. The sneering suspicion of practising lawyers and judges that academics make inept judges lingered, but only for a while because these judges were such an excellent addition to the fresh jurisprudence that the doubters were proved wrong.

Before I joined the Constitutional Court in 2002, two of the original justices were no longer there and had been replaced. The first vacancy was created when in 1998 Ismail Mahomed was elevated to the position of chief justice at the Supreme Court of Appeal. President Mandela appointed Zakeria Mohammed 'Zak' Yacoob SC in his place. I called to congratulate him.

His sense of humour got the better of him. 'DM,' as he fondly called me, and does to this day, 'Madiba has appointed like for like.' I knew exactly what he meant and started chuckling. But I wanted him to say it. I remembered the astute idiom of my mother tongue: *siso se se monate ke se o se ingwaelang sone* (the pimple that is most bearable is the one you scratch yourself). It is a little like the wisdom that only Jewish people ought to tell Jewish jokes. Another as wise is the observation that only 'niggers' may call each other 'nigger'.

I asked Zak: 'What do you mean, *Yaaacooob*?' as he had taught me to pronounce his last name.

Zak fired back: 'Madiba has appointed one Indian for another and one Muslim for another!' We both had a hearty laugh. Our mutual appreciation of the humour, however, did not conceal our mutual grasp of the importance of Zak's elevation to the highest court and his personal triumph despite the obstacles that had littered his way.

Zak and I have been friends and professional colleagues for some 44 years, since 1975 when we were in our late 20s. Back then he practised as a junior advocate side by side with Adv Thembile Skweyiya in chambers located in an area in Durban reserved under apartheid laws for use by black people. Zak, Thembile and I were activist lawyers who sought and aided the broader liberation movement to destroy apartheid. We appeared as counsel in many political trials in defence of detained and charged activists. None of us knew then that we would be required to help clean up the apartheid legal debris or that for many years we would serve together as justices of the Constitutional Court.

Justice John Mowbray Didcott was one of the first to go, when he passed away on 20 October 1998 after a battle with cancer. He is well remembered for his firm support of human rights during his 23 years on the bench during and after the apartheid era. Although I had never appeared before him as counsel during apartheid, I knew the feisty and thoughtful John Didcott even in those days. In the 1980s we met several times at the so-called Mount Grace human rights conferences involving progressive judges, activist lawyers and academics.[7] However, my association with John Didcott continued after his demise and without any overt act on my part. By an arrangement with his family and presumably the leadership of the Constitutional Court, his remains were buried on a place located directly behind and below my chambers at the court building. In his memory a bench was built on the spot. This meant that for my full stay at the court I saw the marble-clad bench in memory of John Didcott through my window.

The vacancy left by John Didcott made possible another early and worthy addition to the court. It came in the person of Adv Sandile Ngcobo. After completing a master's degree at Harvard Law School in the USA from 1985 to 1986, he went on to clerk for A Leon Higginbotham Jr, a United States federal court judge. Ngcobo was appointed to the Constitutional Court in 1999 by Nelson Mandela, having served as a judge in the Cape High Court and in the Labour Appeal Court.

CHAPTER 10

Reporting for duty

With the approval of the JSC, on 29 November 2002 the president of the Republic, Thabo Mbeki, signed my letter of appointment to the Constitutional Court. This thrilled me no end. I knew what an opportunity it was to join and serve on a court which, since its inception eight years earlier, had tended the infant democratic project and had acquitted itself well. I saw my selection as an undisguised invitation to join in the rebuilding of country and society.

A vacancy occurred when Justice Johann Christiaan Kriegler retired from the Constitutional Court in 2002. In many ways he was a legendary figure in law circles. He was an advocate at the Johannesburg Bar for 25 years, prior to becoming a provincial and thereafter appellate judge. He bore the reputation of a penetrating legal mind and he rarely suffered fools. As a judge he was known to get down to the decisive law question in a flash and was always somewhat mystified as to why counsel before his court roamed all over except towards the 'bull point'. He was part of a small cohort of judges on the apartheid bench who opted for common sense and judicial activism. These, and his cutting judicial brain, earned him a nod from President Mandela and a seat on the first Constitutional Court bench of 1994, which court he served for seven years.

Johann Kriegler and I were already well acquainted. Just before he took his seat at the Constitutional Court he and I, as chair and deputy chair, and supported by other excellent domestic and international commissioners, found ourselves holed up together for six months at the Independent Electoral Commission (IEC), whose historic task it was to conduct the first democratic elections South Africa had ever held. Despite our vastly different backgrounds, Johann and I found each other, stuck together and got the mammoth electoral task over the line. By any measure ours was a tight and tough national assignment. We ducked many bullets together in order to deliver a credible election outcome that brought in democratic rule to our land. We became unlikely friends and colleagues in useful combat. In the Afrikaans language one could have said Johann and I used up a bag of salt together.[1] The glue must have been the silent fear that we had to produce a credible electoral outcome or invite a violent transition.

In *My Own Liberator* I relate how Johann and I also accomplished much together in community and public work. With others, under apartheid, we managed Project Literacy. This was a project teaching domestic workers how to read and write after hours in 'whites-only' schools. We also served on the board of the Nelson Mandela Children's Fund for over 20 years, trying to alter the manner in which society treated its children.

And now Justice Kriegler was retiring and I was to take his place at the Constitutional Court. I was well aware that I had big shoes to fill. We met for coffee in his court chambers, soon to be mine, and when we had finished he opened his cabinet and pulled out the green gown (which colour, I confess, had not grown on me over the years). He held it out to me and said: 'Hier is jou toga, kleinboet. Dalk is dit 'n bietjie kort.'[2] Then, in his piercing but wise way, he warned me of a few unrepeatable things about my new role at the court, gave me a tight hug and wished me well. That was the sum total of the handover. Johann had already cleared his drawers and was ready to go. Before he left, his blue eyes lit up with childlike excitement. 'Do you want me to show you the building you will be working in?' he asked. 'I mean the new court building under construction?' I jumped at the offer and we set an appointment.

The site was a typical construction place with cranes, scaffolding, concrete beams and wet cement, dust, noisy machines and drills, and many workmen. To my untrained eye it looked like one big mess, but not so for Johann. He knew the building plans and so, too, the actual layout like the back of his hand. He showed me every crevice, nook, angle and corner of the construction. He knew where the foyer, entrance hall and courtroom would be. He pointed out the sites of the judges' chambers, the art gallery and the Great African Steps.[3] Johann lived and loved the construction, and although he himself would never occupy the building – it would be many, many months before completion and his time on the bench was up – his passion for its design and construction was infectious and he continued to watch its progress all the way to completion.

When I reported for duty at the Constitutional Court in 2002, I went at once to pay my respects to the chief justice and deputy chief justice. Thereafter I went round to every chamber to greet and introduce myself to each of my other eight new colleagues. I did this out of good professional habit. In my time at the Bar a new member was obliged to pay a visit to the chamber of every existing member to greet and introduce themselves. Older members of the Bar would walk past you and refuse to recognise you until you had performed the ritual.

Zak Yacoob and Sandile Ngcobo were the rookies – the newest additions ahead of me – and I was naturally attracted towards them. Also they were of my generation of lawyers. Although we each had impeccable academic credentials and solid practical experience, we were yet to earn the respect of the initial colleagues who had done so much to build the institution from ground zero. In time Thembile Skweyiya would be appointed in place of Richard Goldstone and Johann van der Westhuizen would replace Laurie Ackermann – this would happen in 2004. By that time three of Nelson Mandela's original choices would have retired, and two had sadly passed on. In the preceding decade they had constructed the new court 'brick by brick, stone by stone', as Robert Gabriel Mugabe would have said when talking to his people.[4] We, the beginner justices, did not come with the huge reputations of the founding judges who were retiring. They assembled the early foundation stones of the jurisprudence. We had to bow in respect and yet know that it fell on us to inherit and add on to what they had started. We five – Yacoob, Ngcobo, Skweyiya, Van der Westhuizen and I – were the start of the change of guard.

The Constitutional Court spent nearly a decade from 1994 in rented accommodation in Braamfontein. That location was ahistorical. Although we had had no hand in how the history had unfolded, Tshwane (formerly Pretoria) was still the seat of the national executive government and so the Union Buildings was where the new president sat; parliament was still in Cape Town, so that was where the legislators assembled; and Bloemfontein was still regarded as the judicial capital of the country.

Johannesburg was not known for hosting national state institutions and was better suited for the high-rise headquarters of mining and finance houses, commercial entities and non-state activity. But Arthur Chaskalson, who was to head the new court, had other ideas. I suppose his newly appointed colleagues and the minister of justice, Dullah Omar, supported him. And in time the national treasury advanced the money for renting the temporary home of the court and for constructing its permanent home in Johannesburg. In fact there was no cogent reason for a new court to be bound by the geography of the past.

The site upon which the Constitutional Court proudly stands today was an inspired choice, and one that is rich in history and symbolism. The extended precincts, now known as Constitution Hill, were first a prison for white men, the Old Fort Prison. A section for black men was later introduced, popularly known as Number Four, and a women's jail was added shortly thereafter. The site was deliberately chosen by the judges because of its painful past. The Old Fort Prison was built in 1893 and was no longer used for its original purpose – in fancy language, it was 'decommissioned' in 1983.

In it, hundreds of thousands of people were imprisoned. The legend goes that first the British gaoled Afrikaner soldiers in the Old Fort during the Anglo-Boer War and later imprisoned the anti-British 'rebels' during World War I. But once the Afrikaners gained power from 1948 they used the same site to imprison us. The prisoners included famous figures of our liberation struggle like Robert Mangaliso Sobukwe, Nomzamo Winifred Mandela (Winnie Madikizela-Mandela), Zephania Mothopeng, Deborah Nikiwe Matshoba, Mahatma Gandhi, Fatima Meer, Albertina Sisulu, Barbara Hogan, Joe Slovo, Albert Luthuli and Nelson Rolihlahla Mandela. It may be added that when we acquired political power, we had another idea about how this otherwise miserable hill might be used.

On 21 March 2004, President Thabo Mbeki formally opened the new court precincts.[5] It was a moving occasion at which all eleven justices robed in honour of the induction of the Constitutional Court's permanent home. Now the site is the home of the court, a beacon of the rule of law, achievement of equality, human dignity, fundamental rights and freedom.

The courthouse is a real architectural marvel. The design was inspired by the concept of justice under a tree, paying homage to traditional dispute resolution mechanisms where legal disputes are resolved under a tree. It represents transparency and openness, inclusivity and accountability – and in keeping with these qualities, the building is noted for its transparency and enthralling volumes and graceful proportions. The foyer as well as all lounges, library reading rooms, conference rooms and judges' chambers is flooded with natural light. In contrast to conventional court buildings, this one is open, welcoming and filled with the natural light, brightness and warmth that symbolise open justice.

At eye level the courtroom has a low-lying ribbon of glass windows which allow passers-by to peep into the court proceedings. Coming from the high court where the courtrooms are fully sealed off during sittings, I was fascinated to notice people, and especially schoolchildren, looking in while the proceedings were in session.

The building has no conventional marble cladding or wood panelling. Instead the interior walls of the courthouse are raw and unpretentious red brick, which was retrieved from demolished prison walls. The judges had certainly not run out of budget to clad the bricks. They sought rather to make the poignant point that bricks can help imprison or free us. Another striking feature is the judges' bench. Here, too, convention was broken: the covering is not the usual wood panels but cowhide. I've heard the flippant mockery about whether the cowhide is of the native Nguni cow or of the non-indigenous Friesland cow ... but frankly, it matters not. When does an animal or plant introduced into our country hundreds of years ago become local and homegrown?

The Constitutional Court boasts remarkable artwork in its galleries, open spaces and lounges, most of these donated mainly by South African artists. The library is located on three floors of rising ramps and was designed as the biggest human rights library in the southern hemisphere.

All of these deliberate and enlightened changes regarding what a place of justice should be were refreshing and inspiring, but the change I found when I arrived at the Constitutional Court was certainly not only captured by the magnificent courthouse. The more abiding changes were in the way the court dispatched its business and the culture that went with it.

CHAPTER 11

New ways of doing things

The founding justices of the Constitutional Court understood the historic role they were called to perform. They sought to discard the harmful and useless practices of the past. They were mindful of the ongoing impact of colonial and apartheid culture on the practice of the law and so, too, its impact on judicial culture.

The first of the outward changes was the direction of the Constitutional Court that the conventional mode of address would be discontinued. Counsel were notified that the form of address was to be 'Justice' and not 'My Lord' or 'My Lady'. Importantly, 'Justice' was a gender-neutral form of address. This meant 'Madame Justice' or 'Mr Justice' was also out of bounds. Together with 'My Lord' and 'My Lady', out, too, went the use of 'Honourable'. In the beginning, occasionally during our hearings counsel would stumble and used the archaic form of address, then quickly correct themselves.

The substantive import of the change of the form of address was to rid our judicial system of the useless remnants of colonial trappings and to move closer to the values of our constitutional state. High-flown titles in themselves don't render incumbents any more diligent or honest or effective in their tasks. They add nothing useful; in fact they may impede the delivery of justice. Addressing public office-bearers as 'Honourable' and 'Your Excellency' tells the world nothing about their competence, dutifulness and honour. Respect is ordinarily earned and not self-gifted. The high-flown labels encourage false civility and undue deference which in the end stand in the way of accountability. The bigger the title, the less likely will subordinates and the public demand answers and the higher the likelihood of impunity. In any event, a fresh start deserves a fresh look at tags and titles.

The judges of the Constitutional Court chose the recognised and less excessive form of address of apex courts in most democratic countries. The judges of these courts call themselves 'justices', which describes what they do without undue flourish.

Over time the respect that the justices at the court earned was from their sterling work and not the titles they gave themselves. We all know that in other arms of the state many have chosen inflated labels but the actual honour or excellence is often strikingly absent. If you like, the demand to be called honourable becomes a sleight of hand or an act of public deceit.

The Constitutional Court was careful, however, not to impose its newly inspired decision on the form of address on other courts. The high courts continue to use the old forms of address to this day.

Without detracting in any way from the importance of the matter, I cannot resist introducing a lighter note to repeat a conversation Zak Yacoob reportedly had with the former chief justice of India, PN Bhagwati.[1] When he heard that our court had chosen to drop the 'My Lord' form of address Bhagwati bewailed the decision, saying, 'No, no, no, we are indeed Lords because ours is a divine function.'

Another important change was dispatching the seniority system among judges. In all the other courts, including the high court, all tasks and processes are performed in terms of a strict seniority system. The pecking order decides the allocation of court cases, duties and resources. It decides the order in which judges enter a courtroom, where they sit on the bench and the sequence in which they leave the courtroom. In the case of a panel sitting, seniority is a factor in deciding which judge will write the judgment.

In the Constitutional Court all that was stopped. Some precedence is accorded the chief justice and deputy chief justice, who always lead on administrative matters and enter the courtroom first. The rest of the judges are deemed equal in their judicial roles. Every term there is a sitting roster which rotates sitting slots without seniority coming into play.

The salutary impact of doing away with the seniority system was to affirm each justice and accord them an equal voice on all judicial matters. It is saying that all views are valuable and all are worthy of attention. That point is made even clearer by the fact that each of the eleven judges in the Constitutional Court (and in any other court) has one equal vote on judicial decisions, thus demonstrating that judges do not work for or under the chief justice or any other head of court. The head of court is no more than first among equals in administrative and external relations matters. Unlike in an administrative or executive setting, a majority of judges in a panel can and often do outvote the head of court, who also has only one vote.

Our judicial system requires of every judicial officer sitting alone or in a panel or college to apply their mind independently and without succumbing to the influence or pressure from a fellow judicial officer. In appeals, judicial officers normally sit in a panel varying from two to eleven, depending on the level of the appellate court. The law does this to ensure that justice is done. In an appeal more minds are required to ponder and decide the same issues in order to gain the wisdom and judgement of each judge so as to reduce, if not eliminate, the margin of error in decision-making. So, it is in the public interest and in the interest of justice that institutional arrangements ensure that judges are affirmed, encouraged and supported to exercise full individual independence even within the judicial institution.

In furtherance of the same principle, once Arthur and Pius had chosen chambers in the new vacant courthouse, Laurie Ackermann, who chaired the building committee of the Constitutional Court, used lots to allocate chambers to each of us. The chambers, including those of Arthur and Pius, were all the same size, furnished with same number of pieces of furniture and rugs, and identical in every way save perhaps the colour scheme.

Those of us who had come from the high court could not help but notice that the brand-new judges' chambers did not have private toilets en suite as was the case at the high court. This, of course, meant that justices would share toilets with all staff members. What was more, the toilets were unisex. It must be said that the founding justices of the Constitutional Court had pushed the equal access principle to its full limit.

The core business of the people of a court is to make decisions and to account for the outcomes openly and in writing for access by the immediate litigants and the public. That is what judicial officers are there for – to listen to all sides of a dispute and to make a decision. This calls to mind the words of a referee of a boxing contest after collecting the scores from the judges: 'Ladies and gentlemen: we have a decision ... And the winner is ...'

With this core task in mind, the most telling culture shift at the Constitutional Court was the way judgments were produced. The initial judges put up an admirably efficient support system. Foremost was the law clerks system which had become practice in most apex and other senior courts around the world.

Every judge at the Constitutional Court is assisted by at least two law clerks or researchers appointed from a pool of diverse law graduates who apply annually. Law clerks are involved with all aspects of the court's work. They prepare memos on whether cases should be heard and what the key issues are for hearing. They check judgments, both for substantive consistency and grammatical correctness. They research particular issues that their judge might be interested in and they help prepare media summaries. Since the position is considered as a training one, they are encouraged to debate the outcome of cases with their judges and each other. There are also pre-hearing seminars on each case so that they can practise these skills.

During all my years at the Constitutional Court it was certainly a matter of joy and pride among judges to see how hard-working and eager to please were our young and diverse researchers and law clerks. Most of them were fresh from law school. Those young women and men, bright-eyed and keen to learn, with their eager, expressive faces, looked better (and younger) with each passing year. They were energetic and prepared, ready to start their duties and to take on their world. Their pasts might indeed have been very different but their worlds had a fair chance of converging. But the most mirth and joy came to us judges as we started observing sprouting friendships and even love affairs among those lovely human beings. They ignored the fault lines of our jaundiced society and made friends as they chose. Proudly so, a good few pairs of law clerks during my time went on to marry or to form stable life partnerships as they populated some of the most potent social justice causes and public interest law firms and commercial practices. Yes, indeed – ideal court precincts and people can nurture love.

Central to the role of a law clerk is confidentiality. Law clerks come to know of outcomes of all cases about to be made public. By the time I left the court there had been no breach of this trust by at least 22 law clerks annually. One pleasing feature was to introduce at least one foreign law clerk in every judge's chamber from other African countries and elsewhere in the world. This addition enriched the training of the law clerks and the comparative law capability of the court. Unlike domestic ones, foreign law clerks had to secure their own funding through scholarships. My law clerks from Kenya and Ghana and from Canada and Australia still stay in contact with me, reporting on their career trajectories.

The law clerk programme has gained satisfying purchase, with hundreds of law graduates vying for 22 posts every year. After a year's stint, law clerks move on to join the profession in a wide variety of roles. At the time of my retirement my law clerks of fourteen years had formed a little alumni arrangement and gathered for a farewell function. It was most rewarding to learn how they had become significant actors in the profession and that many soon would be ready for elevation to the bench.

Let me make the point emphatically. In our system law clerks are valuable support for but are not themselves judges. They make no final decision nor do they usurp the judgment writing duty of the judge. In my time I truly relished the sparky debates these very bright, young but inexperienced lawyers had on every case I had to decide. But I would never relinquish the duty and joy of doing what judges have to do: to decide disputes independently and write out the reasons with elegance and clarity for each and every outcome.

In the past, judgments – the key commodity that courts produce – lacked a predictable size, form and style. Even citation of legal sources of precedents occurred randomly, in the middle of the text and often imprecisely. The Constitutional Court got down to reforming this.

By the time I arrived at the court, they had developed a house-style manual that regulated just about the full format of judgment production. In it one found uniform and predictable use of type font, size and spacing; design, including titles and subtitles; page layout, including margins, spacing and indents; paragraph and page numbering; headings, headnotes and footnotes; domestic and international references; and citation style. Ready judgment templates were useful and ensured uniformity and speed.

Having just arrived from the high court, I was able immediately to compare the gulf between the judgment writing practice there and that at the Constitutional Court. I needed to go no further than my own high court reported judgments to see the fundamental shift that the style of the Constitutional Court had made. This new writing culture improved the most vital and public output of the judicial function. The new way had to and did percolate remarkably quickly to other courts and, happily today, barring a few errant exceptions, that is the judgment format in our country.

It is so that relative to other courts, the Constitutional Court was better resourced. Its budget tended to provide for the ample support that modern technology offered. For me the most prominent was the digital platform the court enjoyed. Every judge – and so, too, every law clerk and judge's secretary and support staff – worked online with 24-hour access to the internet. This digital access instantly promoted efficiency and industry. Judges and law clerks could readily access bulky digitised and searchable court records. Law clerks could avail themselves of desktop research and in that way enhance accuracy and comparative features of judgment writing.

Among judges only there was an efficient intranet system, which allowed real-time conversations on cases. This meant that much of the debate occurred online and ahead of judges' conferences where firm decisions on outcome would be taken. All important steps before hearing a case were circulated online. These included a pre-hearing note outlining the issues and time estimates in a case to be heard.

After hearing a case a chosen judge writes a post-hearing note that suggests an outcome and reasons for it. Once it is circulated to the other judges and law clerks online, the debate on the correct outcome and reasons for it starts – all online. Indeed very robust debates among judges were had online. Each judge is expected to say whether they support the proposed outcome or not and why. Some email notes were written during regular office hours but many others carried times well after midnight and into the early hours of the morning. The computer remote access facility threw out of the window conventional working hours. It allowed judges to enter the court network and work from anywhere and at any time for any duration.

As one would have expected, many people, starting with parties to a dispute, would have been curious to peep into the working notes and debates of judges before the delivery of the judgment. The state was a frequent litigant and it, and particularly its intelligence operatives, would have been foremost in wanting to anticipate the decisions of the Constitutional Court. In their wisdom the initial justices declined to place the court information technology on the government platform. The Constitutional Court found a discrete service provider on a separate domain and set in place high-level privacy and security protocols and multiple firewalls. The court also appointed a full-time information and technology officer whose task included reporting monthly on attempts to hack the system. On any given week there would be multiple attempts at hacking the court system.

Another marvel I found when I joined the Constitutional Court was its website. It gave the public and many other institutions access to information about the court, its work and people. More importantly, the website carried the court roll and judgments of the court. Within a few minutes of the delivery of a judgment it was accessible to the public. The court tracked the frenzy of visits and downloads immediately after a high-profile judgment. The website boasted tens of thousands of hits from home and abroad. Part of the high hit rate was the digitised material of the well-resourced library.

Twenty to 25 years ago the Constitutional Court and its founding judges had done so much to make it a centre of excellence. I know that much has been done to bring other courts in line with the support they may draw from information technology, but so much more is still to be done. The workload continues to increase, as do the piles of paper. In this scenario, it isn't difficult to see how the administration of justice might be the casualty. Judicial officers who work in busy courts regularly report on lost court files or their contents, to the detriment and at the cost of blameless litigants. Electronic filing must be a mandatory norm with a sensitive caveat for those in need of justice. Our state, judicial officers, legal practitioners and people must set as an uppermost priority the digitisation of justice. A continued failure to do so will render justice impossible.

CHAPTER 12

A clean slate

The Mandela years felt like the best of times. They were to mark the end of the worst of times. Optimism floated everywhere within and beyond our country. At his induction as commander-in-chief of the nation, Mandela's voice rang across wide spaces like a bell on a still and clear morning:

> Let there be justice for all.
> Let there be peace for all.
> Let there be work, bread, water and salt for all.
> Let each know that for each the body, the mind and the soul have been freed to fulfil themselves.
> Never, never and never again shall it be that this beautiful land will again experience the oppression of one by another and suffer the indignity of being the skunk of the world.
> Let freedom reign.
> The sun shall never set on so glorious a human achievement!
> God bless Africa![1]

I am not saying pain and hurt never was or that it was gone and forgotten. How could I? At the time of Mandela's near-scriptural address the world stood by and watched as 800 000 fellow Africans – Tutsis and moderate Hutus – were slaughtered in the three-month Rwandan genocide.[2] The picture of Chris Hani lying in a pool of his own blood in his driveway a year earlier on 10 April 1993 still flashes in my mind.[3] How can I forget the hundreds of Pan-Africanist Congress combatants who were executed by the apartheid government in the gallows of Pretoria Central Prison for claiming freedom?[4] How could I forget the many, many other women and men and children – yes, children – whom I have not called by name who died for our freedom?

However, we had just escaped a horrific nightmare for a possible idyllic dawn. Most of us trusted that we were on the cusp of renewal – of a new beginning. It was that singular hope that I celebrated.

The air of rebirth and triumph seemed to have cascaded across the nation. Even the manner we played and competed showed. We even tended to celebrate achievements in unison. To this day I remember 24 June 1995. At Ellis Park, in the heart of Johannesburg, the Springboks had beaten the All Blacks 15–12 in extra time in a nerve-racking Rugby World Cup final. How does one forget Joel Stransky's spectacular winning drop goal in the 92nd minute of extra time and Nelson Mandela stepping onto the field to share in the glory of victory? Then on 3 February 1996, at FNB Stadium near Soweto, Bafana Bafana beat Tunisia 2–0 in the final of the Africa Cup of Nations to become champions of Africa. Again, how does one overlook the stunning 73rd-minute goal by Mark Williams, followed by another goal by Mark again in the 75th minute? Again, the talisman, Nelson Mandela, was at hand to step onto the field and cheer when the trophy was lifted.

Kabonina and I and our two sons Sedise and Botshelo were in Atlanta, USA, for the 1996 Olympics. Then I was chairman of Telkom SA, which had sponsored our Olympic team. On 21 July 1996 we were privileged to watch Penny Heyns break the world record for the 100 metres breaststroke in the heats and that evening she won the first of her two gold medals.

Then it was Josia Thugwane's turn for glory. He was an unknown mineworker from Bethal in Mpumalanga who stunned South Africa and the world by winning the 1996 Olympic marathon. On the morning of 4 August 1996 we had chosen to catch our breath and to sleep in a bit. The two boys ran from their hotel room to ours breathlessly shouting, 'Daddy, Mummy, please open the door! Switch on the television! One of our people is winning the marathon!' And there was the diminutive Josia Thugwane in national colours. He was left with only a few kilometres and was comfortably striding to golden victory. The four of us cheered Josia very loudly – as if he could hear us. There's something sublime about seeing and cheering on one's countrywomen and -men as they reach their full potential up to these blinding heights.

*

The first five years of the life of the Constitutional Court, during Mandela's stewardship, were honeymoon years. Its bond with the executive government was most cordial. The nascent court was a vital part of the reconstruction of society. It enjoyed ample support from the new ruling elite but was viewed with much suspicion and dread by the old judicial elite.

Much was made of the prior friendship between Chaskalson and Mandela and yet, I think, both men were well suited for their respective roles and respected the new lines between the executive and the judiciary. A court had to be founded and both of them got on with that job. The early decisions of the Constitutional Court on the presidency demonstrate that healthy and principled distance.

President Mandela attended the opening of the Constitutional Court and oversaw the swearing-in of the judges. His commitment to the rule of law and support for an effective and independent judiciary were well known. Besides being a leader of a liberation movement, he was a trained lawyer and knew how essential courts were to police and uphold constitutional promises. The state favoured the court with a substantial budget, which made the running and ultimate construction of the court complex possible. Such was his interest that Mr Mandela visited the construction site on Constitution Hill and the court has preserved a wonderful photo of him on site wearing a hard-top helmet – to the absolute delight of the construction workers. As he was wont to do, he probably greeted and shook each by hand to the silent disquiet of his bodyguards.

In 1995 the Constitutional Court started its task with a clean slate. This was both a blessing and a curse. The blessing was that the new court could chart a new constitutionalism informed by the values prefigured in the Bill of Rights and the new democratic project. The curse was that the structure of the judiciary that the interim Constitution had set up locked the court into a narrow specialist stream and left the appellate division as the apex court on all other law. In that architecture of judicial power there would be little or no change in the judicial culture. The common law and its colonial pedigree would remain supreme and untouched and the transformative impact of the Constitution would be slim and at best a matter of last resort only.

Before I say more about the curse in the form of the powers of the new court, I have a confession to make. The chapter on judicial authority in the interim Constitution, like the rest, was drafted by a technical committee made up of lawyers.[5] Arthur Chaskalson, Bernard Ngoepe and I served on it. Its mandate was to reduce the agreements or compromises of the negotiating politicians into legal text. We were agents and not principals. The negotiations yielded a specialist court with exclusive constitutional power on top of pre-existing courts which could not hear constitutional disputes. The new court was not connected to the rest of the court system. All appeals would still go through the appellate division, which would have the final word; an exception would be if, in the course of a case before it, it threw up a constitutional issue.

I must now also confess that most of this is said with hindsight. At the time I did not foresee that the court structure would fence in the new court and would not be adequately effective and useful for changing the historical legal and judicial culture. Even if I had foreseen the problem, the mandate of the technical committee was to write out a legal text that was faithful to the compromises made by the political principals.

The problem arose in this way. The source of the authority of the Constitutional Court was the interim Constitution, which would be supreme and enforced through judicial review. The court had the power to decide only constitutional disputes. It had the final word on 'all matters relating to the interpretation, protection and enforcement of the provisions of [the] Constitution'.[6] The Supreme Court of Appeal had the final word on everything else.[7] In effect the Constitutional Court was a specialist court of an exclusively constitutional variety along the lines of European constitutional courts – the German example being foremost.

There were matters in which the Constitutional Court had concurrent jurisdiction with the high courts and the Supreme Court of Appeal, and in others it had the sole power or so-called original jurisdiction: this meant that the Constitutional Court would be the first and last court to test the constitutional validity of any law made by parliament or to review the constitutional validity of bills of parliament or hear disputes between organs of state at national level. On these specified matters the Constitutional Court had original jurisdiction or first and last word.

Constitutional issues that arose midstream in a case before the high courts or appellate division could be referred to the Constitutional Court by some difficult route.[8]

In simple terms the interim Constitution established a dual carriage system of constitutional and non-constitutional issues. The high court and the appellate division could carry on as they had already done for many decades; the courts were expected to dispose of the disputes before them without reaching the constitutional question.

This difficulty preoccupied the early cases of the Constitutional Court, which understood the hierarchy to mean that other courts had to avoid reaching a constitutional issue if the dispute could be resolved through the common law only. In this way the space to decide a dispute under the Constitution became exceptional and ordinarily a forensic plague to be avoided.

Perhaps the clearest statement on the exceptionalism of the Constitution was found in *S v Mhlungu*.[9] Kentridge AJ explained: 'I would lay it down as a general principle that where it is possible to decide any case, civil or criminal, without reaching a constitutional issue, that is the course which should be followed."[10] Other early decisions of the Constitutional Court followed this unfortunate and contested route to sideline the supreme law.[11]

Despite its diversion over the true reach of its power to decide constitutional matters, the Constitutional Court made remarkable headway on substantive issues that otherwise came to it. These were cases where the court had original power or jurisdiction given to it directly by the Constitution or constitutional issues referred to it by the other courts.

Of these cases, the first in 1995 was *Makwanyane*[12] on whether the death penalty was competent under the Constitution. On multiple counts, this was a historical and ground-breaking decision. It was the first case that came before the newly founded court. As many as 400 people were on death row at that time, awaiting the date of their execution.

At the very outset, the president of the Constitutional Court, Justice Chaskalson, defined the core question:

> It would no doubt have been better if the framers of the Constitution had stated specifically, either that the death sentence is not a competent penalty, or that it is permissible in circumstances sanctioned by law. This, however, was not done and it has been left to this Court to decide whether the penalty is consistent with the provisions of the Constitution. That is the extent and limit of the Court's power in this case.[13]

At the end of a remarkably scholarly and bursting judgment, Chaskalson declared that the death penalty offended the Constitution and he ordered that the state and all its organs were forbidden to execute any person already sentenced to death; all such persons would remain in custody, under the sentences imposed on them, until the sentences had been set aside and replaced by lawful punishments.[14]

All other ten justices agreed with the outcome and each wrote a concurring judgment to record a chosen emphasis in the reasoning or simply to express themselves. No other dispute has since attracted a comparable judicial response from all eleven justices in the same case.

After the order of the Constitutional Court, the legislature made a law that required high courts to review the death sentences and, after hearing submissions on appropriate sentence in each case, impose a fresh punishment – other than the death penalty.[15]

Makwanyane did so much more than simply consign capital punishment to its death. One might describe the judgment as a lift-off for the Constitutional Court's enterprise and jurisprudence. It gave content to fundamental rights to life, human dignity and the guarantee against cruel, inhuman and degrading punishment. The main judgment laid the foundations of our embryonic jurisprudence. It displayed new value-based legal reasoning. It anointed purposive interpretation as the correct approach for protecting and advancing fundamental rights and freedoms. It demonstrated the place and usefulness of international law and comparative foreign law in our new way of making decisions and embracing global standards of human decency. *Makwanyane* led the path in introducing the two-stage limitation of fundamental rights and freedoms analysis which later found its way fully into the final Constitution.[16]

Despite the 'curse', and before the start of the final Constitution of 1996,[17] the Constitutional Court resolved some sizeable disputes that were the upshot of the new season of constitutionalism.

Low-hanging fruit included challenges to the validity of provisions in the old-order law regulating criminal justice. The court was quick on the draw. It changed the existing notion of fair trial stating, that 'it embraces a concept of substantive fairness which is not to be equated with what might have passed muster in our criminal courts before the Constitution came into force.'[18] The sequel was that a series of features of the criminal justice system fell away.

In several cases the Constitutional Court decided that certain provisions that offended substantive fairness were not good law and might not be applied again. Examples were the law that allowed a court to make the presumption that a confession made by an accused person before a magistrate was made voluntarily and that it was the accused person who had to show that the confession was not made freely;[19] the law that allowed a court to sentence a juvenile offender to a punishment of whipping was disallowed and stopped as inhuman and degrading.[20] The court required, as the Constitution promised, that an accused person be represented by a legal practitioner of her or his choice, where substantial injustice would otherwise result, at state expense, and also that the accused person be informed of these rights.[21]

The court set aside the legislation that allowed the imprisonment of a judgment debtor who cannot or has not paid a civil debt.[22] In another claim, the court granted an accused person a qualified right to be given copies of certain documents in a police dossier provided they are necessary to help the accused person to prepare their defence.[23] The court intervened and removed the rule that a judge's certificate is required by a person who seeks to appeal, as contrary to fair trial requirements.[24] The court held that a presumption that an accused person is guilty or a reverse onus or duty on the accused to show his innocence was not in keeping with the right to be presumed innocent until proven guilty.[25] The court streamlined and trimmed down the requirements of the bail provision to accord with constitutional dictates.[26] On balance the court came down on the side of a substantive notion of fairness in criminal cases as it sought to give content to the fair trial guarantees of the interim Constitution.

As these fair trial rulings increased, some critics felt that the Constitutional Court had become lenient towards 'criminals' and was only concerned with protecting the accused persons and not the victims of the crime. It is plainly not so. Correctly so, the Constitution was concerned that every person accused of a crime should be afforded a fair hearing by application of the law and before an independent court or tribunal. This is a very important principle in an open, democratic and just society. There is an inherent risk of assuming that people are guilty even before credible and sufficient evidence before a court has found that they are indeed guilty as charged. It cannot be that a mere accusation or suspicion of having committed a crime should suffice to establish guilt.

If we don't keep a strict line on the fairness of the trial of even the 'worst' offender among us, we may end up with many innocent and vulnerable people in jail on mere accusation. During the dark days of apartheid security police detained many opponents of the state on the suspicion that they had or might have committed a political crime against the state. Activists were detained for long and indefinite periods without a fair trial, let alone before an independent court. In fact often the government would declare a state of emergency, which meant that the law was suspended. A person's liberty could be taken away at the whim of the police and without a charge or appearance before a court. The detention was indefinite and the courts were not allowed to decide on the reason for or the length or lawfulness of the detention.

Closer to home, my brother Malatse Moseneke was detained without charge under the state of emergency regulations together with other activists of the time like Zoli Kunene, Moses Chikane *(Robala ka kagiso Mokwena)* and Dr Joe Variawa for well over a year at Modderbee Prison and was released only when the security police chose to release them. My other brother, Tiego Moseneke, was detained together with Zwelakhe Sisulu *(Lala ngoxolo Mfokabawo)* for well over three years at Sun City, as Johannesburg Prison was mockingly nicknamed.

Our notion of a just society must never tolerate such rank injustice. The Constitution promises that no person will be deprived of their liberty or have it taken away without a valid and lawful cause or reason.

A conviction before a court may result in the loss of liberty. That is a serious limitation of the right to human dignity, equal protection of the law and freedom of the person, not to mention the impact imprisonment might have on the family and friends of a wrongly convicted person. We are better off being careful and dutiful in applying rules in order to ensure criminal justice. As the saying goes, we are better off with a guilty person walking free (God forbid, my judicial instinct tells me) than a truly innocent person ending up in gaol.

I have had more than a passing encounter with the miscarriage of justice.

I know something about a person being kept in prison for many years after a mistaken conviction by a court. During my term on the Constitutional Court we had to grapple with a case of wrongful conviction and imprisonment. The court ordered the release of Mr Thembekile Molaudzi, who had served more than ten years in prison on a conviction of murder, armed robbery and two other counts.[27] On the facts, Mr Molaudzi was charged, convicted and sentenced for the murder of a police officer that occurred in August 2002. It was alleged that Mr Molaudzi, together with a group of six other men, shot the policeman in his home and planned to steal his vehicle.

The case of Mr Molaudzi raised very difficult questions for our criminal justice system. He, together with fellow accused, was convicted by the trial court on 22 July 2004 and his appeal was dismissed by a full bench of the high court. The Supreme Court of Appeal dismissed his petition for leave to appeal his conviction and sentence. Mr Molaudzi approached the Constitutional Court without legal representation but it, too, dismissed his application for leave to appeal, citing that it did not raise proper constitutional issues and that the appeal had no reasonable prospects of success.[28] He remained in prison.

After two of his co-accused were successful in appealing their convictions on constitutional grounds,[29] Mr Molaudzi approached the Constitutional Court again, seeking leave to reopen his conviction on the grounds that the conviction was unlawful. He argued that the trial court relied on constitutionally invalid hearsay utterances of a fellow accused made outside court that Mr Molaudzi had been part of the robbery in which the police officer was disarmed and murdered. No other evidence during the trial linked Mr Molaudzi to the commission of the fatal robbery.

The second approach to the Constitutional Court forced the justices to look into the mirror. Ordinarily, the law does not allow a court to reopen a case in which it has given a final decision. The reason for the rule is to achieve certainty and finality. Once all the legal steps in a case have been exhausted, the case should not be reopened. The principle in fancy language is called *res judicata*. A court is required not to overlook the *res judicata* principle unless there are truly compelling reasons that make it in the interest of justice to reopen a finalised and closed case.

In order to decide whether there were compelling reasons to relax *res judicata*, the court had first to find the injustice in the trial that Mr Molaudzi relied on. A closer look at the evidence showed that the trial court had failed to apply the law of evidence correctly and that had it done, so it would have found that there was insufficient evidence upon which a court could find him guilty of the charge. What was more, the Supreme Court of Appeal and the Constitutional Court had both failed to detect the mistake of law which the trial court made.

The obvious but difficult question was whether the court should refuse to relax the rule of *res judicata* and not get to the claim of injustice or whether it should go in there and correct the injustice despite the rule not to reopen finalised cases. The court made the decision to rectify the injustice. Mr Molaudzi's appeal was upheld and the court ordered his immediate release from the undeserved imprisonment.

The horrific experience of Mr Molaudzi tells us that judicial officers do make mistakes. The case is humbling for judges and reminds us and society of judicial fallibility. It is so that to err is human. But it is intolerable when one's mistake, particularly as one who ought to dispense justice, ends in hardship for another person. The judicial role calls for an unfailing attention to detail. First, the facts must be understood in their proper context and sequence and care must be taken to make findings supported by credible facts. A judicial officer must know the law, and if they do not, they must take urgent steps to find the right law and apply it to the properly proven facts in the dispute. Even more important is for the judge to decide on an outcome and formulate an order which the facts and the law permit and which is fair and just.

Experience over the years has taught that a good judicial officer must listen. They must listen patiently to the parties and their counsel on all aspects of the case. Usually, at the beginning of the hearing, the litigating parties and their counsel know a lot more about the case than the judge does. They would have lived with the intricacies of the dispute much longer. They would have given greater attention to the facts and the law than a judge. So listening carefully to them can only help. But in the end, it is the judge who must decide. Adequate moments of reflection by the judge after hearing a case are most helpful.

I add lastly that our court system is indeed premised on judicial fallibility. It is so that ordinarily a judge strives for a fair hearing for the parties and a just outcome in accordance with the law, but this does not always happen. Things can go wrong on the weighing of and making findings on the facts or on identifying or applying the law.

Most court systems entitle a litigant to a right of appeal. Usually a litigant is allowed at least two levels of appeal from the original level of decision. In our country, in theory, a party may have up to four levels of appeal: from the magistrate's court to the high court; within the high court from a single judge to a full bench of the high court; thereafter to the Supreme Court of Appeal; and, lastly, to the Constitutional Court.

The higher the level of appeal the more the number of judicial officers: three judges on appeal in the high court, five in the Supreme Court of Appeal and eleven in the Constitutional Court. The rationale or objective of the appeal system is to stop or reduce the prospect of a wrong judicial outcome. The system works like a sieve that gets finer the higher up in the system one goes. So the more pairs of eyes and individual brains studying and considering a dispute, the greater the prospect of reducing or excluding poor judgments. We know that the appeal system is not foolproof, but we are yet to find one that is absolutely fault-free.

It was therefore quite correct for the new Constitutional Court to make such a fuss about adhering to the new notions of substantive fairness in the criminal justice system.

CHAPTER 13

Judicial architecture reformed

The interim Constitution had a finite life. Its terms predicted its end by creating a constituent assembly that would craft and adopt a final constitution that had to be consistent with pre-set principles. The Constitutional Court was given the power and duty to certify that the draft of the final constitution was consistent with the principles.[1]

The arrangement was both unique and smart. The drafters of the interim Constitution were political parties with no proven democratic support. Their support was apparent but as yet untested by elections. At the same time, representatives of the parties that stood for perceived minorities sought the assurance that the agreed principles in the interim Constitution would be followed by the electoral majority when the final constitution was composed. The principles were a yardstick and safeguard for those who might not be in the majority after the first open and inclusive election.

The constituent assembly was made up of elected representatives of the people in the National Assembly. When they were so gathered, the primary task was to write up a final constitution. The further agreement was that the text of the final constitution would be given to the Constitutional Court to test whether it was faithful to the agreed constitutional principles.

Nearly two years after the start of the new parliament of 1994 the draft constitution was placed before the Constitutional Court for certification. In two monumental judgments the court certified that the draft constitution was consistent or in line with the pre-set principles.[2] The two certification judgments, additional to the death penalty album of eleven judgments,[3] earned the court much of its judicial respect. The court displayed a remarkably high ethic of hard work, a meticulous attention to detail and rational prowess. The decision in relation to the text of each clause of the draft constitution was fully reasoned and tested against the relevant prescribed principle. The certification judgments remain the cornerstone and a foundational understanding of the architecture of our Constitution.

The draft text was assented to and promulgated and the final Constitution took root on 4 February 1997.

The newly found constitutionalism did many good things for our democracy. This I say amidst the full-throttle debate on the historical usefulness of the constitutional transition. Some raise the doubt whether the Constitution was a sufficient platform for true transformation towards an equal and just society, and I will ponder over that critical conversation in a little while. For the present, however, I limit myself to the change and the courts.

The new text reformed the hierarchy of courts, granted constitutional jurisdiction to all superior courts and located the Constitutional Court at the top of the hierarchy.[4] The implications were huge and salutary. The judicial authority vested in the courts under a unified hierarchy. There was one legal system in which the constitutional adjudication was not exceptional and peripheral but the core function of the entire legal system. The judicial artifice or ploy of avoiding the Constitution and using it as the last option fell by the wayside. What was more, every superior court had the power to hear constitutional matters, including setting aside statutes that offended the constitutional prescripts subject to confirmation by the Constitutional Court.

The Constitution made it plain that all law, including the common law and customary law, derived its force from and must be adapted to be in harmony with the Constitution. Equally clear from the Constitution was that the review of the exercise or use of public power must occur within the environs or limits of the Constitution. The Constitutional Court finally laid to rest the split notion that the common law was a body of law that was separate and distinct from the Constitution. If that were so, our uneven past and its legal culture would escape scrutiny and change. Equally worrying was that our legal system would be riddled with multiple streams of the law which were at times different.

On this important issue, since I cannot do any better, I let the vintage Chief Justice Chaskalson speak:

> I cannot accept this contention which treats the common law as a body of law separate and distinct from the Constitution. There are not two systems of law, each dealing with the same subject matter, each having similar requirements, each operating in its own field with its own highest court. There is only one system of law. It is shaped by the Constitution which is the supreme law, and all law, including the common law, derives its force from the Constitution and is subject to constitutional control.[5]

With the full benefit of a reformed judicial architecture in the Constitution, in the following eight years the Constitutional Court went on to decide important cases which gave body to constitutional norms. Many of the early cases of the court related to 'unconstitutional amendments' and the form of government. The cases were a relic of the battle at the constitutional negotiations between those parties that supported a federal state and those that desired a unitary state. The liberation movement opted for a strong, centralised, unitary state. Parties representing minorities or former homelands tended to support a loose federation of multiple self-governing states.

At its core, the debate was over the spread of government power. The liberation movement argued for an integrated and unitary state with power concentrated at the centre and flowing to the extremities or provinces at the behest and pleasure of the central government. They argued that a unitary state would improve efforts to transform society. The other parties argued for a federal state in which the bulk of the power would reside in the federal units and only the residue of the power would be reposed at the centre. The different approaches were as ideological as they were claims for the least or the most control from the centre.

The compromise was to have a unitary state that would devolve specified powers and competences to the provincial and local governments. The provinces were accorded executive and legislative power within their areas of competence, which were specified in the Constitution. These were to be original powers derived directly from the Constitution. This meant that the provinces did not exercise delegated power. They did not depend on the kindness or whim of the central government. More so, the legislature of a province was allowed to adopt provincial constitutions.

In quick pace the two foremost supporters of federalism at the time – the provinces of the Western Cape and of KwaZulu-Natal – initiated the process to adopt provincial constitutions.[6] It was not surprising that in its early life the Constitutional Court heard disputes that one might say were turf battles on federalism, even though sometimes the disputes were dressed up as challenges to intrusive changes to the Constitution.

As early as 1995 the premier of KwaZulu-Natal approached the court seeking an order declaring an amendment to the interim Constitution unconstitutional because it impeded the provincial government in exercising its power to fix appropriate salaries for their public office-bearers.[7] The court dismissed the claim. The argument of the province was quite a poser. The essence of the argument appeared to be that an amendment of the Constitution was unconstitutional even if it was properly adopted by parliament. The contention was truly astonishing. It was difficult to know when and how a properly amended constitutional provision could become unconstitutional or inconsistent with itself.

Another related case of federal contestation[8] was when the KwaZulu-Natal legislature passed a provincial constitution with a two-thirds majority and presented it to the Constitutional Court for certification, as was required by the interim Constitution.[9] The provincial constitution would come into force only if the court certified it not to be inconsistent with the interim Constitution. At the certification hearing the Government of National Unity and the African National Congress objected to the provincial constitution on several grounds. The court, in a unanimous judgment, declined to certify the provincial constitution because it was, in specified respects, inconsistent with the national Constitution.

The same argument arose again in *United Democratic Movement*[10] when, after the 1999 national and provincial elections, the ruling party, the ANC, acquired an electoral super-majority in parliament. Shortly thereafter, in 2002 members of parliament of the ruling party, supported by a few smaller parties, passed constitutional amendments and laws that allowed for floor-crossing by members of parliament, provincial legislatures and municipalities without the members losing the seats they had acquired before the floor-crossing. The court considered floor-crossing to be less than desirable, but none the less chose to respect the will of the super-majority in parliament and dismissed the claim that the amendments were unconstitutional. Once properly passed, a constitutional amendment forms part of the Constitution and cannot be viewed as unconstitutional.

In the Western Cape province the federalism challenge came in a different guise. As we have seen, the province was entitled to adopt a provincial constitution subject to certification by the Constitutional Court.[11] The province passed a provincial constitution with a super-majority of two-thirds. The provincial constitution provided for elections that were to be regulated by provincial legislation and not national legislation. Its legislation envisaged a mainly constituency electoral system. The court took the view that the power the national Constitution gave to a province did not include the power to deviate from the national electoral system.[12] Put another way, the electoral system of a province may not be in conflict with the national electoral system.

As we have seen, in its early life the Constitutional Court had to settle disputes between organs of provinces and national government. More closely, the court had to decide whether the national legislature had impinged on the authority of the province or whether the provinces had acted beyond their remit.[13]

One other such example was the dispute in *Liquor Bill*.[14] The national legislature made a full law that regulated the entire liquor sector. The regulation included the grant of licences for the manufacture and sale, wholesale and retail, of liquor. And yet the Constitution had given the provinces the exclusive power to make laws on liquor licences.[15] The court held that the national legislature had encroached on the exclusive functional areas of the province as authorised by the Constitution. While a case may be made for a national uniformity in liquor licensing, that power must be read to mean 'intra-provincial liquor licences'.[16]

And yet the national Constitution anticipated this kind of contestation among organs of state and required them to resort to the principle of co-operative governance in order to anticipate and resolve inter-governmental disputes.[17] Co-operative governance was not always available or useful. Some challenges were mounted by non-state organs and yet others stemmed from the continuing contest over federalism and the push to limit the overarching power of the national state over provinces.

The post-democracy honeymoon between the president and the Constitutional Court did not stand in the way of the court testing the lawfulness of the official conduct of the president. In fact the early rulings of the court make it plain that even the president had to exercise his powers within the limits set by the Constitution. In *President of the Republic of South Africa v Hugo*,[18] President Mandela exercised his presidential prerogative by granting pardon and reprieve to convicted offenders serving an imprisonment term. In doing so he favoured female parents in custody and excluded male parents. The court, albeit in a split decision, held that the power to pardon or grant reprieve to prisoners must occur within the limits set by the Bill of Rights and in particular with due respect to the requirement of equality between men and women.

In another matter the Constitutional Court held that there is a limit to how far parliament may delegate its power to legislate to the president. On the facts of the particular case, parliament had given the president the power to amend parliamentary legislation. The court baulked at this and held that parliament may not outsource to the president its legislative power to amend legislation[19] and upheld the complaint of the aggrieved Western Cape legislature.

The practice of outsourcing legislative power of parliament to the president of the country may have remarkably deleterious consequences for good governance and the public good. When the legislature does so, in truth, it surrenders its prime and primal responsibility to one person, the president, who may override the will of the representatives of the people. That is a step closer to rule by one person – autocracy. Separation of powers and checks and balances are useful constitutional tools to moderate the relationship between the three arms of the state. So when one conflates the executive and legislative roles in this way, a good few things go down the drain. These would include the duty of the executive to act lawfully, to put laws into practice for the public good, and to account to parliament.

You may remember that I alluded earlier to a close example, that of Zimbabwe, our neighbours. During our judicial observer mission to monitor the 2002 election in that country, we found that their parliament had passed a law that permitted President Mugabe to amend existing laws or make new laws by presidential decree. The result was that electoral laws changed on the trot by presidential decree as and when elections came nearer and nearer. So to speak, there was no legal certainty. Everyone interested in the election was left guessing. The resultant injustice smelled foul to high heaven.

In a government of the people there may indeed be other forms of neglect by the legislature which are equally toxic and bad for the country and its people. Think of a situation where the legislature does not formally outsource its legislative power but almost never holds the national executive government to account. Instead it develops a sweetheart relationship with the executive. Think of a legislature that never genuinely demands full answers from a recalcitrant president and his cabinet. Imagine a legislature that shies away from demanding financial probity from the national executive, which ought to look after, and use wisely and effectively, public resources. Or a legislature that never fully and frankly asks difficult questions about government services to the people. Ponder a majority in parliament that votes against and drowns out minority parties that clamour for openness and accountability from the executive government. Think of a majority in parliament that resists multiple parliamentary motions of no confidence in the president and it later turns out that the motions may have been justified, given that the ruling party ultimately itself ended his presidency before its full term. Imagine the hundreds of billions of rand seemingly lost from the government and its entities.

A parliament, acting for the people, can be a powerful instrument but only if it does what parliament is duty-bound to do: to consider and adopt legislation; to hold the executive to account; and to provide a platform to debate matters of national importance.[20]

Even in those early cases, the Constitutional Court was warning that parliament may not give away or fail to exercise its responsibilities in favour of even a 'darling' president, let alone a 'delinquent' president and his national executive.

The court did not only censure the president and require him to act within the discipline of the Constitution; it also came to the rescue of the president in a set of facts that appeared to demean his office. Mr Mandela set up a commission of inquiry into the affairs of the South African Rugby Football Union (SARFU). Its chairperson, Dr Louis Luyt, on behalf of the union, brought an application in the high court seeking to have the decision to set up a commission reviewed and set aside. The high court judge who heard the review issued an order compelling the president to appear before him and be cross-examined in an open court. Mr Mandela, despite his better judgement, obeyed the order of the judge, appeared before the high court and submitted to cross-examination on the reasons why he had set up the commission.

The Constitutional Court was highly critical of the order of the high court.[21] It held that in civil matters the president should not be required to testify orally about the conduct of his official business save in exceptional circumstances. The court emphasised that when the president is 'called upon to testify, respect for the office, the need to preserve the dignity and status of that office and an understanding of the implications of his busy schedule must be sensitively and carefully considered'.[22]

I could not find a precedent or prior example in our law of a head of state or president who was hauled before a court to testify in a civil suit relating to his conduct as president. Of course a head of state is expected to file affidavits explaining his conduct, but requiring him to submit to cross-examination in an open court on his decision or decisions is probably unheard of. As a matter of passing historical interest, the judge who made the order against Mr Mandela, the president, was the same man who opposed a change to the constitution of the Pretoria society of advocates to admit black people to membership and in particular opposed my admission as a member of the whites-only society of advocates. It is also true that he later regretted his racist conduct and personally apologised to me for having opposed my membership of the Bar.

One of the huge boulders in the path of the Chaskalson Court was the vexed question of amnesty and reparation – questions that resurface frequently in the present-day debate on the efficacy of our transition from a colonial to a democratic society. The issues of amnesty and reparation for past crimes trouble every post-conflict society. The conflict is marked by past patterns of egregious crimes by the ruling regime against an uprising or rebellious population or other opponents of the regime. Besides economic abuse, which is inherent in a repressive system, the crimes take the form of unlawful killings such as assassinations, disappearances, deaths in police detention and prolonged detentions, rape, torture and maiming, and also emotional abuse.

The clamour for amnesty and so, too, for reparation usually comes to the fore when there is reasonable chance of a post-conflict renewal or new beginning. The army generals and other state securocrats, in our country and indeed elsewhere in the post-conflict world, are generally in the front row demanding amnesty for their crimes. They are in essence demanding to be absolved from criminal or civil liability.

As we ended the drafting of the interim Constitution, the word came through to the technical drafting committee that the army and police generals would not subscribe to the new draft text if there was no express provision for amnesty. The result was the so-called postamble to the interim Constitution under the heading 'National Unity and Reconciliation'. It was drafted by the political actors and not the drafting committee. It was in prose and not the customary pithy text and was not numbered into paragraphs. In relevant part it read:

> The adoption of this Constitution lays the secure foundation for the people of South Africa to transcend the divisions and strife of the past, which generated gross violations of human rights, the transgression of humanitarian principles in violent conflicts and a legacy of hatred, fear, guilt and revenge. These can now be addressed on the basis that there is a need for understanding but not for vengeance, a need for reparation but not for retaliation, a need for ubuntu but not for victimisation. In order to advance such reconciliation and reconstruction, amnesty shall be granted in respect of acts, omissions and offences associated with political objectives and committed in the course of the conflicts of the past. To this end, parliament under this Constitution shall adopt a law determining a firm cut-off date, which shall be a date after 8 October 1990 and before 6 December 1993, and providing for the mechanisms, criteria and procedures, including tribunals, if any, through which such amnesty shall be dealt with at any time after the law has been passed. With this Constitution and these commitments we, the people of South Africa, open a new chapter in the history of our country.

Within a year of its life, in 1995 parliament adopted the truth and reconciliation law.[23] The law established the Truth and Reconciliation Commission (TRC) and provided for the granting of amnesty to people who made full disclosure of all the relevant facts relating to crimes or delictual acts or omissions committed with a political objective. The TRC also had to ascertain the fate or whereabouts of victims and restore their human and civil dignity by affording them an opportunity to relate their own accounts of the violations and by recommending 'reparation measures' for the violations. A particular clause of the law[24] provided that no person who had been granted amnesty in respect of an act, omission or offence should be criminally or civilly liable for the crime or act or omission.

The Azanian People's Organisation, a political organisation that enjoyed considerable following during the 1970s and 1980s, was aggrieved by the amnesty clause and approached the Constitutional Court to attack its constitutional validity on the grounds that its results were not allowed by the Constitution.[25] The main contention in *Azanian People's Organisation* was described aptly by Mahomed DP, who wrote the judgment:

> They aver that various agents of the state, acting within the scope and in the course of their employment, have unlawfully murdered and maimed leading activists during the conflict against the racial policies of the previous administration and that the applicants have a clear right to insist that such wrongdoers should properly be prosecuted and punished, that they should be ordered by the ordinary courts of the land to pay adequate civil compensation to the victims or dependants of the victims and further to require the state to make good to such victims or dependants the serious losses which they have suffered in consequence of the criminal and delictual acts of the employees of the state. In support of that attack Mr Soggot SC, who appeared for the applicants together with Mr Khoza, contended that section 20(7) was inconsistent with section 22 of the Constitution which provides that
>
>> '[e]very person shall have the right to have justiciable disputes settled by a court of law or, where appropriate, another independent or impartial forum.'
>
> He submitted that the Amnesty Committee was neither 'a court of law' nor an 'independent or impartial forum' and that in any event the Committee was not authorised to settle 'justiciable disputes'. All it was simply required to decide was whether amnesty should be granted in

respect of a particular act, omission or offence. The effect of an amnesty undoubtedly impacts upon very fundamental rights. All persons are entitled to the protection of the law against unlawful invasions of their right to life, their right to respect for and protection of dignity and their right not to be subject to torture of any kind. When those rights are invaded those aggrieved by such invasion have the right to obtain redress in the ordinary courts of law and those guilty of perpetrating such violations are answerable before such courts, both civilly and criminally. An amnesty to the wrongdoer effectively obliterates such rights.[26]

Mahomed DP readily conceded that there was 'very considerable force' in the contention of the Azanian People's Organisation that the amnesty clause violated the right of victims who sought justice and reparation in the ordinary courts of the land. But the deputy president reasoned that the violation would be unconstitutional only if there was nothing in the Constitution itself which permitted or allowed such violation. In his reasoning, the crucial issue which needed to be decided was whether the Constitution, indeed, permitted the violation of fundamental rights caused by the granting of amnesty.

A unanimous court concluded with Mahomed DP that

the epilogue to the Constitution authorised and contemplated an 'amnesty' in its most comprehensive and generous meaning so as to enhance and optimise the prospects of facilitating the constitutional journey from the shame of the past to the promise of the future. Parliament was, therefore, entitled to enact the Act in the terms which it did.[27]

The conversation on the proper place of accountability and retribution for historical crimes fuelled by political motives is nowhere near the end. The debate is sometimes cast in the dichotomy of justice versus peace, the question being whether the quest for peace should trump the demand for justice. As recently as June 2019 a national newspaper reported on an open letter of family members of victims of historical crimes requesting the president to ask the National Prosecuting Authority (NPA) to take steps to charge perpetrators of the crimes.[28] The context of the request is this. At the end of its work in 1999, the TRC referred more than 300 cases of people who were denied or had not applied for amnesty to the NPA for further investigation and possible prosecution for historical crimes in defence of apartheid.

As I conclude, let me sing my final praise to the Chaskalson Court. It lorded over what may arguably be called the golden age of rights jurisprudence. The Constitutional Court continued to test many statutes for compliance with fundamental rights and freedoms in the Bill of Rights.[29] The rights jurisprudence extended to the achievement of equality and unfair discrimination;[30] the right to privacy;[31] the right to a fair trial and judicial bias;[32] the right to a fair hearing and access to courts;[33] free expression and statutory censorship;[34] best interest of the child;[35] the right to vote;[36] the right to cultural and religious practice;[37] the right of access to specified socio-economic rights;[38] labour rights;[39] property rights;[40] the right to bodily integrity and development of the common law;[41] the right to life;[42] and the right to education.[43]

By any measure, in any democracy, these are achievements to be proud of.

CHAPTER 14

A common purpose

When I joined the Constitutional Court in November 2002 Thabo Mbeki was firmly in the saddle as the president of the country and of the ruling party, the African National Congress. Having served one presidential term, which ended in 1999, with a second term beckoning and there for the taking, Nelson Mandela was nevertheless content to bow out and to leave room for his younger successor. His model has not travelled far on the African continent. One has only to call to mind the terms of office of a few African presidents, such as those of Equatorial Guinea,[1] Zimbabwe,[2] Uganda,[3] Sudan,[4] and Cameroon.[5]

At the 1999 national election, under Mbeki's stewardship the ANC earned its highest electoral approval at the time. He appointed Jacob Zuma as his deputy president. The ANC was returned to power just a whisker short of a super-majority of two-thirds of parliamentary seats. In the national election of 2004, the ruling party exceeded the two-thirds majority, also under Mbeki's watch.[6] He again anointed Jacob Zuma as his deputy. This sizeable majority meant that the ANC could, except for section 1,[7] amend the Constitution of the country without the support of any other political party in parliament.

Even so, the relationship between the judiciary and the executive government had remained cordial and useful save for one big bust-up – the *Treatment Action Campaign* case.[8] This proved to be the severest test of the relationship between the government and the Constitutional Court thus far.

At the time the country was facing a deadly HIV/AIDS pandemic. The antiretroviral treatment Nevirapine reduced the risk of mother-to-child transmission of the disease. The Treatment Action Campaign (TAC),[9] an activist movement that represented people who were infected or affected by HIV/AIDS, brought a claim before the Pretoria High Court asking that government be directed to make the drug Nevirapine accessible to pregnant women and their babies if medical advice so required.

The high court granted the order sought.[10] On appeal by government before the Constitutional Court, the TAC persisted that the government should be directed to make the drug available. The government resisted the court order that the TAC asked from the Constitutional Court. The government's stance was to oppose making the drug available throughout the country.

The leading lights from the government's side were seen as President Thabo Mbeki and Minister of Health Dr Manto Tshabalala-Msimang. The spat between the TAC and the minister was public and emotive. It must surely be so that the president and the minister concerned acted with the concurrence or implicit support of their cabinet colleagues.

A unanimous court ordered the minister of health and all provincial members of executive councils for health to make the drugs available without delay in all cases medically necessary to prevent mother-to-child transmission. Before the order was issued the minister was reported to have threatened not to obey the court order if it were to go against the government. This was a matter of considerable concern but the court had a duty to perform and it did. Once the order was issued, the minister was reported to have said that the government had no intention of frustrating the order and that it stood ready to abide by the final decision of the court.[11]

Some court watchers praised the Constitutional Court for the judgment's masterful tone. It was said to be firm and unwavering and yet avoided critical attack, which might have invited a backlash from the government. The government did well, too, by abiding by the decision of the court and avoiding a crisis that might have endangered the democratic project.

When I joined the Constitutional Court in 2002 it had heard and decided about 174 cases over eight years, which translated to nearly 22 cases a year. This is not a full picture of the judicial workload of the court, however. The number 174 relates only to cases heard in an open court. Every year the court received and decided a few hundred written requests or applications for leave or permission to appeal a court order of a court below.[12] Some applicants were allowed to appeal the court order which they were unhappy about; others were denied permission or leave to appeal. This part of the court's chamber work is not generally in the view of the public but it is a very important aspect of its work nevertheless.

The Constitutional Court is the final court an aggrieved party can go to for relief. For that reason the judges know that a refusal of an application for leave to appeal is a definitive and serious matter. A refusal to grant leave to appeal is made by way of a court order in which all judges must agree and the names of the judges who made the decision must appear on the face of the order.

One of the established and more pleasing conventions I found at the Constitutional Court was that if any one or more judges believed that an appeal might have a reasonable chance or prospect of success, the application had to be set down for hearing even if the majority of justices thought it should be dismissed. The reasoning was that if one of us believed an appeal might succeed, that was a sufficient indication that we all ought to hear full argument before we finally made up our minds. The rule was prudent for another reason. There were a few instances where the majority of judges thought a request to hear an appeal ought to be dismissed summarily or without a hearing and a minority would want to hear argument in the case. Once argument was heard, the majority were persuaded to hold for the appellant.

That the judges were able to achieve all this while at the same time overseeing the building of a courthouse and the setting up of the operational support I described earlier was nothing short of extraordinary. Not only did they work extremely hard, but in so doing they laid the foundation for the future growth of our jurisprudence. Their judgments were remarkably erudite and thorough but also quite long and explicit. The justices had to explain themselves and justify the choices they made as they gave content to important but new constitutional provisions. They had no ready domestic examples of how to decide the bold new claims born of the equally new and brave constitutionalism.

That I was about to join this remarkable team of justices, most of whom had worked together for up to eight years, caused strong emotion within me. I wanted to do the very best I could to contribute and to continue along the stellar path they had set.

I arrived for duty at the Constitutional Court with Bongani Khoza, who was to double as my law clerk and secretary and had clerked for me at the Tshwane High Court. He has come a long way: he has since built a sizeable and respected law firm of his own. In addition I took over the law clerks and researchers who had worked for my forerunner, Justice Johann Kriegler.

I spent time with Justice Zak Yacoob and Justice Sandile Ngcobo to learn more about the lie of the land. For quiet but wise counsel I went to the chambers of Justice Tholi Madala, who had been there from inception. My new colleagues were all welcoming and more than ready to provide guidance and support.

By the time I joined, the court had developed a work routine which newcomers had to learn. Its annual work calendar was divided into four quarters or terms: starting on 15 February, 1 May, 15 August and 1 November.

Each term, during which time the court held actual hearings, was six to eight weeks long. Before each term a judge would have the appeal records and written heads of argument of each party in a case. The records were as many as the cases on the roll for the term. The roll for the term carried an average of eleven to fifteen cases to be heard. The record in each case invariably ran into hundreds and sometimes thousands of pages built up when the matter ran through the courts below the Constitutional Court. This required that the recess period before the actual hearings during a term had to be used to study the appeal record, read heads of argument and study the decided cases which the parties would rely on in oral argument.

The chief justice and his deputy compiled a roll or list of cases for the term. The roll allocated each case to a specified judge – the scribe; who was the person who would write the judgment after the hearing. The convention of the Constitutional Court was that the identity of the scribe was known to the judges and law clerks only. It was a secret to be held from the parties and the public. The reason for this was to avoid planting unhelpful speculation about what outcome a particular scribe might argue. Also it would be undesirable for the counsel to target their arguments at a particular justice in the knowledge that they would be writing the judgment. Lastly, announcing the name of the judge who would be writing the judgment might be unhelpful because their judgment might not become the majority judgment.

In the first term of 2003, I was allocated to write the judgment in *Thebus v S*.[13] I was as excited as I was anxious. The appeal record included the transcript of the evidence before the trial court and was voluminous. But that was the least of my worries – in the many years of my career I had had to read lengthy court records and I was accustomed to this. My unease related to the main issue that arose in the appeal: the legal rule in the field of criminal justice known as common purpose.

Common purpose applies when two or more people acting together and by agreement commit a crime. Once the evidence shows that the accused agreed or made a joint plan to commit a crime, the court may impute the unlawful act of one or more of the actors to one or more of the perpetrators or actors. A vivid example would be where two or more accused are charged with planning and committing murder but only one of them pulls the trigger that kills the deceased. The rule or doctrine of common purpose requires the trial court to find all accused guilty of murder as if they, too, pulled the trigger.

The essence of the appeal before the Constitutional Court was whether the common law rule of common purpose was consistent with the notions of substantive justice set by the new constitutional norms.

I am relating this not to anticipate my decision and that of the other justices who sat in the case, but rather to recount how, in my very first case at the Constitutional Court, I had to struggle with many demons of the past. At fifteen years old, I had been convicted and imprisoned on the doctrine of common purpose. The court had found that I had made common cause with the plan or agreement to overthrow the state unlawfully. The conduct of my fellow accused and of others who were part of the 'conspiracy' against the apartheid government was imputed to me and put on my shoulders.

But this wasn't actually what bothered me; it had happened 40 years before and by then was water under the bridge. However, in the many political trials where I had appeared as defence counsel the indictment invariably relied on common purpose. The accused were guilty because they acted with a common purpose to riot or assemble or march, or wanted to overthrow the state 'by unlawful means'. Perhaps the most celebrated case of common purpose was that of the Sharpeville Six who, in *S v Sefatsa*,[14] were sentenced to death. Mercifully, all six accused were spared execution because of very valiant interventions, clever lawyering and public awareness.[15]

But now my task was judicial. I had to assess whether in an open and democratic society observing fundamental rights and freedoms, it was permissible to rely on common purpose where more than one accused had agreed to commit a crime and together did so. I managed to put aside my personal history, my distaste for the doctrine of common purpose and its past abuse for political suppression. I brought to the fore my duty as a judge to shut the door on my personal prejudice in favour of fidelity to the law. I held that the doctrine of common purpose was a necessary and useful rule of criminal justice to combat joint or planned crime and did not offend the Constitution. That outcome of the case was supported by the chief justice, deputy chief justice and the other eight justices. In short the judgment on common purpose was unanimous.

In the same case there was another important issue that had to be decided. This was whether a trial court might make an adverse inference against an accused person who had chosen not to testify during his trial. The views of the judges of the Constitutional Court were divided in answering this question. Besides my judgment, which was supported by two other judges, the remaining eight judges wrote three separate judgments setting out their respective approaches to the right of the accused person to remain silent.[16]

From this came useful lessons. I was the scribe but each of my colleagues was fully engaged with the issue to be decided. Each approached the issue with an open mind and displayed independent thinking. They were collegial in the robust debates but in the end they freely agreed or disagreed. The concurrences or agreements and dissents or differences were crystallised into written pieces of reasoning and made public.

I must say something about how a draft judgment is brought to finality. Within seven days after the hearing the scribe circulates by email a post-hearing note. It is usually short and crisp, stating whether the appeal should fail or succeed and, if so, to what extent and the reasons for the conclusion. In very short order, the rest of the justices respond online saying whether they support the outcome proposed and, if not, why not. Some members of the court may support the same outcome but for different or additional reasons. If all judges agree with the scribe, the scribe must go ahead and produce a first draft by a certain date. However, if there is no full agreement, the differences on outcome or reasoning are aired at a judges' conference, which is held at least one fixed day every week. The chief justice or deputy chief justice presides over the conference. Only judges attend; support staff are not present.

The table in the judges' conference room is round. Its shape is symbolic of their equal worth and a judge may sit anywhere around the table. Each judge has an equal opportunity to debate their (or any other) view on the case at hand. And, most importantly, every judge has one equal vote, as do the chief justice and the deputy chief justice. In some instances, as has been the case, the chief justice might well be outvoted, in which event his judgment becomes a minority judgment. This means that any judge can gather support for and a majority around their judgment only by force of persuasion. The chief justice does not appoint judges and cannot fire them. He has no sway over what decision another judge might make. In respect of judicial decision his only arsenal is being the ethical and intellectual leader of the court.

During my time on the Constitutional Court bench the debates were always collegial and directed at refining the reasoning that might find its way into judgments. But it must be said: most judges do not shy away from robust debate. Many are where they are after many illustrious years of law practice. They know the law, and if they do not they know it, they know how to find it. They have grown up in the arena of legal battles. They have been reared in the terrain of debate or argument. They are not people with small egos, nor are they people without views on matters legal. What is more, the core function of a judge is to form a view from the facts and the law and make a decision. For better, for worse. A judge may not suffer from indecision. There is no room for intellectual constipation or for a pen that dries up. In the end, after listening carefully, thinking hard, and finding and following the law, a judge must choose a side, write down the choice and say why, and then make public the decision.

At the end of conference the scribe will know who will and who will not support their outcome and route. None the less the scribe must go and write. Even those judges who choose to resolve the matter differently wait for the first draft in order to pinpoint the differences in the approaches with precision. Once the scribe's final draft is at hand and the drafts of the concurring or dissenting judgments have been completed, they return to conference.

The ritual that follows was one I had not seen before, certainly not at the high court. The judges of the Constitutional Court call it 'read-through'. Richard Goldstone spent time helping me understand what a read-through was, as well as its genesis and how it became a part of the ritual of the court.

My final draft in *Thebus* came for read-through before a conference over which Arthur Chaskalson presided. The practice was to read through the draft line by line as colleagues suggested changes of grammar, syntax, word order in sentences, the sequence of sentences or the flow of paragraphs. Some proposed changes were to avoid contradiction or inconsistency in the legal reasoning.

My first read-through was gut-wrenching. It allowed for no authorial pride and tested one's patience for other views or even styles of writing. Some colleagues would insist on even the punctuation they thought was correct. But it was the right thing to do. I had become a member of a court which sat as a college, or *en banc*.[17] Unlike in the high court, in the Constitutional Court, as I would learn, I was writing a judgment for more than just myself. Colleagues who were going to sign on or agree with my judgment were therefore perfectly entitled to want to improve its technical presentation. Even those colleagues who disagreed with my draft had a right to insist that the judgments of their court ought to reflect a level of expertise and standard befitting an apex court. They carried some of the reputational risk.

In time I became the chief disciple of the cult of read-through, particularly when I got into the leadership of the Constitutional Court. Pius Langa and I reduced the harshness of the read-through process at conference by requesting colleagues to send their read-through proposal to the scribe well in advance. This allowed the scribe the option to include the suggestions and save all of us a long, gruelling read-through session.

To my mind, the ritual of read-through is a useful quality-assurance tool, which should be followed by every court that sits as a college of two or more judges.

Thebus was my maiden judgment at the Constitutional Court and a baptism of fire. It presented an opportunity to learn about collegiality and how to agree or disagree fearlessly but without rancour or nastiness. I am thankful that it posed severe tests about my judicial role and yet set me well on my way to a long career on the court.

Some scribes are not as swift as others when it comes to producing that first draft. I like to remember myself as one of those who tried not to hold up the reading process. Justice Tholi Madala – may he rest peacefully – wasn't always as prompt when he was appointed scribe. One morning, to an enquiry from Chief Justice Arthur Chaskalson as to the whereabouts of his first draft, he produced a classic response. 'CJ, the draft is in the pipeline,' he said, to which Chaskalson retorted: 'How long is the pipeline?' Bud Tholi surveyed the ceiling and cleared his throat. 'Well, Arthur, pipelines are notoriously long. The draft will be here, when it is here.'

To a similar enquiry another colleague was said to have answered, 'Arthur, my pen has run dry. The day the ink flows again the draft will be here.'

Every judge hopes for a short pipeline and certainly for a pen that never runs dry.

CHAPTER 15

Tenure and intellectual bonding

Once I had paid my dues as a newcomer to the apex court, and had my first judgment behind me, I got into the drill of the working ways of the Constitutional Court. Like most colleagues, I resigned myself to long hours of reading, thinking, debating and writing. It is so that the court was an appellate court of the final instance, which meant that precedent-setting was core to its mandate. While thinking and writing trumped everything else, prior reading was always a must. One can think and write about a possible outcome only after reading the record.

Sandile Ngcobo and I quickly formed an intellectual bond which came, in part, out of staying late at chambers. After office hours, Sandile would whistle from his chamber to mine to provoke a debate. Over coffee, on many an occasion, we debated intricate issues of law that had arisen out of the submissions made by counsel during a hearing earlier in the day. When it came to getting the law right and producing just outcomes for litigants, both of us cared deeply but, even so, in the same matter we sometimes reached different conclusions – even after a hefty but collegial debate.

Sandile often wrote concurrences and dissents and so did I. *Barkhuizen*[1] was one such case. It concerned the constitutional validity of a time bar clause in an insurance agreement. A time bar clause is intended to prevent an insured person from claiming the amount of the insured loss if he or she does not give notice of the claim to the insurer and file it in a court within the time stipulated in the agreement. Sandile and I debated the legal intricacies at length, although we often ended up with different positions. Our reported judgments and that of Albie Sachs tell the differences.

I soon developed techniques of reading voluminous records of proceedings from other courts. I learned that the best route to the kernel of an appeal was to read the judgment appealed against first, followed by the grounds of appeal or grievances against the order. Only thereafter did I venture into the evidence. An astute judge learns quickly which evidence is core to the decision to be made and which is merely ancillary. This reading skill and technique is vital if a judge is to cope with case records in eleven to fifteen cases on the roll per term. You might be required to lead the writing or be the scribe in one appeal, and yet you must also be ready in all other cases to write a judgment agreeing or differing with the scribe's judgment.

A significant feature of the Constitutional Court bench between 2003 and 2005 was that five of the eleven justices had to step into the shoes of the original justices. The high turnover was a result of the set period of the office of judges of the Constitutional Court, which was different and apart from judges serving in other courts. The interim Constitution fixed the term at seven years,[2] and the final Constitution, read with legislation, extended the term to twelve years if the Constitutional Court judge had served three or more years, or fifteen years if they had never served as a judge before.[3] In my case, because I had served for a year before the high court, I could serve only fourteen years at the Constitutional Court, whereas justices Langa, O'Regan, Mokgoro and Sachs, who had not been judges before, could serve the full term of fifteen years. Even so, the majority of the justices left the Constitutional Court relatively young, a significant example being Kate O'Regan, who left the court at the age of 52.

The initial thinking on the term of judges of the Constitutional Court was much influenced by the European practice. Judges of constitutional courts on the continent of Europe served fixed terms ranging from nine to twelve years.[4] Appointments in those courts were drawn mainly from law professors or the law academy and not from career judges. Judges so appointed would return to their university posts after a short term on the constitutional court. Since constitutional courts policed the use of public power and political governance, it was deemed more expedient to limit their term like other public offices.

That approach differs markedly from the position in the US where justices of the Supreme Court are appointed for life. Some justices have resigned of their own accord,[5] but others have stayed on beyond the age of 80 and still others beyond 90.[6]

The system of judicial tenure for the high court and Supreme Court of Appeal is different. A judge retires at the age of 70 and in a few specified instances they may serve up to only 65 years or up to the outer limit of 75 years of age.[7]

In other judicial systems, particularly in Europe and the US, at the end of their term judges may revert to private legal practice or to a university to teach or join business. Our judicial tenure system is different. After retirement a judge may keep the title and the law considers them as a judge in non-active service.[8] Such a judge is liable to be called up for public duty for up to three months in a year. There are famous examples like Judge Hillary Squires, who was called out of retirement to hear the trial of Mr Schabir Shaik,[9] and Judge Ian Farlam, who presided over the Marikana Inquiry.[10] Several judges since then have been called out of retirement to probe one public or governance indiscretion or another.[11]

On balance our democracy has found a useful role for an ever-increasing pool of retired judges at ages when they are still capable of serving the public well. What is more, retired judges are likely to be truly non-partisan. They have the experience and judicial demeanour acquired over many years. They should seek no patronage or promotion or favour from anyone whatsoever.

*

Returning to my early stay at the Constitutional Court, once the judgment in *Thebus* was out of the way the chief justice allocated me very engaging cases to write. *Minister of Finance v Van Heerden*[12] raised important issues concerning equality, unfair discrimination and restitutionary measures. Mr Van Heerden and a class of members of parliament who belonged to a pension fund associated with the previous parliament were unhappy that the pension scheme for new members of the first democratic parliament offered, in the transition, more benefits to its members. Claimants argued that this differentiation had breached their right to equality and amounted to unfair discrimination. The minister of finance argued that the measures were allowed by the Constitution as restitutionary measures or affirmative action and did not breach the equality clause.

Justices Mokgoro and Ngcobo each wrote a judgment reaching the same outcome as my judgment but on different routes or reasoning. This I recall here only to record and narrate Justice Sachs's unique response. He opened his judgment in this way:

> Paradoxical as it may appear, I concur in the judgment of Moseneke J on the one hand, and the respective judgments of Ngcobo J and Mokgoro J, on the other, even though they disagree on one major issue and arrive at the same outcome by apparently different constitutional routes. As I read them the judgments appear eloquently to mirror each other. In relation to philosophy, approach, evaluation of relevant material and ultimate outcome, they are virtually identical. In relation to starting point and formal road travelled, they are opposite.

Later, Sachs J concludes in near-scriptural terms:

> Thus, I endorse the essential rationale of all the judgments, and explain why I believe that the Constitution obliges us to join together what the judgments put asunder.[13]

I sought to share with you the richness of the debates at the Constitutional Court in a quest to find judicial truth. Equally remarkable were the levels of industry and dedication to found a new jurisprudence under our supreme law.

My next assignment was on the constitutional validity of the conduct of a municipality to levy property rates and taxes on a provisional valuation roll.[14] Mr and Mrs Robertson sought to interdict the City of Cape Town from doing so. The dispute let me into the intricate maze of existing and transitional municipality laws. My task was to make sense of the detailed laws regulating local government and whether they adhered to the new notion of local government under the Constitution.

I moved on to write a judgment in *Laugh It Off*.[15] The case was about the contested space between free expression in the form of parody and the protection of a trademark, which in this case was the beer label 'Carling Black Label'. The owner of Laugh It Off Promotions CC produced for sale T-shirts that carried a parody of the South African Breweries' trademark. It was mocked as 'Black Labour' and 'White Guilt'. In smaller lettering, Laugh It Off converted the slogans 'America's Lusty Lively Beer' and 'Brewed in South Africa' into 'Africa's Lusty Lively Exploitation Since 1652' and 'No Regard Given Worldwide'. In a unanimous judgment the court held for Laugh It Off. Again it was the concurrence by Albie Sachs that caught the public eye:

> Does the law have a sense of humour? This question is raised whenever the irresistible force of free expression, in the form of parody, meets the immovable object of property rights, in the form of trademark protection. And if international experience is anything to go by, it would seem that far from providing clear guidance court decisions on the topic have been as variable as judicial humour itself.[16]

I have described a few of my judgements to show how I eased myself into the culture and work ethic of the Constitutional court. Alongside mine, major precedents were produced by various members of the court.

In a collection of ground-breaking cases the court struck down laws that discriminated on grounds of sexual orientation. In *Satchwell*[17] a sitting judge in the court attacked legislation regulating remuneration and benefits of judges on the ground that it still afforded benefits only to spouses of judges, and did not extend benefits to their permanent same-sex life partners. Under the equality clause the court found that the legislation discriminated on the grounds of sexual orientation and upheld the claim. Shortly thereafter in *J and Another*[18] the court disallowed a provision on the status of children conceived by artificial insemination because it applied to children so conceived within the context of a heterosexual marriage but not of permanent same-sex partners. And later in *Fourie*[19] the court extended the scope of marriage to include same-sex unions.

The Constitutional Court was called upon to decide whether a number of procedural matters offended the Constitution.[20] In *Eisenberg*,[21] the court refused to declare immigration regulations irregular. In *De Reuck*,[22] the court refused to find as unconstitutional the ban on child pornography.

The court was also called upon to resolve a variety of claims. Prominent among these were claims related to land rights. In *Alexkor*[23] the Richtersveld community filed a claim against Alexkor for restitution of land under the law that provided for the restitution of land rights. The court ordered restoration of the land. In *Du Toit v Minister of Transport*,[24] Mr Du Toit asked the court to fix the correct approach for the amount to be paid for compensation for land expropriated under the existing law on expropriation, for the construction of a public road.

In another matter related to property, *Jaftha v Schoeman*,[25] the court had to resolve the question whether a law which permits the sale in execution of people's homes because they have not paid their debts, thereby removing their security of tenure, violates the right to have access to adequate housing, which is protected in the Constitution. The court ordered that every sale in execution that will remove security of tenure of a home must be done under judicial supervision.

In *Mkontwana v Nelson Mandela Metropolitan Municipality*[26] the Constitutional Court had to decide another property-related dispute. This one concerned the constitutional validity of laws which in effect burden owners in relation to consumption charges for water and electricity supplied to other people who occupy their immovable property.

The intersection between delictual liability and the Constitution arose in two matters. In *Rail Commuters Action Group*[27] the question was who bears responsibility for ensuring the safety of passengers travelling on commuter trains. The applicants asserted that Metrorail and the Commuter Corporation and the South African Police Service (SAPS) all bear the obligations to ensure the safety of passengers, and also that all have failed to meet those obligations. Instead the minister of transport argued that SAPS should bear the primary responsibility to ensure the safety of passengers, not the institutions that operate the trains. The Constitutional Court held Metrorail and the Commuter Corporation liable.

In *K*,[28] a case that raises the scope of the vicarious liability of the minister of safety and security, Ms K asked for damages in delict from the minister because she was raped by three uniformed and on-duty policemen after she had accepted a lift home from them when she found herself stranded in the early hours of the morning. Both the high court and the Supreme Court of Appeal dismissed Ms K's claim on the grounds that the respondent was not vicariously liable for the conduct of the policemen who had caused the harm to Ms K. The Constitutional Court found the minister liable and that Ms K was entitled to the compensation she sought.

Minister of Home Affairs v NICRO[29] was an urgent application brought just before the 2004 national election. NICRO challenged, on behalf of prisoners, the validity of provisions which introduced into the electoral law changes that in effect deprived convicted prisoners serving sentences of imprisonment without the option of a fine, of the right to participate in elections during the period of their imprisonment. The crisp point in this application was the constitutionality of these provisions.

Bhe and Others v Khayelitsha Magistrate and Others[30] was a very important case for customary law as codified under apartheid laws. There were two main issues in the case before the court. The first was the constitutional validity of section 23 of the Black Administration Act[31] which purported to give effect to the customary law of succession. The second concerned the constitutional validity of the principle of male primogeniture found in customary law of succession. The court had no difficulty in declaring the rule of custom that elevated male seniority at the expense of women and girls, and prohibited them from inheriting at all, as a violation of the equality promise of the Constitution.

In *Volks v Robinson*,[32] Mrs Robinson came to court contending that the survivor of a stable permanent relationship between two persons of the opposite sex who had not been married to each other during their lifetime, but nevertheless lived a life akin to that of husband and wife, should be afforded the same protection as the survivor of a marriage under the law that provides for the maintenance of surviving spouses.[33] In substance, that law gives surviving spouses the right to claim maintenance from the estates of their deceased spouses if they are not able to support themselves. The high court found that the exclusion of the surviving partner of a permanent life partnership from the ambit of the law was unconstitutional. By a majority the Constitutional Court reversed the decision of the high court and dismissed Mrs Robinson's claim. I invite anyone with an interest to read the four judgments in this case. They are meticulous and well researched; each puts up a compelling case for the outcome it contends for. If I had had another opportunity I might very well have voted differently.

Finally, I reach *Basson*.[34] In 1999, Dr Wouter Basson was charged in the high court on 67 counts, including murder, fraud, certain drug offences and conspiracy to commit various crimes. The majority of the offences were said to have been committed before 1994 when he worked in a division of the South African Defence Force (SADF) called the Civil Co-operation Bureau (CCB) and headed South Africa's bacterial and chemical warfare programme. In April 2002, at the end of a long trial, he was acquitted on all counts. The state's appeal concerned three central issues: whether the conduct of the judge during the trial proceedings gave rise to a reasonable perception of bias; whether the trial court was wrong to exclude the evidence led in bail proceedings from the criminal trial; and thirdly, whether the state was entitled to appeal against the quashing of certain charges at the outset of the trial in the high court and whether those charges were wrongly quashed.

Arthur Chaskalson retired on 31 May 2005 after serving just over ten years. His retirement was of his own volition as he was entitled to lead the Constitutional Court until 2009. I seem to remember him saying if he had stayed on to the end of his term Pius Langa would never have become chief justice. That must be so because his and Pius Langa's terms would have ended roughly at the same time. His early retirement also reduced his retirement benefits, which are calculated on the number of years served. His role as chief justice was acknowledged in many ways. Most prominent was, in 2002, when President Mbeki awarded him the national Order of the Baobab (Gold) for 'exceptional service in law, constitutional jurisprudence and human rights'. At the end of his term parliament held a special session to recognise his immense contribution to the Court, its jurisprudence and the country.

LANGA COURT

CHAPTER 16

Second-generation leaders

During December 2002 the ANC convened its 51st national conference at the University of Stellenbosch in the Western Cape – an unlikely venue, it must be said, when one remembers other venues like Mafikeng, Polokwane, Mangaung and Soweto (Nasrec). There Thabo Mbeki was re-elected as president of the ruling party. Knowing how things work within that movement, he was assured of a second term as president of the country.

On a sunny autumn morning on 27 April 2004 at the Union Buildings, Arthur Chaskalson, the chief justice, swore in Thabo Mbeki as president of the Republic. The day was charged with history. It was our Freedom Day and the 10th anniversary of our democratic rule.[1] President Mbeki, being a historical animal, chose the date and place of his induction with eyes wide open. Good convention and tradition matter.

This reminds me of what I understood to be the swearing-in convention in Ghana. Mfundi Vundla, Peter Vundla and I were privileged to be guests of President Nana-Addo Dankwa Akufo-Addo at his induction in Accra on 7 January 2017. The swearing-in of a president in Ghana always occurs at the exact spot and on the day and month that their inaugural president of the Fourth Republic, Jerry Rawlings, was sworn in.[2] At the ceremony their president-elect wore the traditional *kente* gown similar to the one which was worn by Ghana's first prime minister, Kwame Nkrumah, at a similar occasion. Finding meaning in one's proud past is quite in order. After Mbeki,

President Zuma was sworn in twice under the same canopy at the Union Buildings. I guess it is a way of lamenting the choice of Loftus Versfeld stadium as ahistorical and a breach of maturing national custom.

In his acceptance speech, the president made the awaited assurances:

> Today we begin our Second Decade of Democracy. We are convinced that what has been achieved during the First demonstrates that as Africans we can and will solve our problems. We are equally certain that Africa will record new advances as she pursues the goal of a better life for all.[3]

When he announced his cabinet two days later, Jacob Zuma had been appointed deputy president.

I have already mentioned that the chief justice retired on 31 May 2005. Ahead of that date during April 2005, the president of the country invited me to his office at Mahlamba Ndlopfu.[4] At the meeting, a few members of staff were in attendance, led by Adv Mojanku Gumbi, special adviser to the president. After the initial exchange of pleasantries, the president advised that the chief justice would take early retirement and he asked whether I would consider serving as deputy chief justice alongside Pius Langa as chief justice. My response was predictable. It was indeed a privilege to be asked. But I was not inclined to display right there the excitement and happiness that welled in my bosom. I knew that the process still had some way to go. The law required the president to seek the advice of the JSC. This meant I would have to submit to my third interview before the JSC, and in any event the president had to consult leaders of political parties in parliament about his choices.[5]

The JSC interview with Pius went off ahead of mine. The commission was made up of much the same people who had interviewed me on the two previous occasions. I have recently read again the transcript of my interview before the commission for the post of deputy chief justice and am amazed that I had to respond to so many important questions put to me by the panellists on the law, society and justice. I am deeply grateful that the promises

I made in the interview about our country, its judiciary and its people I have kept. I knew my appointment as deputy chief justice would present an indescribable opportunity to serve but also to find and fulfil my full potential as a jurist.

President Mbeki's letters of appointment for Pius and me as chief justice and deputy chief justice respectively took effect on 1 June 2005.

I was not naïve. I understood that Thabo Mbeki had exercised his presidential prerogative and it was he who had chosen the two of us. He could have chosen someone else for chief justice and overlooked Pius Langa. I was keenly aware that he had bypassed at least five colleagues who came to the Constitutional Court before me. But the Constitution had given the choice to the president and there was nothing I could do to make him not appoint me but rather one of them.

And, frankly, I thought I had been chosen solely on merit. I had been in and out of courts as a practitioner for 30 years. I had been on the high court and on the Constitutional Court for four years and my reported judgments in both courts spoke for themselves. The president chose me knowing that I treasured judicial independence. He had the joint report Judge Khampepe and I had delivered to the presidency on the 2002 Zimbabwe election – which report he chose not to make public – in which we'd concluded that the election had not passed constitutional and legal muster. Also, I was personally confident that if my appointment were confirmed, I would not disappoint. I would do a good job. And, importantly, Pius, who was to become the chief, welcomed and supported my appointment. My colleagues appeared to congratulate me heartily and the collegiality remained in place.

The road ahead for us as leaders of the Constitutional Court was bright and held great promise. The first decade of the court founded a new institution of state, made it work and gave it a proud and respected jurisprudence. We were second-generation leaders who would attract the caution of onlookers until we showed our mettle. I welcomed the challenge and was quietly confident. Under our joint leadership the court would have to grow even further and build on the jurisprudence of the preceding decade as we tied together the gains of our transition to a just society for which both Pius and I had fought relentlessly. We were both activist lawyers who formed and led bodies of lawyers who were opposed to the injustice of apartheid and colonialism,[6] so much so that we had both published journal articles venerating the transformative possibilities of our Constitution.[7] We were children and products of our long struggle for freedom. Now we were being called upon to look after and lead one of the fortresses of the democratic project.

CHAPTER 17

Clouds gathering, storm brewing

Nothing had prepared me for the worst end of the job as deputy chief justice. It was not going to be judicial business as usual. Judges are not soft touches and are used to being called upon to hear difficult cases and make tough decisions, but the Constitutional Court, which was only ten years in existence, had never been exposed to the level of political toxicity I was about to encounter.

Nothing alerted the judiciary to the likely and prolonged political pollution and its resultant climate change. Outside the court, the political weather looked stable and calm and without likely precipitation. This turned out to be a rather poor forecast. The ruling elite were on the verge of a warpath that invariably overflowed into the courts.

On 2 June 2005, a day after Pius and I assumed leadership of the Constitutional Court, Judge Hillary Squires, sitting in the Durban High Court, found Mr Schabir Shaik guilty of corruption and fraud and sentenced him to fifteen years' imprisonment.[1] The judgment talked about a corrupt relationship between Shaik, the accused, and Deputy President Zuma – but Zuma had not been charged as a co-accused.

On Tuesday, 14 June 2005, during a special joint sitting of the two houses of parliament, President Thabo Mbeki dismissed Deputy President Jacob Zuma, citing the conviction of Schabir Shaik for corruption and the findings of the high court which implicated him in corruption and fraudulent activities to assist Mr Shaik in several business interests, including one related to a weapons acquisition deal by the South African government in 1999.

On 22 June 2005, President Mbeki appointed Ms Phumzile Mlambo-Ngcuka as the deputy president. Some drew attention to the fact that the new deputy president was the spouse of Mr Bulelani Ngcuka, the national director of public prosecutions.

Ordinarily these occurrences in the executive arm of the state should have meant nothing for our judicial function. But it was not to be so.

Schabir Shaik appealed his conviction to the Supreme Court of Appeal while on bail. That court gave judgment on 6 November 2006 in which it dismissed all the applications for leave to appeal, and all the appeals in the criminal matter.[2] It partially upheld the appeal against certain confiscation of property orders made by the high court.[3] This meant the fifteen-year imprisonment sentence stood. His further appeal to the Constitutional court was heard and dismissed by a unanimous court.[4]

The judgment was a 'The Court' judgment. Usually at the start or end of a written judgment the names of the judges who sat in the case appear. They are called the coram or bench that sat in the case. The coram of 'The Court' is used when the Constitutional Court is unanimous on every aspect of the decision. With this kind of coram the court conveys that it is speaking with one voice without any exception whatsoever. Even so, at the end of the judgment the names of the judges who made the decision are listed.

Two other examples of 'The Court' judgments were the cases of *Treatment Action Campaign*[5] and *Basson*[6] where the Constitutional Court spoke with one voice on a decision of great import to the nation and one that was likely to divide the nation or a significant section of it. A unanimous outcome in a court of as many as eleven judges does not come easily, but when it does it signifies judicial unison and certainty.

A few days later, on 20 June 2005, the newly appointed national director of public prosecutions, Adv Vusi Pikoli, announced his decision to indict Mr Zuma on corruption charges. Mr Zuma appeared in the Durban Magistrate's

Court on 29 June 2005, but the matter was postponed for further investigation. On 8 August 2005 the scope of the investigation into Mr Zuma was extended to include fraud and tax offences allegedly committed by him.

On 12 August 2005 an application was made in chambers to Judge President Ngoepe of the Pretoria High Court for the issue of search and seizure warrants against the premises of Mr Zuma and of the company Thint. The purpose of the proposed search and seizure operations was said to be to obtain evidence in relation to the investigation of the crimes of which Mr Zuma and Thint were suspected. On the same day Judge President Ngoepe issued the majority of the warrants asked for by the national director of public prosecutions.

On the morning of 18 August 2005, most of the warrants were executed simultaneously at various premises throughout the country. Approximately 250 members of the Directorate of Special Operations, also known as the Scorpions, participated in the operation. They seized approximately 93 000 documents as well as computer equipment.

Mr Zuma and his attorney Mr Michael Hulley approached the Durban High Court and attacked the validity of the warrants of search and seizure. The high court declared the warrants unlawful.[7] Thint challenged them separately in the Pretoria High Court and this time the court dismissed the application, finding the warrants to be lawful.[8] The Supreme Court of Appeal held the warrants to be valid in both the Zuma and Thint matters.[9] They approached the Constitutional Court, which granted leave to appeal and heard submissions in the appeals. The judgment was written by Chief Justice Langa and supported by all justices except Justice Ngcobo, who wrote a dissenting judgment separately.[10] For that reason the judgment was not a 'The Court' judgment.

Soon thereafter, during November 2005, Mr Zuma and Thint companies were indicted to stand trial on 31 July 2006 in the Pietermaritzburg High Court.

But well before the trial date of 31 July 2006, there was an intervening criminal trial. On 6 December 2005, Mr Jacob Zuma was charged with rape in the Johannesburg High Court. On 8 May 2006, the high court dismissed the charges, agreeing that the sexual act in question was consensual. During the trial, Mr Zuma admitted to having unprotected sex with his accuser, whom he knew to be HIV positive, but claimed that he took a shower afterwards to reduce the risk of contracting HIV. This hearing had nothing to do with the Constitutional Court, but the prosecution of Mr Zuma played itself out in a court of law. Again, a powerful political actor was putting judicial independence to the test.

On 31 July 2006 the case against Mr Zuma came before Msimang J for trial on two corruption counts which mirrored the two Shaik corruption counts. The prosecution applied for a postponement to complete its investigations and finalise the indictment. Msimang J refused the postponement and called on the prosecution to proceed with the trial.[11] When the prosecution indicated that it was not ready to do so, he struck the matter from the roll. This of course meant that the case could be brought before a court again for trial. This is so because when Judge Msimang struck the matter off the roll he had not dealt with the substance of the charges and whether they were valid or not.

With a view to the trial, the prosecution approached the high court in separate proceedings and applied for certain documents of and on a company domiciled in Mauritius known as Thales International Africa Ltd, the parent company of Thint, to be requested as a certain domestic law permitted.[12] On 2 April 2007, the high court issued a letter of request to the attorney-general of Mauritius to transmit to South Africa the original fourteen documents in the possession of the Independent Commission against Corruption of Mauritius and to obtain and transmit statements from the relevant authorities as to their authenticity.

Mr Zuma and Thint appealed against the decision of the high court up to the Constitutional Court. The appeal was heard in March 2008 and in July 2008 the Constitutional Court dismissed the appeal in another 'The Court' judgment.[13]

One must keep in mind that Mr Shaik, for his part, continued to litigate

Suzan Mashikoane Maaka (born Moseneke), my beloved aunt with whom I spent my early childhood and schooling.
© MOSENEKE PRIVATE COLLECTION

The Sixth Judicial Colloquium marked the judicial transition from apartheid to constitutional democracy. It was hosted by Chief Justice Corbett, in Bloemfontein in September 1993, and attended by chief justices, senior judges, senior counsel and law academics from several countries. Younger Chaskalson SC and Langa SC and several future Constitutonal Court justices are in the picture. Moseneke SC is eighth from the left in the back row. © MOSENEKE PRIVATE COLLECTION

First official photograph after appointment as a judge in 2001. It still hangs on the Tshwane High Court wall.
© MOSENEKE PRIVATE COLLECTION

In the crimson red robes used by high court judges when sitting in criminal trials, 2002. High court judges use black and white robes in civil trials and other hearings. © MOSENEKE PRIVATE COLLECTION

Formal portrait of the judges of the Transvaal Provincial Division, December 2002.
© MOSENEKE PRIVATE COLLECTION

First National Judges Conference, in 2003, convened by Chaskalson CJ and attended by the minister and deputy minister of justice. © MOSENEKE PRIVATE COLLECTION

Chief Justice Pius Langa and Deputy Chief Justice Dikgang Moseneke at the opening of Fountains Advocates Chambers, 1 September 2005. © MOSENEKE PRIVATE COLLECTION

Addressing a seminar on the founding of the Judicial Education Institute, 2005.
© MOSENEKE PRIVATE COLLECTION

The Chaskalson Court shortly before the retirement of Chaskalson CJ in 2005.
© MOSENEKE PRIVATE COLLECTION

In 2007 Senator Barack Obama visited the Constitutional Court, at that stage unbeknown to any of us that he would become the president of the United States of America for two terms. © MOSENEKE PRIVATE COLLECTION

A judicial exchange between the members of the United Kingdom House of Lords and of the Constitutional Court and the Supreme Court of Appeal of South Africa, held in Edinburgh, Scotland, 2007. © MOSENEKE PRIVATE COLLECTION

An unscheduled but welcome visit to the Constitutional Court by retired President Nelson Mandela and Mrs Graça Machel, 2008. © MOSENEKE PRIVATE COLLECTION

The second judicial conference for South African judges, 6 July 2009, attended by the newly inducted President Jacob Zuma. © MOSENEKE PRIVATE COLLECTION

The Flame of Democracy, a perpetual flame that serves to remind South Africa's citizens of their right to a life free from oppression and injustice, burns inside one of four stand-alone staircases at Constitution Hill. These staircases are the last remaining structures of what was once the precinct's Awaiting Trial Block. © CONSTITUTION HILL

The Constitutional Court sitting to pay tribute and farewell to Chief Justice Pius Langa, Justice Yvonne Mokgoro, Justice Kate O'Regan and Justice Albie Sachs, 2009. © ANTOINE DE RAS

Chief Justice Langa delivering his valedictory address, 2009. © MOSENEKE PRIVATE COLLECTION

Compliment to Justice Kate O'Regan after delivering her valedictory message, 2009.
© MOSENEKE PRIVATE COLLECTION

All five judges (Justice D Moseneke of the Constitutional Court, Judge NM Mavundla of the High Court, Justice N Mhlantla of the Constitutional Court, Judge WL Seriti of the Supreme Court of Appeal and Judge GSS Maluleke) originated from the law practice of Maluleke, Seriti and Moseneke in Tshwane, 2009. © MOSENEKE PRIVATE COLLECTION and seek relief from the courts. By the end of 2006 Mr Shaik and a collection of his related companies filed for leave to appeal to the Constitutional Court. The matter was heard in May 2007 and the judgment dismissing the appeals was handed down on 2 October 2007.[14]

At the end of 2006 Mr Shaik and other corporate applicants asked the Constitutional Court to hear their appeal against an order from the high court of 31 January 2006 requiring Mr Shaik and related companies to pay to the state the value of three benefits which the high court said were proceeds of crime.[15] The agreed value of these benefits at the time was over R34 million. In May 2008, the court in a unanimous decision dismissed Mr Shaik's appeal.[16]

During this period the courts in the country were seized with an avalanche of cases related directly or indirectly to the former deputy president of the country. Much public debate had developed around the role of the courts. Some, particularly many followers of Mr Jacob Zuma, claimed that the courts were being used to settle political scores. A flurry of attacks against the judiciary began to surface. The criticism varied but many claimed that the judiciary was partial and acted unfairly in cases that concerned Mr Zuma.[17] The other line of attack was that the judges were unpatriotic and 'counter-revolutionary'.

Let me readily say that there was not even a scintilla of evidence to support these reckless accusations. The attacks were emotional and uninformed and always at a general level of abuse, without an iota of evidence that judges who made the decisions that had political implications acted improperly or with bias.

In a court such as the Supreme Court of Appeal or the Constitutional Court judges sit in panels of five or eleven. In our constitutional dispensation, one would need a magician or perhaps a hypnotist to dupe so many judges knowingly to act unfairly and impartially.

Throughout these heated and hefty forensic battles, Mr Zuma remained the deputy president of the ANC. Time was ticking towards the 52nd national conference of the ruling party in Polokwane, which was due to be held during December 2007, which is the gathering where national office-bearers are elected.

In the public media arguments came thick and fast on whether, in terms of the ruling party tradition, Mr Zuma, as the deputy president of the ANC, would succeed President Mbeki, whose second term of office was coming to an end. However, Mbeki decided to stand as a candidate for a third term as the ANC president – it seemed this was permissible under the ruling party's constitution. Matters were different when it came to the Constitution of the country; the Constitution does not allow a third term as president of the country. The ruling party structures held their nominations conferences from October 2007, where Zuma appeared favourite for the post of ANC president and, by implication, the president of the country in 2009 if the African National Congress won the national election.

On 18 December 2007, at Polokwane, Jacob Zuma was duly elected president of the ANC with 2 329 votes, beating Mbeki's 1 505 votes.

Just about the time Jacob Zuma was elected president of the African National Congress I celebrated my 60th birthday – I was born on 20 December – with family and a select group of friends. In fact it was a joint birthday party, shared with Peter Vundla, whose birthday was close to mine. I have recounted the celebratory event in *My Own Liberator* but it bears repeating here because of its relevance. Peter and I both made speeches. In mine I chose to walk down memory lane up to the point I became a judge. I said I was privileged to be a judge. It was a job I had thought hard about and chose carefully, understanding that I would perform the judicial duties to the end of my working life. Then there came the judicial mantra: 'In my calling it is not what the ruling party wants; it is not what the delegates want; it is what is good for our people.'

I will explain the underlying ethos of what I said in a moment, but it must wait until I tell you the aftermath of this statement. The *Sunday Times* carried my remarks prominently the following day. Pius Langa called me, asking if I would be available for a meeting with Kgalema Motlanthe, then the newly elected deputy president of the ANC, and Mathews Phosa, then treasurer-general of the ANC, at the court on the Monday morning. The four of us knew each other quite well, so first many pleasantries were exchanged. They then pointed to the concern of some members of the ruling party who understood my statement as an interference in politics when, as a judge, I should not do so; my reference to what was good for our people, it was felt, insinuated that the ruling party did not do what was good for our people, when they were the representatives of the people. I acknowledged that it would be unfortunate if members of the ruling elite understood me that way. I conceded that it might have been less of an issue if I had not talked about delegates at a time when the contest for power in Polokwane was so real and heated. But I made my position clear that as a judge I was duty-bound to do what the law demanded of me and not what the ruling elite and its supporters might demand. Impartiality is a central pillar of the judicial role. Judges have a duty to mediate the vertical power relations between citizens and their government or, to use different terminology, between the ruler and his or her subjects.

If judges were to uphold only the wish of the ruler, whatever the law stipulated, the weaker subjects are damned. They are likely to get the worst end all the time. It must be the law that regulates relationships in society and not the wishes of the powerful. I was doing no more than reciting a judicial chant which I hope young lawyers, judges and other wielders of public power will add to their toolkit of things necessary to advance a just society. Public good and justice must precede the private or political preferences of people who hold public power. As they jostle for public power, the law must constrain their conduct.

The chief justice, our two esteemed guests and I drafted a short public statement as an outcome of the meeting. It was meant to calm the waters within certain quarters of the ruling party. But in truth the criticism by some that judges interfered in political matters kept on rearing its head. This, as you would imagine, was a handy criticism in the arsenal of political supporters given the many legal hostilities that were to lie ahead. And they were indeed many.

Mr Pikoli had in the interim been suspended by Mr Mbeki on an unrelated matter, and Mr Mokotedi Joseph Mpshe, the acting national director of public prosecutions, decided on 27 December 2007 once again to indict Mr Zuma. That decision was followed by an indictment of 87 pages with eighteen main counts of racketeering, corruption, money laundering, tax evasion and fraud. It appeared that many of the allegations were based on the same subject matter that was dealt with in the Shaik trial. The national director of public prosecutions thought differently, however. He insisted that the facts and circumstances differed materially because the evidence against Mr Zuma had grown and the legal impediments to charging him had been reduced.

On 28 December 2007, only days after his victory at Polokwane, the National Prosecuting Authority served Mr Zuma with a charge sheet, ordering him to stand trial in the high court on various counts of racketeering, money laundering, corruption and fraud.

The case went to trial on 4 August 2008 before Judge Chris Nicholson sitting in Pietermaritzburg. Before the hearing, on 23 June Mr Zuma made an application asking the court to make an order declaring that both the Pikoli and the Mpshe decisions to prosecute him were invalid in law and should be set aside.

Judge Nicholson held for Mr Zuma.[18] He slated President Mbeki and his cabinet for meddling in Mr Zuma's prosecution and held that three consecutive national directors of public prosecutions acted unlawfully in relation to charges against Mr Zuma. Nicholson ruled that Zuma should have been given the opportunity to make representations to acting National Prosecuting Authority boss Adv Mokotedi Mpshe before being recharged. Nicholson J set aside the decision of the national director of public prosecutions to prosecute Mr Zuma.

On Saturday, 20 September 2008, ANC Secretary General Gwede Mantashe announced that the party had decided to recall Thabo Mbeki from his position as president.

I pause to observe that our Constitution did not provide for the 'recall' of a sitting president by his own political party, or anyone for that matter. There are constitutional provisions for ending the term of a president prematurely. There are two obvious options. One is to move a motion of no confidence against the president in the National Assembly. In that case the members of the majority party would have had to vote against its own president.[19] The second option is for the president to be removed, or impeached, on certain grounds by a two-thirds majority vote in the National Assembly.[20]

Mbeki chose to resign. He chose the route of least resistance, one that spared his political home the anguish of an open tear.

Kgalema Motlanthe was sworn in as president on 25 September 2008, to serve, or so it seemed, as a caretaker president until after the April 2009 national election.

The order of Nicholson J that set aside the decision to charge Mr Zuma was taken on appeal to the Supreme Court of Appeal by the national director of public prosecutions. Former President Thabo Mbeki sought leave to intervene in the appeal on the ground that he had an interest in the appeal because many findings of the court below impinged on him negatively and he wished to have the record set straight.

The Supreme Court of Appeal declined to grant Mr Mbeki leave to intervene on the narrow premise that while it understood his anxiety to clear his name, his grounds for intervention did not go to the heart of the issues the appeal court had to decide.

In January 2009, the Supreme Court of Appeal delivered a unanimous judgment that set aside the judgment of Judge Nicholson in rather harsh terms. The judgment commended Nicholson for asserting the principle of the judiciary's independence but added that he then 'took his eye off the ball':[21]

> This commendable approach was unfortunately subverted by a failure to confine the judgment to the issues before the court; by deciding matters that were not germane or relevant; by creating new factual issues; by making gratuitous findings against persons who were not called upon to

defend themselves; by failing to distinguish between allegation, fact and suspicion; and by transgressing the proper boundaries between judicial, executive and legislative functions.

The Supreme Court of Appeal found that Nicholson let his subjective view on matters cloud his judgement:

> Judges as members of civil society are entitled to hold views about issues of the day and they may express their views provided they do not compromise their judicial office. But they are not entitled to inject their personal views into judgments or express their political preferences.

In a judgment penned by Deputy President Harms, the Supreme Court of Appeal set aside the order of Nicholson J, which in effect reinstated the charges Mr Zuma had to face. It is so that the judgment of the appeal court was handed down when the horse had bolted. The previous president had been recalled seemingly on the strength of the adverse findings of Judge Nicholson that he and some of his executive colleagues had interfered with and influenced the decision to prosecute Mr Zuma.

On 6 April 2009, three months after the appeal court judgment and less than one month before the national election of 2009, Adv Mokotedi Mpshe, the acting national director of public prosecutions, withdrew all charges against Jacob Zuma, citing the contents of certain 'spy tapes' that showed an improper interference with the prosecutorial decision to charge him.

Later that month the African National Congress won the majority of the votes at the national election and the majority of members of the National Assembly elected Mr Zuma as president of the country. On 9 May 2009, at the Union Buildings under the customary canopy, Chief Justice Pius Langa swore in Mr Jacob Zuma as the new president of the country.

CHAPTER 18

The Hlophe matter

As you would have seen, the Langa Court and, indeed, other superior courts were entrapped in legal disputes that in essence were skirmishes for political power and influence. The skirmishes soon turned into pitched battles. A sizeable chunk of the cases were related to or not far removed from multiple charges that were said to be pending against Mr Jacob Zuma.

One such case before the Constitutional Court was the dispute over the lawfulness of search and seizure warrants that were issued and executed at several premises of or associated with Mr Zuma.

During March 2008, as the previous chapter noted, the court heard full argument[1] and postponed the case to think about and decide the outcome. During that period and while the judgment was awaited by all, remarkable things relating to the judge president of the Cape High Court, Mr Mandlakayise John Hlophe (Hlophe JP), occurred, throwing all the justices of the Constitutional Court, the judiciary and the public into a long and difficult crisis.

The Hlophe matter, as it came to be known, evolved into a prolonged trial of court battles between Hlophe JP and eleven justices of the Constitutional Court.[2] But it did not end there. The Hlophe matter also prompted litigation between certain civil society formations and the judge,[3] and between the JSC and him,[4] and between the JSC and the prime witnesses of the events that led to the complaints against Hlophe.[5]

The genesis of the line of cases was a complaint of judicial misconduct laid with the JSC on 30 May 2008 by Chief Justice Langa (Langa CJ); me, the deputy chief justice (Moseneke DCJ); nine justices: Madala J, Mokgoro J, Nkabinde J, Ngcobo J, O'Regan J, Sachs J, Skweyiya J, Van der Westhuizen J and Yacoob J; and two acting justices – Jafta AJ from the Supreme Court of Appeal and Kroon AJ from the Eastern Cape High Court. Hlophe JP, in turn, on 10 June 2008, laid a counter-complaint against all the justices.

While a decision on the complaint and counter-complaint was pending, Hlophe JP approached the high court for an order declaring that the Constitutional Court had violated certain of his constitutional rights by laying the complaint and by issuing a public media release stating that the complaint had been laid.[6]

The complaint of the justices to the JSC arose from the following facts. Towards the end of March 2008, after the Zuma/Thint hearing, Hlophe JP came to the premises of the Constitutional Court and visited Jafta AJ, who concluded that Hlophe JP had attempted to influence him to find in favour of Mr Zuma in the pending warrants appeal. Knowing that Hlophe JP intended to visit Nkabinde J, he warned her of the possibility that Hlophe JP might repeat his attempt.

As anticipated, on 25 April 2008, Hlophe JP visited Nkabinde J and she, too, concluded that the respondent had sought to influence her to rule in favour of Mr Jacob Zuma and his fellow appellants.

At the beginning of May 2008 and soon after the court term began, Nkabinde J informed Mokgoro J of the visit and through her the matter was taken up with other members of the Constitutional Court. On 29 May 2008, the justices met, discussed the subject and eventually agreed to lodge a complaint of judicial misconduct against Hlophe JP with the JSC based on the information provided to Langa CJ and me by Jafta AJ and Nkabinde J. The complaint was lodged the following day.

We described the core of the complaint as follows:

> A complaint that the Judge President of the Cape High Court, Judge John Hlophe, has approached some of the judges of the Constitutional Court

in an improper attempt to influence this Court's pending judgment in one or more cases is hereby submitted by the judges of this Court to the Judicial Service Commission, as the constitutionally appointed body to deal with complaints of judicial misconduct.

The complaint document explained that the case involved the validity of the search warrants and legal privilege related to Thint and Mr Zuma and added that there was no suggestion that any of the judges involved were aware of or had instigated the action of Hlophe JP. The document described the seriousness of the conduct; the democratic values of the Constitution;[7] the independence of the judiciary and the prohibition of interference with courts;[8] the judicial oath;[9] that attempts to influence a court violates the Constitution and threatens the administration of justice; and that the Constitutional Court and other courts would not yield to or tolerate attempts to undermine their independence.

The justices released a media statement couched in almost identical terms. It was sent electronically to the media houses and other subscribers to the Constitutional Court's distribution platform.

It is so that at that early stage we, the complainants, did not inform Hlophe JP of the allegations or their source. We did not ask for his version once we had heard the accounts of our two colleagues. We did not give him notice of our intention to lodge the complaint and we did not tell him beforehand of our intention to issue a media statement about the complaint.

It is necessary to record that on 10 June 2008, Judge President Hlophe laid a counter-complaint with the JSC against the judges of the Constitutional Court. The basis of that counter-complaint was that the justices of the Constitutional Court had violated his constitutional rights, including his rights to dignity, privacy, equality, procedural fairness and access to courts, by publishing a media release about their decision to lodge the complaint.[10]

On receiving the complaint, the JSC requested Nkabinde J and Jafta AJ to respond to it. In their response our two colleagues stated that they had not lodged a complaint; that they did not intend to do so; and that they were not willing to make statements about the matter.

At the request of the JSC, on 17 June 2008 the chief justice deposed to an affidavit[11] on behalf of the complainant justices. The affidavit, which was also confirmed by Nkabinde J and Jafta AJ, stated that the two justices always considered themselves to have been part of the collective complaint of 30 May 2008 and not as individual complainants. Also, both justices confirmed their accounts of what had occurred by agreeing that the chief justice had correctly narrated their version of events.

A precis of the affidavit, dated 17 June 2008, penned by Chief Justice Pius Nkonzo Langa will not do. I have chosen to restate it, in relevant part, word for word because it is a story well told and it is one of the befitting ways of bringing his strong and wise voice to life. On 4 July 2018, Hlophe JP gave the JSC his response to our sworn statement. I will quote from it extensively as well, in order to give a fair account of his response to the allegations against him.

This I also do because I hope to invite you the reader to be the judge. The complaint was lodged with the Judicial Service Commission. That is a body, and the only body, to which the law has given power to investigate and decide on the conduct of judges.[12] More than twelve years have gone by and up to now the JSC has not itself or through a tribunal tested the veracity of these allegations and counter-allegations. The commission has not made a decision on the complaint.

In fact all the complainant justices barring Justice Jafta have either passed on or retired. It is still unclear whether the JSC will resolve the complaint and, if it were to, when. I am not calling on the commission to do anything; I am simply observing as a complainant, a retired justice of the Constitutional Court and a citizen, that the allegations by two judges about another judge have never seen the light of day. Whatever the reasons might be for this prolonged delay of deciding the complaint, this is unacceptable. The long line of court cases did much to keep in abeyance the adjudication or trial of the merits of the complaint for over twelve years and to this day no hearing has been held to finality to test the truthfulness of the allegations that were made by Justices Nkabinde and Jafta about Hlophe JP. And yet in the twelve years since the complaint, no less than fourteen[13] cases related to our original complaints were decided. The ferocious court battles were about everything technical, procedural or peripheral but nothing about the core complaint. This was by no means a difficult issue to decide: did one judge of a division or court attempt to persuade improperly two judges of another division or court to throw away a decision in a case in favour of Mr Jacob Zuma?

Before I get ahead of myself, I return to what Pius Nkonzo Langa wrote as chief justice and head of the Constitutional Court about the complaint. He started with the explanation that his statement was made following a complaint lodged on 30 May 2008 by eleven justices of the Constitutional Court. In the first two paragraphs he explains:

> This is a consolidated statement made on behalf of all the judges of the Court containing the key information relevant to the complaint. My colleagues Moseneke DCJ, Jafta AJ, Mokgoro J, Nkabinde J and O'Regan J have made confirming statements insofar as the contents of this statement relate to them. The other judges of the Court are willing to make confirmatory statements as well, should the Commission so require.
>
> ...
>
> On 12 June 2008, two of the judges, Jafta AJ and Nkabinde J, lodged a statement to the [Judicial Service Commission] placing on record, among other things, that they were not willing to make any statement to the [Judicial Service Commission], were not at liberty to discuss the contents of their discussion with the Chief Justice and Deputy Chief Justice but that they would not object to their disclosing the contents of those discussions to the [Judicial Service Commission]. The other judges of the Court had no knowledge that Jafta AJ and Nkabinde J had taken this position.

The relevant part of paragraph 3 of the statement reads as follows:

At the outset, I confirm that the complaint having been collectively lodged by the judges of the Court *is being pursued by them*.[14] Those judges are myself, Moseneke DCJ, Jafta AJ, Kroon AJ (Jafta AJ and Kroon AJ acted as judges of the Constitutional Court for the period 15 February 2008 till 31 May 2008), Madala J, Mokgoro J, Ngcobo J, Nkabinde J, O'Regan J (O'Regan J acted as ADCJ for the period 15 February to 31 May 2008 and is sometimes referred to as O'Regan ADCJ in this statement), [Sachs J], Skweyiya J, Van der Westhuizen J and Yacoob J. The basis of that complaint is set out in this statement, and confirmed in the attached statements by Moseneke DCJ, Jafta AJ, Mokgoro J, Nkabinde J and O'Regan J *(my emphasis)*.[15]

In paragraph 5, Langa CJ explained that during March 2008 the Constitutional Court heard argument in the Zuma/Thint cases.[16] These cases are referred to collectively as the Zuma/Thint cases.[17] The panel of judges who heard the cases were Langa CJ, O'Regan ADCJ, Ngcobo J, Madala J, Mokgoro J, Skweyiya J, Van der Westhuizen, Yacoob J, Nkabinde J, Jafta AJ and Kroon AJ. Albie Sachs and I were on long leave and our places were filled by Jafta and Kroon AJ.

Paragraph 8 of the statement explained the nature of the Zuma/Thint cases as follows:

> [They] concerned, *inter alia*, the lawfulness of certain searches and seizures undertaken in terms of section 29 of the National Prosecuting Authority Act 32 of 1998 and the lawfulness of the issue of a letter of request to the authorities in Mauritius in terms of the International Co-operation in Criminal Matters Act 75 of 1996. Both the searches and seizures and the issue of the letter of request related to the criminal investigation concerning, amongst others, Mr J.G. Zuma, Thint Holdings (Southern Africa) (Pty) Ltd and Thint (Pty) Ltd. Judgment in the Zuma/Thint cases has been reserved.

Paragraphs 9 to 15 contain, in concise form, the material facts on which the complaint is based:

9. Towards the end of March 2008, and after argument in the Zuma/Thint cases had been heard –
   (a) without invitation, Hlophe JP visited the chambers of Jafta AJ;
   (b) again without invitation, Hlophe JP raised the matter of the Zuma/Thint cases that had been heard by the Court; and
   (c) in the course of that conversation, Hlophe JP sought improperly to persuade Jafta AJ to decide the Zuma/Thint cases in a manner favourable to Mr J G Zuma.
10. On 23 April 2008, Hlophe JP contacted Nkabinde J telephonically and requested to meet her on Friday 25 April 2008. On that day –
    (a) Hlophe JP visited the chambers of Nkabinde J at the Constitutional Court as agreed;
    (b) without invitation, Hlophe JP initiated a conversation with Nkabinde [J] about the Zuma/Thint cases that had been heard by the Court; and
    (c) in the course of that conversation, Hlophe JP sought improperly to persuade Nkabinde J to decide the Zuma/Thint cases in a manner favourable to Mr J G Zuma.
11. The approach by Hlophe JP to both Jafta AJ and Nkabinde J was then made known to Mokgoro J by Nkabinde J when the court term commenced in May 2008. Nkabinde J invited Mokgoro J to her chambers saying that she needed some advice on a certain matter.
12. Nkabinde J told Mokgoro J in confidence that both she and Jafta AJ had been approached by Hlophe JP. She said that she had been informed by Jafta AJ of the improper approach by Hlophe JP to him prior to her being approached by Hlophe JP and she said that Jafta AJ had warned her of what Hlophe JP might say.
13. Nkabinde J then said that she had been approached by Hlophe JP in her chambers towards the end of April. She told Mokgoro J that Hlophe JP had commenced the conversation enquiring from her 'Which Nkabinde are

you?' Nkabinde J told him where she originated from, whereupon Hlophe JP then said that he had always thought she was from one of the Zulu-speaking Nkabinde families. She told him that she had been married to a 'Nkabinde' and that after their divorce she had retained the surname.

14. Nkabinde J then said that Hlophe JP had told her 'he had a mandate'. He then told her that the privilege issues in the Zuma/Thint cases had to be decided 'properly'. Nkabinde J was concerned because she had been writing a post-hearing note on the aspect of privilege. Both Mokgoro J and Nkabinde J wondered how Hlophe JP had become aware of the fact that Nkabinde J had been writing on that aspect.

15. Hlophe JP told Nkabinde J that he had connections with the national intelligence. He also said that some people were going to lose their positions after the elections. Hlophe JP also said that he had out-grown the Cape High Court, that he was going to make himself available for appointment at the Constitutional Court and that Jafta AJ should also make himself available for appointment to the Constitutional Court.

The statement goes on to explain what transpired next.

16. Mokgoro J advised Nkabinde J to report the matter to Langa CJ and/or Moseneke DCJ. She advised Nkabinde J that the matter would affect the integrity of the judiciary and that, if not attended to, it would place it in peril.

17. Mokgoro J observed that it was deeply worrying that Hlophe JP could approach Nkabinde J in that manner; and wondered if a Judge President could approach a colleague in this manner at the Constitutional Court, what it meant for how he performed his duties as a leader in his own Court. Mokgoro J was of the view that Nkabinde J was under an obligation to make disclosure to Langa CJ or Moseneke DCJ. Mokgoro J was concerned that this is not how we do justice in this country.

18. After reflecting on the matter, Mokgoro J without reverting to Nkabinde J informed O'Regan ADCJ of what she had learnt from Nkabinde J. Mokgoro J and O'Regan ADCJ agreed that Nkabinde J should be encouraged to

report the matter to either Langa CJ or Moseneke DCJ.
19. In the meantime, O'Regan ADCJ informed Moseneke DCJ of what she had been told by Mokgoro.
20. Thereafter, Nkabinde J informed Langa CJ of what had happened. Two meetings were then held between Langa CJ and Nkabinde J at the instance of Langa CJ during which he advised her to make a written statement. At those meetings and subsequently during a telephone discussion with Langa CJ, she expressed her unwillingness to furnish a written statement regarding the matter.

The statement records that on 28 May 2008 a meeting was convened, and attended by Langa CJ, Moseneke DCJ, Nkabinde J and Jafta AJ. At the commencement of the meeting

22. Langa CJ acknowledged that it was a difficult and sensitive matter; but affirmed that it was one that he and Moseneke DCJ viewed seriously and one which had importance beyond the judges concerned.

The latter two judges were asked to recount what had occurred. This is how Langa CJ described the alleged interaction between Hlophe JP and Nkabinde J:

23. Nkabinde J provided the first account. She recounted that Hlophe JP visited her chambers on Friday 25 April. Hlophe JP commenced the conversation by inquiring from her 'which Nkabinde are you?' This was a traditional opening remark aimed at identifying the clan of which she forms part. She explained where she originated from, that she had been married to a 'Nkabinde' from KwaZulu-Natal, and that she retained that name even after their divorce.
24. Hlophe JP then turned to discuss the Zuma/Thint cases; and said they were important cases for the future of Mr Zuma. He said that the issue of privilege was an important aspect of the case for the prosecution. If

the point raised by Mr Zuma's counsel were to be sustained there would be no case against Mr Zuma. Nkabinde J expressed concern to Langa CJ and Moseneke DCJ that she had composed a post-hearing note on the specific issue of privilege and proposed a preliminary conclusion on it. (Post-hearing notes are circulated amongst judges as a precursor to deliberations amongst judges). She was also puzzled as to why Hlophe JP had selected the issue of privilege for discussion and wondered how he could have known that she had written on this issue. She was concerned as to how Hlophe JP had obtained this information about the Zuma/Thint cases.

25. Nkabinde J continued by saying that Hlophe JP had told her that he had a mandate to act as he was doing. He stated that he was politically well connected; and connected to members of national intelligence. The implication was that he was well informed about what was happening at the Court. Hlophe JP added that there was no real case against Mr Zuma and that it was therefore important to hold in his favour. Upon being asked by Nkabinde J what 'besigheid' [the Afrikaans word meaning 'business'] it was of his to discuss the case, Hlophe JP said that Mr Zuma was being 'persecuted' as he (Hlophe JP) had been persecuted. Beyond that Nkabinde J reported that Hlophe JP had made other claims that she referred to as 'hogwash'. Nkabinde J made it clear that she had told Hlophe JP that he is not a member of the Court to talk about the case and that even if he were a member, he would still not be entitled to discuss the case unless he had sat in the case.

26. Nkabinde J stated to Langa CJ and Moseneke DCJ that she had told Hlophe JP that he should not interfere with the workings of the Court; and that Hlophe JP's approach did not influence her.

27. Nkabinde J also told Langa CJ and Moseneke DCJ that after the visit by Hlophe JP she had wrestled with what she should do about the visit for some time. She then decided to speak to Mokgoro J to seek advice, which she did in early May just after the court term commenced.

The statement goes on to provide Jafta AJ's version of his interaction with Hlophe JP:

28. After Nkabinde J had provided her account to Langa CJ and Moseneke DCJ, it was the turn of Jafta AJ. He began by asking whether the meeting was an official or unofficial one. Moseneke DCJ responded that it may have both official and unofficial consequences. He confirmed that Langa CJ and he were acting in their capacity as Chief Justice and Deputy Chief Justice. Jafta AJ then went on to say that he had known Hlophe JP for many years; that they had been colleagues and friends. He said that he did not want to breach a confidence but that he could confirm in general terms what Nkabinde J had said.

29. He stated that in March 2008, after the Zuma/Thint cases had been heard, Hlophe JP had come to his chambers and held a conversation with him. He divided his account of his conversation with Hlophe JP into two parts. The first part he was willing to relate; the second he said he had been told in confidence and refused to relate it. He related the first part of the meeting by saying that Hlophe JP had said that the case against Mr Zuma should be looked at properly or words to similar effect and added words to the effect that you are our last hope ('Sesithembele kinina').

30. In response to a question, Jafta AJ stated that he gained the impression that Hlophe JP wished for a particular result in the matter. Jafta AJ explained that he gained this impression because Hlophe JP mentioned that Mr Zuma was being 'persecuted' just as he (Hlophe JP) had been persecuted. Jafta AJ told Langa CJ and Moseneke DCJ that, particularly after he had heard of the approach to Nkabinde J, he considered the approach to be serious and that it was part of an attempt by Hlophe JP aimed at interfering with the independent exercise of judicial discretion by judges at the Court.

31. Jafta AJ also told Langa CJ and Moseneke DCJ that he had told Hlophe JP in no uncertain terms that the Zuma/Thint cases would be properly decided on its facts and on the application of the law to them.

32. Jafta AJ then stated that when he heard that Hlophe JP planned to visit Nkabinde J, he warned Nkabinde J that Hlophe JP had discussed the Zuma/Thint cases with him.

33. Jafta AJ also told Langa CJ and Moseneke DCJ that he had not planned to

lodge a formal complaint about the conduct of Hlophe JP even though he considered it to have been an improper attempt to influence him. His view was that he had decisively dealt with the matter by rejecting the approach of Hlophe JP.

Both Justices Nkabinde and Jafta viewed the approach by Hlophe JP as inappropriate.

34. Both Nkabinde J and Jafta AJ made it clear that in their view the approach by Hlophe JP had been improper. They also made it clear that after they had dealt with the matter by rejecting the approach of Hlophe JP, they did not consider it necessary to lodge a complaint or make a statement.

It was agreed by all parties in the meeting that the matter should be discussed with other colleagues at the Constitutional Court. The statement records:

35. Langa CJ and Moseneke DCJ then raised the question of how the matter should be taken further. Langa CJ and Moseneke DCJ indicated that in the light of the seriousness of the matter it was their view that a meeting of the judges of the Court should be held to discuss what steps should be taken. Langa CJ and Moseneke DCJ then enquired from Jafta AJ and Nkabinde J whether they would object to the matter being taken to conference. Jafta AJ and Nkabinde J said they had no objection. Jafta AJ then requested that Langa CJ and Moseneke DCJ recount to colleagues what had happened at his meeting with Hlophe JP rather than tell the story himself. Nkabinde J agreed that her story should also be told by Langa CJ and Moseneke DCJ. Langa CJ was approached before the conference and was requested by Nkabinde J (expressing the sentiments of Jafta AJ as well) that conference should be notified on their position on the matter.

36. A meeting was called of judges on Thursday 29 May. The following judges were present: Langa CJ, Moseneke DCJ, O'Regan ADCJ, Jafta AJ, Kroon AJ, Madala J, Mokgoro J, Nkabinde J, Skweyiya J, Van der Westhuizen J

and Yacoob J. Ngcobo J did not attend, nor did Sachs J who was in New York. At that meeting, Langa CJ and Moseneke DCJ recounted the essence of what they had been told at the meeting on 28 May. They asked judges at the meeting not to subject Jafta AJ and Nkabinde J to questioning given the distressing circumstances in which they were. Langa CJ and Moseneke DCJ reported that in their view the conduct of Hlophe JP as reported to them by Jafta AJ and Nkabinde J constituted a serious attempt to influence the decision of the Court in the Zuma/Thint cases.

37. The judges of the court were shocked and distressed at the disclosure by Langa CJ and Moseneke DCJ. A full discussion followed. Various courses of action were debated. It was decided unanimously by all judges present that the appropriate course of action, given the gravity of the matter, was to lay a complaint with the [Judicial Service Commission] against Hlophe JP. If Hlophe JP resisted the complaint, he would have to give oral evidence to the [commission] in due course. The judges agreed that the [commission] would be the appropriate body to determine any dispute of fact that might arise, but decided that it was appropriate given the perceived attack on the integrity of the Court that all judges should be party to the complaint. It was also agreed that a clear and brief press statement should be prepared.

The statement relayed the process of drafting the complaint and press statement that were issued on 30 May 2008:

38. A draft statement was then circulated to colleagues for discussion. During this process, Ngcobo J, who had not attended the meeting, requested that a further meeting be held to discuss whether a press statement should be issued.

39. A meeting was then held on Friday 30 May. Not all judges could be present, but the following judges were present: Langa CJ, O'Regan ADCJ, Jafta AJ, Kroon AJ, Madala J, Mokgoro J, Ngcobo J, Skweyiya J and Van der Westhuizen J. After discussion it was agreed that the terms of the press statement should largely be in the same terms as the complaint to be

lodged with the [Judicial Service Commission]. All judges concurred in the decision, though Langa CJ did note that as chairperson of the [commission], it would not be appropriate for him to issue a media statement. It was also agreed that Langa CJ would call Hlophe JP and inform him of the complaint; that the complaint would be sent to Hlophe JP and thereafter would be lodged with the [Judicial Service Commission]. It was agreed that thereafter the media statement would be issued.

40. On the same day, at approximately noon, Langa CJ then called Hlophe JP to inform him of the complaint and to obtain a secure fax number to which the complaint could be sent. The complaint was then sent to Hlophe JP. Shortly thereafter it was lodged with the [Judicial Service Commission]. And again, shortly thereafter, a media statement was sent to the media list used by the Court.

On 2 June 2008, following the making of the initial complaint, the JSC sent a letter to the Constitutional Court requesting that fuller details about the complaint be forwarded to the commission by 6 June.

Paragraphs 41 to 46 record that counsel was appointed to act for Nkabinde J and Jafta AJ. Counsel was also appointed for the other justices of the Constitutional Court. It was later agreed that counsel representing the court and counsel acting for Nkabinde J and Jafta AJ should work together to finalise what was then contemplated – two separate statements, one for Justices Nkabinde and Jafta and another for the other justices of the court. It became apparent that the deadline of 6 June would not be met and an extension was requested and granted. Discussions ensued to finalise the statements to the JSC:

47. On 11 and 12 June 2008, Moseneke DCJ held a series of conversations with both Jafta AJ and Nkabinde J to finalise the portions of the statement that referred to them. There were repeated delays during the day, but finally, late in the afternoon, the following two proposed paragraphs were forwarded ... for inclusion in the court's statement.

48. The first paragraph referred to the meeting between Hlophe JP and Jafta AJ. It was proposed by counsel for Nkabinde J and Jafta AJ that the following detail be included in the statement: 'In the course of that conversation, Hlophe JP said that the case against Mr J.G. Zuma should be looked at properly (or words of similar effect) and added, "Sesithembele kinina", a rough translation of which is: "you are our last hope".'

49. The second paragraph referred to the meeting between Hlophe JP and Nkabinde J. It was proposed by counsel for Nkabinde J and Jafta AJ that the following detail be included in the statement:

'In the course of that conversation, Hlophe JP said he wanted to talk about the question of "privilege", which in his words formed the gravamen of the National Prosecution Authority's case against Mr J.G. Zuma. He further said the manner in which the case was to be decided was very important as there was no case against Mr Zuma without the 'privileged' information and that Mr Zuma was being persecuted, just like he (Hlophe JP) had also been.'

50. On 12 June at approximately 17h00 a document was delivered by hand to Moseneke DCJ and O'Regan ADCJ which indicated that Jafta AJ and Nkabinde J did not intend to make any statement to the [Judicial Service Commission]. The other judges of the Court had no prior knowledge that the two judges intended to lodge a separate statement of this sort. The statement was circulated to all judges on Thursday evening.

51. A meeting of judges had been convened for 09h30 on Friday 13 June to discuss and settle the statement to be issued to the [Judicial Service Commission]. Present at that meeting were Langa CJ, Moseneke DCJ, O'Regan ADCJ, Kroon AJ, Mokgoro J, Ngcobo J, Van der Westluizen J and Yacoob J. Neither Jafta AJ nor Nkabinde J was present, nor were Madala J, Skweyiya J or Sachs J. It was agreed that a full meeting should be held as soon as possible and that Jafta AJ and Nkabinde J should be asked to attend. The purpose of the meeting was to finalise the formulation of a response to the chairperson of the [commission]. After telephonic conversations, the meeting was set for Monday 16 June 2008 at 12h00.

52. This statement and those annexed to it are a product of that meeting and a subsequent meeting held at the Court on 17 June.

The penultimate section of the statement provided the reason why the complaint was lodged by all the judges:

53. In terms of Section 167(2) of the Constitution, a matter before the Constitutional Court must be heard by at least eight judges. The Constitutional Court has recognised that there is an obligation upon members of the Court to sit in matters unless disqualified or unable to do so for a material reason.
54. The attempt to influence Nkabinde J and Jafta AJ in the manner described above –
    (a) was calculated to have an impact not only on the individual decisions of the judges concerned but on the capacity of the Constitutional Court as a whole to adjudicate in a manner that ensures its independence, impartiality, dignity, accessibility and effectiveness as required by Section 165(5) of the Constitution;
    (b) constituted a breach of Section 165(3) of the Constitution which prohibits any person or organ of state from interfering with the functioning of the courts.
55. In President of the Republic of South Africa and Others v SA Rugby Football Union and Others 1999 (7) BCLR 725 (CC); 1999 (4) SA 147 (CC), the Constitutional Court had to consider an application for recusal against five members of the Court. The Court noted that if one member of the Court is disqualified from sitting in a case, the Court has 'a wider duty to say so, and to take such steps as may be necessary to ensure that the disqualified member does not participate in the adjudication of the case' (at para 31). The Court noted that if one disqualified judge decides to sit in a matter, that 'could fatally contaminate the ultimate decision of the Court, and the other members may well have a duty to refuse to sit with that judge' (at para 32).

56. It follows that every member of the Constitutional Court not only has a direct and substantial interest in any improper attempts to influence the decision-making process required of any member of the Constitutional Court, but a duty to ensure that all judges who sit in a matter are qualified to do so. It is in the light of these obligations and the seriousness with which the *judges of the Court viewed the conduct of Hlophe JP that the judges of the Court (including Moseneke DCJ and Sachs J) unanimously made the complaint* to the [Judicial Service Commission] *[my emphasis]*.

57. Pursuant to the information conveyed by Nkabinde J and Jafta AJ, the Constitutional Court made the complaint on 30 May 2008. Prior to it being lodged, Hlophe JP was telephonically informed of the intention to lodge the complaint with the [Judicial Service Commission] by Langa CJ and a copy of the complaint was furnished to him.

The statement by the Constitutional Court judges ended as follows:

58. In conclusion, it should be noted that this complaint is based on conduct which the judges of the Court view in the most serious possible light. It constitutes a grave threat to the institution of the judiciary, and accordingly to our Constitution. The speedy resolution of the complaint is imperative. Should the [Judicial Service Commission] wish to have any further information or clarification of the above particulars, I will assist to the best of my ability.

On 10 June 2008, Hlophe JP lodged the counter-complaint, and on 30 June 2008 he filed a response to the Constitutional Court justices' complaint against him. In his response, the judge president first addressed the statement filed by Chief Justice Langa on behalf of the judges of the Constitutional Court and alleged that Justices Jafta and Nkabinde were manipulated and pressured by Langa CJ, me and O'Regan ADCJ. This, he said, was evident from their statement of 12 June 2008 to the Judicial Service Commission:

4. On 12 June 2008, a statement was issued by Justice Nkabinde and Justice Jafta in which they indicated that 'we wish to state that we have not lodged a complaint and do not intend to lodge one and, consequently, we are not "complainant judges". Under normal circumstances this would have been the end of the matter. However, the unprecedented conduct of the Judges of condemning me through the media without the details of the complaint does not permit such a graceful exit from the embarrassing situation created by this misguided exercise of judicial solidarity.

Dealing with the series of conversations between Jafta JA, Nkabinde J, Langa CJ and myself, he stated the following:

7. In light of the statement filed by Judges Nkabinde and Jafta the natural result would have been that I am cleared of any alleged wrong-doing by the [Judicial Service Commission]; but that was not to be my fate. It is recorded in paragraph 1 of the statement of the Chief Justice that the 'other judges had no knowledge that Jafta AJ and Nkabinde J had taken this position. The net result was that the lodging of this statement was once again delayed'. What the statement does not say is the following;

7.1. That according to the statement of 12 June 2008, the Chief Justice and the Deputy Chief Justice had known about the position taken by Judges Nkabinde and Jafta since 28 May 2008. The voices of Judges Nkabinde and Jafta were suppressed in the statement issued by the Court on 30 May 2008 and the public was given the impression that there was unanimity by the Judges of the Court. Such a position was incorrect and to a large extent contrived given that in paragraph 2 of the statement of 12 June 2008, Judges Nkabinde and Jafta, state 'We place on record that, from the moment the matter about Judge President Hlophe's visits was reported by O'Regan ADCJ to the Deputy Chief Justice Moseneke, we have on a number of occasions informed Chief Justice Langa and Deputy Chief Justice Moseneke that we were not intending to lodge a complaint and neither were we willing to make statements about the matter.' In paragraph 4 the statement read, 'We further record that on 28 May 2008, we attended a meeting called by Chief Justice Langa and Deputy Chief Justice Moseneke. We had occasion to discuss the issue that formed the subject matter of the complaint against Judge President Hlophe. We again made it clear to them that we were not intending to lay a complaint against Judge President Hlophe and neither did we intend making a statement about the matter.' This position of Judges Nkabinde and Jafta was suppressed in the media statement issued on 30 May 2008 and, as I show, was not disclosed to other judges of the Constitutional Court by Chief Justice Langa and Deputy Chief Justice Moseneke.

Hlophe adopted the narrative that Langa CJ and I manipulated Justices Nkabinde and Jafta into jointly making the statement and concludes:

7.9. It is clear that the process followed and actively encouraged by the Chief Justice and Deputy Chief Justice was designed to subvert the will of their colleagues and the series of conversations were an attempt to persuade them to join the two of them in their view of the matter, a view they recklessly pursued, and has brought this country's judiciary where it is today. On 12 June 2008 and despite the intense interactions between the Deputy Chief Justice and Judges Nkabinde and Jafta recorded in paragraph 47, a joint statement was issued by Judges Nkabinde and Jafta in which they distanced themselves from the complaint.

7.10. The patched up statements pasted in the Chief Justice's statement that are attributed to Judges Nkabinde and Jafta are observably inconsistent with the position that they took on 12 June 2008. The statement by the Chief Justice does not explain the basis on which Judges Nkabinde and Jafta belatedly and inexplicably decided to take a position contradicting their statement of 12 June 2008.

He argued that the complaint and the media statement violated the institution of the judiciary and undermined the judicial office, particularly his:

14. The dilatory tactics that followed the [Judicial Service Commission's] timetable and the seemingly contradictory statements from the two 'complainant judges' further fuel speculations that judges were subjected to undue pressure to change their positions several times in an effort to implicate me in judicial misconduct. The prevarication of the judges in this vicious attempt to remove me as a judge in light of the glaring constitutional errors and procedural missteps, in my respectful submission, certainly runs the risk of eroding the integrity of our judiciary. The duty to protect the Constitution and the judiciary does not give the judges the right to do so in violation of constitutional rights. The suggestion that the judges are exempted from acting in a fair manner since this matter would be decided by the [Judicial Service Commission] is insensitive, overbearing and inconsistent with the office of a judge. Judges are enjoined to give effect to the Constitution and are not exempted from observing constitutional rights and basic decorum even when they file a complaint against me. The office of a judge, and the dignity that attaches thereto, is not only to be accorded respect and dignity by the judges themselves only when they write judgments and sit in Court or some such duties which judges perform on a day to day basis. The office demands strict observance of all rules that inform the office of judgeship. A judge does not throw out of the window basic tenets of the rules of natural justice simply because s/he is a complainant. In any event, judges are bound by the Constitution to respect and protect constitutionally entrenched rights. These judges have not done so by a long shot in this case.

He then relays his version of his visit with Jafta AJ:

23. I visited Justice Jafta in March and approximately three weeks before paying a courtesy visit to Justice Nkabinde. I will follow the sequence of my visits.
23.1. Justice Jafta has described our relationship correctly in paragraph 28 of Chief Justice Langa's statement. We know each other for many years,

have been colleagues and friends. I first came to know Justice Jafta sometime in 1990 when I joined the Department of Public Law at the then University of Transkei as Professor and head of Department. He was in my Department as a lecturer in constitutional law. I had heard that Justice Jafta was on an acting stint at the Constitutional Court and in fact I may have read it somewhere. I had a scheduled trip to Pretoria for my own private business. I called Justice Jafta a few days before my scheduled private business trip to tell him that I was going to be coming to Pretoria and suggested that we meet somewhere if he had time for coffee or something.

23.2. Since he was acting as a judge at the Constitutional Court we agreed that we would meet in his chambers at the Constitutional Court. I was also interested in encouraging him to apply for a permanent position at the Constitutional Court once a vacancy opened up and so was happy to see him in his chambers at the Court. After all he sounded happy and we agreed that I would come to see him at about 11h00 or 11h30 on that day. When I arrived at the Court and announced myself at reception, Justice Jafta was expecting me and I was ushered to his Chambers by someone I believe was his secretary. He received me very warmly and offered me a seat and coffee.

23.3. I was in Justice Jafta's Chambers for approximately 1hr 30 minutes.

We spoke about our families. In particular he asked me about my divorce that he had come to know about fairly recently. We spoke about our past experiences as academics at UNITRA, then as judges and heads of Court. He particularly asked me about my experience in Cape Town and issues of transformation and racism both in the bench and the bar. I asked about his experience as a judge at the [Supreme Court of Appeal] which he said had its own challenges but one that he was particularly enjoying. He also informed me that since his appointment to the [Supreme Court of Appeal] he had bought property in Bloemfontein and moved with his family to live there. Then I asked him about his experience acting as a Judge at the Constitutional Court. He told me that he was enjoying it and would consider availing himself for a permanent appointment if it occurred.

He said some of his colleagues had encouraged him to make himself available for such an appointment. I also encouraged him and said that I believed that he would be a great asset to the Constitutional Court and the development of the constitutional legal culture. I added that I would not mind joining the Constitutional Court in due course after serving the Cape Division for the past 14 years.

23.4. However, he made remarks about what he perceived as a weak management of the Court as a concern for him, in particular that it seemed that Justice O'Regan was running the Court and not necessarily Chief Justice Langa. I then remarked that the Court must be very busy since it was handling very important matters, in particular the Zuma/Thint matter. The reason for my remark was that in one corner of Justice Jafta's chambers were numerous files of the record clearly marked that any person walking into his chambers would be able to see. He agreed with me that there was a lot of work and that the Zuma/Thint case was a brain teaser demanding a focused application of the mind to the complex issues involved. I then added that I believed that the issue of privilege was a very concerning one and had to be dealt with properly. His answer was that the issues in the Zuma/Thint case would be decided correctly and added that the issue of privilege was very critical since it had the potential to alter very firm foundations on which the integrity of our legal system was based.

23.5. I expressed the view that I felt strongly, generally, about privilege and fair trial rights. His response was that he felt the same about the issue of privilege and fair trial rights but was not sure that everyone, particularly his white colleagues, shared the same thinking. My remark is correctly recorded, in that I did say that 'sesithembele kinina' but it was never intended to convey to him that I meant a positive finding on the Zuma/Thint matter. In the context of the conversation that we were having I expressed a view that the issue of privilege would receive satisfactory attention from the Court. That was my view expressed to a friend in a mutually engaged conversation. I would have expressed the same view even if it had not been the Zuma/Thint matter which was involved. The issues in the Zuma/Thint matters were publicly argued and there has been an immense public commentary on the issues. I do not believe that expressing an opinion to an independent minded and competent judge as Justice Jafta would be interpreted as an attempt at influencing him to rule favourably. Such a position in my view is an insult and is demeaning to the Judge concerned. I consider that Justice Jafta is a very experienced Judge of undoubted legal skill and dexterity. His sense of independence is fierce; and, to my mind, he is very unlikely to have considered a conversation with a friend on any legal issues as an attempt to influence him in any manner whatsoever.

23.6. We also spoke about a range of issues and before I left, I once more encouraged him to avail himself for a position at the Constitutional Court if a vacancy occurred. We spoke about the fact that such an opportunity was bound to come since a number of judges would be taking retirement. We mentioned Judge Madala as one of them. I left Justice Jafta's chambers at about lunch time and asked him to show me the way to Justice Ngcobo's chambers to greet him since his chambers were not far from his. Judge Ngcobo is a former colleague who served as a Judge in Cape Town before taking up a position at the Constitutional Court. Justice Jafta accompanied me and we were cordial and friendly as we walked out of his chambers down the passage.

23.7. There was never a time when Justice Jafta for the 1 hour 30 minutes in his chambers suggested that I was acting inappropriately by expressing my views on the many issues that we casually covered. At no stage did Justice Jafta indicate any discomfort about my views expressed to him in the context of a conversation between mutual friends. At no stage did I ever suggest that Justice Jafta should ignore the evidence and rule in any direction in any matter before him. This dialogue between him and me was pleasant and reflected a fondness commonly associated with friends.

Justice Jafta accompanied me to Justice Ngcobo's chambers. He left me there and said that it had been good to see me as a parting shot. I deny that there was ever a time during our one and a half hour's conversation that it became necessary for Justice Jafta to tell me that I was interfering with his work as a judge. There was never a time that he acted or showed signs of being uncomfortable with our discussions, which covered a whole range of issues other than the legal issues in the Zuma/Thint matter. That explains why he waited for almost a month before speaking or warning Judge Nkabinde about the alleged attempt to improperly influence him.

23.8. Justice Ngcobo invited me in and offered coffee. We chatted for about fifteen minutes and when I finished my cup of coffee I left. Justice Ngcobo walked me to my car. Outside Justice Ngcobo's chambers, it is where I met Justice Nkabinde who was with Justice Madala. They stopped to greet me and we exchanged pleasantries. It is then that I said to Judge Nkabinde that I had neither seen nor spoken to her in a long time and particularly after her appointment to the Constitutional Court. She said that she had not seen me too but she had read a lot about me in the papers. We laughed and I promised that I would pay her a visit the next time I had occasion to be at the Constitutional Court.

23.9. Justice Ngcobo and I walked to my car. He left me there and went back. In the car park I saw Deputy Chief Justice's car, and his driver was present. I walked to him and asked if the Deputy Chief Justice was around. The driver told me that he had gone to his chambers. I then left a message with the driver to convey to Deputy Chief Justice my greetings. A few days after that I received a call from the Deputy Chief Justice in which he gave me his private cell number at which he said I could reach him anytime. I must point out that the Deputy Chief Justice and I have, although rarely, had contact with each other, and in one or more of our conversations, he has expressed frustration about what he perceived as the poor leadership of Chief Justice Langa.

23.10. I left the Constitutional Court, carried out my private business in

Pretoria, and went back the same day to Cape Town. Since then I have never called Justice Jafta, but I have on at least two occasions spoken to Justice Ngcobo. There are no allegations that I sought to improperly influence Justice Ngcobo who by far is the most influential judge of the Constitutional Court. He commands a respectable portion of the Constitutional Court's intellectual and legal output and I certainly do not believe that he can be manipulated by anyone into taking a decision against conscience and the evidence.

Hlophe JP's version of the interaction with Justice Nkabinde follows:

24. About two or three weeks after I had met Justice Jafta I was scheduled to attend a meeting of the Local Organising Committee of the Commonwealth Magistrates and Judges Association. I was the Chairperson of the LOC given a mandate by Chief Justice Langa to convene a conference of judges and magistrates in Cape Town in October. There are four judges who are members of the LOC; myself as the Chairperson, Justice Seriti of the Pretoria Division, Justice Joe Rawulinga also in the Pretoria Division and Geraldine Schrider of the Witwatersrand Local Division. The Chief Justice's Chief Director Theo Sifuba co-ordinated the meeting held at the Constitutional Court.

    There were some issues that required resolution relating to the funding of the conference and Mr Sifuba would give us feedback on his efforts to secure funding from the Department and the office of the Chief Justice.

25. This meeting was going to attempt to unlock the red tape in order to fast-track the logistical support required to host a successful conference. Advocate Sifuba was to host lunch at the Court for the members of the LOC prior to the meeting. I called Justice Nkabinde to inform her that I would be at the Court and was going to visit her for a few minutes before my meeting. This was simply a courtesy call and nothing more. Justice Nkabinde and I knew each other, and we share mutual friends. I met her about six years before her appointment to the Constitutional Court when

she was still a trial court judge.

We shared a mutual interest in labour law and had both served in the Labour Court, I at the Labour Appeal Court, and she at the Labour Court.

26. I arrived in Johannesburg a day earlier to meeting Justice Nkabinde because I had been invited to attend a function of the Aspirant Female Judges at Velmo Hotel near Pretoria. I had been invited to this function because I had been one of the examiners of these aspirant female judges. Justice Nkabinde was at the function and she gave the vote of thanks. I only spoke to Justice Nkabinde when she was leaving at which she introduced me to her husband who had accompanied her. We parted with her saying that she would see me the following day and indicated that she was available anytime before lunch since she had plans to travel to the North West that afternoon. She told me that she was on duty with the Chief Justice but would leave around lunch time.

27. I went to the Constitutional Court on the following day and arrived at approximately noon. I announced my arrival at reception and was ushered to her chambers. She welcomed me and offered me tea or fruits which were in a bowl on a table. Somewhere in her chambers are pictures of her family and we chatted about family. I confirm asking her about her family background including her Nkabinde surname. She told me about her previous marriage to a Nkabinde. In fact she said that she was a 'return soldier' meaning that she was divorced. She told me that she retained the Nkabinde surname for the sake of her children who have that surname. I then told her about my divorces as well and we laughed when I said that I was also a 'return soldier'. The conversation was radiant and very jovial. Justice Nkabinde then asked me about my problems in the Cape. In particular she said 'My brother, are all your problems in Cape Town over now?'

28. My response was that they had significantly become less than in the past. We laughed it off and then I asked her about her experience at the Constitutional Court to which she said that she was enjoying herself although she found it very demanding. She said that because the Constitutional Court was the final court it was important that they get

things right first time and all the time. As with Justice Jafta, the record of the Zuma/Thint case occupies a significant space in her chambers, and so, looking at the record, I remarked that it was probably one of the most demanding of the cases that the Court had dealt with, given its importance to the President of the ANC, Jacob Zuma, and the [African National Congress] itself and the country in general since it was clear that Jacob Zuma was a likely contender for the Presidency of the country. I asked her whether judgment was due and she said that there was still a lot of work to be done.

She told me that she was busy doing a note on the issue of privileged communication between attorney and client. The impression created that there is something sinister around the casual discussion on the legal principle of privilege is incorrect. Even if she had not told me that she was writing a post-hearing note on privilege, I am aware that privilege is one of the issues that was argued in the Zuma/Thint matter. There was extensive media coverage of the Scorpions' raid on the offices of Zuma's attorney, an intense media public debate on this issue which was demonstrated by the [General Council of the Bar] and various bodies associated with it issuing press statements on it. It is pretentious to suggest that I specifically chose to discuss the issue of privilege because I had an inappropriate inside knowledge of workings of the Court.

29. Justice Nkabinde said nothing on the merits of the legal privilege as it relates to the Zuma matter, but she did say that it was an important legal issue in the case. I simply agreed with her and stated that I was concerned that the majority in the Supreme Court of Appeal did not attach much weight to the issue of privilege. The conversation was mutual and at no point did Justice Nkabinde indicate any discomfort about the many issues that we discussed, including the issue of privilege. She told me that she was writing a note on privilege but never went into the details of what she was saying about it. I expressed my very strong views on it, but at no point did I think that she was uncomfortable about them to a point that she would consider filing a complaint of improper conduct. I do not

believe that judges are easily influenced by casual conversations, and since all I knew about the case is what I had read mostly in the newspapers, my views could not have been crystallised enough to influence any judge of substance.

30. The allegation that I had a mandate has somehow taken some significance in the complaint against me but was completely misunderstood. Here is where this name mandate comes from. Justice Nkabinde asked me what I was doing in the Constitutional Court. My response was that I had been given a mandate by Chief Justice Langa to chair the LOC for the Commonwealth conference on Judges and Magistrates to be held in Cape Town. I also told her that I would be seeing him for a short time before the meeting to report on some issues. I never said that I had any connections with the national intelligence or that some people would lose their jobs after elections in which Jacob Zuma would be President. Judges enjoy secure tenure and it would be foolishness to use such a blunt threat in such circumstances. Justice Nkabinde, unlike Justice Jafta who was on an acting appointment, is a permanent judge of the Constitutional Court. But again it is unclear how my views expressed with no intimate knowledge of the case could influence a judge of the Constitutional Court.

31. What I found disconcerting is the allegation made on behalf of Justice Jafta that he informed Justice Nkabinde about my alleged improper conduct at his chamber before I visited her. Despite being allegedly warned by Justice Jafta, Justice Nkabinde never cancelled our scheduled meeting, never asked me not to come, but instead welcomed me and spoke with me for approximately 30-45 minutes. I cannot understand how the information that Justice Jafta is alleged to have conveyed to Justice Nkabinde would not have been sufficiently important for Justice Nkabinde to keep me out of her chambers or even meeting her for that matter. As I state above, my conversation with Justice Nkabinde was cordial and friendly up to the end. There was not a single indication from her that my remarks were inappropriate. The suggestion therefore that Justice Jafta warned Justice Nkabinde about my alleged attempts at influencing him is clearly a fabrication aimed

at creating an atmosphere of a united Court on the inappropriate nature of the conversations that I had with these two judges.

I have made the core affidavits supporting the complaint and the response to it speak for themselves. Sadly, Langa CJ passed on before he could testify. While I live I may still be called to testify. So, I am a potential witness on what Justices Nkabinde and Jafta have told me and Langa CJ about their conversations with Hlophe JP. For that reason, it would be unwise to pass any judgment on the facts and circumstances of the complaint. In other words, the case is yet to be decided – it is *sub judice*.

Twelve years have passed and no decision has been reached by the Judicial Service Commission. For that reason, allow me to invite you to be the judge of the complaint, including what you think about the delay of the JSC in reaching finality in a matter of this magnitude for the judiciary and our country.

CHAPTER 19

Jurisprudence – a full repertoire

The narratives in the last two chapters may have left you with a sense of a court under siege. I may have overstated the place of overt and covert political disputes that were couched in terms that demanded mediation or resolution by application of the law. There was indeed abundant political warfare brought into the courts, legal disputes which evoked high public interest and were of immense importance. That was why the publicity around the cases rose high up into the sky.

But, no, that was not the only game in town. That class of case was not the bulk of what the Constitutional Court had to confront. Approaches to the Constitutional Court from claimants seeking relief on matters far removed from the dog fights for public power and influence continued unabated. Ordinary and not-so-ordinary people and big and small corporates and organisations came to our court for relief. Pius Langa and I, supported by all our judicial colleagues, were resolute that the Constitutional Court would remain inward-looking, hard-working and focused on affording effective remedies to those claimants who sought relief.

It had been ten years since the induction of the Constitutional Court. The foundational precedents were helpful and beginning to gain traction and acceptance among would-be claimants. As a result the number of cases to the court by way of direct access or through the channel of appeals from other courts steadily increased. The kind of causes or claims were of many varied origins and offered the court the opportunity to do justice among litigating parties but also to build on the founding precedents and reasoning of our predecessors. We joined the project of building a new legal culture drawn from the broader aspirations of the democratic project and the reconstruction of our society towards a just order.

By some quirk of history the first hearing Pius Langa presided over as Chief Justice in 2005[1] was a case related to the death penalty. The case arose from the order of the Constitutional Court in its very first case of *Makwanyane*[2] on the death penalty. Then the court found that the death penalty violated the Constitution and was invalid and therefore unenforceable.

Ten years later, in 2005, the case of *Sibiya*[3] was about a different but related grievance. The case is perhaps a horrid example of how slowly the wheels of justice might turn. On 6 June 1995, when the Constitutional Court declared that the death penalty was unconstitutional and invalid, there were approximately 400 people on death row awaiting execution. The people on death row had been sentenced to death after having been found guilty by courts for mainly hideous crimes. But the striking down of the death penalty did not suddenly make them not guilty and innocent. It did not mean that they didn't deserve punishment. So in theory their death sentences remained in place until they were replaced or converted by a court to another form of appropriate sentence.

After the death penalty decision of 2005, parliament made a law which regulated how the courts would convert the death penalty sentences to other forms of appropriate sentences.[4] Ten years later the death sentences of 62 people had not yet been converted to another form of punishment and these people were still being held on death row.

Mr Sibiya and other offenders on death row were unhappy that their death sentences remained unchanged despite their very long stay in the death penalty section. As would be expected, the justices of our court were unamused by this callous delay and we ordered full reports to be furnished to us on why it was so and how many death sentences had not been converted. The delay sat somewhere between the passage of the law and finding or transcribing trial and appeal court records of proceedings. Thereafter every record had to be referred to the specific high court where the original sentences of death were imposed. In some instances the sentenced offenders sought a full hearing to make fresh submissions on an appropriate sentence other than the death sentence.

When the *Sibiya* case again came before the court, 33 people were still on death row. The court order required the prosecution and the state to complete all the conversions of sentences by the end of October 2005.[5]

This kind of pernicious delay in doing justice is unacceptable and serves as a big discredit to our and many other democratic justice systems around the world. Tardiness in the legal process is caused by lack of industry or a failure to act as promptly as required. And yet other delays are systemic. It is so that the price for procedural fairness is often delay. The more care the justice system takes, the more delay is inescapable and the more parties may abuse the system. However, a point is certainly reached where, as it is often said, justice delayed becomes justice denied. Judges are well tutored to weigh carefully whether a point has been reached where the delay is so excessive and unreasonable as to throw out a civil claim or criminal charge or other legal process; the test always being whether in all the circumstances, and despite the delay, justice can still be served.

The *Sibiya* decision was only the first for the Langa Court. The eleven justices carried their full and normal load of considering applications or requests for leave or permission to appeal to the Constitutional Court. The law gave the court the prerogative to choose cases it might want to hear. In practice a case serves before the court only with its leave or permission. To make the point finer, one does not ask for leave of the high court to approach it for relief. The party that has a claim approaches the high court as of right and not by its leave. Leave to appeal is simply a mechanism to limit or exclude appeals that are not likely to succeed. They are often said to be appeals without a reasonable prospect of success. It would indeed be futile and a waste of resources to hear an appeal which from the outset it is clear will not succeed.

This of course means that the Constitutional Court must consider every request for leave or permission to appeal a decision of another court. To do that we at the court had to study every request for leave to appeal. Many applications were accompanied by bulky records of proceedings in the courts below. So, as the case flow increased, so did the workload of the justices. Cases which were heard by the Constitutional Court on appeal were always a small fraction of the many applications to the court for leave to appeal.

Every Monday morning during term we gathered in the judges' conference room. The chief justice or I would preside. From the morning to lunch-time, the justices decided whether each request for permission to appeal should be granted. The discussion of each application would be preceded by a memorandum prepared by at least two judges recommending a set-down or dismissal.

If the request was granted, the matter would be allocated a date or set down for fuller argument in a court hearing. At this stage the test is light. Setting the matter down simply means that the appeal has a reasonable prospect of success subject to full argument and later reflection. If the request was refused, the appeal would come to the end of the road. Then the Constitutional Court would issue an order refusing leave or permission to appeal. The order is an order of the full court and bears the names of the judges who reached the decision.

My short account below is made up of broad brushstrokes and limited to cases that the Constitutional Court heard and on which it furnished reasons for its decision or, as we say, handed down a judgment.

One class of disputes related to common law rules and whether they remained consistent with the new rights culture. The court was invited to probe the scope of vicarious liability. This is a rule which determines when one person or legal entity may be held accountable in damages for the wrongful conduct of another. The court held that the rule had now to be applied by the courts in a way in which it was in harmony with the new constitutional dispensation.[6]

Another intriguing matter related to the correct approach to assessing the constitutional validity of a contractual term. In *Barkhuizen*[7] the challenged contractual term was in a contract of short-term insurance. The court held that the proper approach to constitutional challenges to contractual terms was to determine whether the term challenged was contrary to public policy as evidenced by our constitutional values, in particular those found in the Bill of Rights.

In *Steenkamp*[8] the issue was whether financial loss caused by improper performance of a statutory or administrative function should attract liability for damages in delict.[9] The court held that an administrative act that breached a statutory duty was necessarily wrongful in the delictual sense only where there was a legal duty to prevent loss to the plaintiff, and that such a duty existed only where called for by policy considerations of fairness and reasonableness.

The Constitutional Court decided another cluster of cases that related to the common law as encoded or qualified by legislation. Foremost in our equality jurisprudence was the *Fourie* case.[10] There was crisp but highly contested debate about whether the common law understanding of marriage and a provision in the Marriage Act[11] denied same-sex couples equal protection and benefit of the law in conflict with the Constitution, and resulted in same-sex couples being subjected to unfair discrimination. In a ground-breaking decision given the settled meaning of marriage, the court unanimously held that the common law definition of marriage was inconsistent with the Constitution and invalid to the extent that it did not permit same-sex couples from enjoying the status and benefits afforded to heterosexual couples. The failure of the common law and legislation to provide the means that allowed same-sex couples to enjoy the same status, entitlements and responsibilities accorded to heterosexual couples through marriage was held to be an unjustified violation of their rights. The court gave parliament twelve months to correct the defects.

In *Hassam*,[12] our court was invited to test the inheritance regime of a polygamous Muslim marriage against the tenets of the Constitution. The narrow question was whether a provision in the legislation on intestate succession,[13] which excluded a woman in a polygamous Muslim marriage from inheriting, was constitutionally valid. The court thought not. It held that the exclusion of women in this position unfairly discriminated against them on the listed grounds of religion, marital status and gender. The limitation was not justifiable and the challenged provision was constitutionally invalid.

The Marriage Act[14] contained a provision that did not allow a spouse married in community of property to recover delictual patrimonial damages[15] arising from bodily injury inflicted by the other spouse. An obvious example would be damages for bodily injuries of one spouse in a motor vehicle accident negligently caused by his or her spouse in circumstances where they are married in community of property. *Van der Merwe*[16] was such a case where the Road Accident Fund declined to pay for Mrs Van der Merwe's damages arising from her bodily injuries caused by her husband. She challenged whether the provision was constitutionally valid. The court held not. It held that the provision was inconsistent with the Constitution to the extent that it limited the right to equal protection and benefit of the law[17] without any justification.

Next in turn was the recognition of customary marriages and the equality norm. The core issue in *Gumede*[18] was whether legislative provisions that regulated the proprietary consequences of a customary marriage entered into after the commencement of the recognition legislation[19] discriminated unfairly, based on gender and race, against those people who had entered a customary marriage before its commencement. In plain language the question was whether a spouse in a customary union who had married before the new recognition law was excluded from the property benefits of the marriage when she divorced. The court found the distinction untenable. It held that the effect of the challenged provisions was that a wife to a customary marriage entered into before the commencement of the legislation would not be entitled to the matrimonial property upon dissolution of the marriage. The provisions were constitutionally invalid as they discriminated unfairly against women.

In *Gory*,[20] another equality claim, a same-sex life partner challenged the legislation on intestate succession[21] to the extent that it did not provide for same-sex life partners to inherit by intestate succession from one another. The Constitutional Court unanimously decided that the provision unfairly discriminated on grounds of sexual orientation. The defect was cured by a reading-in order to include in the legislation same-sex life partners with reciprocal duties of support.

Geldenhuys[22] posed the enquiry whether legislative provisions[23] setting the age of consent between people of the same sex higher than the age for consenting heterosexual people constituted unfair discrimination. The court concluded that the attacked provisions discriminated unfairly on the ground of sexual orientation and violated the right to equality and the right not to be discriminated against on the ground of sexual orientation. But because the legislation had already been repealed by parliament, the case only concerned those people convicted under the legislation when it was in force.

The Langa Court tested many legislative provisions for constitutional probity. In each case, the question whether the law concerned was valid occurred in a live dispute where a claimant asked for relief from the Constitutional Court and not in an abstract review. Also, unlike the equality cases I have just discussed, the platforms for these challenges were not derived from the equality guarantee but from other protections afforded by the Constitution.

In *Du Toit*,[24] we were concerned with how compensation for expropriation of property must be properly calculated in light of the old-order law of expropriation[25] and the new property clause of the Constitution.[26] We concluded that in the absence of a new expropriation legislation, compensation must be calculated in terms of the existing expropriation legislation and then assessed against the requirements of the property clause in the Constitution.[27] The outcome or compensation arrived at must be just and equitable.

As a personal observation, it struck me that up to then parliament had not made a new-order law of expropriation that was aligned with the property clause in the Constitution. Instead, it was our court that was pushed to reconcile the old-order law of expropriation with the land reform imperatives of the property clause in the Constitution.

Magajane[28] was about a challenge to a North West province gambling law[29] which authorised warrantless searches of unlicensed premises when regulatory inspections were conducted. The question became whether the searches violated the right to privacy. The court held that legislation permitting warrantless regulatory inspections must provide a constitutionally adequate substitute for a warrant. The court asked whether the statute allowing the regulatory inspection could achieve its ends through means less damaging to privacy. The court thought so and declared the disputed provisions constitutionally invalid because the objectives of the searches could be achieved with warrants, which would have been less invasive of the right to privacy.

The court in *Mohunram*[30] was invited to examine whether legislation that allowed the forfeiture of assets[31] was proportionate to the offence committed and therefore constitutionally permissible. The court found the law to be constitutionally compliant but that, in the particular case, the asset forfeiture when weighed against the purpose served was disproportionate.

In *Richter*[32] the core issue was whether a law[33] which limited the right of a South African citizen who was a registered voter but was not in the country at the time of elections was constitutionally valid. The court concluded that all citizens who are registered to vote and who are abroad on voting day are entitled to vote in general elections. The statutory provisions preventing this were found to be unconstitutional and invalid.

The Constitutional Court made a number of rulings in order to protect and advance the rights of accused people to a fair criminal trial and fair appeal. It struck down the legislative provision[34] that required criminal appeals to be heard by a judge behind closed doors as a dangerous inroad on the right to a public trial by denying the right to present oral argument in open court. The court also disapproved of a provision that provided for exemptions from the duty to provide an appeal record as an unjustifiable barrier to the right to appeal or review.[35]

The court expanded the narrow common law definition of 'rape' to include the non-consensual anal penetration of a woman; it did not consider whether the definition should be extended to include the non-consensual penetration of a man as the facts did not require the court to consider the matter.[36]

In a case of the sentencing of a primary caregiver, the court underscored the constitutional injunction that the best interests of a child are paramount in all matters concerning the child. However, the 'best interests' injunction may be limited. The fact that the best interests of a child are paramount does not mean that they are absolute. The interests of the children to be affected must receive due consideration in determining the sentence imposed on their primary caregiver, but this does not mean all other considerations must be overridden.[37]

A man awaiting trial for five years was detained as a sentenced prisoner in a maximum security prison. Was his detention unlawful for the purpose of a claim for delictual damages? The court held that the detention as a sentenced maximum security prisoner violated the man's right not to be deprived of freedom arbitrarily or without just cause and was unlawful and constitutionally invalid.[38]

Employment justice also came for reckoning before the Langa Court. In one claim the issue was whether a regulation conferred a discretion on the national commissioner of the South African Police Service to advertise an upgraded post when it could be held by a satisfactorily performing incumbent. We held that the regulation did confer a discretion but that it must be exercised in a manner that ensures that no incumbents are unfairly retrenched. The court noted that regulations should be interpreted purposively and contextually when they are designed to serve diverse purposes in a complex context.[39]

In *Sidumo*[40] the court sought to resolve the poser caused by the intersection between the administrative law and labour law review standards granted by distinct legislation. The tight poser was whether compulsory statutory arbitration undertaken by the Commission for Conciliation, Mediation and Arbitration[41] under labour legislation[42] constituted administrative action as defined in administrative law legislation[43] and was therefore subject to the standard of review set under the latter legislation. In a highly divided decision, the majority held that an arbitration award by a commissioner is administrative action, but of a kind outside the scope of administrative action legislation.

Chirwa[44] was another complex matter. It sought to resolve the jurisdictional spat regarding whether the high court and the labour court had concurrent jurisdiction to hear disputes involving employment and labour relations. The Constitutional Court resolved that the high court did not have concurrent jurisdiction with the labour court in such matters. The legislative scheme was to empower the labour court to deal with constitutional disputes arising from employment relationships. Therefore, employees must first exhaust statutory remedies in the labour court before approaching the high court.

The court was also required to determine to what extent courts are entitled to exercise supervision over arbitral proceedings, and whether the right of access to courts in terms of the Constitution[45] applied directly to private arbitrations. The court took the attitude that it must construe the statutory requirements for setting aside arbitration awards quite strictly when it comes to private arbitration. The constitutional right of access to courts does not apply directly to private arbitration, but the arbitration process and agreement are still regulated by the law and must be in line with the Constitution. It is an implied term of every arbitration agreement that it be procedurally fair.[46]

The exercise of cultural beliefs and practices and custom also came under constitutional scrutiny. In one dispute, Ms Pillay would not accept that a public school could bar her daughter from wearing a nose stud at school as a cultural practice. The question posed was: to what extent are religious and cultural beliefs protected in public schools? The court ordered the school to allow Ms Pillay to practise her culture. It reasoned that failure to take steps reasonably to accommodate the needs of people on the basis on race, gender, religious or cultural belief amounted to unfair discrimination. The principle of reasonable accommodation was an exercise in proportionality that depends intimately on the facts. Reasonable accommodation is an important fact in determining the fairness of the discrimination. Schools should make exemptions for sincerely held religious and cultural beliefs and practices.[47]

On another terrain, in *Shilubana*,[48] a traditional community broke rank with old custom and installed a woman as a traditional leader. Familial conflict flared up. The issue became whether traditional communities have the authority to develop their customs and traditions to promote gender equality in the succession of traditional leadership in accordance with the Constitution. The court nodded affirmatively. It held that it was constitutionally permissible for a traditional community to develop customary law to align it to the constitutional commitment to gender equality. It followed that the new development of tradition had to be recognised by law.

The many decisions of the Constitutional Court on access to socio-economic rights were avowedly pro-poor. This is hardly surprising if one faces the reality that socio-economic rights are ordinarily justiciable on the back of demonstrable need. She who lives in a mansion is unlikely to make out a proper case that the state owes her access to housing. So the court tends to tilt in favour of the poor with an honest need for the public good that the Constitution affords them.

I cannot resist making the trite observation that the state is the foremost and primary bearer of duties to fulfil socio-economic rights. In a perfect world the state should take all reasonable steps required by law to afford the poor and needy the basic needs of life that translate into socio-economic promises. Even without a wordy constitution, a competent, caring and responsive state will strive to look after its less privileged people.

In a democracy one would expect astute citizens to give their vote only to leaders who are likely to attend to their social needs. In practice this is not so, however. All socio-economic claims in our courts are against the state in its many facets.

In the Langa Court, although we decided a great many socio-economic claims, this did not nearly cover the vast social need that existed. In one, we reminded municipalities of their duties before ejecting unlawful occupants from a dangerous building. Local authorities may use statutory powers to order occupants to vacate dangerous buildings, but before doing so, the government is obliged to take reasonable efforts to engage meaningfully with people who may be rendered homeless by the eviction.[49] The court also ruled as constitutionally invalid a legislative provision that compelled people to leave their homes on pain of criminal sanction in the absence of a court order.

In *Njongi*,[50] a recipient of social grant payments claimed arrears grant payments from a provincial government. The debt resulted from an unlawful decision to terminate the payment of the social grant. Instead of paying, the province pleaded prescription because of passage of time. Prescription is a principle in law which dictates that a debt will lapse, or prescribe, after a certain period of time. It is designed to bring timeous finality to disputes relating to debt. The question posed was whether the state may raise prescription in a claim for arrears of social grant payments. The court frowned at this. It concluded that the debt was caused by an unlawful decision to terminate the payment of the social grant. The prescription period did not begin to run until or unless the administrative decision was set aside or reliance thereon was expressly disavowed by the state. The court expressed doubt as to whether prescription is applicable to constitutional obligations to pay social grants but did not decide the point.

In *Mazibuko*[51] the contested issue was whether the steps taken by a municipality to provide access to sufficient water was reasonable under the Constitution.[52] The court took the view that the state must take reasonable legislative and other measures progressively to achieve the right of access to sufficient water within available resources. This obligation does not confer a right immediately to claim 'sufficient water' from the state. Much indeed has been written by academics and other commentators about the correctness of our decision. I was part of the court that made the decision. Apart from noting the debate around the correctness of the decision, I will not enter it.

In *Joseph*[53] the court ruled on access to electricity supply. On whether electricity supply can be disconnected without notice to the tenants, we held that tenants received electricity as a matter of public law right correlated to the constitutional and statutory duty placed on local government to provide basic municipal services to all people living in its area of jurisdiction. It followed that the municipality was obliged to provide them with procedural fairness, including notice of disconnection.

In *Hoërskool Ermelo*[54] we ruled on the right to receive education in the official language of one's choice in a public school and whether the head of a department of education may revoke the function of the governing body of a public school to determine its language policy. On a proper understanding of the right conferred by the Constitution,[55] the authority to determine the language policy of a public school cannot lie exclusively with the governing body. The state must also ensure effective access to the right to receive education.

On the Constitutional Court's plate during this period there were many other and varied causes: whether an alteration of provincial boundaries was validly made, specifically whether the provincial legislature failed to facilitate public involvement in the process of law-making;[56] whether the granting of amnesty in terms of the law on truth and reconciliation[57] undid the direct legal consequences flowing from the offence that were already complete by the time the amnesty was granted;[58] whether immunity from civil liability given to municipal councillors when carrying out their functions extended to municipal councillors not performing the real and legitimate business of the municipal council;[59] whether legislative provisions[60] served the best interests of the child by providing adequate protection to child complainants of sexual offences;[61] whether adverse costs may be awarded against a private person in constitutional litigation against the state;[62] whether a litigating company must give security for costs, given the right it has to have disputes resolved by courts;[63] whether the duty to exhaust internal remedies should be imposed rigidly or shield the administrative process from judicial scrutiny;[64] whether a private body can exercise a public power that is subject to the Constitution, and, if so, whether that power was properly delegated to it;[65] whether a presidential decision to amend the term of office of the head of the country's intelligence agency or dismiss him is constitutionally permissible;[66] and whether the right to open justice compels the public disclosure of discrete portions of a record of proceedings before a court where the information is alleged to be protected from public disclosure on grounds of national security.[67]

I hope I have left you assured that the Langa Court had a full and engaging repertoire of causes and cases that afforded us the space to do justice alongside the jarring political contestation and threats to other institutions of state. There was indeed a new sheriff in town but no cause for tremor.

CHAPTER 20

'You see, Sboshwa ...'

In April 2008, Pius Langa was left with nearly a year and a half to complete his term of fifteen years on the Constitutional Court. His had been a respectable stay. Unlike some of us, with the dawn of democracy Pius looked to nowhere else but to become a judge. His outstanding contribution attracted a national award. President Mbeki conferred on him the Order of the Baobab in Gold for 'his exceptional service in law, constitutional jurisprudence and human rights', a befitting recognition of a loyal servant of his people.

In 2008 we bade farewell to one of the founders of the court, Justice Tholakele Madala. By this time he had served for fourteen years and we all felt that his quiet and patient wisdom was going to be missed. But Tholi, too, was gradually becoming unwell after running a full race. His retirement made way for President Kgalema Motlanthe to make a new appointment to the Constitutional Court.

He favoured Justice Edwin Cameron from the Supreme Court of Appeal. Full marks must go to President Motlanthe. The appointment of Edwin Cameron was an inspired one at a time when the attitude of most within the ruling party was less than cordial. The Judicial Service Commission was required to furnish the president with three names more than the vacancy to be filled. In other words, the president had a choice from a slate of four appointable judges and he exercised it in favour of Edwin Cameron.

Edwin was a self-evidently excellent choice who would strengthen our court considerably. Not only did he have the gift of an excellent mind; he had outstanding academic accolades as well. Following a stay at the Bar, Edwin took silk and opted for an early judicial appointment, which saw him build considerable experience right up to the Supreme Court of Appeal. He had disclosed openly that he was a gay man and, when very few high-profile people did so, in addition he disclosed that he was living with HIV. Neither of these two facts should have stood – and indeed did not stand – in the way of President Motlanthe to have him grace our bench.

This was not the only inspired decision that President Motlanthe took in relation to the judiciary and other public office-bearers in less than a year in office. I served as chairperson with Dr Anna Mokgokong as deputy chair of the Independent Commission for the Remuneration of Public Office Bearers.[1] The remuneration commission made annual recommendations to the president on appropriate salary packages and, if he agreed, he would table them before parliament for sanction. The remuneration commission started a thoroughgoing review of the remuneration of public office-bearers, including that of judges and magistrates. We compared or benchmarked the office-bearer remuneration packages with a number of comparable sectors. The packages were relatively low and called for a complete restructuring of the salary bands. In any event we had to do away with the complicated notch system inherited from the apartheid state. In relation to judges and magistrates, the remuneration commission strenuously argued that the judicial bench would fail to attract suitable candidates if the salaries were too low. It would be a case of getting monkeys for peanuts. In the cases of all other office-bearers, including the presidency, the remuneration commission argued that higher salaries would prevent if not reduce graft and corruption.

As things stand, I leave it to history to judge whether higher salaries gave us a better judicial bench or other public office-bearers who did not help themselves to public funds.

The remuneration commission proposed a restructuring that would amount to nearly doubling the cash portion of the remuneration of public office-bearers. I was the one who presented the outcome and the commission's recommendations to President Mbeki. He would listen to the presentation pensively, then have a little giggle and say, 'Deputy Chief Justice, I will think about this.' But he just did not bite. A few times I presented to him and a few times he did not bite. I suspected that besides his disdain for money, he was concerned about being viewed as a leader who doubled his own salary and that of others in high places in the state. Having just come from the private sector, I knew better than he did how little he and other senior office-bearers earned. I had no concern with my standing in popularity stakes but he might have had concerns with political rectitude. And yet the commission's proposal to restructure the salary regime of public office-bearers was based on comparative evidence and was well worked and entirely justified. Its prime reason was to attract and keep the best talent in the executive, legislature and the judiciary.

I made one opportunistic presentation to President Motlanthe and he got the point and agreed to sign off on the proposed new salary structure. Parliament approved. I guess President Kgalema could afford to live above or not pander to narrow political sensitivities. He was an interim president and could possibly afford to follow his good judgement or conscience.

Pius's health was deteriorating, but it was his wife of 43 years, Beauty, who, on 30 August 2009, succumbed overnight in hospital after a long illness. Mrs Langa died two days before her 65th birthday, survived by her husband, five children and grandchildren. Pius was grief-stricken; he became even more unwell. I lived close to him and often had to step in to lead the court during difficult moments. He was to retire in October 2009 together with Kate O'Regan, Albie Sachs and Yvonne Mokgoro.

One of the last important things Pius did before he left the Constitutional Court was convene a national judges' conference. This he did in June 2009 and he invited President Jacob Zuma, who was then in his second month as president, to deliver the opening address. The president accepted the invitations and his big motorcade, with an ambulance trailing, motorbikes leading, blue lights flashing and sirens whining, duly arrived at Kievits Kroon, near Tshwane, the conference venue. I had been assigned to keep the president company in the holding room while Pius was attending to opening the plenary session of judges.

So there we were, the two of us, in the holding room. He was the president of the Republic and I was the deputy chief justice of the Republic. On Robben Island Jacob Zuma and I were young men, although he was older than me. We were rank juniors in our respective liberation movements. We each had to serve ten years on the Island. We came to know each other very, very well and were close comrades. In my earlier memoir, *My Own Liberator*, I described how when Kabonina and I planned to go on honeymoon to Durban in 1975, I alerted Msholozi. He met us at the old Durban airport and showed us around Durban. Shortly thereafter, Bhut' Griffiths and Victoria Mxenge and Thembile and Sayo Skweyiya took over and played host. Not long thereafter Zuma left to join the African National Congress in exile.

It crossed my mind as we sat in the holding room that no one of us could have predicted how long it would take in our long struggle to defeat apartheid and colonialism. Less still could anyone have foretold our respective meteoric rise to power and leadership in the affairs of the nation.

On another matter, it was true that since June 2005, when Thabo Mbeki dismissed Mr Zuma as deputy president, a lot of water had run under the bridge. We both knew how many and how intense the court battles were that paved his way to the presidency. Our court was the inevitable terminal. Pius and I sat in some of the cases that affected him directly or indirectly at the Constitutional Court. In a few others I did not sit because I was away on long leave. But we had never had a personal falling-out.

As we met in the holding room we shook hands and then hugged, enthusiastically and warmly, while his security people looked on, a little baffled at our embrace.

I warmly congratulated him for rising to become the country's president. 'Ngiyabonga, Sboshwa[2],' he said. 'Nam' Ngiyabonga, Mongameli[3],' I replied.

After our affectionate greetings, I decided to stick to protocol and take no liberties. In doing so I sought to assure him that I recognised and respected his rise to the presidency. We sat down and an eerie silence crept in until finally the president broke the ice and said, 'You know, Sboshwa, the job of a judge is very difficult. Angithi nina ningabantu ba mafacts[4].' He paused, then added, 'I understand your predicament.' Before I could comment, he continued: 'Let me tell you a nice story about Gaddafi and judges ...' and he giggled a few times. 'You see, Sboshwa, on the sidelines of an African Union meeting, Gaddafi said to me he thought Libya and South Africa are so powerful that together we could rule the entire African continent. Then Gaddafi said we should work together and try to achieve that complete control over Africa.'

All I could say was, 'Auwu, Mongameli[5]?' and wait for the punchline.

The president giggled some more – it went on much longer this time – before continuing with his story. 'I asked Gaddafi what about the judges in his country and Gaddafi said, "What judges?"' The memory seemed to amuse him no end. 'Sboshwa,' he said, 'I told Gaddafi that in my country the judges will never allow me, the president, to do what you say we do if it is not in the Constitution. Wherever you turn to, the judges are all over you.' Another long bout of chortling followed.

I might have grimaced or smiled but I did not have to say anything because at that moment someone knocked at the door of the holding room to say it was time for the president to be ushered into the conference room.

President Zuma delivered a written text affirming his support for the independence of the judiciary. Afterwards he graciously stayed on for tea with all the judges attending the conference and then the big convoy sped off.

Chief Justice Pius Langa had an appointment to meet with President Zuma for a late afternoon discussion about succession. It was scheduled to take place a few days before he was due to retire, the venue being Mahlamba Ndlopfu, the president's official residence in Pretoria. Pius alerted me to the impending meeting.

By then Pius and I had worked together for four years in the leadership of the Constitutional Court and had built a solid bond. He shared his work-related anxieties with me – and they were many – and I shared mine with him. We had endured the Hlophe saga together and we had lived through multiple Zuma-related cases (and there were many of those too). We had been pilloried by a variety of political actors supporting the president as unpatriotic or counter-revolutionary judges. Some critics of the same ilk questioned why the chief justice was given a national award while he was still in office. 'What was he being thanked for?' they insinuated.

On the happy side, we ran a highly efficient and effective court. We wrote some of the finest judgments of the Constitutional Court and continued to hold high the standards of excellence and independence, without fear or favour.

It was quite late in the evening, around 9pm, when Pius returned to the courthouse. I had a lot of judicial work to finish – writing a proper judgment is a detailed and thoughtful enterprise – and was still in my chambers. I was also keen to know from Pius how the meeting had gone. I was dismayed when I saw him. His energy levels had clearly plummeted; his face was ashen and he looked exhausted. He had been made to wait for a few hours before he could see the president, he told me, but no one had cared to explain to him why his meeting was so delayed. If the meeting had not been with the president of the country, he said, he would have walked away. In the end the meeting was short, to the point and not very cordial.

Pius turned to me, his eyes drooping with fatigue, and said simply: 'It is not you. It is SN.'[6]

Then, weeping, he walked away to his chambers.

*

The term of office of Pius Langa as chief justice was marked by concerted turbulence in the social and political space. The honeymoon enjoyed by the Constitutional Court of his predecessor, Arthur Chaskalson, was long gone. The gloves of the political elite within the ruling party were well and truly off and their squabbles for power and influence spilled over into the judicial function. They found ways to clothe their power struggles as legal tussles. And through it all Pius Langa and his court kept good control from the cockpit. He was a patient patriot, a fine jurist and a well-measured chief justice.

We held a number of farewell functions for four very fine jurists: Justice Yvonne Mokgoro, Justice Kate O'Regan, Justice Albie Sachs and Chief Justice Pius Langa. The contribution they made to the democratic project from its inception is displayed in their finely worked and meticulously reasoned judgments that resonate to this day and will for many years to come. Their concrete contribution may also be seen throughout the magnificent court edifice, its locations, its library, its art forms and its enduring symbolism.

One of these functions was a dinner attended by guests drawn from the judiciary, representatives of executive government and the legislature, the legal profession and a collection of notables from civil society and the public. It was a teary affair. The departing justices displayed open departing grief. Their emotional bond with the Constitutional Court and its mission was plain and well justified.

We who were remaining, in turn, were deeply grateful that they had given their all to build the court, literally and figuratively, from ground zero. It is a difficult task, but a happier one, to build public institutions but, as our recent history has attested, it is a much easier task – and horrifically so – to empty them out.

As tradition dictated, we also held a ceremonial court sitting to bid farewell to the chief justice and his three departing colleagues. I was privileged to read a tribute to them on behalf of our remaining colleagues and staff of the court. Several other praises were read from the well of the court by stakeholders in the justice family.

After his retirement, sadly, Pius Langa was struck by illness and he succumbed and passed on at Milpark Hospital, Johannesburg, on 24 July 2013. I was privileged to read the eulogy at his funeral and penned a tribute in a collection of essays in his memory.[7]

NGCOBO COURT

CHAPTER 21

A new political elite

By October 2009 President Zuma was firmly in the saddle as president of the ruling party and of the country. He appointed a new minister of justice, Jeff Radebe, who replaced Minister Enver Surty.[1] Enver Surty was a trained lawyer who had held down a law practice before espousing activism and going to parliament. He was a decent, considerate and listening minster who supported the judicial function and cared about an effective administration of justice. His contribution to the process of writing the final Constitution is well known and documented.[2] It was not clear how and why Surty fell short and was not reappointed.

Surty was replaced by Radebe, who must have pledged to become an ally of the new president, who had survived several skirmishes in the courts and had an obvious and keen interest in the goings-on within the judiciary. Radebe's responsibilities as minister of justice included the monitoring and setting of policy for the institution that was charged with prosecuting crime, the National Prosecuting Authority. Under his watch the Scorpions,[3] who were entrusted with the duty to fight corruption and other economic crimes, were disbanded. Radebe's role was also prominent in the affairs of the Judicial Service Commission, which recommended the appointment of judges to the president. In short, Radebe was right there when vital institutions in the justice sector faced headwinds. He might one day want to explain what his role was in all this.

Chief Justice Langa's term of office ended and the president moved swiftly to formalise his choice of the chief justice. Sandile Ngcobo assumed the post on 1 October 2009 without much ceremony or fanfare. Part of the reason was that a judge, unlike politicians, is sworn in only once and that is when they become a judge for the first time. They do not retake the oath if they are elevated to a higher court or judicial position. Thus it was that when I arrived at the Constitutional Court in 2002, I had already taken an oath of office at the high court so it was not required of me to take it again.

I made time to visit Sandile Ngcobo at his chambers and to congratulate him. We were neither strangers nor enemies. Since my arrival at the court we had become intellectual sparring partners and over time we had built a reasonable collegial liaison. We were not social friends outside the precincts of the court, however, and we did not wine and dine out as I did with some of my other colleagues, such as Zak Yacoob, Thembile Skweyiya, Johann van der Westhuizen, Yvonne Mokgoro and Sisi Khampepe.

Sandile and I both tended to work long and late. He often came to my chambers after hours and in turn I visited his chambers. Over coffee we would debate the difficult law in cases that had been heard and awaited judgment.

It is a well-etched practice that judges of our court never debate the possible outcome of a case or the intricacies of the applicable law until the case has been fully argued in a court hearing. At most a judge who has been assigned to write the main judgment will issue a pre-hearing note listing the issues they believe require resolution. The note will not suggest how the issues in the case, big and small, should be decided. The practice is a welcome and helpful one. Judges sitting as a college are better approaching a hearing with open minds and without the clatter of the initial views of other judges on the outcome.

Sandile had flawless academic qualifications. He had served as a practitioner at the side Bar and the Bar and had built considerable experience as a judge at various courts. Although I was disappointed that I had not been appointed chief justice, I did recognise that Sandile was a worthy appointment. He deserved the post and could do the job just as well. He was a hard-working judge and took time to find what I call 'judicial truth'. This happens when a judge wrestles with the complex crossroads of fact and law in order to reach a truly just outcome.

What was more, Sandile had acquired the skill to write down the workings of his mind. I knew this well because by the time he was appointed chief justice we had debated virtually every complicated case and had written concurring or dissenting judgments side by side. Let me embroider and say it is not everyone who speaks well that can pen his thoughts just as well. So, setting aside my personal disappointment because I had been bypassed, I wholly accepted his leadership and was ready to work as his deputy. He, too, had been bypassed when I was appointed deputy chief justice and this had not unduly interfered with our ongoing jurisprudential sparring and collegial friendship. I was quite content to play my role as deputy chief justice. And I did.

For good reason our Constitution distinguishes between how all other judges are appointed from the manner of appointment of the chief justice and deputy chief justice, and the president and deputy president of the Supreme Court of Appeal. As I have relayed earlier, with all other judges, the president must appoint the candidates declared appointable by the JSC, but when it comes to the senior leadership of the judiciary, the president initiates the process by selecting the person he prefers to assume the role. In effect, barring some horrible mishap, the president appoints the chief justice, deputy chief justice and the president and deputy president of the Supreme Court of Appeal.[4]

The rationale for this constitutional scheme appears to be that the president deserves this power because his role obliges him to interact frequently with the leadership of the judiciary. Another consideration may be one of separation of powers and checks and balances. The executive must have a significant say over judges just as judges influence and sometimes thwart the exercise of executive and legislative power. In any event, in their wisdom, the founding mothers and fathers of the Constitution gave this power to the president and must be respected. The rule of law demands no less.

One of the first tasks the new chief justice had to accomplish was to fill the vacancies of the four justices who had retired just before he was appointed. The selection process of the JSC yielded a number of appointable candidates and President Zuma appointed Justices Johan Froneman, Chris Jafta, Sisi Khampepe and Mogoeng Mogoeng. This meant a complete change of the guard at the Constitutional Court.

After fifteen years none of the founding justices was left. This did not mean the court would veer off its path of travel. The Constitution remained the same. The major building blocks of constitutionalism were well in place. There was a broad line of precedents or decided cases that would bind the new justices and all other justices who served on the court and beyond.

Our courts, like many courts in the world, follow the precedent system of decision-making called, in Latin, *stare decisis*.[5] At its simplest, *stare decisis* lays down that when a court makes a decision in a case that has similar or comparable facts and law, it is obliged to follow the principle or rule established in the earlier binding decision. A precedent is binding on the court making the decision if it was made by a court of similar or higher status. So, everything being equal, decisions of the Constitutional Court bind judges of that court and all other courts below it, unless the precedent is overturned by the court which made it on the grounds that it was clearly wrongly decided. The overturning of an earlier precedent does not occur lightly and, if it does, there has to be a full motivation as to why the precedent was wrongly decided.

The precedent system has several merits. The leading reason is to foster certainty and equality in the application of the law. It would be most undesirable for judges to apply or interpret the law in any odd way in matters with a similar set of facts or circumstances. If that were so, litigants would not know what likely outcome to expect from the courts. They would struggle to arrange their affairs in accordance with the law. They would be faced with arbitrariness and would not get equal protection of the law.

Precedents impose a coherent way in which judicial officers in the entire court structure should reason and come to decisions. Should they depart from precedent, on appeal there would be a clear yardstick to correct the errant decisions and in that way afford litigants equal justice. Of course, a collection of precedents in a field of law exposes how judges and lawyers think about the judicial function. That underlying thinking and the legal norms deduced from precedents are called jurisprudence.

It goes without saying that a judicial system can rely on past examples or precedents or decision-making only if the judiciary lays bare the full reasons for the decisions they take. This means judgments of courts that set binding examples must be recorded and preserved. This is usually done in law reports. These are the stoutly bound books that one often sees on bookshelves in offices of lawyers and judges' chambers. In this digital age law reports are accessible online and may be downloaded and read by everyone. This means anyone within the public may now read exactly why a judge has decided the case in the manner they did and make up their own mind whether he agrees or not. That explains why there is a growing practice and belief that judgments are best cast in everyday language that is free from legal jargon and in that way accessible to everyone.

But here is my point: there can be no effective precedent system without open and reported judgments. During my time at the Constitutional Court at least three countries on our continent approached us for help in rebuilding a precedent system. Their legal systems, citing budgetary constraints, had stopped preserving written judgments a few decades before, and now their courts were seeking support from us. The absence of reported judgments meant that judges, even at the highest level, stopped being accountable. They did not tell the litigants and the public how they arrived at a decision. They issued orders without reasons. Arbitrariness and uncertainty had crept in. Suspicion of bias or impropriety festered with every order made and the administration of justice suffered severely.

In this kind of setting people mistrust the courts. The courts stop being effective and useful arbiters of disputes. In turn courts cannot call the government, or indeed anyone wielding public power, to account. And, as we all know, once the judicial arm of the state collapses, the rule of law will never survive. Anarchy and repression thrive. The country's inhabitants become fair game for lawless government.

In light of this, it is an initiative to be applauded that the Southern African Legal Information Institute (SAFLII) is placing online all judgments that may be found at home and at courts in southern Africa – a valuable and essential resource.

*

The fact that all inaugural judges of the Constitutional Court had retired and that the new president had appointed a new minister of justice and a new chief justice and also that he had added four new judges did not mean that the court would suddenly change its jurisprudence and decide cases of similar legal import differently. And besides the value of precedent, once appointed, any judge worth the title will never be on anyone's leash. A judge's only restraint should be the law and their conscience. As I show below, the court's role was not compromised. In fact it continued to be independent, efficient and effective.

We welcomed our new colleagues and they got down to the business of the Constitutional Court.

The socio-political climate in the country had come to a level of stasis once more. It seemed that the political war was over; as if the storm had blown over and calm had returned. The political power contest had yielded an outcome. There was a clear winner and a new political elite. The court still enjoyed a strong flow of disputes unconnected to the power spat of the body politic. In fact throughout the Ngcobo Court it was regular judicial business. Parties with wide-ranging grievances and disputes approached the court and sought or resisted the relief asked for.

So the jurisprudence of the Constitutional Court flourished in a variety of fields of law. The nation's confidence in the place and its work remained unbending. Many real people, natural or corporate, came forward with pressing grievances seeking judicial relief.

In this time the court resolved a number of procedural matters. These included the first-ever review of the taxation of the court's own taxing master[6] and whether a claimant is entitled to relief for an extended procedural delay in a labour claim.[7] Another procedural challenge was whether the Constitution allowed the use of provisional sentence, a shotgun procedure frequently used in the courts to recover a liquid debt,[8] and when the Constitutional Court should discharge its own supervisory order in an access to housing dispute.[9] The court pondered over a number of fair trial claims. These included the fairness of sentencing in a trial which led to a conviction on dealing in drugs.[10] Another was the power of the president to pardon people convicted of crimes with an alleged political motive.[11] Yet another claimant challenged the constitutional validity of a law[12] that allowed the arrest of a debtor who was suspected of being about to flee the country to avoid paying a debt (known as arrest *tanquam suspectus de fuga*).[13] Another case was about whether an accused person might be fairly convicted and sentenced under an old-order law that still applied in the Transkei[14] after the new Constitution but did not apply in the rest of South Africa.[15] In another criminal justice appeal a woman who had been sentenced to direct imprisonment argued that she would have been punished differently if the correct sentencing principles had been used with due weight to the fact that she was a primary caregiver of her minor children and that the best interests of her children would be harmed.[16] An imprisoned litigant sought the Constitutional Court to direct the responsible minister of government to consider his conditions of parole and possible release.[17] In another claim the issue was whether a life imprisonment sentence was a just sentence where a wife had contracted a murderer to kill her husband.[18]

Disputes took a variety of forms, such as the validity of constitutional amendments which altered the boundaries of two adjacent provinces;[19] the import of international trade agreements and anti-dumping duties;[20] the scope and effect of a law[21] that targeted communal land rights as part of the broader right to fair land restitution;[22] and the respective powers of a metropolitan municipality and a provincial development tribunal over land rezoning and development.[23]

Some of the matters we heard challenged the partiality of decisions taken by judges. In one instance the grievance was that the judgment amounted to a cut-and-paste job from the written argument of one party in the dispute and that the judge concerned did not properly consider the arguments of both parties impartially and had refused to recuse himself from any further proceedings in the matter.[24] In the other appeal the claim was that one of the judges in a panel held a small parcel of listed shares of a bank which was a party in the dispute and another had an alleged prior association with the bank. The question was whether the judges were biased for these reasons only.[25] Another argued that a judgment by the Supreme Court of Appeal infringed on several fair trial rights because of a perceived judicial bias.[26] The Constitutional Court also answered the question whether a law on the prescription[27] of a claim for damages arising from bodily injuries caused by a motor vehicle is constitutionally valid if one considers the right of access to courts.[28] A related case was on the interaction between the right to recover damages arising from personal injuries under the common law and under a related third-party law.[29] Also related was the common law right of mineworkers to recover damages for occupational injury that they could not claim from the employer under an applicable legislation.[30]

As we can see, the citizenry used the court to its full extent, aside from and outside political contests, which were often inward-looking and self-serving. We as a court most of the time kept our heads down as we dispensed justice on a vast range of disputes, all of them hankering for adjudication.

One case brought urgently before us in 2010 concerned the immigration of a Russian exotic dancer, Tatiana Malachi, who was seemingly kept at one of our airports and prevented from leaving the country for contractual reasons concerning unpaid debt to her employers. This case was memorable for me because my colleagues never allowed me to forget the misstep I made in an unguarded moment. It caused them much mirth and me much ragging for years. The picture the court record sketched of Miss Tatiana was of a person of considerable dancing skills with a body and face to match the part. The case did not require Miss Tatiana to be in court. Her counsel, Mr Katz SC, was in attendance. During the court sitting I said: 'Mr Katz, is the applicant, Ms Tatiana, in court?'

My female colleagues were unamused: 'Why should she be here?' they chided me indignantly. My male friends like Cameron, Yacoob and Van der Westhuizen never let me off the hook and jibes about Tatiana have persisted to this day. At my farewell function, my well-loved and esteemed colleague Edwin Cameron related the Tatiana incident to all and sundry at my expense. I had no valid defence except to say that court records should be written in bleak and cheerless terms; that I must have been overcome by a boyish instinct to set my eyes on the fairytale Russian dancer who sat at the centre of the controversy. Even in matters of serious import and consequence, lighter moments do arise.

The court made decisions on issues like urban development and approval of building plans;[31] the import of a failure by an organ of state to make a necessary decision under administrative justice;[32] a preferential procurement scheme vitiated by fraudulent fronting;[33] requirements for the granting of a prospecting licence and the rights of an affected owner or communities;[34] defamation and impairment of dignity in the light of the law granting amnesty for past crimes;[35] defamation and impairment of dignity in the light of fundamental rights enshrined in the Constitution;[36] and whether a law which allows the state to confiscate monies that were paid under an unlawful agreement in terms of the national credit consumer law[37] is arbitrary deprivation of property by the state.[38]

The court decided important cases on unlawful occupiers and just remedies and relocation orders;[39] whether a registrar of a high court may grant an order declaring mortgaged property that is a person's home specially executable;[40] the conduct of a political party in preparation for local government elections;[41] and the eviction of a public school from private property.[42]

The court was increasingly engaged with matters related to employment and labour. It was asked to determine the meaning of 'essential service' under the labour relations laws[43] in relation to members of a police union who were not executing police duties;[44] transfer of a business as a going concern under the labour relations laws;[45] whether the minister of government should be held vicariously liable for damages arising from the brutal rape of a 13-year-old girl by a policeman who was on standby duty;[46] and whether a court that makes provision for the reasonable legal expenses of an accused defendant under the prevention of organised crimes law[47] may extend those expenses to be incurred to assets held by the defendant's wife.[48]

In another important case, the Constitutional Court had to resolve two important issues: first, how the state discharges the burden, under the access to information laws,[49] of establishing that its refusal to grant access to a record is justified; and second, the circumstances under which a court may call for additional evidence in the form of the contested record.[50] In a different matter, the court was asked to consider the circumstances in which it should intervene to infuse the law of contract with constitutional values in the development of the common law of contract in the light of the spirit, purport and objects of the Bill of Rights in our Constitution.[51] The question presented in another proceeding was whether a provincial legislature has the authority to enact legislation dealing with its own financial management.[52] Another question that was brought before the court was when compensation for expropriation of property in terms of the Constitution is to be determined.[53] The court was also asked to decide on the interpretation of and relationship between two South African statutes that deal with restraint orders in criminal matters.[54] The one provided for the issue of restraint orders by courts regarding the property of persons against whom criminal proceedings were pending or about to be instituted, while the other provided for the enforcement in South Africa of restraint orders that had been issued in the course of criminal proceedings in foreign states.[55]

*

One ghost of past political conflict, however, still hovered and occasionally it howled. Its genesis was the much-publicised resolution of the 2007 national conference of the ruling party. The ANC conference resolved that the corruption-busting entity known as the Scorpions, which was located in the office of the National Prosecuting Authority, must be disbanded and replaced with a new policing unit under the South African Police Service. The rationale for disbanding the Scorpions was 'the constitutional imperative that there be a single police service'. For this reason the Scorpions should be dissolved, and those members of it performing policing functions should fall under SAPS. It was decided that the relevant legislative changes should be effected 'as a matter of urgency'.

The Scorpions had been established by a law of parliament and could be undone and replaced only by another law. Parliament duly passed a law terminating the Scorpions and enacting a new entity, the Directorate for Priority Crime Investigation, known as the Hawks. This new unit had considerably less sting and freedom from executive influence and control.[56]

Mr Glenister was a self-appointed crusader against corruption. He was less than pleased by the law that abolished the Scorpions – which unit had carried the reputation of effectiveness in combating corruption. Mr Glenister attacked the constitutional validity of the new legislation that disestablished the Scorpions and created the Hawks. The government defended the validity of the law. All this translated into the *Glenister* case.[57]

In its decision, the Constitutional Court was split midway. We sat in a panel of nine justices and the court was split five to four. Ngcobo CJ wrote one judgment and Edwin Cameron and I collaborated in writing the other. Our joint judgment attracted a majority of one and became the judgment of the court. Portions of the legislation were declared inconsistent with the Constitution and invalid in so far as it failed to secure an adequate degree of independence for the newly established Directorate for Priority Crime Investigation. Parliament was given eighteen months to remedy the defects.

I will not succumb to the temptation of deciding the correctness or otherwise of either of the judgments, nor do I believe it necessary for me to re-sketch here the political and social milieu in which the judgments were penned. Suffice it to note that many subsequent events in the private and public spaces of our country suggested that there was a steady and increasing trend of financial, administrative and other forms of corruption, a matter which is thoroughly borne out by the evidence brought before the commission of inquiry into state capture headed by Deputy Chief Justice Zondo.[58]

Dissatisfied with the amendments made to give effect to the order in *Glenister* and to remedy the defective legislation, the Helen Suzman Foundation, a civil society group, challenged the constitutionality of the legislation. In a majority judgment, Chief Justice Mogoeng confirmed that some legislative provisions improperly allowed undue political interference. It concluded that the provisions inadequately secured the structural and operational independence of a constitutionally mandated anti-corruption body like the Directorate.[59]

When Sandile Ngcobo was appointed chief justice it was understood that he would occupy the position for just under two years. His term of office was to end at midnight on 14 August 2011. Clearly, President Zuma was of a different mind. On 11 April 2011 he requested the chief justice, in a letter to him, to remain in office for an additional period of five years. The letter concluded with the words:

> Having regard to the above, I, in terms of section 8(a) of the [Judges' Remuneration and Conditions of Employment] Act, would like to request you to continue to perform active service as Chief Justice of South Africa from the 15th August 2011 until 15 August 2016.

On 2 June 2011, the chief justice wrote back, accepting President Zuma's invitation to have his term of office extended for five years to 2016. On 3 June 2011 the president went ahead and extended the term of office of Chief Justice Ngcobo. Later that day, President Zuma sent this decision to the Judicial Service Commission and to leaders of the political parties represented in the National Assembly before he announced his decision to the nation in an address to parliament.

Multiple parties were affronted by the decision. Some approached the Constitutional Court seeking an order to set aside as invalid the extension of the term of office of the chief justice on the ground that the legislative provision President Zuma hoped to use, on the advice of minister of justice Jeff Radebe, was plainly unconstitutional and invalid and so, too, was the extension of office. President Zuma and Minister Jeff Radebe resisted the relief asked for by the multiple parties. The chief justice chose to abide by the decision of the court.

A unanimous court of ten justices arrived at a decision. This was a 'The Court' judgment because all justices who sat spoke with one voice. On 29 July 2011 they handed down the judgment, which ruled that the extension of the term of office of the chief justice was not permissible in law. The legislative provision the president sought to rely on was itself inconsistent with the Constitution and invalid. It followed that President Jacob Zuma acted contrary to the Constitution in extending the term of office.[60]

Chief Justice Ngcobo withdrew his acceptance of the extension of his term on 27 July 2011, shortly before the unanimous judgment was delivered and made public.

As convention dictated, the Constitutional Court held a ceremonial court sitting at which his colleagues, the profession and the two other arms of state bade farewell to the departing chief justice. It fell on me, being the most senior after him, to recite the valedictory speech.

MOGOENG COURT

CHAPTER 22

Banishing the elephant

From midnight on 14 August 2011 our country had no chief justice. The Constitution told us that the Constitutional Court consisted of 'the chief justice of South Africa, the deputy chief justice and nine other judges'.[1] This was not a breach of the supreme law, however, because it anticipated a lacuna, or gap, like this. The Constitutional Court has a set quorum. It is competent to perform its judicial role with fewer than the full quota of eleven justices provided that the members of the court sitting are not fewer than eight in number.[2] Remaining was a college of ten justices who could and did sit without a chief justice. Secondly, in the absence of the chief justice the deputy chief justice acts as chief justice in the meantime. I was not formally appointed acting chief justice nor was it necessary in law. I was the *de facto* acting chief justice and I led the court accordingly.

The president wasted no time in taking steps to fill the vacancy. The law was clear. As head of the national executive, the president appointed the chief justice after consulting the JSC and the leaders of parties represented in the National Assembly.[3] To accomplish his desired appointment, the president needed to consult the JSC, which meant the commission had to be convened to ascertain its views on the candidate the president sought to appoint as chief justice. Again the law was clear. If the chief justice was temporarily 'unable to serve' on the commission, the deputy chief justice acted in his or her stead on the commission.[4]

Within two days of the vacancy, on 16 August 2011 President Zuma sent me the letter reproduced below. It speaks for itself. The letter told me what was within my full expectation, namely, that I would not be the next chief justice – I would be overlooked again. The last sentence of the letter invited me to express my views soon. I did not read this as inviting my view on the identity or suitability of the person the president preferred to appoint as chief justice. I read the line as asking me to say when and how soon I would convene the JSC to enable him to consult it on his choice as the law required.

It was unclear to me why filling the vacancy was a matter of extreme urgency. Even so I sensed the speed with which the president wanted his will to be done. I wrote back to him the following day, 17 August, advising that I had convened an urgent meeting of the commission for Saturday, 20 August 2011. That meeting had a limited purpose of settling the procedure by which the commission would be consulted and agreeing on the date and procedure for the interview of the hand-picked candidate.

The designs of the president quickly filtered into the public space. That was so because the president had written to leaders of political parties in parliament in a bid to consult them. Also I had written to members of the JSC about the likely appointment of a new chief. The pending commission meeting to assess the suitability of the chief justice nominate was widely reported and debated in the public media in support or otherwise of the nomination.

I was approached by at least three people and two or so civic bodies who sought my support for a nomination alternative to that of the president's for the post of chief justice. Much as I was flattered, I emphatically declined. For one thing the law was clear. The president made known his choice and had the right and prerogative to appoint. His duty was not to seek permission of the commission or political leaders but only to consult them and then appoint. So, it would have been as silly as it would have been futile to put up nominations other than the president's.

In order to place the matter beyond all doubt for all concerned, I wrote a statement of my response to the decision of the president to nominate someone else and still require me to preside over the consultation ahead of the appointment. I released my written position to the public before chairing the meeting of the JSC which was intended to test the suitability of the person nominated for the position of chief justice.

Again, I think I would do a disservice to the statement if I were to paraphrase it. Here it is:

> Opening Statement by Deputy Chief Justice Dikgang Moseneke at the special meeting of the Judicial Service Commission held in Cape Town on Saturday, 20 August 2011.

Esteemed members of the Judicial Service Commission (Commission), I thank you for attending this special meeting on such short notice. I welcome you all.

In my capacity as Deputy Chief Justice, I have convened this special meeting at the written request of the President of the Republic of South Africa, His Excellency, Mr Jacob Zuma and in accordance with the provisions of section 178(7) of the Constitution. That section provides that if the Chief Justice is unable to serve on the Commission, the Deputy Chief Justice acts as his or her alternate on the Commission.

In a letter to me dated 16 August 2011, the President informs that it is necessary to appoint a new Chief Justice and that in his view 'Justice Mogoeng Mogoeng will be a suitable candidate to assume the position of the Chief Justice of the Republic of South Africa'.

The letter records that section 174(3) of the Constitution requires that the President consult, amongst others, with the Commission on the appointment of the Chief Justice. Pursuant to that provision the President requests the Commission to let him have its views on the suitability of Justice Mogoeng Mogoeng for appointment as Chief Justice.

I caused the letter from the President to be circulated to all members of the Commission. Responses of some members made it clear that there are differences of opinion on the procedure the Commission must follow

MOGOENG COURT

16 August 2011

Dear Honourable Deputy Chief Justice Moseneke

APPOINTMENT OF THE CHIEF JUSTICE OF THE REPUBLIC OF SOUTH AFRICA

The position of Chief Justice of the Republic of South Africa became vacant at midnight on the 14th of August 2011, as a result of the discharge from active service of the incumbent Chief Justice, Mr Justice Sirral Sandile Ngcobo.

It is therefore necessary to appoint a new Chief Justice.

I am of the view that Mr Justice Mogoeng Mogoeng will be a suitable candidate to assume the position of Chief Justice of the Republic of South Africa.

Pursuant to Section 174 (3) of the Constitution of the Republic of South Africa, 1996, I am required to consult, among others, with the Judicial Service Commission, (JSC), on the appointment of the Chief Justice.

I shall appreciate it much if the JSC could let me have its views on the suitability of Justice Mogoeng for appointment as Chief Justice of the Republic of South Africa.

In view of the urgent need to appoint the new Chief Justice, it will be highly appreciated if I could obtain your views at your earliest convenience.

Yours faithfully,

JACOB GEDLEYIHLEKISA ZUMA
PRESIDENT OF THE REPUBLIC OF SOUTH AFRICA

Deputy Chief Justice Dikgang Moseneke
Constitutional Court
1 Hospital Street
Constitution Hill
Braamfontein
2017

Cc: Mr Sello Chiloane, The JSC Secretariat

The Constitutional Court of South Africa

CHAMBERS OF
JUSTICE D MOSENEKE
DEPUTY CHIEF JUSTICE OF SOUTH AFRICA

Constitution Hill
Private Bag X1
BRAAMFONTEIN
2017
Tel: (011)359-7442
Fax: (011)403-8883
E Mail: grobler@concourt.org.za

17 August 2011

Your Excellency
The President of the Republic of South Africa
Mr Jacob Gedleyihlekisa Zuma

APPOINTMENT OF THE CHIEF JUSTICE OF THE REPUBLIC OF SOUTH AFRICA

I write in response to your letter dated 16 August 2011.

I have noted that you are of the view that Justice Mogoeng Mogoeng will be a suitable candidate to assume the position of Chief Justice of the RSA and that under section 174(3) of the Constitution you are required to consult with the Judicial Services Commission.

Pursuant to your request, I have convened an urgent meeting of the Judicial Services Commission to be held in Cape Town on Saturday 20 August 2011 at 10am. At that meeting the Commission will be required to decide on the procedure to be followed by the Commission for the purpose of being consulted by the President as required by the provisions of section 174(3) of the Constitution. The Commission will also determine the place and time for the interview of the President's nominee, Justice M Mogoeng, in accordance with the procedure that would have been adopted.

Shortly after the meeting of 20 August 2011, a further letter reporting on the outcome of that meeting will be directed to the President.

Yours faithfully

Dikgang Moseneke
Deputy Chief Justice of the
Republic of South Africa

when it is consulted by the President as required by section 174(3) of the Constitution.

Thus, this meeting has the singular purpose of determining the procedure to be followed by the [Commission] when its views are required by the President on the suitability of a nominee he or she intends to appoint as Chief Justice. Naturally, when the procedure is certain, the time, date and place where the nominee or nominees would submit to an interview have to be fixed.

Before I invite deliberation on this narrow purpose of the meeting, it is proper and necessary that I banish the elephant out of the room. That elephant is whether I am available to be a nominee or contender or contestant for the position of Chief Justice.

Our country and its people have been exposed to considerable media and public conversations on the nomination of the Chief Justice. Certain media reports have expressed preferences on who the President should nominate. Of course, that constitutional prerogative vests in the President.

Some organisations have gone further and mentioned me by name as a possible nominee. Other media reports and organisations have purported to nominate me or have said that they would do so if the Commission's procedure were to permit them.

I thank those within our nation who have shown trust in me and thought that I could serve our country in that crucial position. Equally, I understand and respect the views of those who take a different view.

Let me make it clear that, much as I consider it an honour to be thought of as a potential nominee for the post of Chief Justice of this country, I have never solicited or accepted any nomination and I am not available to accept any nomination, whatever its source, now or after the deliberations of this Commission. Therefore, I am neither a hopeful, nor a nominee or a contender, present or future, for the position of Chief Justice.

In some instances, public speculation nearly suggests that my very life depends on my being appointed Chief Justice. That is simply not so. As matters stand, it is a rare privilege to serve my country on its highest Court. This came after a long and rewarding career, over more than 30 years, as a candidate attorney, attorney, junior counsel, and senior counsel, judge of the high court and later of the Constitutional Court. I am further honoured to serve as Deputy Chief Justice. I am indeed prepared to serve on any other court below the Constitutional Court. I would hope that the usefulness of my contribution on the Court and to the democratic project to create an equal, cohesive and socially just society does not depend on the position I hold or the position I am given or indeed the position I manage to extract for myself. Every one of us can make a worthy contribution, whatever our position. We need not abandon good sense, the task at hand, or principle in order to get up the ladder of hierarchy or privilege.

If my reckoning is accurate, my term on the Court ends at the end of 2016. Provided that my will and energy to serve do not wilt, I will continue to serve where I am now, dutifully and in the best sense of a patriotic judge who seeks to make a contribution towards achieving a better life for all. To accomplish that, I need not be a Chief Justice.

Having cleared the overgrowth, I now invite debate on the issues at hand.

Cape Town
20 August 2011

The JSC in Cape Town convened for purpose of the inquiry into the fitness of the chief justice nominate to assume office. The proceedings were of very high public interest and were televised for the full two days of the proceedings. The duty fell on me to preside over the process of the commission.

A majority of members of the commission resolved that the nominated candidate was suitable to occupy the position of chief justice. I have chosen not to run a commentary on the long and contested proceedings. I was integral to and immersed in the deliberations and may betray partiality.

I compiled a written account of the proceedings and their outcome. Without delay I sought an audience with the president to deliver the report and to answer questions he might have on the proceedings. I met the president at his official residence in Tshwane on a warm and pleasant evening.

As you might have gathered by now, each time the president and I met there was never a shortage of pleasantries to exchange. We were anything but aliens. Our extended joint stay in Robben Island prison made for easy and ready small talk. I got down to the job of the evening. He thanked me graciously for convening the commission and for reporting on the outcome of its meeting.

He let slip that he had been watching the interview of Justice Mogoeng on the television over two days, so I was surprised when he requested a transcript of the private deliberations. In my view the request for the transcription was a mere gap-filler in the conversation; I didn't think he was really planning to read the voluminous transcript – but then again, perhaps he was. My chambers arranged for the recording of the deliberations to be transcribed and delivered to Mahlamba Ndlopfu.

The president appointed the new chief justice almost immediately, many days before he received the transcript.

We were the only two people in the room that day. It was not my place to ask him why on three occasions when he had the opportunity to appoint me as chief justice, he did not. He could have done so when Pius Langa retired; or when Sandile Ngcobo had to retire and he chose him again and tried to extend his term of office; and when that failed and Ngcobo finally left, he appointed someone else. So not once, not twice but thrice he could have appointed me chief justice but would not. The result was that I served as deputy chief justice under three different chief justices.

As you may have inferred from my statement before the JSC, my secondary role became an unintended blessing and opportunity. I happily led the Constitutional Court from behind. I thankfully escaped the administrative drudgery. I did not have to talk with politicians or consider their expectations or submit to media interviews. I ignored the pomp and ceremony of office and focused on the efficacy of judicial outcomes.

I worked hard on cases, ploughed through useful and not so useful appeal records and written arguments. I read the prime precedents and authorities that counsel relied on in their written argument. I followed commentary on our cases in academic journals. I went to court prepared and ready and looked forward to live hearings in our magnificent courthouse. Thoughtful and skilled oral presentation of argument in court thrilled me no end. I often engaged counsel and tested the cogency of their submissions. I hardly remember missing a hearing. I revelled in that endless search for judicial truth; for a just outcome aptly predicated on the law. I was propelled to look for the sweet spot, for the happy intersection between fidelity to the law and doing justice. The law should never be an ass. Ideally, law and fairness should never part ways. The two should never diverge.

I often told my judicial colleagues that a particular case got my 'judicial juices running', indicating the excitement I always felt at a complex dispute that called for a full and just answer. I carried that enthusiasm into the post-hearing conference that I held with my law clerks and researchers immediately after every court hearing. Hot from the oven, each young, bright mind had to tell me what the outcome in the case should be and why, in a few sentences.

On 8 September 2011, President Zuma appointed Justice Mogoeng as the new chief justice. Earlier on that day I was home in Tshwane for a well-earned private rest when Ms Lakela Kaunda, a presidential aide, called. 'Justice Moseneke, the president has asked to see you at the Sefako Makgatho Guest House today.' She specified the time but not the purpose of this meeting at the official guest house. I did not consider myself free to decline the invitation. On arrival I was led into a holding room. In it, to my surprise, were seated Sandile Ngcobo and Mogoeng Mogoeng, the past and the new chief justice.

It was an uncharted and, indeed, uneasy gathering. Life would have been a little more tolerable if the three of us were not corralled by presidential command in this way. We did not have a chance to exchange anything other than nervous grins before Jacob Zuma entered the room. He gave each of us a bear hug as if we were long-lost chums of his. The hugs went with his signature burst of laughter that, supposedly, was intended to dissipate unease. He cleared his throat and said, 'Thank you for coming! We will shortly be led to a press conference to announce the appointment of the new chief justice.'

The holding room went silent again. Sandile betrayed a light smile on the edge of his lips and broke the tension. 'E-e-eh, Mogoeng!' he said with a deep isiZulu accent. 'You know, Mogoeng, it will not be enough to slaughter a cow in celebration. You will have to slaughter an elephant for this windfall.' Jacob Zuma broke into uncontrollable laughter and so did Ngcobo. I can't remember what Mogoeng did in response. I probably grinned with embarrassment.

I sat through the press conference and its multiple and clicking lenses, smiling through the extensive photo sessions. Then I rushed home to the refuge of our residence in Tshwane.

CHAPTER 23

Harmony and turbulence

It would be less than candid to leave the impression that when Chief Justice Mogoeng assumed office on 8 September 2011 it was a matter of jubilation on my part and all round. Some in the judiciary and the broader public supported his appointment and others did not. It mattered little then as I had publicly disavowed any hope or likelihood or desire to assume the post. President Jacob Zuma had made the appointment and, whatever one's persuasion on the matter might have been, it was a legal fact. What remained was how best to manage the situation in the best interests of the Constitutional Court and the nation.

It would have been a matter of some personal satisfaction to have been appointed. Serving as a leader of the judiciary would have added a terrific climax to a fairy-tale career. As you would have followed, the events afforded me ample time to process the disappointment.

Another soothing consideration was that I had tasted the leadership of the Constitutional Court often. Pius Langa was not blessed with the best of health. He was often away sick and I led in his absence. Also, even when Pius Langa was present at the court, we worked together well and co-led with no friction. Even up to the point of Mogoeng Mogoeng's appointment, I was the *de facto* and, by operation of the law, acting chief justice. After his extended interview before the JSC and before he was formally appointed, Mogoeng rightly sought from me leave of absence from court sittings to travel to his home in Mafikeng for some personal matter. The next time we met was at the press conference hosted by the president at Sefako Makgatho Guest House to announce his rise to the leadership of the Constitutional Court.

I have already stated a few times that we all read too much into positions. We are too readily seduced by titles. We infer more power and influence than a position actually affords one. For one thing, all judicial decisions at the Constitutional Court are taken by all justices together in the judges' conference room where each justice has one equal vote. This deliberate constitutional design defines the court as all eleven of us led by a chief justice and a deputy chief justice.[1] It clothes each of the eleven justices with a vote of equal force. Decisions are made by the court sitting or deciding together as a college or *en banc* over every dispute.

So decisions on disputes between litigants or parties or, shall we say, judicial decisions must be arrived at by a majority of votes. Neither the chief justice nor the deputy chief justice may direct a fellow justice to vote in a particular manner on a judicial decision. That would be a gross transgression of the law and the ethical code of judges.[2] Legitimate judicial difference among or between colleagues is perfectly acceptable, and that is why a judge must publicly say whether she agrees with the reasoning and outcome of a judgment or not. If they do not, the judge concerned must write out the nature and extent of the dissent.

Our structure of authority in each court is a flat one and not hierarchical or ranked. The more senior or experienced judicial officer may not order a junior or another judicial officer how to decide a dispute. This is a vital feature of the personal and institutional independence of the judges. It is also a vital protection to members of the public and litigants alike who are entitled to a fair hearing before a competent, fair and independent tribunal or court. All are entitled to the assurance that each of the eleven justices in our apex court will bring his or her mind to bear on the dispute without bias and free from any command structure. This explains why in some cases the chief justice or his deputy may be outvoted as the minority in a decision. That is all well, perfectly acceptable and lawful. In fact, it may be a welcome indication that judges of a court make up their minds without fear or favour of their judicial seniors nor at their favour.

Outside the judicial function at their court, the chief justice carries enormous and important duties. He (or she) is the overall leader and representative of the judiciary as a whole. He is the head of the administration of the court and of all other courts in the country. He heads the office of the chief justice (which is a state department), which administers the affairs of the judiciary.[3] He sets norms, standards of performance and a code of ethics for the judiciary. He convenes and chairs the Judicial Service Commission, which recommends the appointment of judges and regulates the misconduct or indiscipline of judges. He liaises with the other arms of the state and participates in multiple ceremonial roles such as convening and presiding over parliament after national elections, and the swearing-in of the president of the country and members of the national executive. Convention requires the chief justice to attend joint sittings of parliament on special occasions and presidential banquets and other functions hosted for visiting heads of state by the president. The chief justice also represents the country's judiciary in the region, the continent and the world in bodies on courts, law and justice.

A good few other laws of parliament entrust the chief justice with small but important roles which are nearly invisible to the broader public. One example that comes to mind is the annual process for setting the remuneration and other benefits of judicial officers.[4]

As if all these chores and burdens were not enough, the chief justice is expected to be the intellectual and jurisprudential leader of the Constitutional Court, the judiciary and the country. So there is no doubt that being a chief justice is a full and prestigious job, particularly in a constitutional democracy where the courts sit at the centre of the democratic enterprise. It can also be a thankless job during times of political divisions within party and state.

*

Over fifteen years of the Constitutional Court's life a convention had developed that important non-judicial decisions, such as the administration of the court, were made by the chief justice in consultation with the deputy. This was a practice of common sense to ensure joint leadership, sharing of roles and smooth administration. In any event the law requires the deputy to act in the place of the chief justice during any temporary absence. This smooth running would be possible only if they ordinarily acted together.

Evidently, Mogoeng and I were like Siamese twins of sorts except that no surgical separation was possible. I was to remain his deputy for another five years and he would lead the Constitutional Court for at least ten years. During my term of office I would perforce be his alternate in each of his constitutional and statutory duties. Ordinarily the deputy chief justice or other justices met the chief justice in his or her chambers. This convention was premised on respect for the office and in part on seniority.

Mogoeng moved into the chambers that Ngcobo had occupied on my floor and so, barring a chamber between mine and his, he and I became neighbours. It was certain that we had to meet soon and often thereafter. Mogoeng called and asked to meet and offered to come across to my chambers. I would have met him in his chambers to honour the convention and respect the office he occupied, but he insisted that he would come over. Lesley Grobler, my unfailing executive secretary, whipped up a quick tea and biscuits. Mogoeng and I share a mother tongue. I congratulated him in our Setswana language for his new role and wished him well. However, every time we had to meet to do court business he tended to come across and meet in my chambers.

At the beginning, we kept a respectful but business-like distance. I was not unaware that his were initial but small steps to repair the rupture that might have developed between us during his appointment process. At first I was cautious but amenable to embracing the healing process. He also had to win over the trust of several of his colleagues who were already at the Constitutional Court when he was first appointed as a judge there in 2009. He now had to relate to them as their leader and not their junior. These judges included Zak Yacoob, Thembile Skweyiya, Bess Nkabinde, Johann van der Westhuizen and Edwin Cameron.

Lunches in the judges' common room made for one generally convivial space where conversations were informal and neutral anecdotes were shared, but one such lunch got us near a perilous cliff of one of the unspoken 'no-go' subjects.

The unsaid but well-observed rule of social interaction among judges is not to have conversations about religion, politics and sex. A review of weekend sport serves as an innocent filler. One could merrily praise the weekend performance of Sundowns or the Blue Bulls, as I habitually did as an ardent supporter of both. Happily, my sports clubs won more than they lost. This often drew spirited counters from the Orlando Pirates and Kaizer Chiefs types, even from a Sharks supporter or an AmaZulu Football Club hanger-on. Some judges took sides openly when they narrated provincial cricket runs and wickets.

Showing that kind of sports partiality was rife and fun. It was not viewed as detracting from the dispassionate demeanour of a judge. It was an acceptable escape from the rigour of judging others and saying why you do so.

If we hadn't been watching sport over a weekend but had enjoyed ourselves in social engagements of one sort or another, these might be lightly alluded to; but judges would not boast about intimate exploits or preferences in the common room. Besides it being bad manners, intimacy is a private matter. It is a topic that may enrage passion and divulge partiality in contested issues like gender justice, patriarchy, sexual orientation and reproductive rights.

Politics and religion are the two rather obvious suspect categories that are off the lunch-room table. In our law a judge may not be a member of a political party but as individual citizens they have the right to vote in national, provincial and local government elections. When it comes to religion, a judicial officer may worship, or not, in any manner they choose; they may join any religious tendency. A judge is a bearer of religious, cultural and political rights like any other citizen but they may not allow their politics, culture or religion to intrude into the judicial function. Sternly and consciously, judges must keep out these irrelevant intrusions in judicial decision-making. In saying this, I am not about to ignore the debate sparked by some legal thinkers that every judge brings their 'inarticulate premise' to the job. A judge, willingly or not, brings along with them an array of personal beliefs that must influence their judging job. No judge is fully insulated from personal values. Even so, the one thing each judicial officer must do is to display utmost fidelity to the law at all times to the exclusion of personal fancy.

At this particular 'cliff-edge' lunch, which took place shortly after Mogoeng Mogoeng had been appointed chief justice, it was religion that slipped inadvertently into the conversation. Often, if not always, Mogoeng concluded his emails to colleagues on the court with the words 'God bless you' and today Zak Yacoob had something he wanted to say. He cleared his throat, lifted his head and face higher than usual, cleared his throat again and said politely: 'Mogoeng, please don't finish off your emails to me with the words "God bless you". You see, I do not think you have the authority to order God to bless me, nor do I need the prayer that God bless me. Look at me, I am an atheist and totally reprobate and yet I am just fine. I don't pray but I am doing just fine. Look how far I have come.' He cleared his throat again. 'But what is more, Mogoeng, God does not exist.'

A hush fell over the common room and Mogoeng's face went ashen. We all saw it. Yacoob may not have seen what we saw because he is blind. I am, however, cautious to say what Zak can or cannot see. In the many years of working close to Yacoob on the court, he has described to me accurately details of occurrences or the good looks of ladies I would have expected him not to have seen.

But Yacoob was not done. With the lunch table completely silent, Zak ponderously told the painful tale of his losing his eyesight when he was a boy. His father was an Islamic priest. He prayed devoutly and often for the restoration of his son's eyesight. His mother, too, prayed fervently. Zak prayed for himself too. Other priests, believers and people concerned prayed earnestly and many times for the restoration of his eyesight. Despite the multiple and devout prayers of many, his eyesight was never restored.

'You see, Mogoeng,' Yacoob explained, 'if there was a God, he would have heard these devout prayers.' Then, in a little climb-down from absolute atheism, he conceded: 'Maybe I have done so well and have come up to this court without a God because my dad continued praying for me.'

The debate about the existence of God was never raised again, but after that Mogoeng no longer asked God to bless us on email.

Mogoeng and I had frequent long and short discussions about issues that related to our judicial responsibilities. At a practical level of sharing the leadership burden a quiet and natural consensus between us emerged that he would be left alone to lead and be the face of the judiciary as a whole. This meant that he would run and expand the office of the chief justice; interact with the president and the minister of justice and his department; lead the body of the heads of courts; lead the Judicial Service Commission; manage the entire judiciary and all the external relations, including the media; and represent the judiciary at a variety of bodies.

I would focus on and give support to the actual judicial function at the court. I had developed considerable passion for ensuring that the court considered and decided the high volume of applications for leave to appeal; to sit in court hearings and procure a prompt output of judgments. For that reason I tended to sit in virtually every hearing and presided in a high number of the hearings. I also tended to preside over many judges' conferences when Chief Justice Mogoeng was temporarily absent. In each case Mogoeng alerted me early about a duty that would take him away from the court.

The reason for being taken away from the court was that the role of the chief justice had been expanded by the Constitution[5] and a new law.[6] The chief justice was now the head not of the Constitutional Court only but of the judiciary as a whole. He had to attend to the hygiene of the nation's judicial function. The expanded role was primarily external to the Constitutional Court and included all judicial officers at all courts, besides external roles like representing the judiciary everywhere else.

This meant that alongside my other colleagues on the court, I wrote several main judgments and so, too, concurring or dissenting judgments. I had the space, the energy and excitement to make a contribution to the existing jurisprudence.

As our work dealings continued, Mogoeng and I cultivated considerable professional closeness. We found each other, so to speak. We were in complete agreement about our duty to perform our judicial roles to the best of our abilities and without fear or favour. We reached mutual trust over our fortitude or courage to protect the judiciary in a climate of increasing criticism that it was acting beyond its lawful bounds and was (or so it was claimed) politically partisan.

It was not long before 'MM', as I had come to call him fondly, mooted the idea of his going on long leave. He wondered whether I would agree to a formal appointment as acting chief justice. At first I thought this was unnecessary. I would in any event act as head of the Constitutional Court in his temporary absence. This happened by operation of the law. His stance was more forthright and emphatic, however. MM reasoned that none of his predecessors ever sought to have me formally appointed acting chief justice in their absence. For some obscure reason, they had all avoided doing so. He wanted Jeff Radebe and Jacob Zuma to agree to a formal appointment under the hand of the presidency. 'DM,' as he had come to call me affectionately, 'I ask that you agree to be appointed acting chief justice by the president.' I remember well saying, 'MM, you may go ahead with the appointment you suggest provided neither Minister Radebe nor President Zuma is told that I am asking for it – because I am not. I am happy to serve and act in your absence without formal certification.'

Within a few days MM came back to me in my chambers armed with a document signed by Jacob Zuma. I quietly wondered which of his teeth MM had had to extract to get this done, but the upshot was that I was to bear the title of acting chief justice until MM returned from long leave.[7]

MM's fervent gesture did not go unnoticed by me. He was adding to the confidence-building measures we had mutually undertaken to solidify our camaraderie after a somewhat difficult patch in the past. He was saying privately and publicly that, as we say in our language, 'Re Mmogo' – we are now all in it together. He displayed maturity and foresight in strengthening our relationship and in this he was spot on. We had to find leadership harmony in favour of a vital institution in our democratic journey. It would not be long before together we hit considerable turbulence as politicians attacked the chief justice, me and the judiciary as a whole on many unfounded grounds.[8]

The early attack on the Constitutional Court or the judiciary took the form of an allegedly leaked intelligence report which contained allegations that Justice Johann van der Westhuizen, Justice Johan Froneman and I were US Central Intelligence Agency (CIA) spies who were paid huge US dollar sums in secret offshore accounts abroad.

Oh, there we go again. If you don't like someone or what they do, they're a spy. That easy, lazy, dirty and slimy, tired old card which scoundrels of our long, proud and glorious fight for equality and freedom continue to play.

The three accused quickly sought audience with the chief justice. If it were not so defiling an allegation, it would have been a laughing matter. We told Mogoeng we wanted Jacob Zuma as president to confirm that the so-called leaked report was a true intelligence report and, if it was, we sought proof of the allegations. 'If indeed there is proof,' I remember saying to MM, 'I will resign or accept a dishonourable discharge.' Johann van der Westhuizen took a different and more interesting tack. He asked Mogoeng to help him get the bank account number where 'his' US dollars were kept.

The outcome of the meeting with Mogoeng was the letter of 20 August 2013 to President Zuma reproduced below. We never received any formal letter from the presidency. The chief justice informed us that the presidency had directed that the inspector general of intelligence[9] should investigate the matter and report on it to us and to the chief justice. A couple of weeks later, Adv Faith Radebe, the inspector general of intelligence, and a few spooks set up a meeting at the court premises to interview us. A few more weeks went by and then Adv Jay Govender, the legal adviser to the inspector general, brought me a report on the outcome of their probe (see the photograph section for these findings in full). The report from the outset stated that I was never ever a spy as alleged or at all. Adv Radebe confirmed that the

The Constitutional Court of South Africa

CHAMBERS OF
JUSTICE D MOSENEKE
DEPUTY CHIEF JUSTICE OF SOUTH AFRICA

Constitution Hill
Private Bag X1
BRAAMFONTEIN
2017
TEL: (011) 359 7442
FAX: (011) 403 8883
E-Mail:moseneke@concourt.org.za

20 August 2013

Dear Mr President,

Over the weekend a so-called "intelligence report" was circulated in the press in which it was stated that three Justices of the Constitutional Court (Deputy Chief Justice Moseneke, Justice van der Westhuizen and Justice Johan Froneman) were on the payroll of a United States agency with payments being made into a secret bank account in the Cayman Islands. There is no truth in all the allegations against us. But they are very serious allegations and if true would disqualify any judge from holding office.

We have accordingly requested the Chief Justice to seek the assurance from you that no state agency is involved in any way in relation to the allegations in the report. If any state agency is involved we would expect you to take urgent steps to ensure that the integrity of the judiciary, at the highest level, is ensured.

Thank you,

Sincerely

Dikgang Moseneke

Johann van der Westhuizen

Johan Froneman

allegations against or about me had not emanated from national intelligence and were false. I was an upright, high-ranking and long-service judge and citizen who had performed his judicial role with diligence and patriotism and was unassociated with any foreign power or organisation. It seems as though subversive forces were spreading misinformation for reasons unknown.[10]

After the report, Van der Westhuizen popped into my chambers, quite peeved that we were not going to get any banking details of the US dollar account in the Cayman Islands.

CHAPTER 24

Challenging the courts

Throughout the Mogoeng Court, from 2011 to my retirement in 2016, Jacob Zuma was riding the crest of political power. He had scored a big political victory at the Polokwane elective conference when he became leader of the ruling party. As a sequel, in 2009 he became the president of the country. In 2012 in Mangaung he was re-elected president of the ruling party and in 2014 he again became president of the Republic. He appointed as his deputy Matamela Cyril Ramaphosa, who is now president of the country.

As the Mogoeng Court took root, a collage of events surfaced, most of which – perhaps even all – had a bearing on the judicial function and on later court decisions. The events conspired to lure the judiciary into mediating disputes prompted by the exercise of political or executive power. The head of state and of the national executive made decisions or was drawn into political contests which over time mutated into long fights in our courts. The courts had a duty to decide any and every dispute that was capable of resolution by application of the law. While courts sat passively, once parties to a dispute had couched their conflict in legal terms, the judiciary was obliged to respect their right of access to the courts conferred on 'everyone' by our Bill of Rights.[1]

Those who wielded public power, aggrieved citizens, political parties and civil society formations alike spared no moment to engage the courts. The courts during the Mogoeng era had and still have to mediate a remarkably

intelligence

Office of the Inspector-General of Intelligence
REPUBLIC OF SOUTH AFRICA

PO Box 1175, MENLYN PARK, 0077 Bogare, Cnr Atterbury & Lois Street, MENLYN
Tel: (012) 367 0845/47/61, Fax: (012) 367 0920

OIGI/IG10(IG50)1/5/2
DIR D07* 10000000000006789*

3 December 2014

Deputy Chief Justice Dikgang Moseneke
Constitutional Court of South Africa
1 Hospital Street
Constitution Hill
BRAAMFONTEIN
2017

Dear Deputy Chief Justice

Feedback on the Inspector-General of Intelligence (IG) investigation on the source and origins of the "source reports" document

Reference is hereby made to the above matter and to the meeting held on the 2nd December 2014.

The aforesaid meeting was held at the request of the President of the Republic of South Africa, the honourable Mr Zuma to enable the IG to discuss the concerns of the affected Constitutional Court Justices with regard to the so-called "source reports" document and for us to provide feedback on findings derived pursuant to an investigation conducted on the said matter.

The concerns of the Constitutional Court Justices stems from the fact that the aforesaid document made reference to the South African Constitutional Court and other courts as being used to subvert the South African constitutional democracy. The document further makes reference to your name and those of two other Justices of the Constitutional Court as rendering services in support of an organisation whose objectives is to threaten the democracy of the State and in respect of which funds were arranged for payment abroad to the named Justices.

Our investigation stemmed from a complaint lodged by Mr Z Vavi, the General Secretary of COSATU. The crux of Mr Vavi's complaint was that it was his belief that the "source reports" document emanates from the State Intelligence Services and that the document makes reference to him as one of the key perpetrators of a plan to overthrow the current democratic government of the Republic of South Africa (RSA), which allegations he strenuously deny as alleged or at all.

Ihhovisi Lomhloli Jikelele Wezobunhloli • Kantoro ya Motlhankedimogolo wa tsa Matlhale • Hofisi ya Mulavisisi-Jenerali wa Vunhlorhi • Kantoor van die Inspekteur-generaal van Inteligensiedienste • I ofisi yomHloli omKhulu wezoBuhlakani • Ofisi ya Mohlahlobi Kakaretso wa Bohlwela • Ofisi ya Mutoli-Dzheneralawa Vhusevhi • Ofisi ya Mohlahlobi-pharephare ya Bohlodi • I-Ofisi yoMhloli-Jikelele wobuNtlola • Lihhovisi leMhloli-Jikelele weTebunhloli

---

The findings of the inspector general of national intelligence, Adv Faith Radebe.
© MOSENEKE PRIVATE COLLECTION

Feedback on the Inspector-General of Intelligence (IG) Investigation on source and origins of the "source reports" document

As part of the investigation the "source reports" document was subjected to an analysis by a qualified intelligence analyst and a counter-intelligence assessment.

Our investigation found that the document has been fabricated by an organised information peddling network. This formation looks for areas of conflict within the social, political and economic environments and fabricates information on persons of certain standing and repute in society with a view to tarnish their image and cast aspersions on them and their character.

The investigation also found that the said document first found its way in COSATU with the current President of COSATU, Mr Sdumo Dlamini being the first recipient thereof. During interview with Mr Sdumo Dlamini indicated that he found the document having been slid underneath the door of his office by persons unknown to him at the COSATU Head office. Upon reading the document, he took it to his home where he hid it without first discussing with his colleagues or any other person. Mr Dlamini later discussed the document with few of his colleagues carefully selected by him on different occasions during secret meetings called by him. A copy was made from the document under his possession without his knowledge, which copy was given to Mr Vavi who then made further copies for distribution at a meeting of COSATU delegates. Mr Vavi also called a media press conference whereat he distributed copies of the document.

Mr Dlamini also indicated that he later destroyed the copy that was in his possession. It is worth noting that Mr Dlamini believed that the contents of the "source reports" are true. It is clear from the evidence that Mr Dlamini was either a witting or unwitting client of the information peddlers. It is noted further that COSATU has in recent times being used as the recipient and conveyor-belt of peddled information documents as previously the so-called "Browse Mole report" document also found its way to COSATU before it found its way to the public. Whilst there is no other evidence to corroborate or contradict Mr Dlamini's version, it is our respectful submission that his version of events appears to lack plausibility.

It is found that the contents the document referred to as "source reports" are fabricated in all material respects in so far as it relates to you and other mentioned Justices. Furthermore, we have found that at no stage did you conduct yourself as an enemy of our Constitutional Democracy.

We are attending to advise the President of the outcome of our aforesaid meeting and our communication in relation to the findings of our investigation.

We thank you.

Kind regards

Ambassador (Adv) FD Radebe
INSPECTOR-GENERAL OF INTELLIGENCE

The formal portrait of the Ngcobo Court, 2009. © MOSENEKE PRIVATE COLLECTION

Lighter moments at the Constitutional Court. © MOSENEKE PRIVATE COLLECTION

Chief Justice Arthur Chaskalson's funeral service at Westpark Cemetery, 2012.
© GALLO IMAGES/FOTO24/CORNEL VAN HEERDEN

A courtesy visit to the Supreme Court of the United States as guest of Justice Ruth Bader Ginsburg, the veteran, steadfast and progressive jurist who had earlier found it beneficial to visit our Constitutional Court, 2014. © MOSENEKE PRIVATE COLLECTION

Law clerks and researchers for every year of my full term of office were an invaluable part of the work of the Constitutional Court. © MOSENEKE PRIVATE COLLECTION

In addition to law clerks and researchers, a competent, dependable, loyal and long-serving professional assistant such as Ms Lesley Grobler (third from the left at the back), was indispensable.
© MOSENEKE PRIVATE COLLECTION

Honorary doctorate conferred by the University of Cape Town, together with Ahmed Kathrada and Thuli Madonsela, 2015.
© GALLO IMAGES/BEELD/DEON RAATH

Awarded an honorary doctorate at the end of two terms (of six years each) as chancellor at the University of the Witwatersrand, Johannesburg, 2018.
© MOSENEKE PRIVATE COLLECTION

President Rampahosa confers the Order of Luthuli in Gold in 2018 in a ceremony of National Awards.
© MOSENEKE PRIVATE COLLECTION

Serving as the arbitrator in a dispute between the Gauteng provincial government and families of the victims affected by the death and torture of mental health-care users of Life Esidimeni, 2018. © MOSENEKE PRIVATE COLLECTION

Guest of the chief justice and justices of the Supreme Court of Canada, January 2019.
© MOSENEKE PRIVATE COLLECTION

With the pilots who flew the president, first lady and myself to Mazimbu, Morogoro, 15 August 2019. © MOSENEKE PRIVATE COLLECTION

Recent home visit to Adv George Bizos SC, a salted and highly respected veteran of our profession, a human rights fighter and fellow executor in the deceased estate of the late former President Nelson Rolihlahla Mandela, 2019. © MOSENEKE PRIVATE COLLECTION

high flood and churn of disputes ignited by the exercise of presidential or public executive power or political disagreements. Misgovernance and the lack of financial probity increased the flow. The courts became the place to go to. It was as if there were no other sites where disputes, political or otherwise, could be mediated. This meant that the judiciary attracted undeserved and sometimes unwelcome attention. The case-load swelled as political power contests threatened to burst the judicial dam wall. Litigants who won praised us; those who lost found many unkind words to heap upon us. Even so, rarely did the women and men on the bench blink.

Below I give you no more than a peek into the prominent examples of what I have been talking about, starting from the beginning of the Mogoeng era.

President Zuma appointed Mr Richard Mdluli on 1 July 2009 as the head of crime intelligence in the South African Police Service (SAPS). It is important to note that the person appointed to this leadership position must be someone with the highest degree of integrity. This is because the position allows the head to exercise control over all surveillance that is carried out by the SAPS in any investigation, to have access to highly sensitive and confidential information, and to access funds from the Secret Service Account.

On 31 March 2011, Mr Mdluli was arrested and charged with eighteen counts, including murder, intimidation, attempted murder, kidnapping, assault and intent to do grievous bodily harm.[2] In September 2011, while suspended as crime intelligence head, Mdluli handed himself over to authorities and appeared in the Commercial Crimes Court in Pretoria on separate charges of fraud, corruption, theft and money laundering.[3] In its wisdom, or the lack of it, the National Prosecuting Authority withdrew all the charges against Mdluli. The commissioner of police also reinstated him as crime intelligence boss. Two years later, during September 2013, the high court overturned the decision taken by the NPA to withdraw charges against him.[4] The matter was taken up to the Supreme Court of Appeal, which partly confirmed and upheld the decision of the high court.[5] We know now, in July 2019, nearly eight years later, that Richard Mdluli has been convicted by the high court on multiple offences.[6]

In 2010 an activist citizen, Mr Terry Crawford-Browne, approached the Constitutional Court seeking an order compelling the president to appoint a commission of inquiry into the strategic defence procurement package, known more simply as the armaments acquisition process or the arms deal. The state had bought military equipment and arms with massive amounts of public money. In their court papers, Mr Crawford-Browne and others made incessant allegations that the acquisition was riddled with dishonesty, theft and corruption. Before the matter was heard before the court, on 15 September 2011 the president announced that he would appoint – and during October 2011 *did* appoint – a commission of inquiry into the arms deal. It was chaired by Judge Legoabe Willie Seriti.[7]

It took five years before the report of the commission saw the light of day; it was made public during April 2016. The Seriti Commission investigating the arms deal found no wrongdoing. Parties dissatisfied with the findings of the report have taken them on review, asking the courts to set the findings aside as a whitewash and invalid in law.[8]

Again during October 2011, on another front also related to the security forces, the president announced the suspension of the national police commissioner, General Bheki Cele, pending the outcome of an investigation into allegedly unlawful lease agreements. Later the president fired General Cele from his position as commissioner of police for alleged offences of fraud and corruption in the handling of leases for police headquarters, which were concluded at far above market rates. In April 2019, the Tshwane High Court declared Zuma's decision to dismiss Cele as invalid and set it aside. An uncomfortable irony was that just about the same time Police Commissioner Cele was dismissed, Jackie Selebi, the former police commissioner who had been convicted of corruption and sentenced to fifteen years' imprisonment,[9] was released from prison on medical parole. His conviction, too, went on appeal from the high court through to the Supreme Court of Appeal[10] and ended up in our court – where the appeal also failed.

To complete the picture, again during October 2011 the president dismissed two cabinet ministers, Mr Sicelo Shiceka and Ms Gwen Mahlangu-Nkabinde, who were accused of corruption.

The following year, 2012, was perhaps even more eventful. The national disciplinary committee of the ruling party, the ANC, suspended its Youth League leader, Julius Malema, banning him from all party activities for five years.[11] Within six months of the suspension the former ANCYL leader was charged with money laundering over a government tender awarded to a company partly owned (so it was alleged) by his family trust. Within a month of the charges, Julius Malema launched his own political party – the Economic Freedom Fighters (EFF) – in Marikana.[12] The significance of the choice of the venue at Marikana will emerge right away.

The day of 16 August 2012 was the fateful afternoon of the Marikana massacre. The police opened fire on striking mineworkers gathering on a koppie near the platinum mine at Marikana, killing at least 34 working people and leaving at least 78 seriously injured and arresting more than 200 others.[13] The shock, fear and disgust ran right across our nation and abroad even before we knew the facts. These police killings were too close to our historical bone. We had been there before. The massacre of a protesting populace was the currency that oppressors traded in.

How could we wake up to a police massacre now – under our government? In *My Own Liberator* I recalled how the newspaper front pages of bloodied dead bodies lying on the ground after the Sharpeville massacre of 21 March 1960 affected me profoundly. That devastation had occurred because of a peaceful campaign of protest against the pass laws, led by the Pan Africanist Congress. Now, again, I was confronted by similar front-page footage – how was this possible? I did not yet know what had happened that afternoon, but it hurt. It hurt very deeply.

President Zuma, correctly, observed that we needed to know the true facts and, on 23 August 2012, he established the Marikana Commission of Inquiry to investigate the circumstances surrounding the massacre.

The duty fell on one of my esteemed colleagues and retired judge of the Supreme Court of Appeal, Ian Farlam, to chair the commission, hence its title – the Farlam Commission.[14] Again the proceedings of the commission were a long, hard crunch but up to this day, as I gather, the claims for damages and support of the dependants of the killed miners are in different stages of settlement for compensation by the state.[15] Just short of three years later, the president released the Marikana Commission report.[16]

Following a recommendation from the commission's report, the president established an inquiry into Police Commissioner Riah Phiyega's fitness to hold office.[17] She was placed on suspension until the inquiry was completed and seemingly until the end of her term of office, in June 2017, on full pay. This despite the board of inquiry recommending that she be dismissed as unfit for the position of national commissioner of police – a decision that she took on review.[18]

President Zuma appointed Adv Menzi Simelane as national director of public prosecutions. Following on the Ginwala Inquiry,[19] the lawfulness of the president's appointment was challenged in court. On Friday, 5 October 2012, the Constitutional Court ruled that the appointment was invalid.[20] In reading the unanimous judgment, Justice Zak Yacoob said that the appointment of the national director of public prosecutions was not a matter to be determined by the subjective opinion of the president. It was rather a jurisdictional prerequisite to be determined objectively, he said. Yacoob J added that 'dishonesty is inconsistent with the hallmarks of conscientiousness and integrity that are essential prerequisites to the proper execution of the responsibilities of a national director'.[21]

The president appointed a new national director of public prosecutions, Mr Mxolisi Nxasana, whose appointment was effective from 1 October 2013. Just under a year later, the president informed Mr Nxasana of his intention to establish an inquiry into his fitness to hold office.[22] Some ten months later, in May 2015, the inquiry into Mxolisi Nxasana's fitness to hold office, which never commenced with hearings, was interrupted with the presidency announcing that Mr Nxasana and the president had reached a settlement for Mr Nxasana to vacate his office against payment of an agreed severance package amounting to over R17 million. On 18 June 2015, President

Zuma appointed Shaun Abrahams as the new national director of public prosecutions.

Unsurprisingly, the settlement agreement with Mr Nxasana and the appointment of the incoming national director, Mr Abrahams, were attacked in court as unlawful. The challenge wound its way through the courts until the Constitutional Court.[23] The Constitutional Court upheld the attack and ordered Nxasana to repay the large amount of cash he received from the president to vacate his office. The court also refused to allow him to return to his former position because that would only prolong the instability at the NPA. The court found that Adv Shaun Abrahams's appointment was also invalid and set it aside.

Justice Mbuyiseli Madlanga explained that

> for a few years there has been instability in the office of the [national director of public prosecutions] and, therefore, in the leadership of the [National Prosecuting Authority]. With the court challenge of Mr Nxasana's vacation of office and with the appointment of Advocate Abrahams, that instability persists to this day ... The sooner it is brought to an end the better.[24]

The court went on to state that 'former President Zuma was bent on getting rid of Mr Nxasana by whatever means he could muster',[25] and that he had abused his power when he removed Nxasana as head of the NPA.[26] It added:

> Advocate Abrahams benefited from this abuse of power. It matters not that he may have been unaware of the abuse of power; the rule of law dictates that the office of [national director of public prosecutions] be cleansed of all the ills that have plagued it for the past few years.[27]

The court ordered the new president, Cyril Ramaphosa, to appoint a new prosecutions boss within 90 days of the order.

*

I pause to doff my hat at the painful passing-on of the first president of the democratic Republic, Nelson Rolihlahla Mandela, on 5 December 2013. My voicemail was loaded with several messages summoning me to President Mandela's residence. They were initiated by Mama Graça Machel and the people she had asked to call me to Mr Mandela's home urgently. Unfortunately, I was caught up in a year-end judges' dinner with my phone switched off. It would have been a rare privilege to bid Tata farewell.

In any event, I knew I had been appointed as President Mandela's deceased estate co-executor with Adv George Bizos and Judge President Themba Sangoni. His will was in my custody. The immediate task was to ensure that Mr Mandela was buried in the manner he had devised in his will. To that end I asked for an urgent audience with President Zuma and we were agreed that the state funeral would abide by the wishes of President Mandela as set out in the will. He was buried in Qunu in the Eastern Cape on 15 December 2013.

*

During March 2014, the public protector, Thuli Madonsela, released a report which found that some of the R246 million taxpayer-funded refurbishments and security upgrades at President Jacob Zuma's Nkandla residence were unlawful. Over a year later, police minister Mr Nathi Nhleko prepared and made known a report on the president's Nkandla residence, the findings of which differed materially from the public protector's report.[28] The minister's alternative report was placed before parliament and adopted on 18 August 2015.

The dispute on the validity of the public protector's report and whether it was binding was brought before the highest court in the land. On 31 March 2016, the Constitutional Court held that the remedial action taken by the public protector in her Nkandla report was binding; that President Zuma's failure to comply with the remedial action was inconsistent with the

Constitution and invalid; and that the reasonable costs of the non-security upgrades made to his private residence must be paid by President Zuma personally.[29] On 1 April 2016, the president appeared on national television and apologised to the nation about Nkandla.

On 29 November 2013, the Constitutional Court held that a R10 billion contract which had been awarded through a government tender process to a private company known as Cash Paymaster Services (Pty) Ltd for the distribution of social grants countrywide was constitutionally invalid.[30] The declaration of invalidity was suspended pending the determination of an equitable remedy. The court later ordered the responsible government agency and the South African Social Security Agency (SASSA) to set up a new tender process.[31] The court also issued a structural interdict that required the SASSA to report regularly to the court on the steps taken to secure an alternative service provider. Several court proceedings had to be held to ensure that the dispensing of social grants was not interrupted.[32]

Before 2014 ended, the Supreme Court of Appeal heard an appeal from the full bench of the high court. The appeal before it was on whether the NPA should be ordered to release to certain claimants the taped conversations about corruption charges against President Zuma. These were known as the 'spy tapes' and their footage led to the NPA's decision to drop corruption charges against the president. The Supreme Court of Appeal ordered the NPA to release the full and unedited version of the spy tapes within five days of the order.[33]

At the start of every year the president delivers a state of the nation address, known as the SONA. In 2015 it was held on 12 February. For the first time ever, the joint sitting of parliament was disrupted by violence breaking out in the houses of parliament. Members of parliament belonging to Julius Malema's political party, the Economic Freedom Fighters, were forcibly removed from the house and in turn members of another political party, the Democratic Alliance (DA), walked out of the house in protest at the forced removal of EFF members by the members of the South African Police Service. The DA was of the opinion that the use of police in the removal was unconstitutional and breached the separation of powers doctrine.

Chief Justice Mogoeng and I and other heads of courts were in attendance as convention over many years demanded. We witnessed the preceding protest and disruption by some members of parliament and the forcible removal of members of the EFF by public police officers. Even after most opposition members had left the house, the leaders of the judiciary rightly stayed on and listened to the long speech of self-praise and promises that was subsequently delivered by the president – in a near-empty house. I was saddened by the events of the day. I could not put my finger on the source of my deep disquiet about the hygiene of our democratic project and national transformation.

Even that dispute which arose in parliament and reached a climax in our full sight and hearing ended up in the Constitutional Court. It came before the court not for the facts, but only for resolution of the constitutional contest. On 18 March 2016, the court ruled that the use of police to remove members of parliament, subject to some qualifications, was unconstitutional.[34]

Another dispute in the National Assembly concerned the validity of its rules. The Constitution allows any member of the National Assembly to introduce a bill in parliament. Parliamentary procedures developed by the assembly at the time dictated that a member who wished to introduce a bill first required the permission of the National Assembly before doing so. One member took issue with this as unconstitutional and invalid. The Constitutional Court was asked to determine whether the rules had the effect of preventing members from exercising their constitutional powers. In a majority judgment penned by the chief justice, the court held several rules to be unconstitutional for denying individual members and minority parties the power to initiate, prepare and introduce legislation.[35]

In November 2012, Ms Lindiwe Mazibuko, DA parliamentary leader, gave notice of a motion of no confidence in the president in terms of the Constitution. The relevant committees of the National Assembly were unable to reach consensus, which resulted in the motion not being tabled before the assembly. Dissatisfied with the perceived inaction, Ms Mazibuko instituted urgent proceedings to order the speaker to take the necessary steps that would ensure a debate and vote on the motion. One of the core issues the Constitutional Court had to decide was whether the rules of the National Assembly were inconsistent with the Constitution. The majority of the judges held them to be incompatible to the extent that they did not vindicate the rights of members of the assembly to formulate, discuss and vote on a motion of no confidence in the president within a reasonable time.[36]

The Constitutional Court was also asked to decide disputes that arose within the ruling party, the ANC. In November 2012, we heard an urgent application challenging the propriety of a provincial conference of the ANC in the Free State. The court held that the constitutions and rules of political parties must be consistent with our supreme Constitution. The majority of the judges found that the irregularities violated the party's constitution and guidelines, which in turn nullified the provincial conference.[37]

During June 2015 our country hosted an African Union summit to be attended by heads of states.[38] Sudanese President Omar al-Bashir was one of the attendees of the summit. At the time of his visit to our country, al-Bashir was the subject of International Criminal Court (ICC) warrants of arrest issued in respect of charges of war crimes, crimes against humanity and genocide. The high court was approached on an urgent basis and its full bench, led by Judge President Mlambo, ordered, on 15 June 2015, that the failure of the state to take steps to arrest or detain al-Bashir was inconsistent with the Constitution and compelled the state to take steps to prevent him from leaving South Africa until his application for arrest or surrender was completed in terms of the ICC warrants against him.[39] Despite the court order, al-Bashir left South Africa. The ICC afforded South Africa a period of time to explain why it had not arrested him.[40] The government approached the Supreme Court of Appeal to overturn the order of the high court, but on 15 March 2016 the Supreme Court of Appeal confirmed that South Africa should have arrested Sudanese President al-Bashir.[41]

In another of the many tramlines of litigation against the head of state, on 29 April 2016 the high court ruled that the decision of the NPA to withdraw 783 charges against President Zuma was irrational and set it aside.[42] The decision was unsuccessfully appealed in the Supreme Court of Appeal.[43] In fact, Mr Zuma has since been charged afresh and he is currently an accused person before the high court.[44]

On 6 October 2016 President Zuma appointed Adv Busisiwe Mkhwebane as the new public protector, replacing Adv Thuli Madonsela after her non-renewable term expired.

*

I trust that I have left you with an inkling of the avalanche the judiciary had to weather to see through a period of remarkable political misgovernance and contests in our land. As you will see shortly, the ruling elite was less than happy with the role of the judiciary and they lashed at it hard. And yet many men and women in our society continued to heap praise on judges and their courts and express their gratitude for the fine work they did.

CHAPTER 25

Jurisprudence amid executive hostilities

Just after Chief Justice Mogoeng had been appointed, the Constitutional Court enjoyed a little honeymoon period with the national government led by President Jacob Zuma and its political supporters. But that was only for a while. Right after the start of the Mogoeng Court, in September 2011, controversial cases of political import reached the Constitutional Court. I have spent time in the previous chapter describing some of the cases of that genre. The national government appeared unhappy about the calls that the Constitutional Court made case by case. The national government, or individuals close to it, hurled public scorn at the judiciary, decrying many of the judgments we made of which they did not approve. The disparaging comments ranged from the judges being unpatriotic to being counter-revolutionary or inspired by some or other foreign interests. Another favourite criticism was that the decisions of the courts unduly encroached on the terrain of the executive government.

The accusation against the judiciary occurred in a setting in which our democratic system appeared to have lost the capacity to mediate conflict at sites other than the courts of law. Ordinarily, sites like the national, provincial and local government should have served to mediate power or political differences. Increasingly, however, it seemed as if the courts were the only sites of dispute resolution for the political elite and its devotees.

This seemed to apply to any and all levels of the state. If members fell out with each other, they went straight to the courts. The same applied when it came to other democratic institutions, organs of state or state-owned enterprises. One of the reasons the political elite rushed to court so easily was that the state paid their legal bills; at that time they were never at personal financial risk when pursuing court cases, of having to pay for these out of their own pockets. Whether or not they lost their causes, there was no adverse financial outcome for the officials concerned.

Political party discipline should have sufficed to curb internal insurgency and yet it did not. Many warring party factions did not wait; they did not exhaust internal remedies first. Much to the anger of political party bosses, their followers tended to use the courts not as the last but rather the first resort.

Soon a public stand-off between the government and the judiciary surfaced at the highest level of state. It was between the judiciary, led by the chief justice, and the national government, led by the president of the country.

Even in that frosty setting, judges of the Constitutional Court continued to bear a very high case-load. 'Ordinary' people and other social and corporate entities continued to repose their trust in the court, and disputes were many and varied. In turn the court made many more decisions on 'ordinary' disputes well below the political radar of the ruling elite. Through the incessant power tussles and cases of a political character or public governance, which kept coming, the Constitutional Court remained remarkably resilient as a site of impartial dispute resolution.

Our adjudication work in the 'ordinary' cases is worth spending a little time on in this chapter, even if only in broad brushstrokes. In addition to the cases that were heard in an open court and decided, the court was inundated with applications or requests for leave to appeal. People wanted to hear the final word from the highest court in the land. The Constitutional Court was obliged to weigh their requests carefully before they were set down for hearing or dismissed to finality. This was adjudication work done by us in chambers and collectively decided in a judges' conference. It was an important part of the court's work. Being a court of final instance, our 'no' meant the end of the road for a litigant.

JURISPRUDENCE AMID EXECUTIVE HOSTILITIES

The Mogoeng Court mediated claims that sought to secure or advance the rights of the child in varied contexts.[1] We heard and decided many appeals on labour disputes derived from the Labour Appeal Court.[2] We set down and resolved multiple disputes on the governance or admission policies of public schools (the so-called Model C schools) which, under apartheid, had been reserved for children classified as white.[3] We heard a steady stream of appeals on competition law deriving mainly from the Competition Appeal Court.[4] There was no lack of disputes related to municipal governance. These included contests about town planning, building regulations, and municipal service delivery and municipal levies, rates and taxes.[5] We also adjudicated conflict within and between organs of state.[6] There were claims arising from landownership, occupation and use and other forms of land tenure, legislation relating to land, restoration of land rights, and unlawful occupation of land or buildings and evictions.[7] We had a steady flow of commercial disputes on tax, banking law and credit agreements, mortgage bonds and pensions.[8] We also entertained contests on traditional leadership and governance.[9] Expectedly, we resolved a good few claims on mineral and mining rights.[10] On an occasion we were called upon to adjudicate a dispute over the extradition of Zimbabwean citizens.[11] Some of our decisions were called on to adapt the common law in a manner that made it consistent with the norms of the Constitution.[12] The Constitutional Court also grappled with difficult questions of equality, race and quotas in the workplace in the context of remedial or restitutionary measures of the Constitution.[13]

We decided several matters that, in varying degrees, were *causes célèbres*, that is, much in the public eye and where court decisions on them inevitably evoked public interest and response.

One of these concerned a social movement known as the Opposition to Urban Tolling Alliance (OUTA) and a few others. They approached the high court seeking an order that the decision to establish road tolling in the Gauteng province was unlawful. As an interim measure, the high court issued an interdict prohibiting the South African National Roads Agency Limited (SANRAL) from levying and collecting tolls pending the main review. The dispute ended up on appeal in the Constitutional Court. In a unanimous judgment the court held that the legislative choice to toll roads at a fee payable by motorists may be an interesting political debate or even an unpopular choice, but the harm that would confront government, including the national treasury, and the South African National Roads Agency would be too great if the temporary order was granted.[14] The Constitutional Court's setting aside of the interim relief allowed tolling to continue, pending the main review of the decision to toll.[15]

I can't resist relating the story of an elderly gentleman who met me at a Sunday church service a few days after I had delivered the *E-tolls* judgment in the full glare of television cameras. He chuckled and said: 'Judge, I know where you live. I will be dropping all my e-toll statements at your home for payment by you.' If I had had any response, he did not wait to hear it, but shuffled away, chuckling again, only this time slightly harder.

In 2008, parliament adopted the Mineral and Petroleum Resources Development Act.[16] The relevant provisions of the Act were encapsulated by a judgment handed down by the Constitutional Court:

> On behalf of all the people of South Africa, the state is now the custodian of the mineral and petroleum resources of this country which is their common heritage. One of the objects of the [Act] is to give effect to this principle by granting various kinds of rights to successful applicants. Prospecting, mining, exploration or production rights granted in this manner are regarded as limited real rights. Detailed provision is made for the grant, content and duration of the rights. If these rights are not appropriately exercised, they may be suspended or cancelled. Whenever the common law is inconsistent with the [Act], the latter prevails.[17]

Writing for the majority of the court, Mogoeng CJ summarised the impact of the concerned legislation in this way:

> Its commencement had the effect of freezing the ability to sell, lease or

cede unused old order rights until they were converted into prospecting or mining rights with the written consent of the Minister for Minerals and Energy. It also had the deliberate and immediate effect of abolishing the entitlement to sterilise mineral rights, otherwise known as the entitlement not to sell or exploit minerals.[18]

Agri South Africa, an advocacy entity that represented the interests of commercial farmers, attacked the constitutional validity of the legislation on the ground that it amounted to expropriation of mineral rights without compensation.[19] The majority of the court thought not and held the legislation to pass constitutional muster.

Another matter that evoked considerable debate among the justices of the Constitutional Court and within the broader public was the appeal of Mr Dudley Lee. Justice Nkabinde, who wrote for the majority, captured the facts that underpinned the delictual claim for damages in this way:

> [Mr Lee] was incarcerated in the admission section at the maximum security prison at Pollsmoor from 1999 to 2004, but was released on bail for a period of approximately two months in 2000. He attended court on no fewer than 70 occasions. When inmates were transported for court attendance, they were stuffed into vans like sardines. At court they were placed into cells which were jam-packed. Those who appeared before the regional court were taken to a separate, smaller cell which was not overly full.
>
> ...
>
> [Mr Lee] was not infected with TB [tuberculosis] when he arrived at Pollsmoor; the responsible authorities were 'pertinently aware of the risk' of inmates contracting TB; TB is an airborne communicable disease which spreads easily especially in confined, poorly ventilated and overcrowded environments; Pollsmoor is notoriously congested and inmates are confined to close contact for as much as 23 hours every day – this providing ideal conditions for transmission; on occasion, the lock-up

total was as much as 3 052 inmates and single cells regularly housed three inmates; communal cells were filled with double and sometimes triple bunks; the responsible authorities relied on a system of inmates self-reporting their symptoms upon admission to the prison and during incarceration; and the control of TB at Pollsmoor depends upon effective screening of incoming inmates, the isolation of infectious patients and the proper administration of the necessary medication over the prescribed period of time.'[20]

The question before us was whether the breakdown of the health-care system at Pollsmoor prison and the inadequacy of nutrition which played a role in the development and uncontrollable spread of TB during Mr Lee's incarceration were an omission that constituted a negligent breach of the prison's constitutional and statutory duty to protect Mr Lee's rights while in their custody.

In its decision, the court was split midway. We sat as a bench of nine.[21] Five justices thought the prison and government were liable to Mr Lee for delictual damages because the negligent omission of the prison authorities was causally linked to Mr Lee's infection with TB. Four justices thought not. This meant that Mr Lee was successful on appeal. How would you have voted? You be the judge!

*

It is not often that judicial officers resort to courts over their remuneration. The convention in the judiciary was to soldier on quietly. Here a judicial officer went to court for an increase in pay.

The Association of Regional Magistrates of Southern Africa, the applicant, was a non-profit professional association that represented over 90 per cent of regional court magistrates in South Africa. The regional magistrates and regional court presidents were unhappy with President Zuma's decision to increase their annual remuneration by only five per cent when the statutory body that was charged with recommending their remuneration had recommended seven per cent and the consumer price index was higher than five per cent. The high court granted the order against the president. It set aside the determination of five per cent and directed that the increased remuneration was to continue to be of full force and effect until the president had taken the decision afresh. A unanimous Constitutional Court refused to follow the decision of the high court, holding that the president had weighed all relevant factors and thereafter exercised his executive discretion lawfully and rationally.[22]

Mr Imraahn Ismail Mukaddam came to our court asking for leave to appeal a decision of the Supreme Court of Appeal. During the relevant period, he conducted a business distributing bread in the Western Cape province. He purchased bread from some of the respondents, who were major bread producers, and sold it to informal traders, from whom consumers bought their bread. The record showed that there were approximately 100 distributors like Mr Mukaddam in the Western Cape.

In 2006, the Competition Commission launched an investigation into the major bread producers. Their finding was that these producers were involved in anti-competitive behaviour in dealing with bread distributors in the Western Cape. In the end some major bread producers admitted to, and others were adjudged to have been involved in, anti-competitive behaviour. They paid sizeable fines ranging from R99 million to R196 million.

Aggrieved by this price-fixing and collusive conduct, Mr Mukaddam approached the high court for a certificate or permission to institute a class action against the bread producers on behalf of the affected bread distributors of the Western Cape. It was argued all the way to the Constitutional Court. Justice Jafta, who wrote for the majority, recalled the right of access to courts afforded everyone by the Constitution and upheld the claim for a certificate to institute a class or group action for damages, if any, incurred by the bread distributors. The matter was remitted to the high court to be dealt with in the light of the Constitutional Court's judgment.[23]

Southern African Development Community (SADC) member states established a regional tribunal by a treaty, which later was amended and then known as the Amended Treaty.[24] Under it, the tribunal had the power to hear human rights-related complaints particularly by citizens against their states.

The government of Zimbabwe later expropriated the land of certain Zimbabwean farmers without compensation. The farmers instituted a claim in the tribunal on the ground that their human rights to property and to access to courts had been violated. The tribunal upheld the claim and ordered Zimbabwe to restore the violated human rights and to pay the legal costs incurred by the farmers. Zimbabwe did not honour the order of the tribunal. The aggrieved farmers approached the high court in South Africa to have the costs order against Zimbabwe enforced in South Africa. Both the high court and the Supreme Court of Appeal maintained that the costs were capable of enforcement by a writ of execution issued authorising the attachment and sale in execution of property owned by Zimbabwe in Cape Town.

Zimbabwe appealed to the Constitutional Court. Writing for the majority, Mogoeng CJ held that when the farmers' human rights to property and to access to courts were violated, Zimbabwe was, in terms of the Amended Treaty, obliged to co-operate with the tribunal in the adjudication of the dispute.[25] After the tribunal had delivered its judgment, Zimbabwe was duty-bound to assist in the execution of that judgment and so was South Africa. The Constitutional Court considered and dismissed Zimbabwe's claim for immunity as it was diminished by its free assent to the terms of the Amended Treaty. The Constitutional Court ordered the government of Zimbabwe to pay the legal costs that were ordered by the tribunal.

The non-compliance of Zimbabwe with the order of the tribunal was tabled before the Summit of Heads of State, as the Amended Treaty directed. They took no steps to require Zimbabwe to comply with the order of the tribunal. If anything, the heads of state disbanded the tribunal's power to adjudicate the cases brought by individuals against their state.[26]

I must add with considerable disgust and sadness that political impunity trumped accountability and the rule of law. To this day, citizens of the SADC region have no legal recourse against the conduct of their governments beyond domestic courts. When domestic courts flounder, citizens are left with no recourse. Put otherwise, impunity will flourish as big men and women of the ruling elite of Africa do as they please in complete disregard of the law and their obligations to foster a just and inclusive society.

*

Mr Mzoxolo Magidiwana and others were members of a class of people who were arrested or injured after the shooting of a number of people by members of SAPS at the Marikana mine during August 2012. The commission of inquiry – the Farlam Commission – into the events at Marikana began its work in October 2012. At the time when Mr Magidiwana and his comrades approached the high court in Pretoria, the commission's term had been extended up to a year. Their funding for their participation in the commission proceedings lasted only six months and the applicants had been unable to secure funding for a further six months of sittings; neither had they been able to secure contingent funding should the commission's term be extended once again. The minister of justice refused their request for funding because the government could find 'no legal framework through which government can contribute to the legal expenses of any of the parties who participate[d] in the commission of inquiry'.[27] Legal Aid South Africa also declined the funding request. Mr Magidiwana and other affected miners sought relief from the courts by way of an urgent interim order for funding.

When the interdict application reached the Constitutional Court we observed that

> absent a fair opportunity, the search for truth and the purpose of the Commission may be compromised. This means that unfairness may

arise when adequate legal representation is not afforded. But this does not mean that courts have the power to order the executive branch of government on how to deploy state resources. And whether the desirable objective of 'equality of arms' before a commission translates into a right to legal representation that must be provided at state expense is a contestable issue.[28]

A unanimous court turned down the claim as an urgent interdict and required the full hearing in the high court to resolve the validity of the claim.[29]

For my part this was a correct decision in law because there was no legislation that compelled the state to fund the appearance of a person who does not work for the government before a commission. But the decision was bitter in justice. Every representative of the government before the commission was fully funded by public funds, including the police who shot at the miners, but the injured and arrested and moneyless miners were not.[30]

*

I trust that I have brought to you the textured richness of the work the Constitutional Court was privileged to do in a rarified public space. 'Ordinary' citizens not favoured with huge public or private power or purse trusted the courts and sought relief within a setting that promised an efficient, effective and impartial adjudication. I was left with the distinct impression that the general populace trusted the courts and in particular the Constitutional Court and the work it did.

I am not blind to the dire difficulty of access to justice by aggrieved people with little money to spend on asserting their rights or claims. I am not making light of the heavy case-load most courts below the Constitutional Court had to, and continue to, suffer under. Budgetary resources were always way short of the material needs of the officers of the court and the bench. Even so, we judicial officers did our utmost to be good and to preserve and advance the stated public purpose of the judiciary.

The political elite, starting with President Zuma and his cabinet, thought differently about how the judiciary performed. They charged that we displayed a fixed and untransformed mindset in our decision-making. They were plainly unhappy that some contests, important to them, were resolved by the courts in a manner of which they did not approve.

One constant refrain was that of judicial trespass. The charge was that the courts usurped the decision-making power of the executive and legislature. In other words some decisions of the courts 'trespassed' into the terrain of the executive or law-making terrain. The dissatisfaction was summarised by calling our system of governance a 'judiocracy' – a rule by the judges. There is, indeed, a simple question to the charge of breaching separation of powers. Does the Constitution or other law authorise a court to decide the dispute put before it? If the Constitution and other law confer the power on the courts to decide an issue, that is a complete answer to the charge of judicial trespass.

The judicial function is passive. Judges don't look for cases; but rather cases look for judges. Once a case formulated in legal terms finds a judge, however, they are – if they have the jurisdiction – obliged to hear it and produce an outcome. In our democracy everyone has a right of access to courts about any dispute that is capable of resolution by application of the law. So, judges are obliged to decide disputes within their power. If there is any trespass, as one of my esteemed colleagues once said, it is a trespass the Constitution directs and permits.

Often judges were accused of bias or lack of impartiality. The accusations even suggested that the judges had taken sides with opposition parties or civil society who, they said, sought to govern the country through the courts. The charges surfaced each time the government or its supporters disliked a particular judicial outcome. The grievances were usually couched in generic terms and lacked any evidence to support the claim of bias. The law is intolerant of partial judges. It provides for a widely known procedure for the recusal of a judge from hearing and deciding a dispute. Recusal applications surface from time to time, particularly in criminal trials, and yet I know of no full-blown application by the government or the ruling party in any case seeking the recusal of a judge on the grounds of bias or partiality.

The other bone of contention raised by the president and his cabinet colleagues related to public lectures that were delivered on occasion by Mogoeng or me. They perceived the public lectures to be inimical towards the government of the day. I do not propose to rehash the public lectures concerned as mine are published and some ended up on the official website of the Constitutional Court. In my view, the lectures dealt with the judicial function or the constitutional project or jurisprudence in general. The point is that judges are not only judgment machines but also thought leaders in their field. When not in court, many senior judges are visiting professors in law schools and also deliver prestigious public lectures on questions of law, society and justice at conferences, institutes and other sites of public discourse. This they must do with careful caution in respect of their judicial role and the need to safeguard their neutrality and avoid undue controversy.

In the first half of 2015 this judicial haranguing by the ruling elite gained such currency that it became necessary to meet with President Zuma and his cabinet, identify the sources of conflict and seek possible solutions.

While the cutting end of the criticism was directed at me and the chief justice, the two of us agreed that our meeting with the president and his cabinet should be a matter that included and engaged heads of courts and senior judges of all divisions. This united front of the judiciary was plainly important.

Increasingly, the Supreme Court of Appeal and high courts of various divisions made decisions of which the ruling elite also disapproved. Those courts, too, were beginning to attract the wrath of the governing elite and their devotees. One ready example was the order of the high court led by Judge President Mlambo requiring that the government prevent the departure from the country of President al-Bashir of Sudan.[31] The appeal of the national government was dismissed by the Supreme Court of Appeal and never reached the Constitutional Court. Another example was the decision to give the Democratic Alliance, a political party in parliament, and the public access to the so-called spy tapes that were relied on by the national director of public prosecutions to withdraw the criminal charges against President Zuma.[32] It was the judiciary as a whole that was under siege – and not only me and the chief justice or the apex court.

Heads of courts and senior judges met on 8 July 2015 to deliberate on the incessant attacks on the judiciary and to prepare for the meeting with the president, deputy president and his cabinet. The leadership of the judiciary spoke with one voice in a public statement. Here is the text:

Statement issued by the Chief Justice, the Heads of Courts and Senior Judges of all divisions

On 8 July 2015

The Judiciary's Commitment to the Rule of Law

A judge's principal article of faith is to adjudicate without fear, favour or prejudice. When each judge assumes office she or he takes an oath or affirmation in the following terms: to be faithful to the Republic of South Africa; to uphold and protect the Constitution and the human rights entrenched in it; to administer justice to all persons alike without fear, favour or prejudice and in accordance with the Constitution and the law.

To judges this obligation and the oath are sacred.

Our Constitution, like others of its kind, sets out the powers of each arm of State. No arm of the State is entitled to intrude upon the domain of the other. However, the Constitution requires the judiciary ultimately to determine the limits and regulate the exercise of public power.

Judges, like others, should be susceptible to constructive criticism. However, in this regard, the criticism should be fair and in good faith. Importantly the criticism should be specific and clear. General gratuitous criticism is unacceptable.

In the adjudication process, judges do not act as a collective with a collective mindset. Each judge is informed by constitutional values, her or his conscience and brings to bear an individual judgment.

Of course, judges, like other mortals, err. There are several levels of courts that serve a corrective purpose when judges make a mistake. That explains why the Constitution provides for an appeal mechanism. Moreover, judgments are often subjected to intensive peer and academic scrutiny and criticism.

There have been suggestions that in certain cases judges have been prompted by others to arrive at a pre-determined result. This is a notion that we reject. However, in a case in which a judge does overstep, the general public, litigants or other aggrieved or interested parties should refer the matter to the Judicial Conduct Committee.

The Rule of Law is the cornerstone of our constitutional democracy. In simple terms it means everybody whatever her or his status is subject to and bound by the Constitution and the law. As a nation, we ignore it at our peril.

The heads of courts and senior judges of all divisions have requested the Chief Justice, as head of the judiciary, to meet with the head of state to point out and discuss the dangers of the repeated and unfounded criticisms of the judiciary. It has the potential to deligitimise the courts. Courts serve a public purpose and should not be undermined.

The historic meeting between the national executive and judiciary was held at Sefako Makgatho State Guest House. The president attended with the deputy president and several members of his cabinet. Most heads of courts joined me and Mogoeng. The executive rolled out afresh the usual and, I must add, tired accusations of judicial bias against the government and of judicial overreach. I choose not to repeat the goings-on in that meeting. Not everyone who was there present would today be proud of the accusations that were levelled with such gusto against our judiciary and particularly against the chief justice and me.

We remained unbending. We stuck to the mantra of judicial office repeated in our statement above. And, in practice, the judiciary tried hard not to veer far off the high ethical standards we had set for ourselves in line with our and, indeed, the global code of judicial ethics.

The judiciary policed the nation and its rulers and, in turn, judges owed everyone the duty to do their utmost and be worthy of the privilege and charge.

CHAPTER 26

Final sitting

As was the tradition, a formal ceremony to mark the end of a judge's term on the Constitutional Court takes place on a normal working day. The date set for mine was 20 May 2016 and that morning I would deliver my final judgment.

Perhaps one way of approaching the difficult question I posed to myself as I began considering this judicial memoir – had I been a good judge? – is to look at my level of industry and dedication to my role on the Constitutional Court. I was part of the decision-making in 411 written judgments over just under fourteen years. Of the total, 273 were unanimous judgments, 114 were split outcomes or reasoning arrived at by a majority decision. In my time, I had participated in and co-decided many thousands of applications or requests for leave or permission to appeal to our court. Of the total workload I can confirm proudly that in each of the judgments I assented to, I had fully immersed myself to ensure proper and just outcomes consistent with the law and justice. Also, I had the privilege to write over 50 substantive judgments, which included concurring judgments and no less than fifteen dissenting judgments.

A formal ceremony, such as was held for me, was by then well etched in our judicial convention. The judiciary knows no better way of celebrating judicial excellence, service and fidelity than in the very forum in which it dispenses justice as required by the oath of office. It is a time-honoured tradition. Fellow colleagues who hold judicial office robe and come in attendance as a mark of homage to the departing justice.

Allow me the liberty to repeat the first few paragraphs of my valedictory judgment. It may seem sentimental to reproduce my own words, but this judgment sits close to my heart. I choose it because access to education, more importantly access to quality education, also sits at the heart of our entire liberation project:

> Teaching and learning are as old as human beings have lived. Education is primordial and integral to the human condition. The new arrivals into humankind are taught and learn how to live useful and fulfilled lives. So education's formative goodness to the body, intellect and soul has been beyond question from antiquity. And its collective usefulness to communities has been recognised from prehistoric times to now. The indigenous and ancient African wisdom teaches that '*thuto ke lesedi la sechaba*'; '*imfundo yisibani*' (education is the light of the nation) and recognises that education is a collective enterprise by observing that it takes a village to bring up a child.
>
> Of this Aristotle, Immanuel Kant, Karl Marx, Mahatma Gandhi, Helen Keller, Nelson Mandela, Kofi Annan, Malala Yousafzai, the Holy Bible, Buddha, and the Holy Quran have said:
>
> 'Education is an ornament in prosperity and a refuge in adversity.' – Aristotle
>
> 'How then is perfection to be sought? Wherein lies our hope? In education, and in nothing else.' – Immanuel Kant
>
> 'The education of all children, from the moment that they can get along without a mother's care, shall be in state institutions.' – Karl Marx
>
> 'If we want to reach real peace in this world, we should start educating children.' – Mahatma Gandhi
>
> 'Education should train the child to use his brains, to make for

himself a place in the world and maintain his rights even when it seems that society would shove him into the scrap-heap.' – Helen Keller

'Education is the great engine of personal development. It is through education that the daughter of a peasant can become a doctor, that the son of a mineworker can become the head of the mine, that a child of a farmworker can become the president of a great nation. It is what we make out of what we have, not what we are given, that separates one person from another.' – Nelson Mandela

'Education is a human right with immense power to transform. On its foundation rest the cornerstones of freedom, democracy and sustainable human development.' – Kofi Annan

'There are many problems, but I think there is a solution to all these problems; it's just one, and it's education.' – Malala Yousafzai

'My people are destroyed for lack of knowledge.' – The Holy Bible: Hosea 4:6

'To have much learning, to be skilful in handicraft, well-trained in discipline, and to be of good speech – this is the greatest blessing.' – Buddha

'Are those equal, those who know and those who do not know? It is those who are endowed with understanding that receive admonition.' – The Holy Quran: Surah Az-Zumar 39:9

Despite these obvious ancient virtues, access to teaching and learning has not been freely and widely accessible to all people at all times. All forms of human oppression and exclusion are premised, in varying degrees, on a denial of access to education and training. The uneven power relations that marked slavery, colonialism, the industrial age and the information economy are girded, in great part, by inadequate access to quality teaching and learning. At the end of a long and glorious struggle against all forms of oppression and the beginning of a democratic and inclusive society, we, filled with rightful optimism, guaranteed universal access to basic education. We collectively said: 'everyone has the right to basic education, including adult basic education'.

Even so, disputes on access to basic education in our society are not scarce. There are continuing contests on the governance of public schools and policies on admission of learners. This despite a number of precedents of our courts that were meant to clear the murky waters of the shared space between school governing bodies and provincial executives charged with the regulation of public schools.[1]

After delivery of the judgment and taking in the many tributes, I read a farewell address, which can be found in full in the Appendix, acknowledging and thanking guests, colleagues and the many friends I had made along the way to the highest court in our land.

My words were no less sincere than heartfelt. I was then, and I remain, grateful for the opportunity I had to be part of the serious end of our work at the Constitutional Court. It was truly rigorous in a climate of respectful debates as we justices of the court shared in the search for legal truth.

This is so because at its very essence, a judge must have an unquenchable thirst for arriving at an outcome that is just and equitable. In the course of doing so, each individual judge owes to himself or herself, owes to each litigant and owes to the public at large the highest level of fidelity. With unflinching industry and sense of duty, a judge must dig deep to ensure that only justice flows from his or her determinations. This is not a collective duty; it is an individual duty. However, where judges sit together, they are indeed duty-bound to make clear their own stances in order to ensure optimal outcomes.

I hope and trust that I brought the requisite integrity beyond all question. I hope that I had an unsurpassed determination to defend and protect the gains of our hard-won struggle for liberation, freedom and democracy. I trust that each time there were storms that swelled around our institution I, together with my colleagues, stood firm. Unpopular decisions I never flinched from making provided that they were consistent with my honest judicial judgment. I knew that in a country such as ours, where want, poverty, illness and inequality abound, I had to be part of a pro-poor court. I unflinchingly supported and protected worker rights. Together as colleagues, we were the first out of the blocks each time we had to consider disputes relating to the vulnerable sitting on the margins of society.

We, as a collective, understood that everybody exercising public power had to do so within the constraints of the law. We knew well that, uncomfortable as it often was, executive and legislative excesses had to be curbed. In short, I was true to the oath of office. That is, I always acted without fear, favour or prejudice. I kept the highest standards and traditions of judicial excellence. And I hope that I never failed to defend fearlessly the independence of the judiciary, the rule of law and the full realisation of the basic rights our Constitution affords to each of our people.

I strove to support the transformation project, to make our country reflect the text and living spirit of our Constitution. Fidelity to our oath of office is important, not because we are important but because, without it, not we but our people will suffer. By our people, I mean the full diversity, poor and rich, white and black, female and male, urban and rural, the marginalised and the powerful. They all deserve our unwavering protection, which our Constitution demands we provide. After all, we are the ultimate guardians of our Constitution.

If I had ever forgotten it, this responsibility would be brought home to me most forcefully in a role I would take on in 2017, that of arbitrator in the Life Esidimeni Commission of Inquiry.

For now, however, my judicial journey as a member of the court had come to its end.

AFTER THE CONSTITUTIONAL COURT

CHAPTER 27

The Life Esidimeni Commission of Inquiry

Earlier in this memoir, I admired the unique distinction our country had drawn between judges in active and non-active service. On that regime judges are appointed for a lifetime. They keep their title and terminal earnings but remain bound by ethics, discipline and duty. They are liable to be called up for short stints of judicial service while in non-active service. Aside from formal judicial postings, judges in non-active service are used extensively to chair public probes and commissions of inquiry of a wide variety. Others are also favoured by parties to a dispute to serve as arbitrators in sizeable private commercial disputes. Our system, unlike that in many other countries, encourages the inflow of new and younger judges while retaining access to older and veteran judges. One may say we strive to enjoy the best of the two worlds of renewal and experience.

During 2017, Gauteng Premier David Makhura called me, seeking a meeting. At the appointed time, his sizeable motorcade snaked up my driveway. The victims of the Life Esidimeni tragedy and his provincial government had agreed on a possible mediator or arbitrator in their stand-off, the premier told me. That person, he said, was me. I was impressed by the premier's obvious commitment to righting the wrong suffered by the victims of Life Esidimeni. An injustice had occurred, he said, and government must confess its wrong, take responsibility and atone.

At the time I had not followed the media reports on that tragedy closely, but I thought a good place to start would be to hear everyone out – the government and the families of the victims. I needed to know that I was the choice of all of them as the person to act in the dispute resolution process. A mediator or arbitrator must be trusted and wanted by all parties to a dispute. I chaired a series of meetings with representatives of the families of victims and senior officials of the provincial government. The negotiations yielded an arbitration rather than mediation. The victims sought a process with definitive and binding outcomes. This led to an arbitration agreement with elements that went beyond the possible compensation.

Truth, accountability and closure were crucial needs of the families of the victims. They wanted to know how the deaths and mistreatment of the health-care users had occurred, and by whom and why. They also hoped for therapy for the families of all victims and for survivors of the mistreatment in order to confront and overcome the tragedy. It seemed plain to me that this would be arbitration of its own kind. A monetary award, if any, would be important. But excavating the truth, healing the loss and hurt, and possible emotional closure were as important. So, too, were the criminal accountability of the concerned government officials and the governance responsibility of government. In all fairness, the provincial government did not resist the stance assumed by the victims and it openly confessed its wrongdoing and conceded the merits of the central grievance of the victims.

When I agreed to the role of arbitrator, I had no idea what I was getting myself into. The arbitration hearing started on 9 October 2017 and continued until 9 February 2018. It was open to the affected families, the provincial government, the public and all media. The hearings sat for 43 days and an additional two days of legal argument. Sixty witnesses took the stand and gave evidence under oath. Out of the 60 witnesses, twelve were senior government officials of the province. They included the former head of the department of health; the acting head of the department; a former member of the executive council for health; the member of the executive council for health; the member of the executive council for finance; the premier; and the national minister of health. Five witnesses were middle-management government employees and one was a senior officer in the South African Police Service. The managing director of Life Esidimeni during the period of the tragedy also testified. The witnesses included three managers or owners of non-governmental organisations to which mental health-care users were moved, six were expert witnesses, 22 were family members of the deceased people, and nine were family members of the surviving victims. Fifty-nine affidavits were submitted by attorneys for the deceased in relation to the witnesses who chose not to testify orally and 42 affidavits were handed in by attorneys of survivors. In addition to the arbitration record, which ran into 3 000 pages, 173 documentary exhibits were admitted to the record.

The hearing divulged a harrowing account of the death, torture and disappearance of utterly vulnerable mental health-care users in the care of an admittedly delinquent provincial government. It was also a story of the searing and public anguish of the families of the affected patients and of the collective shock and pain of many other caring people in our land and elsewhere in the world. These inhuman narratives were rehearsed before me amidst a public display of agony and grief as some victims and their families cried out loud during the hearing.

It is now undisputed that as a result of their move out of Life Esidimeni facilities after 1 October 2015, 144 mental health-care users died and 1 418 were exposed to trauma and morbidity, among other results, but survived. Of the known survivors, the provincial government reported that the whereabouts of 44 patients then remained unknown. It is my hope that by now, in 2020, the government has done its utmost to find certainty about the fate of the missing people.

The arbitration was a sequel to the recommendation of Professor Malegapuru Makgoba, the Health Ombud, in a report into the circumstances surrounding the deaths of mentally ill patients. The Ombud's report was most helpful and formed the factual foundation for the arbitration process. All parties to the arbitration accepted its accuracy and credibility. The dispute between the parties was not about the facts or the identity of the people who were entitled to redress. It was also not whether the conduct of employees of the state was negligent and unlawful. These elements were admitted. The core dispute was the nature and extent of the equitable redress, including compensation, due to the patients and their families who were adversely affected by the so-called Marathon Project which led to the closure of Life Esidimeni facilities after 1 October 2015, resulting in death or trauma.

For its part, the provincial government argued that it was liable to compensate the families of the deceased and the mental health-care users who survived the Marathon Project or their families for estimated funeral expenses and common law general damages arising from pain, suffering and emotional shock, and nothing else. To that end, the government offered to pay a globular amount of R200 000, which some claimants accepted conditionally.

For their part, the claimants, in slight variations, were emphatic that beyond the general damages for which the government was obviously liable, the pervasive, egregious, uncaring and wanton violations of the constitutional rights of all mental health-care users and their families called for equitable redress, which must include constitutional damages. The state resisted this claim.

After all was said and done, that was the residual but intractable difference and dispute I was called upon to resolve.

It did not end there. The hearing had to contain elements intended to achieve the related objectives of 'closure'. These were to uncover the full circumstances of the death or survival of affected patients; to afford the affected families the space to mourn or grieve as they related what they knew about the demise or survival of their loved ones; to give the provincial government decision-makers an opportunity to account for the deaths and torture of the people who were in their care; to grant an opportunity to the political representatives of the government to tender public apologies and hopefully facilitate emotional closure on the part of the affected families of those who died and those who survived the ordeal of the Marathon Project. The victims also hoped that the disclosures of wrongful conduct towards the victims would lead to a government recovery programme that would accrue to the benefit of all other mental health-care users at facilities within the country.

The genesis of this terrible tale of death and torture was the termination of the contract between the Department of Health and Life Esidimeni. The contract, which had been in operation for over 30 years, was ended on 29 September 2015 by a formal notice authorised and signed by the head of department, Dr Tiego Ephraim Selebano. On 21 October 2015, then member of the executive council Ms Qedani Mahlangu announced the formal end of the contract of service. In her evidence before me, Ms Mahlangu was adamant that the decision to terminate the contract was taken by a 'collective'. In contrast, Dr Selebano claimed that he signed the notice ending the contract only because he feared his political principal, Ms Mahlangu, on whose instructions he terminated the contract.

The contract was ended on a 'six-month' notice. This meant that all mental health-care users would be moved out of Life Esidimeni facilities by 31 March 2016. Random and mass discharges of patients on the orders of the department started immediately. The date for the closure of the facilities was later extended to 30 June 2016. The end of the contract compelled the move of 1 711 patients out of Life Esidimeni between October 2015 and the end of June 2016. They were moved to hospitals, to non-governmental organisations handpicked by the department or to their family homes.

Before and after the termination of the contract, the families of patients, civil society, professional bodies and clinicians practising outside and within the Health Department made attempts to persuade the department to devise a plan that would protect the rights and meet the needs of the people being moved out of Life Esidimeni. The department did not heed any of these pointed warnings of potential harm. Ms Mahlangu, Dr Selebano and the former head of the Mental Health Directorate, Dr Makgabo Manamela, obstinately went ahead with mass removals, without the involvement of and consultation with families and concerned health professionals. As a result, at least 144 people in their care died and, barring the missing patients, just over 1 500 patients survived the torturous conditions after their forced displacement from Life Esidimeni to all kinds of inadequate facilities.

The most incredible part of the response of these three high-ranking government officials was that they had no reason to believe that the displaced patients would die or suffer severe ill-treatment and torture. On the facts as a whole, I found that this response of highly placed officials was so improbable that it must be false.

Aside from the probabilities, the reasons that Ms Mahlangu and Dr Selebano and their department advanced for terminating the service contract with Life Esidimeni were shown in evidence to be untrue. Also, the reasons were not properly related to the outcomes they claimed they were pursuing. In short, besides the reasons being untruthful, the decision on which the reasons were based was irrational and in blatant breach of the law and the Constitution.

The member of the executive council for finance told the hearing that the claim that the contract was stopped because the province confronted resource constraints was not true.

However, even if the resource constraint was real, if the organ of state concerned had budgeted according to a mistaken understanding of its constitutional and statutory obligations, this could not provide an acceptable justification for the failure to protect the constitutional rights of victims.

The Constitution goes further to impose overarching duties on wielders of public power. As elected office-bearers and so, too, all those in the public service, as they go about their duties, they must first and foremost be faithful to the law. They must act within the strictures of the law and eschew unlawfulness. They may not elevate their personal or arbitrary or political or other preferences above or in a breach of binding law. That is a bare minimum of the constitutional tenet of the rule of law. Absent a respect for the law, we head down the slippery slope of disorder and anarchy. The weak, poor and vulnerable will bend in oppression while the powerful and ruling elite minister to their needs and do as they please. That is why we have embedded in our democratic practice the foundational values of openness, responsiveness and accountability in the exercise of public power. If these values were given full rein, the people in our land, and certainly the defenceless mental health-care users of Life Esidimeni and their families, would have been spared death, torture and trauma.

Our democratic project sets admirably high principles for officials in the public service. Public administration must occur within the precincts of set values and principles. These include a high standard of professional ethics using public resources in an efficient, economic and effective manner; providing services impartially, fairly, equitably and without bias; and being responsive to people's needs. In addition, public administration must be accountable and transparent by providing the public with timely, accessible and accurate information.

Here, it is useful to record that the Constitution expressly, albeit self-evidently, imposes duties of fidelity to the law, transparency and accountability on a member of the provincial executive council. To cut to the chase: Ms Mahlangu was responsible for the executive function related to health care in the province, as assigned by the premier. She was obliged to act in accordance with the Constitution. She was 'accountable collectively and individually' to the legislature for the performance of her functions and duties, and she bore the duty to give full and regular reports to the legislature. The evidence showed that these obligations were not honoured.

In the reasons for the award I made, I spelled out the regulatory regime in considerable detail. In my view this was necessary given the vast human tragedy, in the form of death, torture and survival of defenceless mental health-care users. Also, because since 1994 our state has erected a globally admirable and compliant regulatory regime for the care of such patients. Its provisions are by and large in sync with international human rights and mental healt-care norms of a very high order. But what stands out is the breadth and depth and frequency of the arrogant and deeply disgraceful disregard of constitutional obligations, other law, mental health-care norms and ethics by an organ of state, its leaders and employees.

In sum, besides the reasons for being untruthful, the decision to terminate the contract was irrational and in blatant breach of the law and the Constitution. Absent rationality in the use of public power, arbitrariness and tyranny will flourish. The death and torture in the Life Esidimeni tragedy stemmed from the irrational, arrogant and uncaring use of public power.

I invited Ms Mahlangu and Dr Selebano several times to explain the true reason why they ended the contract. They failed to do so. They diverted responsibility, so they thought, by saying it was a 'decision of the collective'. Both admitted that each had the power to stop the termination of the contract but never explained why they did not do so. Neither could explain why it was urgent to cancel the contract. Here is the point. Their irrational and thus unconstitutional decision was the reason for the death and torture that ensued. And still the claimants, and indeed the nation, do not know the true reason why the triggering decision was taken by powerful government officials against defenceless mental health-care users and their families. Without the truth, 'closure' for the claimants was a distant possibility.

This wanton, arbitrary and unaccounted-for decision caused so much pain and suffering, stress, trauma and morbidity. It was a material breach of the constitutional obligations of the government and its servants. Such a breach, together with other considerations, weighed heavily on me in determining the character of the just and equitable redress I opted for.

Every element of the Marathon Project trampled heavily on dignity: on the human dignity of the mental health-care users when they were still alive, their dignity after they had passed away, and the dignity of their family members who watched their loved ones waste away and die, powerless to do anything to prevent it.

The violations of the right to dignity here were as many as they were plain to see. Not only were the patients stripped of their dignity, in life and in death, but their families were also treated as subhuman and devoid of any worth. Their entitlement to participate in the decisions about the health care of their loved ones was disregarded, as was their right to information. Their grief was brushed off. Their emotional distress arising from the trauma they went through was undermined and used to marginalise them.

The evidence showed the efforts of many family members who took to searching for their loved ones. The indignity of being confronted with dehydrated, emaciated and unwell patients in dingy and unkempt non-governmental organisation facilities might seem a fairly obvious indignity, but it needs to be visualised. For those families who found their loved ones deceased – and in some instances their bodies were decomposed – not only must their pain be deemed immeasurable, but this was an affront to the human worth of the families and at odds with the values of Ubuntu, which teach us mutual respect, caring, communal sharing and human solidarity.

I found that the claimants, in the extended sense, of patients and their families or next of kin, were stripped of their dignity in the way that the government treated them. Before their death they were owed a duty of protecting and upholding their dignity. The state failed them dismally. In fact the state proactively invaded their dignity despite warning and protests from organised clinicians, psychiatrists, psychologists and formations of families.

The right not to be treated in a cruel, inhuman or degrading way is a self-standing right in the Constitution. It is related to the right to dignity but its reach travels further. It does not only require that people be treated in a respectful and dignified manner and in accordance with their human worth but also targets proactive and systematic acts that are not only unkind but also hateful and directed at bodily and psychological hurt and harassment. All the facts here point to cruelty – an antithesis of empathy and caring.

The final question facing me was to find what would be just and equitable redress, including compensation. The claimants contended that severe constitutional breaches against the mental health-care users who had died, and those who had survived, and their families had occurred. Their claims, they said, were for damages beyond common law damages and flowed from severe breaches by the government of the constitutional rights of the claimants not covered by redress allowed by the common law or statutory law.

The arbitration agreement had stipulated that, in the absence of an agreement on the quantum of compensation, the arbitrator must make a binding award on equitable redress and on measures to facilitate closure. The redress, the agreement explained, included appropriate compensation for affected families whether on a group or individual basis.

AFTER THE CONSTITUTIONAL COURT

At the end of the hearing, the government tendered a globular amount of R200 000 per claimant family as full and final settlement for estimated funeral expenses and common law general damages arising from psychological injury and emotional shock. Some of the claimants accepted the tender. Claimants, in slight variations, were emphatic that beyond the general damages for which the state was evidently liable, the equitable redress must include constitutional damages. The violations of the constitutional rights of mental health-care users and their families were pervasive, egregious, uncaring and wanton.

The government resisted an award for 'constitutional' damages in the region of R1 million to R1.5 million. The principal reasoning of the government was twofold. First, once a claimant has been compensated under the common law, they may not rely on the Constitution to seek equitable redress. All civil claims, the argument ran, must be brought only under the rubric of the common law. On this reasoning the stratagem of the government was to settle 'common law' damages and then contend that the claimants might no longer rely on the Constitution for equitable redress.

The government went on to submit that once the constitutional right alleged to be breached has been identified, there remains a further issue of whether constitutional damages are appropriate constitutional remedy for that breach. I find no fault in this submission. But here is the rub. In this arbitration there can be no doubt that a legion of constitutional rights had been breached and each had been meticulously identified and proven by uncontested facts.

In effect, the government was arguing that the claimants should have converted all their claims to common law claims and, if not, they would be non-suited. There is no body of judicial authority that supports this proposition. The cases simply state that the common law mode of pleading may be resorted to, to vindicate a constitutional breach. The cases do not mean that a party is barred from relying on the Constitution where the breaches defy common law formulation. The cases do not also mean that a constitutional injury does not exist outside the scope of the common law. It would be strange, if not bizarre, if a claim under the supreme law of the land would be denied vindication simply because it could not fit into the common law framework. If that were so, the constitutional remedies would be granted only subject to the common law. That would be remarkably retrogressive and show an uninformed understanding of the hierarchy of sources of law. The common law continues to exist only because the Constitution so permits it provided it is consistent with the supreme law. Delictual harm caused by a breach of constitutional guarantees is and must be capable of appropriate redress.

More importantly, the claim for invasive and pervasive violation of constitutional guarantees by the state cannot readily or always be couched in common law terms. I have set out in some detail what the families of the deceased mental health-care users had to endure; the torture that the survivors had to endure; the wanton violation of nearly every protection the legislation was meant to provide so as to give effect to the constitutional promise of access to health care; the wanton disregard of our international obligations on mental health care; and the blatant abuse and disregard of professional ethics. All these breaches together led to amazing devastation for families of the deceased and survivors.

In effect, the government had invited me to squeeze these pervasive and putrid and reeking violations of our Constitution and many valuable laws into common law strictures of psychological injury and shock for which R180 000 might be the going rate in trial courts under the common law. I declined that invitation. This was a matter of massive proportion for the utterly defenceless mental health-care users who deserved every care in the world and every protection and vindication a tribunal like this could afford them.

The parties have agreed on equitable redress in the form of compensation and wisely allowed the arbitrator discretion to determine the form of equitable redress. I can find no hint that the parties sought to leave their fate in the narrow strictures of the common law, which well predates our modern and transformative Constitution.

AFTER THE CONSTITUTIONAL COURT

When I made the award I was mindful of the fact that many other potential claimants were not before me in these proceedings. I was aware of the many public announcements and media advertisements that invited potential claimants to come forward. Even so, not all have joined the process. I trusted that when they find their voice or way, the government would choose to meet their claim in terms identical to the award I was to make rather than to set up new litigation of another arbitration process.

I found it salutary to thank the families of the claimants and the national minister of health, the premier of Gauteng province and the member of the executive council for health who stayed the course to bring this arbitration to fruition. The logistical and material support to families and the arbitration staff was considerable. They represented a contrite, responsive and accountable government that readily came along to help heal the gaping and personal wounds of so many in our nation. More so, they publicly apologised. In my award I required them to do it again in a manner I specified.

I made an award that sought to vindicate the constitutional breaches. The damages were sourced outside the ordinary ambit of the common law. They were animated by and justified in order to vindicate the high promises of our supreme law. The size or quantum of the compensation to the victims and other features of the award are now a matter of public record.

One can only trust that the horror of death and torture of defenceless health-care seekers caused by a recalcitrant government in open breach of its own laws will never ever happen again in our land or anywhere else.

CHAPTER 28

'Retirement'

Life within the judiciary is less glamorous than meets the eye. Past the glitz of public power, titles, decorum, bibs and gowns, and courthouses sit punishing labour and a cloistered lifestyle.

A judicial officer dedicated to the task works very hard over long hours. An average trial court judicial officer sits the better part of the working day in public hearings where one's patience, listening skills and emotional intelligence are drawn out to the full. A court hearing is not a game but a scarce public amenity with severe outcomes. That makes courtroom time precious.

A day of trial is a hard slog that continues into the evening. A judge is beset with the task of summarising the evidence or reading up the authorities relied upon or writing a short opinion to decide a legal point raised in the course of the hearing. Oftentimes, the judge has to read up and prepare for a different hearing or argument coming up the very next day. It is rough out there.

In appellate courts, judges have just as much, if not more, to do. Foremost, they must know the detailed facts of the case on appeal. The facts are found only from reading and mastering the record of appeal. The law that governs the case may be ascertained only when the facts in the record are fully grasped. No judge worth the title can or should decide or join a decision in a matter in which he or she has not properly studied the record. The reputation of the judiciary can only be harmed when litigants or their counsel gain the warranted impression that a judge in a hearing was not on top of the record.

Well-crafted judgments come at a huge personal and social cost to their author. Making important decisions takes time. But thinking the route to the outcome is even harder.

I will confess that, none the less, I did manage to sneak in a round of golf on most Saturday mornings, but those breaks, I believe, were important. I would also make time for a long walk-run when I had to agonise over a just outcome in an intractable case, and the exercise helped both to clear and focus my mind.

Judicial ethics, too, impose a cloistered lifestyle. Ethics instruct a judge to avoid apparent or real conflict of interest. A judge must avoid any conduct or association that might compromise his impartiality. On this score a judge does not have to be, in fact, biased. If the judge allowed an impression to be formed by others that they might be partial towards a cause, person or organisation, that may be a valid ground for recusal. A well-founded perception of bias may be just as fatal. It is a bit like saying birds of a feather flock together.

Well, that stern rule of ethics should dispose of a judge frequenting shebeens, pubs, stokvels, hotel foyers or rowdy and drunken rugby and soccer stadium suites. A loud and drunken judge in a public place is not only an eyesore but also a distinct threat to his calling.

One well-publicised incident of a drunken judge in our country left all of us reeling and deeply embarrassed. My golfing mates and other friends were well on my case. '"Sober as a judge"?' they teased. 'What? Should we not say "drunk as a lord" instead?'

The social exclusion of judges travels quite far. Many weddings and other open parties would be out of bounds. Powerful and not-so-potent politicians, big or small business leaders, social entrepreneurs and other power brokers in private and public spaces ought to fall off a judge's social calendar. It is only a matter of time before the host of that wedding of the year or that chief executive of that business behemoth or the leader of that powerful political formation is before the courts. The powerful tend to have sharp elbows. Any prudent judge would know that it is only a matter of time before the mighty are embroiled in court battles.

Even if the case does not come before you as judge, you don't want to leave the impression that the litigant might be favoured because he consorts with judges. So, most judges take care to live away from the public glare. They tend to skip celebrity affairs and rather go out or dine with a partner, family, close friends or other judges.

For much the same reason, the norm demands that a judge must keep their mouth shut and pen dry on public debates lest they are seen as nursing a fixed notion or partiality. The rule was seemingly inherited from our English colonial masters. They taught that judges spoke only through their judgments. Beyond that, they had to keep their peace forever.

But the bar to public expression by judges was by no means universal. On the European continent, for instance, senior judges are drawn mostly from university law professors and for a fixed term. At the moment of their appointment they would have published extensively in their various fields of academic expertise. Some during their tenure continue to teach and write and speak at conferences. After the fixed term, some senior judges resume teaching or even business or political roles. This model of extra-judicial expression one also finds, with some variation, in Latin America where judges are drawn mainly from the law academy and tend to hold known views on social and other causes.

The other model might well be that of the United States of America where most state court judges campaign for and are elected into judicial office. Their views on public matters are no secret. They bare their political and social views to impress and gain the support of the electorate. As they serve as judges in state courts, they hope to be re-elected in the future. So, expectations of solitude and silence would hardly apply and so, too, concerns about perception of bias.

US federal judges and justices of the Supreme Court are appointed by the president subject to confirmation proceedings. Even so their tradition is not to silence judges. Many write and speak often outside their court opinions. They teach at or address law schools and some often visit law schools as justices in residence. In my time I was struck by the many judicial memoirs produced by US federal judges as against judges of other jurisdictions in the world.

African judiciaries have not yet worked out a fresh model that offers guidance on when and how far judges may express themselves outside their judgments. There is no hardened convention on extra-judicial expression. It is sad but true that many of our judges have been consumed by life-and-death battles to do their public duty without the interference of the executive arm of state.

For many of our judges, advocacy and critical debate about their craft and justice in society seemed far removed from their minds in the face of more pressing challenges around institutional hunger, a punishing workload, survival and integrity. Most executive governments in Africa and elsewhere are deeply intolerant of judges who rule independently, albeit rightly, against them. Such governments are much like the burly bullies of rugby or soccer fields who swear and threaten to beat up the referee who blows against them. They like their judges compliant and silent as executive impunity flourishes.

Rather than allow myself to get carried away on this issue, I will return to the point I sought to make. A sitting judge ought to be free to follow and engage in critical thinking about the law, justice and society outside their formal judgments. It should be open to the judge to engage in extra-judicial expression. This stance stems from the view that a sitting judge ought not to disengage from their social setting. They should avoid being hived off into an elitist bubble away from the lives of inhabitants of all classes and stations. This permits a judicial officer to engage in analytical thinking and take advantage of the taxonomy of the academy. It is so that the judiciary's regular function is casuistic. A judge resolves disputes case by case and within the limits of fixed facts. Research lends to academics the benefit of hindsight and a systematic overview.

'RETIREMENT'

*

In my time I wrote many formal judgments but I also refused to be fenced in. I wrote and delivered papers and thought pieces on law, justice and society at conferences, at law schools and at judicial conferences, at gatherings of the legal profession and before other formal audiences at home and abroad. The choice of extra-judicial expression I made had vast unintended consequences for the last years of my judicial life and the days of my retirement. Shortly after my retirement an enthusiastic desktop researcher unearthed electronic links to the published papers and recorded addresses during my tenure on the bench and thereafter. To my surprise and delight I wrote and spoke incessantly. I was published far more than I imagined. I was struck by the breadth of the subjects I wrote on side by side with my day job at the Constitutional Court. I was by no measure a quiet judge.

I was privileged to write on many matters of the history of our struggle for freedom and its heroes. Starting with progressive lawyers, I wrote and delivered praises in memory of Godfrey Mokgonane Pitje, the founding president of the Black Lawyers Association and Bram Louis Fischer, that veteran and brilliant senior counsel who broke loose from his limiting lineage to join a crusade of freedom and equality at the cost of his life. I penned a published memorial lecture in honour of Justice Oliver Deneys Schreiner (1890–1980), that renowned judge of the Appellate Division of the Supreme Court of South Africa who was passed over twice for the position of chief justice. I read eulogies at the memorial services of our departed chief justices Arthur Chaskalson and Pius Nkonzo Langa and at the funeral of my well-loved colleague Justice Thembile Skweyiya. I wrote posthumous tributes to Griffiths and Victoria Mxenge, that brave couple of attorneys and activists who were murdered so brutally by apartheid agents.

It fell often on me to compose and read memorial lectures for a motley collection of stalwarts of our struggle for freedom. I read no less than three memorial lectures in honour of Robert Mangaliso Sobukwe – in Kimberley, hosted by the Black Lawyers Association, at the University of South Africa and at the University of the Witwatersrand. Each of these universities had renamed a major building in honour of Sobukwe. I wrote published tributes to Ruth First and to Jafta Kgalabi Masemola; to Nelson Rolihlahla Mandela and Stanley Mmutlanyane Mogoba; Helen Suzman; Oliver Reginald Tambo, Peter Storey, Lot Ndlovu and, more lately, to Govan Mbeki.

During my time on the court, I needed to engage with conversations of young lawyers in training and their law teachers. Murmurs were beginning to get louder amongst law students and their young professors that our transition to democracy had come to naught; that the resultant Constitution and the meaning the court had given to it were not fit for purpose and that the farce about the rule of law was an excuse to entrench colonial power relations and historical privilege. This debate implied that the Constitution was not a sufficient condition for altering social power relations in society. It was indeed a valid debate to be had; I entered that debate with a good few papers.

I scripted multiple public lectures for virtually every law school in our land, starting with my alma mater, the University of South Africa. I straddled our land from university to university – from Fort Hare to Stellenbosch; Western Cape to Johannesburg; from Cape Town to Pretoria; from North West to Rhodes; from Nelson Mandela to Limpopo; and at Wits many times. The papers I read included the history of our law; the legal mechanics of our transition from apartheid to democracy; the resultant transformative constitutionalism and its core values such as democracy, human dignity, the rule of law, the attainment of equality, respect for fundamental rights and freedoms, governance that is open, accountable and responsive. I wrote about social justice and access to public goods that make our lives liveable and tolerable. I pondered over the architecture of our state, including the presidency and executive authority, the law-making function and the place of judicial power. I explored the new hierarchy of sources of law, including the place of the common law, indigenous law and the plural streams of law. I have agonised over gender injustice. I have written about the land question and restitutionary measures and other constitutional means to achieve land justice. I have had occasion to consider the place of foreign and international law and other comparative jurisprudence.

Even isolated but newsworthy events would prompt me to write. When Oscar Pistorius's trial and appeal ended, I published a piece pondering the detailed but wise terms of the judgment and order of Mlambo JP on a fully televised criminal trial and what that meant for our notions of open justice. When the #FeesMustFall movement within our universities swung into full revolt, again I wrote on whether their claim to state-funded higher education was in accord with our constitutional promises. Both peer-reviewed articles are published in university law journals in the United Kingdom.

The salutary benefits of my pronounced writing were to escape the intellectual and social solitude of judicial life and continue to wrestle with the trajectory of the democratic project and the larger march of the progressive world towards a more just society within the strictures of the law. The unintended benefit and perhaps bother of my intellectual restlessness was the flood of invitations to me from our universities, social movements and other diverse domestic formations concerned about law, society and justice. I was joining what Joel Netshitenzhe famously called 'a festival of ideas', even though political platitudes were distinctly louder.

*

During the latter days of my stay on the bench and more so after my retirement, many universities and supreme courts around the world extended invitations for me to teach and deliver papers. A few examples should suffice. During my sabbatical I was favoured to lecture at the Maryland University law school, where I crafted the first part of the manuscript of *My Own Liberator*. For that I am grateful to Professor Taunya Lovell Banks, who made it possible. In New York, thanks to Professor Gay McDougall, I addressed the law school at Fordham University. On another occasion, in the same city I was the guest of Professor Penny Andrews and spoke on our Constitution and jurisprudence at CUNY School of Law in a conversation with Professor Emeritus Frank Michelman of Harvard Law School.

AFTER THE CONSTITUTIONAL COURT

At Cambridge University I pondered the pro-poor jurisprudence of the Constitutional Court and whether one could properly be pro-poor and an unbiased umpire. Then also I acknowledged the beneficial influence on us of the Canadian Supreme Court jurisprudence on proportionality and the limitation analysis of fundamental rights and freedoms in our Constitution.

Not long thereafter I was invited as a distinguished fellow at the University of Georgetown in Washington. I taught comparative constitutional law. Here, I cannot resist relating that while in Washington, Kabonina and I visited the White House as guests of the president and first lady, Barack and Michelle Obama. It was an annual cocktail evening of music and culture hosted by the first couple. For reasons I know, the president of the USA heard that we were in Washington and extended the invitation, which we received on a gold-lettered personal notecard. But the intriguing beginning of this story is the following. One Senator Barack Obama had visited our land during the tenure of President Mbeki. For reasons unclear to me, the senator did not secure an invitation from our presidency. Being the trained lawyer the senator was, he opted to visit the Constitutional Court. I was then acting chief justice, and my colleagues and I gladly received him and his party in our common room. He expressed his admiration for the jurisprudence of the court.

I remember asking the senator, somewhat irreverently, what the origin of his last name, 'Obama', was. He called up his African lineage originating in Kenya with remarkable gusto. It was impressive. I had to swallow my fine cheek. None of us, his hosts, ever imagined that he would rise to become president of the United States. The rest, as the saying goes, is history.

At Zurich University in Switzerland I was a distinguished fellow and co-taught with Professor Matthias Mahlmann models of executive powers in constitutions. At Oxford University I was the guest of my erstwhile colleague Professor Kate O'Regan and talked about our transition to democracy and separation of powers. I subsequently visited New York University law school as a distinguished scholar and joined in comparative constitutional law seminars.

'RETIREMENT'

On two occasions after my retirement I was favoured with an invitation to become a guest and resident writer at the renowned creative retreat at the Rockefeller Foundation Centre in Bellagio, Italy. My host was the executive director, Ms Pilar Palacia, and it was in the harrowing beauty of Bellagio that I was moved and privileged to write much of this judicial memoir. More recently, the Munk Institute invited me to deliver a lecture at the inauguration of the Nelson Mandela Lectureship in Human Rights at the University of Toronto, Canada. I remain grateful to Professor Cotler for that invitation.

During my stay on the court and more so after retirement I have been privileged to visit supreme courts in many jurisdictions of the world. These include Zimbabwe, Namibia, Lesotho, Zambia, Ghana, Tunisia, England, Greece, Italy, the Netherlands, Belarus, Switzerland, Australia, Sri Lanka, Canada and the USA. I've also been received at international and regional tribunals, among them the SADC Tribunal in Namibia, the African Court of Justice and Human Rights in Arusha, Tanzania, the International Court of Justice, and the International Criminal Court.

In turn, our court was favoured to receive judges and justices of supreme courts from many parts of the world. These included almost all democracies and some countries which had experienced strife. Among the latter were Lebanon, South Sudan, Yemen, Palestine, Sri Lanka and Libya. One distinguished visitor who comes to mind was Justice Ruth Bader Ginsburg of the US Supreme Court, who became the first justice in residence at our court; later, in another visit, we received her colleague Justice Stephen Breyer. Both reciprocated the courtesy when I visited Washington and even helped arrange an invitation to lunch in the court building with Chief Justice Roberts and other justices at the Supreme Court.

*

If I thought retirement would bring me hard-won rest and peace, I soon learned that this was not going to happen. I cannot say I didn't receive plenty of coaching from judges who had retired before me, and their advice was on similar lines: 'Dikgang, remember to say no.' My partner, Kabonina, was the head coach and, in fact, I did say no to many an invitation. One invitation I could not have declined, however, was the one to sit as arbitrator in the Life Esidimeni inquiry. How could I possibly have said no to that request?

Shortly before I was approached by the premier of Gauteng province to sit as arbitrator, I had been engaged by Adv Karen McKenzie, the head of the Human Rights Unit within the Secretariat of the Commonwealth of Nations, to travel to Colombo in Sri Lanka in order to explore a possible facilitation of constitutional reforms in that country. The conflict and deaths relating to the Tamil Tigers posed the possibility for a truth and reconciliation process. We engaged with the head of government, the prime minster and the minister of foreign affairs, members of parliament and a variety of activist groups. A week's stay in that scenic country quickly revealed how close to the surface were the deep and difficult fissures in a post-conflict society consumed by religious and associated loyalties. My conclusion was that progress on reform was not going to be easily made in the short term and my services were required closer to home.

On the authority of a SADC resolution aimed at bringing constitutional and security reforms in the Kingdom of Lesotho, I was appointed by President Ramaphosa to serve as the leader of the facilitation team in a process of national reforms that were under way in that country. This role is ongoing and much progress has been achieved as Basotho get down to implementing the agreed reforms. Twice, in Windhoek, Namibia, and in Dar es Salaam, Tanzania, I was directed by President Ramaphosa to appear before SADC heads of state and report on the facilitation work in Lesotho.

It does indeed seem that there is no rest for the wicked. Or, as they say in isiZulu: 'I donki sishaya le idontsayo' (You had better lash the donkey that pulls the most).

*

I may have worked myself into the ground and given up a meaningful social life and material acquisitions, but I believe that my judicial role has significantly enriched my life. As I moved to the end of my judicial term and immediately thereafter, I received an astonishing number of awards and honorary doctorates from law schools at home and abroad in recognition of what I regard as the small contribution I was able to make while I enjoyed judicial office. Such accolades were truly humbling – from the prestigious judicial awards both at home and abroad, high awards I have received from churches, and also from a wide range of professional bodies. In 2018 I was presented with the Order of Luthuli in Gold, our nation's highest national honour, in recognition of my 'exceptional contribution to the field of law and the administration of justice' – recognition that brought great joy to me, my wife Kabonina, our children, grandchildren and extended family.

But even more meaningful to me than official awards and accolades are the many, many citizens of our land who walk up to me with kind words of gratitude. To be so profusely honoured for fulfilling my judicial calling is satisfaction of a deep and lasting kind.

Acknowledgements

My wife, Kabonina, and her brood and grand-brood had to endure the labour. The grandchildren were more forthright: 'Koko, why does Tata sit so long in the study and work on the laptop?' I am most grateful for their forbearance. At the end of 2019 all twelve of us – four children, six grandchildren, Kabo and myself – went to the same holiday resort over the same time and lived in joint, adjacent chalets. Pure joy! It was my way of saying: 'The manuscript is done and thank you all.'

In my first memoir, *My Own Liberator*, I spoke out of turn. I promised this additional instalment. Damn, never do that to yourself! Everyone who had read the first book would charge somewhat impolitely: 'When is your second book coming out?' I am not thanking these over-eager followers, but they certainly kept me on my toes. How could I have slept on the job at hand or simply failed to do it or caved in?

The other people I should thank are those who took concrete steps to lend a hand toward this modest accomplishment.

Michelle Toxopeus served as a law clerk and researcher in the last year of my term on the Constitutional Court. She has since moved on, as I have. At my request she offered to read every word in every chapter I composed. She proffered helpful editorial suggestions. But foremost, she did accuracy checks and the research reflected in the endnotes, which are an emporium of legal history and citation for future researchers. I am most thankful for her unfailing support and contribution. All the shortcomings in the memoir are certainly mine.

Lesley Grobler, my personal assistant of over 25 years, provided invaluable

AKNOWLEDGEMENTS

logistical support during the compilation of the manuscript. I am most grateful.

In a work of this kind it has not been easy deciding what is in and what is out – how high should I lift the judicial gown and how far should I bare my judicial soul? My brother, Tiego Moseneke, and Vincent Maleka, now an acclaimed senior counsel, were at hand to hear me out but left the final decision to me. I am indebted to them for helping me keep my sanity.

Not once, but twice I was an invited resident during 2018 and 2019 at the Rockefeller Centre in Bellagio, Italy. I was privileged to write a substantial part of this memoir at that magnificent villa located on manicured grounds and presenting harrowingly beautiful vistas over Lake Como. My chief hostess was that inimitable governess, Pilar Palacia. I am most grateful.

The final praise is due to my publishers, the Pan Macmillan team, and in particular Andrea Nattrass, who cannot help coming across as a convent mother superior and yet is polite and always making sure the work gets done. A book is difficult to do. Thank you, Andrea, for repeatedly saying: 'This is an important book. It must be done.'

Alison Lowry has worked her way into my intellectual heart. She served as my editor for both my memoirs. Her soft suggestions have been thoughtful and elegant. She is an artist in her own right. Alison, I repeat here what I have told you a good few times: thank you.

I am grateful to Edwin Cameron for gracing this work with a Foreword. A more suitable honour would be hard to come by. Edwin and I, although in different contexts, are not strangers to childhood adversity. I adore how he brushed off that inhibiting upbringing and deservedly rose to our judicial summit. He openly bore the scourge of illness with both anguish and bravery, and in so doing, helped millions of others to regain their self-worth. He is blessed with an unmatchable intellect and even more with an abiding human solidarity – Ubuntu. I often call him my jurisprudential lover. Together we have won a few battles in the court. Ke a leboga Cameroooon!!!

Dikgang Moseneke
Tshwane
December 2019

APPENDIX

Farewell address

Chief Justice, former President Thabo Mbeki and Mrs Mbeki; former President Kgalema Motlanthe and Mrs Motlanthe, President and Deputy President of the Supreme Court of Appeal, Justices of the Constitutional Court – both currently sitting and retired, Judges President, Heads of Courts and Judges of all our courts, the Chairperson of the National Council of Provinces, Deputy Minister of Justice and Constitutional Development, leaders of political parties and of social movements, all formations within the legal fraternity, Deans of Law Schools, members of my family, and in particular my wife, Kabo Moseneke, and my mother, Karabo Moseneke. Allow me also to welcome all patriots, compatriots and citizens of our land and friends who have cared to come and observe this moment with us.

I will cease to hold office as a Deputy Chief Justice of the Republic and retire from the Constitutional Court of South Africa at midnight today, 20 May 2016.

I have had the distinct privilege of serving the judicial bench for fifteen years; of which no less than a continuous period of fourteen years I served in the Highest Court of the Republic.

A formal ceremony, such as the present, is by now well etched in our judicial convention. The Judiciary knows no better way of celebrating and sending off one of its own than in the very forum in which it dispenses justice. It is a time-honoured tradition that on an occasion like the present, fellow colleagues who hold judicial office would robe and so would counsel and be in attendance as a mark of homage to the departing Justice.

And that explains, in part, why this morning commenced with an actual court sitting in which I had the honour of delivering my last judgment ever in this Court. It is a symbolic way of a final salute or, if you want to change the imagery, it is a moment to discard one's judicial robes and gavel.

In a formal farewell, like the present, representatives of the Bar would appear in formal robes. I thank the representative of the General Council of the Bar, Adv Jeremy Muller SC and Adv Dumisa Ntsebeza SC from Advocates for Transformation, who delivered tributes on behalf of the advocates of our country. I am grateful to attorneys Mvuzo Notyesi, President of the National Association of Democratic Lawyers and co-chairperson of the Law Society of South Africa, and Lutendo Sigogo, President of the Black Lawyers Association, who are here to represent attorneys of the entire Republic. I am also grateful to receive Adv Andrew Chauke, Director of the National Prosecuting Authority, Gauteng Local Division.

In deep recognition that in our part of the constitutional arrangement the Judiciary is an arm of the State, a formal ceremony such as the present will be hardly complete without high representatives and leaders of our Legislative and Executive arms of the State. I am humbled and delighted by the tribute of Honourable Chairperson of the National Council of Provinces, Ms Thandi Modise MP – *re a leboga Mma*.

We are equally pleased to receive the Honourable Deputy Minister of Justice and Constitutional Development, Mr John Jeffery MP, representing the Executive arm of the State.

I am thankful and honoured by the presence of formations in the legal profession and these include the General Council of the Bar, Advocates for Transformation, the Law Society of South Africa, Black Lawyers Association and the National Association of Democratic Lawyers. I thank public interest law entities, which include the Aids Law Project, the South African Institute for Advanced Constitutional and Public Law, Human Rights and International Law, the Centre for Human Rights, the Legal Resources Centre and the National Movement of Rural Women.

I ask to make special mention of deans of Law Schools. Legal education for our young people and indeed for sitting judges and magistrates is my passion. I have found time throughout my term to lecture at law schools both at home and abroad. Equally, I thank leaders of Chapter 9 and other institutions which are charged with the protection and advancement of our constitutional democracy. These include the Human Rights Commission, the Public Protector and the Independent Electoral Commission. We have also in our midst many attorneys, advocates, social activists, members of the public who have kindly agreed to join us and grace this occasion. I am deeply appreciative.

I have talked a little about my life story last night at a dinner held by the Chief Justice in my honour. I will avoid doing so again. Mine is a long tale. I have written it up in a memoir. The tale meanders from the dusty streets of Atteridgeville through to my secondary tuition and my untimely residence on Robben Island. Then, I had no idea that my perilous experiences were to set me up for a life of remarkable fulfilment. The pain and adversity in my childhood prepared me for a life-long commitment to conduct that will bring true and full liberation of our land and all its remarkable people. The sojourn on Robben Island set me on a course of constantly asking: what are the features of a good society?

Out of all that emerged two cardinal lessons. First, you cannot merely dream about your revolutionary ideals. You have to take real and concrete steps to pursue legitimate ideals. The second lesson was that I was my own liberator. A line copied from the inimitable revolutionary thinkers like Anton Muziwakhe Lembede and Robert Mangaliso Sobukwe. They must in turn have copied it from Amílcar Cabral. These thinkers in essence were urging young people like me to pursue *inkululeko nge xesha lethu* – freedom in our lifetime.

This to me was the ultimate statement of personal and collective agency. We have to identify worthy causes which might change our lot and the world. Immediately thereafter we must ask the question that Lenin famously posed:

What is to be done? And then we must get up and do things. Things that will move us closer to our idealised collective condition.

So I knew when I came out of Robben Island that I had to make a choice either to go into exile or to remain a combatant in the domestic struggle. I chose to do things the way I know best. To become a lawyer of remarkable excellence, of unfailing integrity and of commitment to the broader struggle of our people in all their kinds, shapes and colours for an equal and just society.

To that end, I wanted to become an attorney even if I was a convicted terrorist. I did everything to achieve that. I litigated against the Law Society to let me in. I went on to the Bar Council which had a race clause that excluded black people. There too I kicked the door open. I was very determined to become a spokesperson for our people in difficult times in our troubled past.

I defended every activist you care to remember. I searched and found uMkhonto weSizwe cadres in solitary confinement. I saved a number of the Azanian People's Liberation Army combatants from further hangings. I have appeared in trials of Azanian National Liberation Army fighters. I had the privilege of defending Dr Fabian Ribeiro, Titus Mafolo, Smangaliso Mkhatshwa, Winnie Madikizela-Mandela, Jan Shoba, Clement Zulu, Achmad Cassiem, Nkosinathi Nhleko, Ingoapele Madingoane, Zwelakhe Sisulu, Thami Mazwai, Mathatha Tsedu, Ronnie Mamoepa, Don Nkadimeng and scores of other activists as well as numerous trade union formations.

I had the blessing of a vast, varied and progressive law practice that was well aligned with my personal and collective mantra that I was my own liberator and that our people are their own liberators.

Before I knew it, I was a senior counsel with only ten years of practice at the Bar after five years of practice as an attorney.

Before the democratic transition had gained traction I made a conscious choice not to be a politician but to remain a freedom fighter and a revolutionary. That I thought I could best achieve by resigning from all political formations and by concentrating on being a full-time legal practitioner. Aside from a little digression into business, I concentrated on becoming as good a lawyer and later a judge as I could be.

It was Arthur Chaskalson who pestered me to come to the bench. But even more emphatic was the President of the time, Mr Thabo Mbeki, who, in his characteristic way, said: 'Chief, you are one of the leaders of our people.' Utatu' Nelson Mandela was a little more blunt. I suspect he was set on me by the Chief Justice and the President of the Republic. He said: 'Dikgang, your people need you.' I relented and became a judge. Fifteen years later here am I, deeply thankful to all who urged me on to assume this onerous responsibility.

As my mother often says, *di tshegofatso tsa Modimo ga dina tekanyetso* – the blessings of the Lord know no limit. The first of the blessings was near-perfect health. This allowed me energy without end. In the fifteen years of service, I have never taken sick leave and the only time when I was away from work for a week was when my beloved son, Bo, succumbed. So that lifetime dedication of hard work I brought to my judicial obligations.

The second blessing was the love I have and continue to have for our people. They are entitled to live in a just and socially inclusive society where their dignity and self-worth are intact and well cherished. They must access quality education, universal health care, water and sanitation, a place that they can call home, an environment that is well preserved and, in all this, the space to simply be human. That explains why at my 60th birthday, I made the point and I make it again: it is not what the ruling party wants, it is not what any other political party wants, it is what is good for our people. That is what makes me wake up in the morning and be a good Justice of this Court as all my faculties permitted me.

What a privilege it was to serve you all and I am thankful for that. I had the space to work, to think and to write to my heart's content. I have had the pleasure of writing on virtually every big political, social and commercial dispute in our land. I have had the joy of going to law schools in this land and in other lands only to find extensive passages of what I have written taught to young lawyers at law schools. I have been blessed with remarkable colleagues who made judicial collegiality appear natural and inbred.

APPENDIX

As I end, going back to where I started, I am my own liberator. Our people are their own liberators. In the last instance, the people are the bedrock of our democracy. It is they who matter and we as institutions that wield public power, like courts, are in their service.

Lastly, let me turn to my family. None of my fascinating legal and judicial journey of 40 years would have been possible without my mother and father (May his soul rest in peace). And none of it would have been possible without my sibling brothers and sisters. In all of these travails I had the sheer warmth of a big robust family which was there throughout and it is here today and will be there towards my last days. That is the magic of a loving, cohesive and supportive family.

Chief Justice, it was a wonderful experience to work with you and I hope that I provided a joint and supportive leadership to our Judiciary. I said last night that despite our past uncomfortable encounter, we have found each other. We have made common cause on a principled and honest footing. We share the love for our people and their right to be well as it is our duty to serve them. I say without any fear of contradiction that your integrity is beyond question. Your fervour to defend and protect the gains of our hard-won struggle for liberation, freedom and democracy is unsurpassed. Each time there were storms that swelled around our institution, you stood firm. You never flinched from making unpopular decisions provided that they were consistent with your honest and rigorous judicial judgement. But sadly, much turbulence lies ahead. But that is what good pilots learn to live with. You are a safe pair of hands and I wish you well as I make my last salute.

I always understood that everybody exercising public power had to do so within the constraints of the law. I knew well that uncomfortable as it often was, Executive and Legislative and indeed corporate and business excesses had to be curbed. I truly hope that I was faithful to my oath of office. I pray that I kept its highest standards and tradition of judicial excellence.

To my remaining colleagues in this Court and all of our Judiciary, I urge you to remain on this hallowed bench not unaware of what a privilege it is. You must recognise that we are standing on the shoulders of giants. You must promise that you shall remain true and faithful to all that you have been, as a colleague. You must promise to defend fearlessly the independence of the Judiciary, the rule of law and the full realisation of the basic rights that our Constitution affords to each one of our people. You will be very much part of the transformation enterprise and the democratic project to make our country reflect the text and living spirit of our Constitution.

Fidelity to our oath of office is important, not because we are important but because without it, it is not us but our people who will suffer. By our people, I mean the full diversity, poor and rich, white and black, female and male, urban and rural, the marginalised and the powerful, all deserve our unwavering protection, which our Constitution demands of us to provide. After all, you are the ultimate guardians of our Constitution for and on behalf of our people.

May God bless Africa. May God bless her people. May God give us leaders the wisdom and the care that we need to deliver our people, and may all of us be granted the wisdom to know that each is his or her own liberator and may find the space to make a real difference. A space which my nation favoured me to have, love, cherish and use.

God bless.

Dikgang Moseneke
20 May 2016

Notes

EARLY CAREER

1 CHOOSING LAW

1 In Chapter 8 of *My Own Liberator*, I explain in some detail my hearing that took place in the Old Synagogue. It was the site of several high-profile political trials, chief among them the infamous Treason Trial, where leaders of the Congress Alliance, including Nelson Mandela, were arrested and tried for high treason. All the accused were acquitted in 1961. The inquest, in 1977, into the death of Steve Biko also took place there.

2 *Messages of Imam Sultan Muhammad Shah: Message No 1*, by Shia Imami Ismailia Association for Africa, 1955.

3 Scholars included Hugo Grotius, Johannes Voet and Dionysius Godefridus van der Keessel.

4 Jan van Riebeeck, a Dutch official, first landed at the Cape in 1652, marking the beginning of European colonialism in South Africa. English settlers arrived in the early 1800s. Clashes between the Dutch and the English ensued and continued until 1902 when a peace agreement was arrived at, followed by the formation of the Union of South Africa in 1910.

2 THE RIGHT TO ROBE

1 *Ex Parte Moseneke* 1979 (4) SA 884 (T).

2 *Case and Another v Minister of Safety and Security and Others*; *Curtis v Minister of Safety and Security and Others* [1996] ZACC 7; 1996 (3) SA 617 (CC); 1996 (5) BCLR 608 (CC); *Midrand / Rabie Ridge / Ivory Park Metropolitan Substructure v Mofokeng NO and Another* 1996 (1) SA 375 (T); *Hintsho and Another v Minister of Public Service and Administration and Others* 1996 (2) 828 (TkS); *Bogoshi v National Media Ltd and Others* 1996 (3) SA 78

NOTES: CHAPTER 2

(W); *Berco Sameday Express v McNeil and Others* [1996] 4 All SA (W); *Bogoshi v Van Vuuren NO and Others; Bogoshi and Another v Director, Office for Serious Economic Offences, and Others* [1995] ZASCA 125; 1996 (1) SA 785 (SCA); *Lifestyle Amusement Centre (Pty) Ltd and Others v The Minister of Justice and Others* 1995 (1) BCLR 104 (C); *Rainbow Farms (Pty) Ltd v FAWU and Others* [1995] 1 BLLR 87 (IC); *Tseane v Get Ahead Foundation* (1995) 16 ILJ 202 (IC); *Phathela v Chairman, Disciplinary Committee, SA Medical and Dental Council* 1995 (3) SA 179 (T); *Chief Pilane v Chief Linchwe and Another* 1995 (4) SA 686 (B); *Bogoshi v Van Vuuren NO and Others; Bogoshi and Another v Director, Office for Serious Economic Offences, and Others* 1993 (2) SACR 98 (T); *S v Theledi* 1992 (1) SACR 336 (T); *Deneys Reitz v South African Commercial, Catering and Allied Workers Union and Others* 1991 (2) SA 685 (W); *S v Tshoba en Andere* 1989 (3) SA 393 (AD); [1989] 4 All SA 667 (AD); *Majele v Guardian National Insurance Co Ltd* 1986 (4) SA 326 (T); *Mokoele v National Employers' General Insurance Co Ltd and Another* 1984 (1) SA 27 (T); *Karstein v Moribe and Others* 1982 (2) SA 282 (T); *S v Mathope and Others* 1982 (3) SA 296 (B); *Maluleke v Minister of Internal Affairs* 1981 (1) SA 707 (B).

3 The Southern African Catholic Bishops' Conference is an organisation that was created in 1947 to 'foster the spirit of communion within the universal Church and between the particular churches'. In the 1970s the conference began participating actively in various forms of Christian protest, spearheaded by the South African Council of Churches and the Christian Institute. Since 1990, it has focused its attention on issues relating to conflict resolution, education, democracy and development. The conference is currently based in Waterkloof, Tshwane.

4 The South African Council of Churches is an interdenominational forum of churches and organisations that was founded in 1968 to promote and advance justice, skills development and community projects, and theological reflection. The council strongly condemned the injustices and human rights violations under apartheid. It also provided practical assistance to those oppressed under the regime by offering emergency services to victims, caring for the families of those unjustly detained, campaigning for international sanctions, raising funds for legal services for apartheid victims and funding community development programmes, among other things. The Council continues its work today on issues of justice, reconciliation, poverty and the empowerment of marginalised people. Its offices are in Johannesburg.

5 The International Defence and Aid Fund was established in 1956 by Canon L John Collins of St Paul's Cathedral in London primarily in response to the Treason Trial, where 156 leaders of the Congress Alliance were arrested and charged with high treason. Its core mission was to raise and distribute funds for legal assistance in the political trials of anti-apartheid activists and to financially support the families and dependants of political prisoners. The Fund was dissolved once apartheid ended, but not before it formally handed over its resources to organisations based in South Africa.

6 Carruthers and Co was a firm of solicitors in London that often acted as an intermediary for funds flowing from individuals in the United Kingdom to anti-apartheid attorneys in South Africa.

NOTES: CHAPTER 2

7 The Southern Africa Project of the Lawyers' Committee for Civil Rights under Law was founded in 1967 to provide financial and legal assistance to political prisoners and anti-apartheid lawyers in South Africa and Namibia. Apart from its funding activities in South Africa, the project drew considerable international attention to the injustices suffered under apartheid by initiating various campaigns, publishing research reports and raising concerns within the United States in attempts to influence US foreign policy. It was headed by Gay J McDougall from 1980 to 1994. After the inauguration of Nelson Mandela as president of South Africa, the project closed its doors in August 1994.

8 Ismail Mahomed SC was the first person of colour to take silk in South Africa and the first black person to receive a permanent appointment to the Supreme Court. His 35 years as an admitted advocate saw him practising in various countries, including England and neighbouring Lesotho, Botswana, Swaziland and Zimbabwe. In South Africa, his practice focused on civil rights. He represented several anti-apartheid activists in political trials and continually challenged decisions made by the apartheid state. After co-chairing the Convention for a Democratic South Africa (CODESA), the multi-party negotiations to achieve South Africa's democracy, Ismail Mahomed was appointed a judge in the Constitutional Court in 1994. He became the deputy president of the court in 1995 and, a year later, its chief justice – a position in which he served until his death in 2000. Recognised for his contribution to human rights advocacy and jurisprudence, Justice Mahomed received numerous awards and honorary doctorates in his lifetime. An annual academic competition encouraging critical legal writing of law reform by law students is named in honour of him.

9 Philemon Pearce Dumasile Nokwe, known as Duma Nokwe, was a teacher before he obtained a law degree and later became the first black advocate of the Supreme Court of the Transvaal. He was a staunch political activist and member of the ANC, leading to his arrest, together with 155 others, in what became known as the Treason Trial. During the trial, a state of emergency was declared that compromised the ability of their legal team to perform their duties. Duma and Nelson Mandela temporarily took the baton and served as members of the legal defence team as well as accused in the trial. He was elected secretary-general of the African National Congress in 1958 and subsequently hounded by the security police until he fled into exile in 1963. He became the ANC's director of international affairs in Lusaka, Zambia, and a well-known figure at international meetings, urging foreign states and international organisations to act against the South African apartheid state.

10 Thembile Lewis Skweyiya SC practised as an advocate for 25 years. He was called upon to occupy a permanent position as a judge of the high court in KwaZulu-Natal in 2001 and appointed to the Constitutional Court in 2004. After ten years of service at the court, he retired in 2014.

11 Zakeria Mohammed Yacoob SC was admitted as an advocate in 1973 and took silk in 1991. He was appointed to the Constitutional Court in 1998, serving as a justice for fifteen years.

NOTES: CHAPTERS 3 AND 4

3 DETOUR TO THE BENCH

1 Tholakele 'Tholi' Hope Madala first qualified as a teacher from the University of Fort Hare in the Eastern Cape before graduating in law, becoming a lecturer at the University of Transkei and later moving on to practise as an attorney. In 1982 he was admitted as an advocate, with a practice and legal career characterised by a pursuit of human rights and access to justice for all. Shortly after taking silk in 1993, Tholi Madala became the first black judge in the Eastern Cape when he was appointed to the high court bench in 1994. Later that year, he was appointed by President Nelson Mandela to serve as a judge of the Constitutional Court. He served on the court's bench for fourteen years, retiring in 2008.

2 Judge Frederik 'Frikkie' Eloff was judge president of the Transvaal provincial division from 1991 to 1998, when he retired. He was born and lived in Pretoria for most of his life, apart from a stint in a boarding school in England. After serving his articles, in 1947 Judge Eloff was called to the Pretoria Bar, where his practice, spanning 25 years, focused mainly on commercial litigation. He received silk status in 1965 before being elevated to the bench in 1973. He was appointed Deputy Judge President of his division in 1985 before taking the reins as judge president.

3 Stephanus Johannes Paulus Kruger, known as Paul Kruger, was elected president of the Transvaal Republic, formerly known as the Zuid-Afrikaansche Republiek, in 1883. He negotiated independence from Britain in 1884 at the London Convention. He served as president for four terms, with his last re-election in 1898, shortly before the Tweede Vryheidsoorlog.

4 Arthur Chaskalson was appointed by President Nelson Mandela in June 1994 as the Constitutional Court's inaugural president. He was later appointed as the court's second chief justice from 2001 until his retirement in 2005.

5 *Moseneke and Others v Master of the High Court* [2000] ZACC 27; 2001 (2) BCLR 103 (CC); 2001 (2) SA 18 (CC).

6 Adv Mojanku Gumbi was the legal adviser to President Thabo Mbeki from 1999 to 2008.

4 A PERMANENT APPOINTMENT

1 Sections 174 and 178 of the Constitution outline the requirements for permanent judicial appointment. The Judicial Service Commission Act 9 of 1994 states that, once appointed, a judge may not hold or perform any other office of profit and must disclose all registrable interests.

2 The Judicial Service Commission is established in terms of section 178 of the Constitution. Its primary functions are to advise national government on issues relating to the judiciary or the administration of justice, to interview prospective judges in order to make a recommendation of appointment to the president, and to manage complaints against judges. Its composition and processes are further regulated in the Judicial Service Commission Act 9 of 1994.

3 Section 174(3) of the Constitution.

NOTES: CHAPTERS 4 TO 6

4 The Black Lawyers Association, formerly known as the Black Lawyers Discussion Group, was established in 1977 in response to actions taken by the apartheid state against black lawyers, including a decision to prohibit them from practising in white areas without a Group Areas permit. The group fought against these unjust and discriminatory practices which prevented black lawyers from practising their profession. The present-day Black Lawyers Association serves as a voluntary association open to all lawyers in South Africa, regardless of race, sex, political belief, religion, area of practice or type of practice, and strives to promote transformation in the legal profession.

5 A FORMIDABLE WORKLOAD

1 The oath of judicial officers is found in Schedule 2 of the Constitution.
2 *S v Makwanyane and Another* [1995] ZACC 3; 1995 (6) BCLR 665 (CC); 1995 (3) SA 391 (CC) is the landmark judgment by the Constitutional Court, handed down in 1995, declaring the death penalty inconsistent with the newly established constitutional order.
3 The Judicial Conduct Committee of the JSC is established by section 8 of the Judicial Service Commission Act to receive, consider and deal with complaints against judges. The committee is made up of the chief justice, the deputy chief justice and four other judges.
4 Magistrates' courts are divided into regional and district courts, and ordinarily deal with less serious criminal and civil cases than those cases brought before higher courts.
5 Section 302 of the Criminal Procedure Act 51 of 1977.
6 *S v Ndou* JDR 0884 (T); *S v Mokoena* 2003 (1) SACR 74 (T); *Nxumalo v First Link Insurance Brokers (Pty) Ltd* 2003 (2) SA 620 (T); *S v Mofokeng* 2003 JDR 0073 (T); *Kyle and Others v Maritz & Pieterse Incorporated* 2002 JDR 0401 (T); *Harris v Absa Bank Ltd t/a Volkskas* 2006 (4) SA 527 (T); *Northern Province Development Corporation v Attorney Fidelity Fund Board of Control* 2003 (2) SA 284 (T); *O'Hagan's Franchising (Pty) Ltd v Mathu Restaurant Nelspruit CC and Others* 2002 JDR 0166 (T); *Schoonbee & Others v MEC for Education, Mpumalanga & Another* (2002) 23 ILJ 1359 (T); *S v Congola* 2002 (2) SACR 383 (T); *Mkatshwa v Mkatshwa and Another* 2002 (3) SA 441 (T); *Chesterfin (Pty) Ltd v Contract Forwarding (Pty) Ltd and Others* 2001 JDR 0594 (T); and *S v Nel* 2002 (1) SACR 425 (T).

6 FREE AND FAIR

1 The acronym AU brings to mind the EU – the European Union – a political and economic union of 27 member states located primarily in Europe. It was formally established by the Maastricht Treaty on 1 November 1993, just under six years before the resolution to form the AU was adopted.
2 The African Charter on Human and Peoples' Rights, also known as the Banjul Charter, was adopted by the OAU Assembly in June 1981 and came into force in 1986. Apart from

it being Africa's leading human rights instrument, the African Charter also established the African Commission on Human and Peoples' Rights to interpret the Charter. Other important human rights instruments adopted by the AU or its predecessor include the African Charter on the Rights and Welfare of the Child, 1990; the Protocol to the African Charter on Human and Peoples' Rights on the Rights of Women in Africa, 2003; the African Charter on Democracy, Elections and Governance, 2011; and the Protocol to the African Charter on Human and Peoples' Rights on the Rights of Persons with Disabilities in Africa, 2018.

3 The Sirte Extraordinary Session (1999) decided to establish an African Union, the Lomé summit (2000) adopted the Constitutive Act of the Union, the Lusaka summit (2001) drew the roadmap for the implementation of the AU, and the Durban summit (2002) launched the AU and convened its first Assembly of the heads of states.

4 The 37th Summit of the Organisation of African Unity in July 2001 formally adopted the strategic framework document and the African Union ratified it at its first summit in 2002.

5 The Electoral Supervisory Commission was mandated by the Zimbabwean Constitution to oversee the registration of voters and the conduct of elections. It was subsequently abolished in 2005 and its functions were transferred to the Zimbabwe Electoral Commission.

6 *M & G Media Ltd and Another v President of the Republic of South Africa and Others* [2010] ZAGPPHC 43.

7 *The President of the Republic of South Africa and Others v M & G Media Ltd* [2010] ZASCA 177; 2011 (2) SA 1 (SCA).

8 *President of the Republic of South Africa and Others v M & G Media Ltd* [2011] ZACC 32; 2012 (2) BCLR 181 (CC); 2012 (2) SA 50 (CC).

7 CONSTITUTIONAL COURT: GENESIS AND NOMINATION

1 See a discussion of the cases that we argued together in *My Own Liberator*.

CHASKALSON COURT

8 WHO WILL GUARD THE GUARDIANS?

1 The Convention for a Democratic South Arica (CODESA) was a multi-party negotiation forum established in 1991 to negotiate an end to apartheid and forge a new path for South African democracy. The primary task at the convention was ensuring a peaceful transition to democracy by negotiating the principles of a new constitution, the composition of an interim government to manage the transition, the future of the homelands, and the structure of a new electoral system.

2 See Chapter 1.

NOTES: CHAPTERS 8 AND 9

3 The Constitution Seventeenth Amendment Act 72 of 2012 amended section 167(3) of the Constitution, extending the Constitutional Court's jurisdiction to include any matters that raise an arguable point of law of general public importance which ought to be considered by the court, with its leave or permission.

4 Magisterial districts were aligned to apartheid-era territories, even post-1994. This made it difficult for ordinary citizens to access justice as they often had to travel far distances to reach the district court that had jurisdiction to hear their matter. The Department of Justice and Constitutional Development, in 2014, recognised the need to redress the spatial imbalances created by old-order jurisdictions. It embarked on a process of rationalising the magisterial districts and realigning them to population settlement trends since democracy. The process, which has been undertaken gradually and is still ongoing, will improve spatial justice and ensure easier access to courts.

5 Regional magistrates' courts, on the one hand, have criminal jurisdiction over serious crimes, including murder, rape, armed robbery and serious assault. Sentencing in regional courts may include life imprisonment for serious offences like rape or murder. The court may also impose a fine not exceeding R300 000. Regional courts now also have civil jurisdiction over divorce matters. District courts, on the other hand, only have jurisdiction over less serious crimes. They may not hear matters involving murder, rape or treason, for example. The maximum sentence a district court may impose is three years' imprisonment or a fine not exceeding R100 000. District courts also have jurisdiction over civil matters where the claim does not exceed R100 000.

6 These new courts include the Limpopo division of the high court, Polokwane, and the Mpumalanga division of the high court, Mbombela. This means that all nine provinces now have a high court.

7 Other local divisions are found in Bhisho, Mthatha and Port Elizabeth in the Eastern Cape.

8 Specialised courts have the same status as a high court and include the Labour Court, the Land Claims Court, the Competition Tribunal and the Electoral Court.

9 The creation of the Union of South Africa in 1910 brought together the British colonies of the Cape, Natal, Transvaal and the Free State. One of the major political issues during negotiations toward a union was that of its new capital. A compromise was eventually reached, with Pretoria (now Tshwane) holding the executive seat, Cape Town embracing the legislative seat and Bloemfontein (now Mangaung) becoming the judicial capital of South Africa.

9 THE CLASS OF '95

1 From August 1994 to September 1996, Justice Richard Goldstone's service to the Constitutional Court was held in abeyance while he served as chief prosecutor of the UN International Criminal Tribunals for the former Yugoslavia and Rwanda. In his absence, Sydney Kentridge QC was appointed to serve as an acting judge and penned the court's

first judgment – *S v Zuma and Others* [1995] ZACC 1; 1995 (2) SA 642 (CC); 1995 (1) SACR 568 (CC).

2 Section 176 of the Constitution was amended in 2001 to extend the term of office of a Constitutional Court judge from seven years to twelve years or until the judged turned 70, whichever came first. Section 4(1) of the Judges' Remuneration and Conditions of Employment Act 47 of 2001 further states that a Constitutional Court judge whose twelve-year term of office expires before they have completed fifteen years of active service must extend their stay at the court until a full fifteen years as a judge have been served.

3 In *S v Makwanyane and Another* [1995] ZACC 3; 1995 (6) BCLR 665 (CC); 1995 (3) SA 391 (CC), the Constitutional Court considered the death penalty as a punishment in light of the newly established constitutional values and held that the death penalty constituted cruel, inhuman and degrading punishment, which is prohibited by the Constitution. It held that capital punishment was not justifiable as a penalty in an open and democratic society based on freedom and equality. On the question of public opinion, the court held firmly that 'the issue of the constitutionality of capital punishment cannot be referred to a referendum, in which a majority view would prevail over the wishes of any minority. The very reason for establishing the new legal order, and for vesting the power of judicial review of all legislation in the courts, was to protect the rights of minorities and others who cannot protect their rights adequately through the democratic process.'

4 The appointment meant that Justice Ismail Mahomed was South Africa's first black chief justice.

5 *Case and Another v Minister of Safety and Security and Others; Curtis v Minister of Safety and Security and Others* [1996] ZACC 7; 1996 (3) SA 617 (CC); 1996 (5) BCLR 608 (CC).

6 Moseneke D.E. 'Personal tribute to former Chief Justice Pius Langa' (2015) *Acta Juridica* (1) pp 3–9.

7 Mount Grace was a conference venue in the Magaliesberg in Gauteng province. The conferences were organised by the Centre for Applied Legal Studies of the University of the Witwatersrand, Johannesburg.

10 REPORTING FOR DUTY

1 '*'n Sak sout met iemand opeet*' is an Afrikaans idiom, which means that one has gained so much experience with someone that you get to know one another very well.

2 'Here's your toga, little brother. It might be a bit short for you.'

3 The Great African Steps form a walkway between the Constitutional Court and the old stone wall of the Number Four prison, symbolising a path between the hurtful past and a hopeful future.

4 Speaking at an official handover of $1 million by Robert Mugabe to the African Union Foundation, the former president of Zimbabwe called on all Africans to work together to build their continent 'brick by brick, stone by stone'.

NOTES: CHAPTERS 10 TO 12

5 At present, 21 March is a holiday in South Africa known as Human Rights Day. Historically the day was observed as Sharpeville Day. It was declared a public holiday in remembrance of the Sharpeville massacre of 1960 in which 69 unarmed black protestors were shot dead by policemen, and 180 others seriously wounded, in non-violent protests led by the Pan-Africanist Congress against apartheid's pass laws.

11 NEW WAYS OF DOING THINGS

1 Prafullachandra Natwarlal Bhagwati served as India's seventeenth chief justice from 12 July 1985 until his retirement on 20 December 1986. While he made many contributions to law in India, he is best known for pioneering public interest litigation in the 1980s. He died aged 95 in 2017.

12 A CLEAN SLATE

1 Statement of the president of the African National Congress, Nelson Mandela, at his inauguration as president of the democratic Republic of South Africa, Union Buildings, Pretoria, 10 May 1994.

2 The United Nations estimates that 800 000 people were slaughtered during 100 days of the Rwandan genocide, while some commentators estimate the death toll to be higher.

3 Thembisile Chris Hani was the former chief of staff of Umkhonto weSizwe (MK), the military wing of the African National Congress. He was also leader of the South African Communist Party (SACP) at the time of his assassination in 1993.

4 Between 1960 and 1989, the apartheid government enforced the death penalty against 134 political prisoners who were hanged for politically motivated murders and acts of sabotage or treason. Of these, 101 were put to death in the 1960s. Poqo, the military wing of the Pan Africanist Congress, suffered the greatest loss at the gallows, with at least 66 of its members being hanged by the apartheid state in the 1960s alone. In 2016, the government initiated the Gallows Exhumation Project to exhume the remains of the political prisoners from unmarked graves and hand them over to their families for reburial.

5 The Technical Committee on Constitutional Issues was chaired by Prof François Venter and comprised Adv Arthur Chaskalson, Adv Dikgang Moseneke, Adv Bernard Ngoepe, Prof George Devenish, Prof Marinus Wiechers, Prof Firoz Cachalia, Prof Michèle Olivier and Prof Willem Olivier.

6 Section 98(2) of the Constitution of the Republic of South Africa Act 200 of 1993 (interim Constitution).

7 Section 100 of the interim Constitution.

8 Section 102 of the interim Constitution.

9 *S v Mhlungu and Others* [1995] ZACC 4; 1995 (3) SA 867 (CC); 1995 (7) BCLR 793 (CC).

10 *S v Mhlungu* at para 59.

NOTES: CHAPTER 12

11 *S v Bequinot* [1996] ZACC 21; 1997 (2) SA 887 (CC); 1996 (12) BCLR 1588 (CC); *Du Plessis and Others v De Klerk and Another* [1996] ZACC 10; 1996 (3) SA 850; 1996 (5) BCLR 658 (CC); *Zantsi v Council of State, Ciskei and Others* [1995] ZACC 9; 1995 (4) SA 615 (CC); 1995 (10) BCLR 1424 (CC); and *S v Vermaas, S v Du Plessis* [1995] ZACC 5; 1995 (3) SA 292 (CC); 1995 (7) BCLR 851 (CC).

12 *S v Makwanyane and Another* [1995] ZACC 3; 1995 (3) SA 391 (CC); 1995 (6) BCLR 665 (CC).

13 *S v Makwanyane* at para 5.

14 *S v Makwanyane* at para 151.

15 Criminal Law Amendment Act 105 of 1997.

16 In giving content to the limitation of rights in section 33 of the interim Constitution, the *Makwanyane* judgment introduced the concept of proportionality as implicit in assessing a limitation to a right. It called for a 'balancing of different interests', which included taking into account relevant considerations which were not explicitly found in the constitutional text. These considerations were later expressly incorporated in the limitation clause of the final Constitution (section 36).

17 The Constitution of the Republic of South Africa, 1996 was adopted by the Constitutional Assembly on 8 May 1996 and forwarded to the Constitutional Court for certification. After sending it back to the Constitutional Assembly for revision, which was finalised by 11 October 1996, the Constitutional Court certified the final text on 4 December 1996. It was signed into law by President Nelson Mandela on 10 December 1996 in Sharpeville, promulgated on 18 December 1996 and became effective from 4 February 1997.

18 *S v Zuma and Others* [1995] ZACC 1; 1995 (2) SA 624 (CC); 1995 (4) BCLR 401 (CC) at para 16.

19 *S v Zuma and Others* above.

20 *S v Williams and Others* [1995] ZACC 6; 1995 (3) SA 632 (CC); 1995 (7) BCLR 861 (CC).

21 *S v Vermaas; S v Du Plessis* [1995] ZACC 5; 1995 (3) SA 292 (CC); 1995 (7) BCLR 851 (CC).

22 *Coetzee v Government of the Republic of South Africa; Matiso and Others v Commanding Officer Port Elizabeth Prison and Others* [1995] ZACC 7; 1995 (4) SA 631 (CC); 1995 (10) BCLR 1382 (CC).

23 *Shabalala and Others v Attorney-General of the Transvaal and Another* [1995] ZACC 12; 1996 (1) SA 725 (CC); 1995 (12) BCLR 1593 (CC).

24 *S v Ntuli* [1995] ZACC 14; 1996 (1) SA 1207 (CC); 1996 (1) BCLR 141 (CC).

25 *S v Mello* [1998] ZACC 7; 1998 (3) SA 712 (CC); 1998 (7) BCLR 908 (CC); and *S v Van Nell and Another* [1998] ZACC 8; 1998 (8) BCLR 943 (CC).

26 *S v Dlamini, S v Dladla and Others; S v Joubert; S v Schietekat* [1999] ZACC 8; 1999 (4) SA 623 (CC); 1999 (7) BCLR 771 (CC).

27 *Molaudzi v S* [2015] ZACC 20; 2015 (8) BCLR 904 (CC); 2015 (2) SACR 341 (CC).

28 *Molaudzi v S* [2014] ZACC 15; 2014 (7) BCLR 785 (CC). While the court dismissed Mr Molaudzi's application for leave to appeal, it wrote a short judgment lamenting the

unacceptable delay in his appeal. Mr Molaudzi was sentenced on 22 July 2004 but his appeal to a full bench of the high court was only heard more than eight years later, on 7 December 2012.

29 In *Mhlongo v S; Nkosi v S* [2015] ZACC 19; 2015 (2) SACR 323 (CC); 2015 (8) BCLR 887 (CC), the Constitutional Court was asked by two of Mr Molaudzi's co-accused to determine the constitutional validity of extra-curial statements of an accused in a criminal trial. They claimed that the common law position that rendered extra-curial admissions, but not confessions, by an accused against a co-accused admissible violated their right to equality. The court held that the different treatment of extra-curial admissions and confessions creates a differentiation that unjustifiably limits the right to equal protection and benefit of the law in terms of section 9(1) of the Constitution. The court ordered the immediate release of the applicants after they had served more than a decade in prison.

13 JUDICIAL ARCHITECTURE REFORMED

1 Section 71 of the interim Constitution ensured that the final constitutional text would not be of any force or effect unless the Constitutional Court certified that all its provisions complied with the 34 constitutional principles set out in Schedule 4 of the interim Constitution. Once it was certified, no court would have the authority to enquire into the validity of the text or provision.

2 *Certification of the Constitution of the Republic of South Africa, 1996* [1996] ZACC 26; 1996 (4) SA 744 (CC); 1996 (10) BCLR 1253 (CC) and *Certification of the Amended Text of the Constitution of the Republic of South Africa, 1996* [1996] ZACC 24; 1997 (2) SA 97 (CC); 1997 (1) BCLR 1 (CC).

3 *S v Makwanyane and Another* [1995] ZACC 3; 1995 (3) SA 391 (CC); 1995 (6) BCLR 665 (CC).

4 Chapter 8 of the Constitution

5 *Pharmaceutical Manufacturers Association of South Africa and Another: In re Ex Parte President of the Republic of South Africa and Others* [2000] ZACC 1; 2000 (2) SA 674 (CC); 2000 (3) BCLR 241 (CC) at para 44.

6 The constitution of the Western Cape was duly adopted by a two-thirds majority in the provincial legislature and certified by the Constitutional Court on 18 November 1997 in *Certification of the Amended Text of the Constitution of the Western Cape, 1997* [1997] ZACC 15; 1998 (1) SA 655 (CC); 1997 (12) BCLR 1653 (CC). It was assented to on 15 January 1998. While the KwaZulu-Natal legislature adopted its provincial constitution on 15 March 1996, the Constitutional Court refused to certify it. The province has not yet brought an amended text before the court to certify.

7 *Premier of KwaZulu-Natal and Others v President of the Republic of South Africa and Others* [1995] ZACC 10; 1996 (1) SA 769 (CC); 1995 (12) BCLR 1561 (CC). The province also contested amendments to the interim Constitution relating to traditional authorities and local government.

NOTES: CHAPTER 13

8 *Certification of the Kwazulu-Natal Constitution* [1996] ZACC 17; 1996 (4) SA 1098 (CC); 1996 (11) BCLR 1419 (CC).
9 In terms of section 160(4) of the interim Constitution, the Constitutional Court could only certify the provisions of a province's constitutional text if it was satisfied that none of its provisions was inconsistent with the interim Constitution or the constitutional principles in schedule 4, subject to a few permissible deviations.
10 *United Democratic Movement v President of the Republic of South Africa and Others (African Christian Democratic Party and Others Intervening; Institute for Democracy in South Africa and Another as Amici Curiae) (No 2)* [2002] ZACC 21; 2003 (1) SA 495 (CC); 2002 (11) BCLR 1179 (CC).
11 The Western Cape initiated the process to adopt a provincial constitution after the national Constitution was adopted in 1996. While the court is still required to certify the text, the standard against which it must comply is slightly different from what was stipulated in the interim Constitution. Section 142 of the Constitution empowers provincial legislatures to adopt a constitutional text and submit it to the court for certification. The court must ensure that the provincial text is not inconsistent with the Constitution, subject to a few permissible deviations, that it complies with the founding values entrenched in section 1 of the Constitution and the constitutional provisions of co-operative governance, and that it does not confer on the province any powers or functions that fall outside those conferred on it by the Constitution.
12 *Certification of the Constitution of the Western Cape, 1997* [1997] ZACC 8; 1997 (4) SA 795 (CC); 1997 (9) BCLR 1167 (CC) at paras 42-51. The court, in refusing to certify the Western Cape constitution, also took issue with provisions relating to the administration of oaths of office and cabinet ministers undertaking 'paid work'. The Western Cape's amended constitutional text was subsequently certified by the court.
13 *Western Cape Provincial Government and Others: In re DVB Behuising (Pty) Limited v North West Provincial Government and Another* [2000] ZACC 2; 2001 (1) SA 500 (CC); 2000 (4) BCLR 347 (CC).
14 *Ex Parte President of the Republic of South Africa: In re Constitutionality of the Liquor Bill* [1999] ZACC 15; 2000 (1) SA 732 (CC); 2000 (1) BCLR 1 (CC).
15 Schedule 5 of the Constitution provides the functional areas of exclusive provincial legislative competence.
16 *Ex Parte President of the Republic of South Africa: In re Constitutionality of the Liquor Bill* [1999] ZACC 15; 2000 (1) SA 732 (CC); 2000 (1) BCLR 1 (CC) at para 73.
17 Chapter 3, particularly section 41(3), of the Constitution.
18 *President of the Republic of South Africa and Another v Hugo* [1997] ZACC 4; 1997 (4) SA 1 (CC); 1997 (6) BCLR 708 (CC).
19 *Executive Council of the Western Cape Legislature and Others v President of the Republic of South Africa and Others* [1995] ZACC 8; 1995 (4) SA 877 (CC); 1995 (10) BCLR 1289 (CC).
20 Section 42(3) of the Constitution stipulates that the National Assembly is elected to

NOTES: CHAPTER 13

represent the people and to ensure government by the people by selecting the president, providing a national forum for public consideration of issues, passing legislation and scrutinising and overseeing executive action. The Constitution also affords the National Assembly the necessary law-making powers, in terms of section 55, and further enjoins it to provide mechanisms to ensure executive accountability and oversight.

21 Reported in *SARFU and Others v President of the RSA and Others* 1998 (10) BCLR 1256 (T).
22 *President of the Republic of South Africa and Others v South African Rugby Football Union and Others* [1999] ZACC 11; 2000 (1) SA 1 (CC); 1999 (10) BCLR 1059 (CC) at para 245.
23 Promotion of National Unity and Reconciliation Act 34 of 1995 ('the Act').
24 Section 20(7) of the Act.
25 *Azanian People's Organisation (AZAPO) and Others v President of the Republic of South Africa and Others* [1996] ZACC 16; 1996 (4) SA 672 (CC); 1996 (8) BCLR 1015 (CC) (*Azanian People's Organisation*).
26 *Azanian People's Organisation* at paras 8-9.
27 *Azanian People's Organisation* at para 50.
28 *Business Day*, 20 June 2019, accessed at https://www.businesslive.co.za/bd/national/2019-06-19-apartheid-victims-families-want-closure-from-cyril-ramaphosa/.
29 *Du Toit and Another v Minister of Welfare and Population Development and Others* [2002] ZACC 20; 2003 (2) SA 198 (CC); 2002 (10) BCLR 1006 (CC); *Ex Parte Minister of Safety and Security and Others: In re S v Walters and Another* [2002] ZACC 6; 2002 (4) SA 613 (CC); 2002 (7) BCLR 663 (CC); *Moise v Greater Germiston Transitional Local Council* [2001] ZACC 21; 2001 (4) SA 491 (CC); 2001 (8) BCLR 765 (CC); *Potgieter v Lid van die Uitvoerende Raad: Gesondheid Provinsiale Regering Gauteng en Andere* [2001] ZACC 4; 2001 (11) BCLR (CC); *Moseneke and Others v Master of the High Court* [2000] ZACC 27; 2000 (2) SA 18 (CC); 2001 (2) BCLR 103 (CC); *Dawood and Another v Minister of Home Affairs and Others; Shalabi and Another v Minister of Home Affairs and Others; Thomas and Another v Minister of Home Affairs and Others* [2000] ZACC 8; 2000 (3) SA 936 (CC); 2000 (8) BCLR 837 (CC); *S v Manamela and Another (Director-General of Justice Intervening)* [2000] ZACC 5; 2000 (3) SA 1 (CC); 2000 (5) BCLR 491 (CC); *Lesapo v North West Agricultural Bank and Another* [1999] ZACC 16; 2000 (1) SA 409 (CC); 1999 (12) BCLR 1420 (CC); *Mistry v Interim National Medical and Dental Council and Others* [1998] ZACC 10; 1998 (4) SA 1127 (CC); 1998 (7) BCLR 880 (CC); *De Lange v Smuts NO and Others* [1998] ZACC 6; 1998 (3) SA 785 (CC); 1998 (7) BCLR 779 (CC); *Larbi-Odam and Others v Member of the Executive Council for Education (North-West Province) and Another* [1997] ZACC 16; 1998 (1) SA 745 (CC); 1997 (12) BCLR 1655 (CC); *S v Coetzee and Others* [1997] ZACC 2; 1997 (3) SA 527 (CC); 1997 (4) BCLR 437 (CC); *Fraser v Children's Court Pretoria North and Others* [1997] ZACC 1; 1997 (2) SA 261 (CC); 1997 (2) BCLR 153 (CC); *Scagell and Others v Attorney-General, Western Cape and Others* [1996] ZACC 18; 1997 (2) SA 368 (CC); 1996 (11) BCLR 1446 (CC); *Ynuico Ltd v Minister of Trade and Industry and Others* [1996] ZACC 12; 1996 (3) SA 989 (CC); 1996 (6) BCLR 798

NOTES: CHAPTER 13

(CC); *S v Ntuli* [1995] ZACC 14; 1996 (1) SA 1207 (CC); 1996 (1) BCLR 141 (CC); *Ferreira v Levin NO and Others; Vryenhoek and Others v Powell NO and Others* [1995] ZACC 13; 1996 (1) SA 984 (CC); 1996 (1) BCLR 1 (CC); *S v Bhulwana, S v Gwadiso* [1995] ZACC 11; 1996 (1) SA 388 (CC); 1995 (12) BCLR 1579 (CC); *Coetzee v Government of the Republic of South Africa, Matiso and Others v Commanding Officer Port Elizabeth Prison and Others* [1995] ZACC 7; 1995 (4) SA 631 CC); 1995 (10) BCLR 1382 (CC); and *S v Williams and Others* [1995] ZACC 6; 1995 (3) SA 632 (CC); 1995 (7) BCLR 861 (CC).

30 *S v Jordan and Others (Sex Workers Education and Advocacy Task Force and Others as Amici Curiae)* [2002] ZACC 22; 2002 (6) SA 642 (CC); 2002 (11) BCLR 1117 (CC); *Satchwell v President of Republic of South Africa and Another* [2002] ZACC 18; 2002 (6) SA 1 (CC); 2002 (9) BCLR 986 (CC); *Moseneke and Others v Master of the High Court* [2000] ZACC 27; 2000 (2) SA 18 (CC); 2001 (2) BCLR 103 (CC); *Hoffmann v South African Airways* [2000] ZACC 17; 2001 (1) SA 1 (CC); 2000 (11) BCLR 1211 (CC); [2000] 12 BLLR 1365 (CC); *National Coalition for Gay and Lesbian Equality and Others v Minister of Home Affairs and Others* [1999] ZACC 17; 2000 (2) SA 1 (CC); 2000 (1) BCLR 39 (CC); *National Coalition for Gay and Lesbian Equality and Another v Minister of Justice and Others* [1998] ZACC 15; 1999 (1) SA 6 (CC); 1998 (12) BCLR 1517 (CC); *City Council of Pretoria v Walker* [1998] ZACC 1; 1998 (2) SA 363 (CC); 1998 (3) BCLR 257 (CC); *Larbi-Odam and Others v Member of the Executive Council for Education* [1997] ZACC 16; 1998 (1) SA 745 (CC); 1997 (12) BCLR 1655 (CC); *Harksen v Lane NO and Others* [1997] ZACC 12; 1998 (1) SA 300 (CC); 1997 (11) BCLR 1489 (CC); *Prinsloo v Van der Linde and Another* [1997] ZACC 5; 1997 (3) SA 1012 (CC); 1997 (6) BCLR 759 (CC); *President of the Republic of South Africa and Another v Hugo* [1997] ZACC 4; 1997 (4) SA 1 (CC); 1997 (6) BCLR 708 (CC); *Fraser v Children's Court Pretoria North and Others* [1997] ZACC 1; 1997 (2) SA 261 (CC); 1997 (2) BCLR 153 (CC); *Brink v Kitshoff NO* [1996] ZACC 9; 1996 (4) SA 197 (CC); 1996 (6) BCLR 752 (CC); and *S v Ntuli* [1995] ZACC 14; 1996 (1) SA 1207 (CC); 1996 (1) BCLR 141 (CC).

31 *Investigating Directorate: Serious Economic Offences and Others v Hyundai Motor Distributors (Pty) Ltd and Others: In re Hyundai Motor Distributors (Pty) Ltd and Others v Smit NO and Others* [2000] ZACC 12; 2001 (1) SA 545 (CC); 2000 (10) BCLR 1079 (CC); *National Coalition for Gay and Lesbian Equality and Another v Minister of Justice and Others* [1998] ZACC 15; 1999 (1) SA 6 (CC); 1998 (12) BCLR 1517 (CC); *Mistry v Interim National Medical and Dental Council and Others* [1998] ZACC 10; 1998 (4) SA 1127 (CC); and *Bernstein and Others v Bester NO and Others* [1996] ZACC 2; 1996 (2) SA 751 (CC); 1996 (4) BCLR 449 (CC).

32 *Beyers v Eleven Judges of the Constitutional Court* [2002] ZACC 19; 2002 (6) SA 630 (CC); 2002 (10) BCLR 1001 (CC); *S and Others v Van Rooyen and Others (General Council of the Bar of South Africa Intervening)* [2002] ZACC 8; 2002 (5) SA 246 (CC); 2002 (8) BCLR 810 (CC); *S v Boesak* [2000] ZACC 25; 2001 (1) SA 912 (CC); 2001 (1) BCLR 36 (CC); *S v Dzukuda and Others; S v Tshilo* [2000] ZACC 16; 2000 (4) SA 1078 (CC); 2000 (11) BCLR 1252 (CC); *S v Manamela and Another (Director-General of Justice Intervening)* [2000] ZACC 5; 2000 (3) SA 1 (CC); 2000 (5) BCLR 491 (CC); *S v Dlamini; S v Dladla*

NOTES: CHAPTER 13

and Others; *S v Joubert; S v Schietekat* [1999] ZACC 8; 1999 (4) SA 623 (CC); 1999 (7) BCLR 771 (CC); *Mphahlele v First National Bank of South Africa Ltd* [1999] ZACC 1; 1999 (2) SA 667 (CC); 1999 (3) BCLR 253 (CC); *Sanderson v Attorney-General, Eastern Cape* [1997] ZACC 18; 1998 (2) SA 38 (CC); 1997 (12) BCLR 1675 (CC); *S v Coetzee and Others* [1997] ZACC 2; 1997 (3) SA 527 (CC); *Key v Attorney-General, Cape Provincial Division and Another* [1996] ZACC 25; 1996 (4) SA 187 (CC); 1996 (6) BCLR 788 (CC); *Scagell and Others v Attorney-General, Western Cape and Others* [1996] ZACC 18; 1997 (2) SA 368 (CC); 1996 (11) BCLR 1446 (CC); *Prinsloo v Van der Linde and Another* [1997] ZACC 5; 1997 (3) SA 1012 (CC); 1997 (6) BCLR 759 (CC); *S v Rens* [1995] ZACC 15; 1996 (1) SA 1218 (CC); 1996 (2) BCLR 155 (CC); *Nel v Le Roux NO and Others* [1996] ZACC 6; 1996 (3) SA 562 (CC); 1996 (4) BCLR 592 (CC); *S v Bhulwana, S v Gwadiso* [1995] ZACC 11; 1996 (1) SA 388 (CC); 1995 (12) BCLR 1579 (CC); *Shabalala and Others v Attorney-General of the Transvaal and Another* [1995] ZACC 12; 1995 (1) SA 725 (CC); 1995 (12) BCLR 1593 (CC); *Coetzee v Government of the Republic of South Africa, Matiso and Others v Commanding Officer Port Elizabeth Prison and Others* [1995] ZACC 7; 1995 (4) SA 631 CC); 1995 (10) BCLR 1382 (CC); *S v Williams and Others* [1995] ZACC 6; 1995 (3) SA 632 (CC); 1995 (7) BCLR 861 (CC); and *S v Zuma and Others* [1995] ZACC 1; 1995 (2) SA 642 (CC); 1995 (4) BCLR 401 (CC).

33 *Moise v Greater Germiston Transitional Local Council* [2001] ZACC 21; 2001 (4) SA 491 (CC); 2001 (8) BCLR 765 (CC); *De Beer NO v North-Central Local Council and South-Central Local Council and Others (Umhlatuzana Civic Association Intervening)* [2001] ZACC 9; 2002 (1) SA 429 (CC); 2001 (11) BCLR 1109 (CC); *Potgieter v Lid van die Uitvoerende Raad: Gesondheid Provinsiale Regering Gauteng en Andere* [2001] ZACC 4; 2001 (11) BCLR (CC); *Dormehl v Minister of Justice and Others* [2000] ZACC 4; 2000 (2) SA 825 (CC); 2000 (5) BCLR 471 (CC); *Beinash and Another v Ernst & Young and Others* [1998] ZACC 19; 1999 (2) SA 116 (CC); 1999 (2) BCLR 125 (CC); *Mohlomi v Minister of Defence* [1996] ZACC 20; 1997 (1) SA 124 (CC); 1996 (12) BCLR 1559 (CC); *Azanian People's Organisation (AZAPO) and Others v President of the Republic of South Africa and Others* [1996] ZACC 16; 1996 (4) SA 672 (CC); 1996 (8) BCLR 1015 (CC); and *Besserglik v Minister of Trade, Industry and Tourism and Others (Minister of Justice Intervening)* [1996] ZACC 8; 1996 (4) SA 331 (CC); 1996 (6) BCLR 745 (CC).

34 *Khumalo and Others v Holomisa* [2002] ZACC 12; 2002 (5) SA 401 (CC); 2002 (8) BCLR 771 (CC); *Islamic Unity Convention v Independent Broadcasting Authority and Others* [2002] ZACC 3; 2002 (4) SA 294 (CC); 2002 (5) BCLR 433 (CC); *S v Mamabolo* [2001] ZACC 17; 2001 (3) SA 409 (CC); 2001 (5) BCLR 449 (CC); *President of the Ordinary Court Martial and Others v Freedom of Expression Institute and Others* [1999] ZACC 10; 1999 (4) SA 682 (CC); 1999 (11) BCLR 1219 (CC); *South African National Defence Union v Minister of Defence* [1999] ZACC 7; 1999 (4) SA 469 (CC); 1999 BCLR 615 (CC); *JT Publishing (Pty) Ltd and Another v Minister of Safety and Security and Others* [1996] ZACC 23; 1997 (3) SA 514 (CC); 1996 (12) BCLR (CC); and *Case and Another v Minister of Safety and Security and Others, Curtis v Minister of Safety and Security and Others* [1996] ZACC 7; 1996 (3) SA 617 (CC); 1996 (5) BCLR 608 (CC).

NOTES: CHAPTER 13

35 *Bannatyne v Bannatyne and Another* [2002] ZACC 31; 2003 (2) SA 363 (CC); 2003 (2) BCLR 111 (CC); and *Fraser v Children's Court Pretoria North and Others* [1997] ZACC 1; 1997 (2) SA 261 (CC); 1997 (2) BCLR 153 (CC).

36 *New National Party v Government of the Republic of South Africa and Others* [1999] ZACC 5; 1999 (3) SA 191 (CC); 1999 (5) BCLR 489 (CC); and *August and Another v Electoral Commission and Others* [1999] ZACC 3; 1999 (3) SA 1 (CC); 1999 (4) BCLR 363 (CC).

37 *Islamic Unity Convention v Independent Broadcasting Authority and Others* [2002] ZACC 3; 2002 (4) SA 294 (CC); 2002 (5) BCLR 433 (CC); *Prince v President of the Law Society of the Cape of Good Hope* [2002] ZACC 1; 2002 (2) SA 794 (CC); 2002 (3) BCLR 231 (CC); *Christian Education South Africa v Minister of Education* [2000] ZACC 11; 2000 (4) SA 757 (CC); 2000 (10) BCLR 1051 (CC); *S v Lawrence; S v Negal; S v Solberg* [1997] ZACC 11; 1997 (4) SA 1176 (CC); 1997 (10) BCLR 1348 (CC); and *Gauteng Provincial Legislature: In re Gauteng School Education Bill of 1995* [1996] ZACC 4; 1996 (3) SA 165 (CC); 1996 (4) BCLR 537 (CC).

38 *Minister of Health and Others v Treatment Action Campaign and Others (No 2)* [2002] ZACC 15; 2002 (5) SA 721 (CC); 2002 (10) BCLR 1033 (CC); *Government of the Republic of South Africa and Others v Grootboom and Others* [2000] ZACC 19; 2001 (1) SA 46 (CC); 2000 (11) BCLR 1169 (CC); and *Soobramoney v Minister of Health (KwaZulu-Natal)* [1997] ZACC 17; 1998 (1) SA 765 (CC); 1997 (12) BCLR 1696 (CC).

39 *National Union of Metal Workers of South Africa and Others v Bader Bop (Pty) Ltd and Another* [2002] ZACC 30; 2003 (3) SA 513 (CC); 2003 (2) BCLR 182 (CC); *National Education Health & Allied Workers Union (NEHAWU) v University of Cape Town and Others* [2002] ZACC 27; 2003 (3) SA 1 (CC); 2003 (2) BCLR 154 (CC); *Fredericks and Others v MEC for Education and Training Eastern Cape and Others* [2001] ZACC 6; 2002 (2) SA 693 (CC); 2002 (2) BCLR 113 (CC); and *South African National Defence Union v Minister of Defence* [1999] ZACC 7; 1999 (4) SA 469 (CC); 1999 BCLR 615 (CC).

40 *First National Bank of SA Limited t/a Wesbank v Commissioner for the South African Revenue Service and Another; First National Bank of SA Limited t/a Wesbank v Minister of Finance* [2002] ZACC 5; 2002 (4) SA 768 (CC); 2002 (7) BCLR 702 (CC).

41 *Carmichele v Minister of Safety and Security* [2001] ZACC 22; 2001 (4) SA 938 (CC); 2001 (10) BCLR 995 (CC).

42 *Ex Parte Minister of Safety and Security: In re S v Walters and Another* [2002] ZACC 6; 2002 (4) SA 613 (CC); 2002 (7) BCLR 663 (CC); *Mohamed and Another v President of the Republic of South Africa and Others* [2001] ZACC 18; 2001 (3) SA 893 (CC); 2001 (7) BCLR 685 (CC); *Soobramoney v Minister of Health (KwaZulu-Natal)* [1997] ZACC 17; 1998 (1) SA 765 (CC); 1997 (12) BCLR 1696 (CC); and *S v Makwanyane and Another* [1995] ZACC 3; 1995 (3) SA 391 (CC); 1995 (6) BCLR 665 (CC).

43 *Gauteng Provincial Legislature: In re Gauteng School Education Bill of 1995* [1996] ZACC 4; 1996 (3) SA 165 (CC); 1996 (4) BCLR 537 (CC).

NOTES: CHAPTER 14

14 A COMMON PURPOSE

1 Teodoro Obiang Nguema Mbasogo has been president of Equatorial Guinea for four decades, commencing on 3 August 1979.
2 Robert Mugabe served as Zimbabwe's prime minister from 1980 to 1987, followed by 30 years at the helm as its president from 31 December 1987 to 21 November 2017.
3 Yoweri Kaguta Museveni has held the office of president of Uganda for 33 years since 29 January 1986.
4 Omar Hassan Ahmad al-Bashir was president of Sudan from 16 October 1993 until his ousting in a military coup on 11 April 2019. Prior to his presidency, he had already resumed power in 1989 as chairman of the Revolutionary Command Centre for National Salvation (RCC), which was established as a 'transitional government' after the military coup against Sadiq al-Mahdi.
5 Paul Biya has been president of Cameroon for almost four decades since 6 November 1982.
6 In 1999 the ANC attained a majority of 66.35% and in 2004 it attained 69.69% of the national vote.
7 Section 1 of the Constitution establishes South Africa as one sovereign, democratic state and lays out its founding values. These include human dignity, equality and the advancement of human rights and freedoms; non-racialism and non-sexism, the supremacy of the Constitution and the rule of law; and universal adult suffrage, a national common voters' roll, regular elections and a multi-party system of democratic government. Section 74(1) of the Constitution stipulates that section 1 may only be amended by a vote supported by 75 per cent of the National Assembly. The remaining provisions of the Constitution may be amended by a two-thirds majority.
8 *Minister of Health and Others v Treatment Action Campaign and Others (No 2)* [2002] ZACC 15; 2002 (5) SA 721 (CC); 2002 (10) BCLR 1033 (CC).
9 The Treatment Action Campaign (TAC) was founded in December 1998 to campaign for access to HIV/AIDS treatment. While it has continued to be instrumental in securing HIV/AIDS programmes, it also campaigns for important issues affecting the quality of and access to health care in the public sector.
10 *Treatment Action Campaign and Others v Minister of Health and Others* 2002 (4) BCLR 356 (T).
11 See Heywood M. 'Preventing mother-to-child HIV transmission in South Africa: Background, strategies and outcomes of the Treatment Action Campaign case against the Minister of Health' (2003) 19 *SAJHR* 278-315.
12 Over the last three years, well over 300 applications have been filed annually in the Constitutional Court.
13 *Thebus and Another v S* [2003] ZACC 12; 2003 (6) SA 505 (CC); 2003 (10) BCLR 1100 (CC).
14 In *S v Sefatsa and Others,* Transvaal Provincial Division, unreported, cc 698/85, Mojalefa

NOTES: CHAPTERS 14 AND 15

Reginald Sefatsa, Reid Malebo Mokoena, Oupa Moses Diniso, Theresa Ramashamole, Duma Joshua Khumalo and Francis Don Mokhesi were convicted and sentenced to death for the murder of the deputy mayor of Sharpeville, Mr Kuzwayo Jacob Dlamini, during a protest against corrupt councillors. The accused appealed their convictions and sentences, but the Appellate Division held in *S v Sefatsa and Others* [1987] ZASCA 150; [1988] 4 All SA 239 (AD) that there was no room to interfere with the trial court's decision.

15 The Sharpeville Six spent four years in prison on death row. During that time, State President PW Botha ignored emphatic appeals from the United Nations and several foreign states and refused to intervene in their case to grant clemency. International outcry, including direct appeals from British Prime Minister Margaret Thatcher and United States President Ronald Reagan, was strongly related to the lack of evidence directly linking the six accused to Mr Dlamini's death. Local organisations continued to protest against their sentences. New evidence calling into question witness testimony provided a month-long postponement of their execution. On 11 July 1988, amid local and international pressure condemning their sentences, Justice Minister Kobie Coetsee granted the Sharpeville Six an indefinite stay of execution just hours before they were scheduled to be hanged. Their sentences were commuted to prison sentences but they were later released during negotiations which saw the liberation of all political prisoners from jail.

16 Separate judgments were produced by Goldstone and O'Regan JJ, Yacoob J and Ngcobo J.

17 The French term *en banc* means 'in full court'; it signifies that a decision is made by a full bench of all the judges in a court.

15 TENURE AND INTELLECTUAL BONDING

1 *Barkhuizen v Napier* [2007] ZACC 5; 2007 (5) SA 323 (CC); 2007 (7) BCLR 691 (CC).

2 Section 99(1) of the interim Constitution.

3 Section 176 of the Constitution read with section 4(1) of the Judges' Remuneration and Conditions of Employment Act 47 of 2001.

4 Judges from France, Italy, Poland, Portugal, Romania and Slovenia are appointed to their respective constitutional courts for a non-renewable term of nine years. Georgia affords constitutional court judges ten years on the bench without the option of renewal, while judges from Germany's Federal Constitutional Court are elected to serve a non-renewable twelve-year term.

5 For example, Justice Sandra Day O'Connor, the Supreme Court's first female judge, retired in 2006 at the age of 75, while Justice David Souter was 69 years old when he retired in 2009.

6 Notably, Justice Thurgood Marshall, the first and only African-American justice at the time, served beyond 80 years, retiring at the age of 82. Justice Anthony Kennedy retired in 2018 after serving 30 years on the bench. He was 82 years old at the time. Justices John

NOTES: CHAPTER 15

Paul Stevens and Oliver Wendell Holmes Jr were both 90 years old when they retired.

7   Section 3(2) of the Judges' Remuneration and Conditions of Employment Act 47 of 2001 stipulates that a judge must retire at the age of 70 years if they have served at least ten years on the bench. They may request to retire at the age of 65 if they have performed active service for fifteen years. Section 4(4) of the Act allows a judge who is 70 years old but who has not yet completed fifteen years of active service to continue serving on the bench until they complete their fifteen years of active service or attain the age of 75 years, whichever comes first.

8   Section 7 of the Judges' Remuneration and Conditions of Employment Act states that a judge must be available to perform service for three months a year until 75, and may voluntarily perform such service beyond that age if their mental and physical health permits.

9   *S v Shaik and Others*, Durban Local Division, unreported, cc 27/04.

10 The Marikana Commission of Inquiry was mandated to investigate the incidents that occurred in August 2012 at the Lonmin Mine in Marikana, North West, which led to the death of 44 people.

11 The Mokgoro Commission of Inquiry, chaired by retired Constitutional Court Justice Yvonne Mokgoro, was established in 2018 to investigate the fitness and propriety of two senior officials in the NPA. Also in 2018, the commission of inquiry into allegations of impropriety regarding the Public Investment Corporation (PIC) was chaired by former president of the Supreme Court of Appeal, Justice Lex Mpati. The Commission of Inquiry into Tax Administration and Governance by the South African Revenue Service was established in 2018 and chaired by Justice Robert Nugent. In 2017, Justice Bernard Ngoepe was appointed to inquire into and report on defined actions taken by the minister of social welfare and development in the payment of social grants, known colloquially as the SASSA Inquiry. Retired Deputy Chief Justice Dikgang Moseneke was appointed in 2017 as arbitrator, in what was known as the Life Esidimeni Arbitration, to determine equitable redress due to mental health-care users and their families as a result of state actions which caused multiple deaths and severe trauma. The Competition Commission initiated the Health Market Inquiry in 2013, headed by retired Chief Justice Sandile Ngcobo, to evaluate the explanations for observed increases in pricing and expenses in the private health-care sector. Justice Kate O'Regan, together with Adv Vusi Pikoli, was appointed in 2012 as chair of the Khayelitsha Commission of Inquiry into allegations of police inefficiency in Khayelitsha, a township in the Western Cape. The Presidential Remuneration Review Commission, also established in 2012, is chaired by Justice Kenneth Mthiyane to review the remuneration policy and conditions of the public service.

12 *Minister of Finance and Other v Van Heerden* [2004] ZACC 3; 2004 (6) SA 121 (CC); 2004 (11) BCLR 1125 (CC).

13 *Minister of Finance and Other v Van Heerden* at para 135.

14 *City of Cape Town and Another v Robertson and Another* [2004] ZACC 21; 2005 (2) SA 323 (CC).

NOTES: CHAPTER 15

15 *Laugh It Off Promotions CC v South African Breweries International (Finance) BV t/a Sabmark International and Another* [2005] ZACC 7; 2006 (1) SA 144 (CC); 2005 (8) BCLR 743 (CC).
16 *Laugh It Off Promotions CC* at para 71.
17 *Satchwell v President of the Republic of South Africa and Another* [2003] ZACC 2; 2003 (4) SA 266 (CC); 2004 (1) BCLR 1 (CC), per O'Regan J.
18 *J and Another v Director General, Department of Home Affairs and Others* [2003] ZACC 3; 2003 (5) SA 621 (CC); 2003 (5) BCLR 463 (CC), per Goldstone J.
19 *Minister of Home Affairs and Another v Fourie and Another* [2005] ZACC 19; 2006 (1) SA 524 (CC); 2006 (3) BCLR 355 (CC), per Sachs J. A minority judgment on the question of remedy was penned by O'Regan J.
20 In *National Director of Public Prosecutions v Mohamed NO and Others* [2003] ZACC 4; 2003 (4) SA 1 (CC); 2003 (5) BCLR 476 (CC), the court, per Ackermann J, refused to declare constitutionally invalid a procedure established by legislation permitting an *ex parte* application by the head of public prosecutions. Yacoob J, writing for the court in *Swartbooi and Others v Brink and Another (2)* [2003] ZACC 25; 2006 (1) SA 203 (CC); 2003 (5) BCLR 502 (CC), determined that municipal councillors should not be held personally liable for costs in civil proceedings for anything said, produced or submitted before a municipal council. An application for leave to appeal a matter of access to information was dismissed by the court in *Ingledew v Financial Services Board* [2003] ZACC 8; 2003 (4) SA 584 (CC); 2003 (8) BCLR 825, per Ngcobo J. In *Shaik v Minister of Justice and Constitutional Development and Others* [2003] ZACC 24; 2004 (3) SA 599 (CC); 2004 (4) BCRL 333 (CC), the court, per Ackermann J, dealt with the constitutionality of a legislative provision regulating inquiries by an investigating director.
21 *Minister of Home Affairs v Eisenberg & Associates: In re Eisenberg & Associates v Minister of Home Affairs and Others* [2003] ZACC 10; 2003 (5) SA 281 (CC); 2003 (8) BCLR 838 (CC).
22 *De Reuck v Director of Public Prosecutions (Witwatersrand Local Division) and Others* [2003] ZACC 19; 2004 (1) SA 406 (CC); 2003 (12) BCLR 1333 (CC), per Langa DCJ.
23 *Alexkor Ltd and Another v Richtersveld Community and Others* [2003] ZACC 18; 2004 (5) SA 460 (CC); 2003 (12) BCLR 1301 (CC).
24 *Du Toit v Minister of Transport* [2005] ZACC 9; 2006 (1) SA 297 (CC); 2005 (11) BCLR 1053 (CC), per Mokgoro J. A minority judgment was written by Langa ACJ.
25 *Jaftha v Schoeman and Others, Van Rooyen v Stoltz and Others* [2004] ZACC 25; 2005 (2) SA 140 (CC); 2005 (1) BCLR 78 (CC), per Mokgoro J.
26 *Mkontwana v Nelson Mandela Metropolitan Municipality* [2004] ZACC 9; 2005 (1) SA 530 (CC); 2005 (2) BCLR 150 (CC), per Yacoob J. A separate judgment was penned by O'Regan J.
27 *Rail Commuters Action Group v Transnet Ltd t/a Metrorail* [2004] ZACC 20; 2005 (2) SA 359 (CC); 2005 (4) BCLR 301 (CC), per O'Regan J.

NOTES: CHAPTERS 15 AND 16

28 *K v Minister of Safety and Security* [2005] ZACC 8; 2005 (6) SA 419 (CC); 2005 (9) BCLR 835 (CC), per O'Regan J.
29 *Minister of Home Affairs v National Institute for Crime Prevention and the Re-Integration of Offenders (NICRO) and Others* [2004] ZACC 10; 2005 (3) SA 280 (CC); 2004 (5) BCLR 445 (CC), per Chaskalson CJ. Separate minority judgments were written by Madala J and Ngcobo J.
30 *Bhe and Others v Khayelitsha Magistrate and Others* [2004] ZACC 17; 2005 (1) SA 580 (CC); 2005 (1) BCLR 1 (CC), per Langa DCJ. A minority judgment was penned by Ngcobo J.
31 38 of 1927.
32 *Volks NO v Robinson and Others* [2005] ZACC 2; 2005 (5) BCLR 446 (CC), per Skweyiya J. Ngcobo J wrote a separate concurring judgment while two separate dissents were penned by Mokgoro and O'Regan JJ, and Sachs J.
33 Section 1 of the Maintenance of Surviving Spouses Act 27 of 1990.
34 *S v Basson* [2004] ZACC 13; 2005 (1) SA 171 (CC); 2004 (6) BCLR 620 (CC).

LANGA COURT

16 SECOND-GENERATION LEADERS

1 Freedom Day celebrates South Africa's first democratic election held in 1994.
2 The inauguration of all five elected presidents of Ghana since the birth of its Fourth Republic has taken place on 7 January at Independence Square in Accra. It marks the day in 1993 that the Constitution of the Fourth Republic of Ghana came into effect. In 2019, the day was declared 'Constitution Day' to commemorate Ghana's longest undisrupted period of stable constitutional order. Independence Square, also known as Black Star Square, was commissioned in 1961 by its revolutionary leader, Prime Minister Kwame Nkrumah, to celebrate Ghana's independence from Britain.
3 Address by the president of South Africa, Thabo Mbeki, on the Occasion of His Inauguration and the 10th Anniversary of Freedom, Pretoria, 27 April 2004.
4 Mahlamba Ndlopfu means 'the new dawn' in Shangaan. It is the official residence of the president.
5 Section 174(3) of the Constitution obliges the president to consult the JSC and leaders of parties in the National Assembly before appointing the country's chief justice and deputy chief justice.
6 Justice Pius Langa was active in the formation of the National Association of Democratic Lawyers, serving on its steering committee and acting as its president from 1988 to 1994. Justice Dikgang Moseneke was a founding member of the Black Lawyers Association, serving as its first national secretary, and NADEL, serving as its founding national treasurer.

NOTES: CHAPTERS 16 AND 17

7 See Langa P. 'Transformative Constitutionalism' (2006), *Stellenbosch Law Review,* 351-60 and Moseneke D. 'Transformative Constitutionalism: Its Implications for the Law of Contract (2009)', *Stellenbosch Law Review,* 20(1) 309-17.

17 CLOUDS GATHERING, STORM BREWING

1 *S v Shaik and Others* 2007 (1) SACR 142 (D).
2 *S v Shaik and Others (Criminal appeal)* [2006] ZASCA 105; 2007 (1) SA 240 (SCA).
3 *S v Shaik and Others (Civil appeal)* [2006] ZASCA 106; [2007] 2 All SA 150 (SCA).
4 *S v Shaik and Others* [2007] ZACC 19; 2008 (2) SA 208 (CC); 2007 (12) BCLR 1360 (CC).
5 *Minister of Health and Others v Treatment Action Campaign and Others (No 2)* [2002] ZACC 15; 2002 (5) SA 721 (CC); 2002 (10) BCLR 1033 (CC).
6 *S v Basson* [2005] ZACC 10; 2007 (3) SA 582 (CC); 2005 (12) BCLR 1192 (CC).
7 *Zuma and Another v National Director of Public Prosecutions and Others* [2006} ZAKZHAC 5; 2006 (1) SACR 468 (D).
8 *Thint (Pty) Ltd and Others v National Director of Public Prosecutions and Others* Case no. 268/2006, unreported, 4 July 2006.
9 *National Director of Public Prosecutions and Others v Zuma and Another* [2007] ZASCA 137; 2008 (1) SACR 298 (SCA) and *Thint (Pty) Ltd v National Director of Public Prosecutions and Others* [2007] ZASCA 136; 2007 JDR 1140 (SCA).
10 *Thint (Pty) Ltd v National Director of Public Prosecutions and Others, Zuma and Another v National Director of Public Prosecutions and Others* [2008] ZACC 13; 2009 (1) SA 1 (CC); 2008 (12) BCLR 1197 (CC).
11 *S v Zuma and Others* [2006] ZAKZHC 22.
12 Section 2 of the International Co-operation in Criminal Matters Act 75 of 1996.
13 *Thint Holdings (Southern Africa) (Pty) Ltd and Another v National Director of Public Prosecutions, Zuma v National Director of Public Prosecutions* [2008] ZACC 14; 2009 (1) SA 141 (CC); 2009 (3) BCLR 309 (CC). The high court judgment was delivered by Levinsohn DJP as *National Director of Public Prosecutions v Zuma and Others* Durban and Coast Local Division Case no. 13569/2006, unreported, 2 April 2007. The Supreme Court of Appeal unanimously dismissed the applicants' appeal against the high court's decision in *Zuma and Others v National Director of Public Prosecutions* [2007] ZASCA 135; 2008 (1) SACR 298 (SCA).
14 *S v Shaik and Others* [2007] ZACC 19; 2008 (2) SA 208 (CC); 2007 (12) BCLR 1360 (CC).
15 As contemplated by the Prevention of Organised Crime Act 121 of 1998. The high court order is cited as *National Director of Public Prosecutions v Shaik and Others* Durban and Coast Local Division Case no. 27/04, unreported, 31 January 2006.
16 *S v Shaik and Others* [2008] ZACC 7; 2008 (5) SA 354 (CC); 2008 (8) BCLR 834 (CC).
17 In an insightful article titled 'A few reflections on the role of courts, government, the legal profession, universities, the media and civil society in a constitutional democracy', retired

judge of the Constitutional Court, Justice Van der Westhuizen, traces South Africa's history of political interference in judicial affairs contrasted with our now constitutionally entrenched principles of judicial independence and separation of powers. He analyses the relationship between the courts and various stakeholders, including government, between 1994 and 2008. In doing so, he addresses some remarks mounted against the Constitutional Court and its judgments in particular. He concludes by emphasising the importance of informed criticism and debate within South Africa's constitutional democracy.

18 *Zuma v National Director of Public Prosecutions* [2008] ZAKZHC 71; 2009 (1) BCLR 62 (N); [2009] 1 All SA 54 (N).

19 Section 102(2) of the Constitution.

20 Section 89 of the Constitution.

21 *National Director of Public Prosecutions v Zuma* [2009] ZASCA 1; 2009 (2) SA 277 (SCA); 2009 (4) BCLR 393 (SCA).

18 THE HLOPHE MATTER

1 *Thint (Pty) Ltd v National Director of Public Prosecutions and Others; Zuma and Another v National Director of Public Prosecutions and Others* [2008] ZACC 13; 2009 (1) SA 1 (CC); 2008 (12) BCLR 1197 (CC).

2 *Langa and Others v Hlophe* [2009] ZASCA 36; 2009 (8) BCLR 823 (SCA); and *Hlophe v Constitutional Court of South Africa and Others* [2008] ZAGPHC 289.

3 *Hlophe v Premier of the Western Cape Province, Hlophe v Freedom Under Law and Others* [2012] ZACC 4; 2012 (6) SA 13 (CC); 2012 (6) BCLR 567 (CC); *Hlophe v Premier of the Western Cape Province, Hlophe v Freedom Under Law and Others* [2011] ZACC 29; 2012 (1) BCLR 1 (CC); *Freedom Under Law v Acting Chairperson: Judicial Service Commission and Others* [2011] ZASCA 59; 2011 (3) SA 549 (SCA).

4 *Hlophe v Judicial Service Commission and Others* [2009] ZAGPJHC 19.

5 *Nkabinde and Another v Judicial Service Commission and Others* [2016] ZACC 25; 2017 (3) SA 119 (CC); 2016 (11) BCLR 1429 (CC); *Nkabinde and Another v Judicial Service Commission and Others* [2016] ZASCA 12; 2016 (4) SA 1 (SCA); *Nkabinde and Another v Judicial Service Commission President of the Judicial Conduct Tribunal and Others* 2015 (1) SA 279 (GJ).

6 *Hlophe v Constitutional Court of South Africa and Others* [2008] ZAGPHC 289.

7 The constitutional values, enshrined in section 1 of the Constitution, that are particularly relevant to the complaint include the supremacy of the Constitution and the rule of law.

8 Section 165(2) of the Constitution establishes the independence of the courts. They are subject only to the Constitution and the law, which they must apply impartially and without fear, favour or prejudice. Section 165(3) of the Constitution prohibits any person or organ of state from interfering with the functioning of the courts.

NOTES: CHAPTER 18

9 As contained in Schedule 2 of the Constitution.
10 Hlophe J further argues that the judges violated Principles 17 and 19 of the United Nations Basic Principles on the Independence of the Judiciary, Article 26 of the African Charter on Human and Peoples' Rights and Article 14(1) of the International Covenant on Civil and Political Rights. For details of the counter-complaint see the decision of the Supreme Court of Appeal in *Langa and Others v Hlophe* [2009] ZASCA 36; 2009 (4) SA 382 (SCA).
11 An affidavit is a sworn written statement that is used as evidence in court.
12 Section 8 of the Judicial Service Commission Act 9 of 1994 establishes a Judicial Conduct Committee of the JSC to receive, consider and deal with complaints relating to the conduct of judges. Grounds upon which a complaint may be lodged in terms of section 14(4) of the Act include gross misconduct, a breach of the Code of Judicial Conduct, or any conduct that is incompatible with or unbecoming the holding of judicial office, including any conduct that is prejudicial to the independence, impartiality, dignity, accessibility, efficiency or effectiveness of the courts. In terms of section 16 of the Act, the committee may recommend to the JSC that a Tribunal be appointed in respect of impeachable complaints. In turn, the JSC must request the chief justice to appoint a Tribunal. Chapter 3 of the Act regulates Judicial Conduct Tribunals.
13 In chronological order by date, the cases relating to the Hlophe complaint include: *Hlophe v Constitutional Court of South Africa and Others* [2008] ZAGPHC 289; *Langa and Others v Hlophe* [2009] ZASCA 36; 2009 (8) BCLR 823 (SCA); *Hlophe v Judicial Service Commission and Others* [2009] ZAGPJHC 19; *Premier, Western Cape v Acting Chairperson, Judicial Service Commission* 2010 (5) SA 634 (WCC); *Freedom Under Law v The Acting Chairperson: Judicial Service Commission and Others* Case No 63513/09 North Gauteng High Court, unreported, 10 December 2010; *Acting Chairperson: Judicial Service Commission and Others v Premier of the Western Cape Province* [2011] ZASCA 53; 2011 (3) SA 538 (SCA); *Freedom Under Law v Acting Chairperson: Judicial Service Commission and Others* [2011] ZASCA 59; 2011 (3) SA 549 (SCA); *Hlophe v Premier of the Western Cape Province, Hlophe v Freedom Under Law and Others* [2011] ZACC 29; 2012 (1) BCLR 1 (CC); *Hlophe v Premier of the Western Cape Province, Hlophe v Freedom Under Law and Others* [2012] ZACC 4; 2012 (6) SA 13 (CC); 2012 (6) BCLR 567 (CC); *Nkabinde and Another v Judicial Service Commission President of the Judicial Conduct Tribunal and Others* 2015 (1) SA 279 (GJ); *Nkabinde and Another v Judicial Service Commission and Others* [2016] ZASCA 12; 2016 (4) SA 1 (SCA); and *Nkabinde and Another v Judicial Service Commission and Others* [2016] ZACC 25; 2016 (11) BCLR 1429 (CC); 2017 (3) SA 119 (CC).
14 My emphasis.
15 While Justice Sachs was not included in the list of judges in paragraph 3 of the complaint, he formed part of the cohort of justices who collectively laid the complaint against Hlophe JP to the JSC. This is clear from paragraph 56 of the complaint:
'It is in the light of these obligations and the seriousness with which the judges of the Court viewed the conduct of Hlophe JP that *the judges of the Court (including ... Sachs J)*

NOTES: CHAPTERS 18 AND 19

unanimously made the complaint to the [Judicial Service Commission]' *(my emphasis)*.
16 *Thint (Pty) Limited v National Director of Public Prosecutions and Others* (CCT89/07); *J.G. Zuma and Another v National Director of Public Prosecutions and Others* (CCT91/07); *Thint Holdings (South Africa) (Pty) Limited and Another v National Director of Public Prosecutions* (CCT90/07); and *J.G. Zuma v National Director of Public Prosecutions* (CCT92/07).
17 The outcomes – the judgments – in these matters are now reported as:
Thint (Pty) Ltd v National Director of Public Prosecutions and Others, Zuma and Another v National Director of Public Prosecutions and Others [2008] ZACC 13; 2009 (1) SA 1 (CC); 2008 (12) BCLR 1197 (CC); and *Thint Holdings (Southern Africa) (Pty) Ltd and Another v National Director of Public Prosecutions, Zuma v National Director of Public Prosecutions* [2008] ZACC 14; 2009 (1) SA 141 (CC); 2009 (3) BCLR 309 (CC).

19 JURISPRUDENCE – A FULL REPERTOIRE

1 18 August 2005 – the first hearing in the third court term of 2005.
2 *S v Makwanyane and Another* [1995] ZACC 3; 1995 (3) SA 391 (CC); 1995 (6) BCLR 665 (CC).
3 *Sibiya and Others v Director of Public Prosecutions: Johannesburg High Court and Others* [2005] ZACC 6; 2005 (5) SA 315 (CC); 2005 (8) BCLR 812 (CC); *Sibiya and Others v Director of Public Prosecutions: Johannesburg High Court and Others* [2005] ZACC 16; 2006 (2) BCLR 293 (CC); [2005] JOL 15699 (CC); and *Sibiya and Others v Director of Public Prosecutions* [2006] ZACC 22; 2006 (2) BCLR 293 (CC). While Justice Pius Langa presided over the first *Sibiya* hearing as the deputy chief justice, the second *Sibiya* hearing was his inaugural hearing as chief justice.
4 Criminal Law Amendment Act 105 of 1997.
5 *Sibiya and Others v Director of Public Prosecutions: Johannesburg High Court and Others* [2005] ZACC 16; 2006 (2) BCLR 293 (CC); [2005] JOL 15699 (CC).
6 *K v Minister of Safety and Security* [2005] ZACC 8; 2005 (6) SA 419 (CC); 2005 (9) BCLR 835 (CC).
7 *Barkhuizen v Napier* [2007] ZACC 5; 2007 (5) SA 323 (CC); 2007 (7) BCLR 691 (CC).
8 *Steenkamp NO v Provincial Tender Board of the Eastern Cape* [2006] ZACC 16; 2007 (3) SA 121 (CC); 2007 (3) BCLR 300 (CC).
9 Delict is a civil law claim for liability against a person for causing injury or damage to another.
10 *Minister of Home Affairs and Another v Fourie and Another* [2005] ZACC 19; 2006 (1) SA 524 (CC); 2006 (3) BCLR 355 (CC).
11 Marriage Act 25 of 1961.
12 *Hassam v Jacobs NO and Others* [2009] ZACC 19; 2009 (5) SA 572 (CC); 2009 (11) BCLR 1148 (CC).
13 Intestate Succession Act 81 of 1987.

NOTES: CHAPTER 19

14 Marriage Act 25 of 1961.
15 Simply put, patrimonial damages arise from a monetary loss whereas non-patrimonial damages recognise personality interests like bodily integrity, a person's good name or dignity.
16 *Van der Merwe v Road Accident Fund and Another* [2006] ZACC 4; 2006 (4) SA 230 (CC); 2006 (6) BCLR 682 (CC).
17 Guaranteed by section 9(1) of the Constitution.
18 *Gumede (born Shange) v President of the Republic of South Africa and Others* [2008] ZACC 23; 2009 (3) BCLR 243 (CC); 2009 (3) SA 152 (CC) (8 December 2008).
19 Recognition of Customary Marriages Act 120 of 1998.
20 *Gory v Kolver NO and Others* [2006] ZACC 20; 2007 (4) SA 97 (CC); 2007 (3) BCLR 249 (CC).
21 Intestate Succession Act 81 of 1987.
22 *Geldenhuys v National Director of Public Prosecutions and Others* [2008] ZACC 21; 2009 (2) SA 310 (CC); 2009 (5) BCLR 435 (CC).
23 Sexual Offences Act 23 of 1957.
24 *Du Toit v Minister of Transport* [2005] ZACC 9; 2006 (1) SA 297 (CC); 2005 (11) BCLR 1053 (CC).
25 Expropriation Act 63 of 1975.
26 Section 25 of the Constitution.
27 Section 25(3) of the Constitution.
28 *Magajane v Chairperson, North West Gambling Board* [2006] ZACC 8; 2006 (5) SA 250 (CC); 2006 (10) BCLR 1133 (CC).
29 North West Gambling Act 2 of 2001.
30 *Mohunram and Another v National Director of Public Prosecutions and Another (Law Review Project as Amicus Curiae)* [2007] ZACC 4; 2007 (4) SA 222 (CC); 2007 (6) BCLR 575 (CC).
31 Prevention of Organised Crime Act 121 of 1998.
32 *Richter v The Minister for Home Affairs and Others (with the Democratic Alliance and Others Intervening, and with AfriForum and Another as Amici Curiae)* [2009] ZACC 3; 2009 (3) SA 615 (CC); 2009 (5) BCLR 448 (CC).
33 Electoral Act 73 of 1998.
34 Criminal Procedure Act 51 of 1977.
35 *S v Shinga (Society of Advocates (Pietermaritzburg) as Amicus Curiae), S v O'Connell and Others* [2007] ZACC 3; 2007 (4) SA 611 (CC); 2007 (5) BCLR 474 (CC).
36 *Masiya v Director of Public Prosecutions Pretoria (The State) and Another* [2007] ZACC 9; 2007 (5) SA 30 (CC); 2007 (8) BCLR 827 (CC).
37 *S v M* [2007] ZACC 18; 2008 (3) SA 232 (CC); 2007 (12) BCLR 1312 (CC).

NOTES: CHAPTER 19

38 *Zealand v Minister for Justice and Constitutional Development and Another* [2008] ZACC 3; 2008 (4) SA 458 (CC); 2008 (6) BCLR 601 (CC).

39 *South African Police Service v Public Servants Association* [2006] ZACC 18; 2007 (3) SA 521 (CC); [2007] 5 BLLR 383 (CC).

40 *Sidumo and Another v Rustenburg Platinum Mines Ltd and Others* [2007] ZACC 22; 2008 (2) SA 24 (CC); 2008 (2) BCLR 158 (CC).

41 The Commission for Conciliation, Mediation and Arbitration (CCMA) is an independent dispute resolution body established in terms of the Labour Relations Act 66 of 1995.

42 Labour Relations Act 66 of 1995.

43 Promotion of Administrative Justice Act 3 of 2000 (PAJA).

44 *Chirwa v Transnet Limited and Others* [2007] ZACC 23; 2008 (4) SA 367 (CC); 2008 (3) BCLR 251 (CC).

45 Section 34 of the Constitution.

46 *Lufuno Mphaphuli & Associates (Pty) Ltd v Andrews and Another* [2009] ZACC 6; 2009 (4) SA 529 (CC); 2009 (6) BCLR 527 (CC).

47 *MEC for Education: KwaZulu-Natal and Others v Pillay* [2007] ZACC 21; 2008 (1) SA 474 (CC); 2008 (2) BCLR 99 (CC).

48 *Shilubana and Others v Nwamitwa* [2008] ZACC 9; 2008 (9) BCLR 914 (CC); 2009 (2) SA 66 (CC) (4 June 2008)

49 *Occupiers of 51 Olivia Road, Berea Township and 197 Main Street Johannesburg v City of Johannesburg and Others* [2008] ZACC 1; 2008 (3) SA 208 (CC); 2008 (5) BCLR 475 (CC). This duty is grounded in section 26(2) of the Constitution.

50 *Njongi v Member of the Executive Council, Department of Welfare, Eastern Cape* [2008] ZACC 4; 2008 (4) SA 237 (CC); 2008 (6) BCLR 571 (CC).

51 *Mazibuko and Others v City of Johannesburg and Others* [2009] ZACC 28; 2010 (4) SA 1 (CC); 2010 (3) BCLR 239 (CC).

52 In terms of section 27(1)(b) of the Constitution.

53 *Joseph and Others v City of Johannesburg and Others* [2009] ZACC 30; 2010 (4) SA 55 (CC); 2010 (3) BCLR 212 (CC).

54 *Head of Department: Mpumalanga Department of Education and Another v Hoërskool Ermelo and Another* [2009] ZACC 32; 2010 (2) SA 415 (CC); 2010 (3) BCLR 177 (CC) (14 October 2009).

55 Section 29(2) of the Constitution.

56 *Merafong Demarcation Forum and Others v President of the Republic of South Africa and Others* [2008] ZACC 10; 2008 (5) SA 171 (CC); 2008 (10) BCLR 968 (CC).

57 Promotion of National Unity and Reconciliation Act 34 of 1995.

58 *Du Toit v Minister for Safety and Security and Another* [2009] ZACC 22; 2010 (1) SACR 1 (CC); 2009 (12) BCLR 1171 (CC).

59 *Dikoko v Mokhatla* [2006] ZACC 10; 2006 (6) SA 235 (CC); 2007 (1) BCLR 1 (CC).

NOTES: CHAPTERS 19 TO 21

60 In the Criminal Procedure Act 51 of 1977.
61 *Director of Public Prosecutions, Transvaal v Minister for Justice and Constitutional Development and Others* [2009] ZACC 8; 2009 (4) SA 222 (CC); 2009 (7) BCLR 637 (CC).
62 *Biowatch Trust v Registrar Genetic Resources and Others* [2009] ZACC 14; 2009 (6) SA 232 (CC); 2009 (10) BCLR 1014 (CC).
63 *Giddey NO v JC Barnard and Partners* [2006] ZACC 13; 2007 (5) SA 525 (CC); 2007 (2) BCLR 125 (CC).
64 *Koyabe and Others v Minister for Home Affairs and Others* [2009] ZACC 23; 2010 (4) SA 327 (CC); 2009 (12) BCLR 1192 (CC).
65 *AAA Investments (Proprietary) Limited v Micro Finance Regulatory Council and Another* [2006] ZACC 9; 2007 (1) SA 343 (CC); 2006 (11) BCLR 1255 (CC).
66 *Masetlha v President of the Republic of South Africa and Another* [2007] ZACC 20; 2008 (1) SA 566 (CC); 2008 (1) BCLR 1 (CC).
67 *Independent Newspapers (Pty) Ltd v Minister for Intelligence Services (Freedom of Expression Institute as Amicus Curiae): In re Masetlha v President of the Republic of South Africa and Another (Independent)* [2008] ZACC 6; 2008 (5) SA 31 (CC); 2008 (8) BCLR 771 (CC).

20 'YOU SEE, SBOSHWA ...'

1 The commission was established by the Independent Commission for the Remuneration of Public Office Bearers Act 92 of 1997. It makes recommendations concerning the salaries, allowances and benefits of defined public office-bearers.
2 Thank you, fellow prisoner. 'Sboshwa' was a term of endearment we used on Robben Island.
3 I am also grateful, Mr President.
4 You people are bound by the facts before you.
5 Oh, Mr President?
6 In internal notes we all used initials (PL for Pius Langa, DM for Dikgang Moseneke, AS for Albie Sachs, COR for Catherine O'Regan and SN for Sandile Ngcobo).
7 'A Transformative Justice: Essays in Honour of Pius Langa' (2015), Bishop M & Price A (eds.) Pretoria: Juta.

NGCOBO COURT

21 A NEW POLITICAL ELITE

1 Minister Enver Surty served as minister of justice and constitutional development from September 2008 to May 2009.

NOTES: CHAPTER 21

2 Surty E., 'In Pursuit of Dignity' (Awqaf 2019).
3 Officially known as the Directorate of Special Operations.
4 Section 174(3) of the Constitution.
5 The Latin maxim is *stare decisis et non quieta movere* which, simply put, means 'to stand by decisions and not to disturb settled matters'.
6 *Hennie De Beer Game Lodge CC v Waterbok Bosveld Plaas CC and Another* [2010] ZACC 1; 2010 (5) SA 124 (CC); 2010 (5) BCLR 451 (CC).
7 *Billiton Aluminium SA Ltd t/a Hillside Aluminium v Khanyile and Others* [2010] ZACC 3; 2010 (5) BCLR 422 (CC); 2010 31 ILJ 273 (CC).
8 *Twee Jonge Gezellen (Pty) Ltd and Another v Land and Agricultural Development Bank of South Africa t/a The Land Bank and Another* [2011] ZACC 2; 2011 (3) SA 1 (CC); 2011 (5) BCLR 505 (CC).
9 *Residents of Joe Slovo Community, Western Cape v Thubelisha Homes and Others* [2011] ZACC 8; 2011 (7) BCLR 723 (CC).
10 *Moloi and Others v Minister of Justice and Constitutional Development and Others* [2010] ZACC 2; 2010 (2) SACR 78 (CC); 2010 (5) BCLR 497 (CC).
11 *Albutt v Centre for the Study of Violence and Reconciliation and Others* [2010] ZACC 4; 2010 (3) SA 293 (CC); 2010 (5) BCLR 391 (CC), which deals specifically with whether the President is required, prior to the exercise of the power to grant pardon, to afford the victims of the offences a hearing; and *Chonco and Others v President of the Republic of South Africa* [2010] ZACC 7; 2010 (6) BCLR 511 (CC).
12 In the Magistrates' Courts Act 32 of 1944.
13 *Malachi v Cape Dance Academy International (Pty) Ltd and Others* [2010] ZACC 13; 2010 (6) SA 1 (CC); 2010 (11) BCLR 1116 (CC).
14 Dangerous Weapons Act (Transkei) 71 of 1968.
15 *S v Thunzi and Another* [2010] ZACC 12; 2011 (3) BCLR 281 (CC); and *S v Thunzi and Another* [2010] ZACC 27.
16 *S v S* [2011] ZACC 7; 2011 (2) SACR 88 (CC); 2011 (7) BCLR 740 (CC).
17 *Van Vuuren v Minister of Correctional Services and Others* [2010] ZACC 17; 2010 (12) BCLR 1233 (CC); 2012 (1) SACR 103 (CC).
18 *S v Marais* [2010] ZACC 16; 2011 (1) SA 502 (CC); 2010 (12) BCLR 1223 (CC).
19 *Poverty Alleviation Network and Others v President of the Republic of South Africa* [2010] ZACC 5; 2010 (6) BCLR 520 (CC); and *Moutse Demarcation Forum and Others v President of the Republic of South Africa and Others* [2011] ZACC 27; 2011 (11) BCLR 1158 (CC).
20 *International Trade Administration Commission v SCAW South Africa (Pty) Ltd* [2010] ZACC 6; 2012 (4) SA 618 (CC); 2010 (5) BCLR 457 (CC).
21 Communal Land Rights Act 11 of 2004 (CLARA).
22 *Tongoane and Others v National Minister of Agriculture and Land Affairs and Others* [2010] ZACC 10; 2010 (6) SA 214 (CC); 2010 (8) BCLR 741 (CC).

NOTES: CHAPTER 21

23 *City of Johannesburg Metropolitan Municipality v Gauteng Development Tribunal and Others* [2010] ZACC 11; 2010 (6) SA 182 (CC); 2010 (9) BCLR 859 (CC),
24 *Stuttafords Stores (Pty) Ltd and Others v Salt of the Earth Creations (Pty) Ltd* [2010] ZACC 14; 2011 (1) SA 267 (CC); 2010 (11) BCLR 1134 (CC).
25 *Bernert v Absa Bank Ltd* [2010] ZACC 28; 2011 (3) SA 92 (CC); 2011 (4) BCLR 329 (CC).
26 *De Lacy and Another v South African Post Office* [2011] ZACC 17; 2011 (9) BCLR 905 (CC).
27 The prescription principle in law is primarily regulated in South Africa by the Prescription Act 68 of 1969 but is also provided for by other Acts of parliament regulating specific areas. It is designed to bring timeous finality to disputes relating to debt.
28 *Road Accident Fund and Another v Mdeyide* [2010] ZACC 18; 2011 (2) SA 26 (CC); 2011 (1) BCLR 1 (CC).
29 *Law Society of South Africa and Others v Minister of Transport and Another* [2010] ZACC 25; 2011 (1) SA 400 (CC); 2011 (2) BCLR 150 (CC).
30 *Mankayi v AngloGold Ashanti Ltd* [2011] ZACC 3; 2011 (3) SA 237 (CC); 2011 (5) BCLR 453 (CC).
31 *Camps Bay Ratepayers and Residents Association and Another v Harrison and Another* [2010] ZACC 19; 2011 (4) SA 42 (CC); 2011 (2) BCLR 121 (CC).
32 *Offit Enterprises (Pty) Ltd and Another v Coega Development Corporation (Pty) Ltd and Others* [2010] ZACC 20; 2011 (1) SA 293 (CC); 2011 (2) BCLR 189 (CC).
33 *Viking Pony Africa Pumps (Pty) Ltd t/a Tricom Africa v Hidro-Tech Systems (Pty) Ltd and Another* [2010] ZACC 21; 2011 (1) SA 327 (CC); 2011 (2) BCLR 207 (CC); and *Viking Pony Africa Pumps (Pty) Ltd t/a Tricom Africa v Hydro-Tech Systems (Pty) Ltd and Another* [2011] ZACC 5; 2011 (6) BCLR 646 (CC).
34 *Bengwenyama Minerals (Pty) Ltd and Others v Genorah Resources (Pty) Ltd and Others* [2010] ZACC 26; 2011 (4) SA 113 (CC); 2011 (3) BCLR 229 (CC).
35 *The Citizen 1978 (Pty) Ltd and Others v McBride* [2011] ZACC 11; 2011 (4) SA 191 (CC); 2011 (8) BCLR 816 (CC).
36 *Le Roux and Others v Dey* [2011] ZACC 4; 2011 (3) SA 274 (CC); 2011 (6) BCLR 577 (CC).
37 National Credit Act 34 of 2005.
38 *Cherangani Trade & Invest 107 (Pty) Ltd v Mason and Others* [2011] ZACC 12; 2011 (11) BCLR 1123 (CC).
39 *Pheko and Others v Ekurhuleni Metropolitan Municipality* [2011] ZACC 34; 2012 (2) SA 598 (CC); 2012 (4) BCLR 388 (CC); *Occupiers of Portion R25 of the Farm Mooiplaats 355 JR v Golden Thread Ltd and Others* [2011] ZACC 35; 2012 (2) SA 337 (CC); 2012 (4) BCLR 372 (CC); *Occupiers of Skurweplaas 353 JR v PPC Aggregate Quarries (Pty) Ltd and Others* [2011] ZACC 36; 2012 (4) BCLR 382 (CC); and *City of Johannesburg Metropolitan Municipality v Blue Moonlight Properties 39 (Pty) Ltd and Another (CC)* [2011] ZACC 33; 2012 (2) SA 104 (CC); 2012 (2) BCLR 150 (CC).
40 *Gundwana v Steko Development CC and Others* [2011] ZACC 14; 2011 (3) SA 608 (CC); 2011 (8) BCLR 792 (CC).

NOTES: CHAPTER 21

41 *Electoral Commission of the Republic of South Africa v Inkatha Freedom Party* [2011] ZACC 16; 2011 (9) BCLR 943 (CC).
42 *Governing Body of the Juma Musjid School and Others v Essay N.O. and Others* [2011] ZACC 13; 2011 (8) BCLR 761 (CC).
43 Labour Relations Act 66 of 1995.
44 *South African Police Service v Police and Prisons Civil Rights Union and Another* [2011] ZACC 21; 2011 (6) SA 1 (CC); 2011 (9) BCLR 992 (CC).
45 *Aviation Union of South Africa and Another v SAA (Pty) Ltd and Others* [2011] ZACC 31; 2012 (1) SA 321 (CC); 2012 (2) BCLR 117 (CC).
46 *F v Minister of Safety and Security and Another* [2011] ZACC 37; 2012 (1) SA 536 (CC); 2012 (3) BCLR 244 (CC).
47 Prevention of Organised Crime Act 121 of 1998.
48 *Naidoo and Others v National Director of Public Prosecutions and Another* [2011] ZACC 24; 2012 (1) SACR 358 (CC); 2011 (12) BCLR 1239 (CC).
49 Promotion of Access to Information Act 2 of 2000.
50 *President of the Republic of South Africa and Others v M & G* [2011] ZACC 32; 2012 (2) SA 50 (CC); 2012 (2) BCLR 181 (CC).
51 *Everfresh Market Virginia (Pty) Ltd v Shoprite Checkers (Pty) Ltd* [2011] ZACC 38; 2012 (1) SA 256 (CC); 2012 (3) BCLR 219 (CC).
52 *Premier: Limpopo Province v Speaker: Limpopo Provincial Legislature and Others* [2011] ZACC 25; 2011 (6) SA 396 (CC); 2011 (11) BCLR 1181 (CC).
53 *Haffejee NO and Others v eThekwini Municipality and Others* [2011] ZACC 28; 2011 (6) SA 134 (CC); 2011 (12) BCLR 1225 (CC). In terms of section 25(2) of the Constitution.
54 Prevention of Organised Crime Act 121 of 1998, and the International Criminal Matters Act 75 of 1996 (ICCMA).
55 *Falk and Another v National Director of Public Prosecutions* [2011] ZACC 26; 2012 (1) SACR 265 (CC); 2011 (11) BCLR 1134 (CC).
56 The National Prosecuting Authority Amendment Act 56 of 2008 and the South African Police Service Amendment Act 57 of 2008.
57 *Glenister v President of the Republic of South Africa and Others* [2011] ZACC 6; 2011 (3) SA 347 (CC); 2011 (7) BCLR 651 (CC).
58 The Judicial Commission of Inquiry into Allegations of State Capture, Corruption and Fraud in the Public Sector including Organs of State, known as the Zondo Commission of Inquiry into State Capture, was formally appointed on 25 January 2018 to investigate matters of public and national interest concerning allegations of state capture, corruption and fraud.
59 *Helen Suzman Foundation v President of the Republic of South Africa and Others; Glenister v President of the Republic of South Africa and Others* [2014] ZACC 32; 2015 (2) SA 1 (CC); 2015 (1) BCLR 1 (CC).

60 *Justice Alliance of South Africa v President of Republic of South Africa and Others, Freedom Under Law v President of Republic of South Africa and Others, Centre for Applied Legal Studies and Another v President of Republic of South Africa and Others* [2011] ZACC 23; 2011 (5) SA 388 (CC); 2011 (10) BCLR 1017 (CC).

MOGOENG COURT

22 BANISHING THE ELEPHANT

1 Section 167(1) of the Constitution.

2 Section 167(2) of the Constitution.

3 Section 174(3) of the Constitution.

4 Section 178(7) of the Constitution.

23 HARMONY AND TURBULENCE

1 Section 167(1) of the Constitution.

2 The Code of Judicial Conduct, adopted in terms of section 12 of the Judicial Service Commission Act 9 of 1994, expressly states that a judge must uphold independence of mind in the performance of judicial duties.

3 The office of the chief justice was established as a national department by proclamation by the president in the *Government Gazette* (GN 335500) on 23 August 2010. Its objectives include ensuring the chief justice can properly execute his or her mandate as head of the Constitutional Court and the judiciary; enhancing the institutional, administrative and financial independence of the office of the chief justice; and improving organisational governance and accountability, and the effective and efficient use of resources.

4 Section 2 of the Judges' Remuneration and Conditions of Employment Act 47 of 2001 stipulates that the annual salary and benefits of judges is determined by the president by notice in the *Government Gazette*, after taking into account the recommendations made by the Independent Commission for the Remuneration of Public Office Bearers. The commission, when investigating salaries and benefits, must consult with, among others, the chief justice.

5 Section 165(6) of the Constitution, which was added by the Constitution Seventeenth Amendment Act, 2012, stipulates that the chief justice is the head of the judiciary and exercises responsibility over the establishment and monitoring of norms and standards for the exercise of the judicial functions of all courts.

6 Section 8(2) of the Superior Courts Act 10 of 2013 reiterates that the chief justice, as the head of the judiciary, exercises responsibility over the establishment and monitoring of norms and standards for the exercise of the judicial functions of all courts.

NOTES: CHAPTERS 23 AND 24

7 Justice Moseneke acted as chief justice from 1 November 2013 to 31 March 2014.
8 The court, and the judiciary as a whole, was continually accused of judicial overreach and an alleged disregard for the doctrine of separation of powers. Some also alleged a partiality against the ruling party and the government of the day. Similar to allegations against the court during Langa CJ's term, summarised by Justice Van der Westhuizen in his article titled 'A few reflections on the role of courts, government, the legal profession, universities, the media and civil society in a constitutional democracy', the court was criticised for allegedly avoiding issues on which judicial guidance would be welcomed. It was also criticised for avoiding substantive issues by dismissing matters on procedural grounds. Strong academic critique continued against the court for alleged judicial failures to advance transformative justice, particularly regarding socio-economic rights. On this, Justice Van der Westhuizen notes:

'Much of the criticism may certainly have merit and must be taken into account. The world of the judge is, however, not always the world of the scholar, philosopher or artist, no matter how much some of us – including myself – would like it to be a little more open than it is. Philosophers (to use a broad term) have to ask questions. Judges have to provide answers to questions brought before them by litigants. No matter how much I as a judge may hope that, for example, certain socio-economic issues be brought to court, we cannot go and look for them.'

9 Section 210(b) of the Constitution read with section 7(1) of the Intelligence Services Oversight Act 40 of 1994.
10 See 'Chief Justice Speaks Out about Sex Smear', *Mail & Guardian*, 11 June 2015. Available at https://mg.co.za/article/2015-06-11-chief-justice-speaks-out-about-sex-smear/.

24 CHALLENGING THE COURTS

1 Section 34 of the Constitution.
2 The charges related to the alleged murder of Mr Tefo Ramogibe, the husband of Mr Mdluli's former lover, in February 1999.
3 These charges related to the alleged unlawful utilisation of funds from the Secret Service Account for personal benefit.
4 *Freedom Under Law v National Director of Public Prosecutions and Others* [2013] ZAGPPHC 271; 2014 (1) SA 254 (GNP).
5 The Supreme Court of Appeal reversed the high court's order, setting aside the decision to withdraw the murder and related charges. Therefore, the withdrawal of those charges stood. *National Director of Public Prosecutions and Others v Freedom Under Law* [2014] ZASCA 58; 2014 (4) SA 298 (SCA).
6 Mdluli was found guilty of intimidation, kidnapping and assault.
7 The Commission of Inquiry into Allegations of Fraud, Corruption, Impropriety or Irregularity in the Strategic Defence Procurement Package, known as the Arms Procurement Commission or the Seriti Commission, would be chaired by Justice

NOTES: CHAPTER 24

Seriti, with Justice Hendrick Mmolli Thekiso Musi and Justice Francis Malesela Legodi as his co-commissioners. Justice Legodi resigned from the commission in 2013. The President decided that the commission would continue with only two judges. The terms of reference were published on 4 November 2011; these outlined that the commission should inquire into the rationale for the deal; whether the equipment acquired was used; whether job opportunities and offsets anticipated to flow from the deal materialised; whether any person improperly influenced the award or conclusion of any contracts awarded in the procurement process; and whether any contract concluded pursuant to the procurement process was tainted by any fraud or corruption capable of proof, such as to justify its cancellation and the ramifications of such cancellation.

8 Two non-governmental organisations, Corruption Watch and Right2Know, filed an application to review and set aside the findings of the Seriti Commission due to its failure properly to investigate the allegations of fraud and corruption.]

9 *S v Selebi* [2010] ZAGPJHC 53 and *S v Selebi (Judgment on sentence)* [2010] ZAGPJHC 58.

10 *Selebi v S* [2011] ZASCA 249; 2012 (1) SA 487 (SCA).

11 The decision to suspend Julius Malema was first taken on 10 November 2011. The suspension was upheld on appeal in 2012.

12 The Economic Freedom Fighters launched in Marikana, in the North West province, on 13 October 2013. Its founding manifesto described it as:

'a radical and militant economic emancipation movement that brings together revolutionary, fearless, radical, and militant activists, workers' movements, non-governmental organisations, community-based organisations and lobby groups under the umbrella of pursuing the struggle for emancipation. The [Economic Freedom Fighters] is a radical, leftist, anti-capitalist and anti-imperialist movement with an internationalist outlook anchored by popular grassroots formations and struggles. The [Economic Freedom Fighters] will be the vanguard of community and workers' struggles and will always be on the side of the people. The [Economic Freedom Fighters] will, with determination and consistency, associate with the protest movement in South Africa and will also join in struggles that defy unjust laws.'

13 The conflict related to an unprotected strike that the miners at Lonmin platinum mine had embarked on in protest for higher wages. In addition to the 34 people killed on 16 August, ten others were killed in incidents related to the strike in the four days preceding the massacre.

14 The terms of reference of the Marikana Commission of Inquiry were published on 12 September 2012. It mandated the commission to investigate matters of public, national and international concern arising out of the tragic incidents at the Lonmin Mine in Marikana, which took place from 11 August to 16 August. In particular, the commission was asked to investigate the conduct of Lonmin; the conduct of the South African Police Service; the conduct of the Association of Mineworkers and Construction Union (AMCU), their members and their officials; the conduct of the National Union of Mineworkers (NUM), its members and its officials; the role played by the department

NOTES: CHAPTER 24

of mineral resources or any other government department or agency in relation to the incidents, whether it was appropriate in the circumstances, and consistent with their duties and obligations in terms of the law; and the conduct of individuals and loose groupings in fomenting or otherwise promoting a situation of conflict and confrontation which may have given rise to the tragic incident, whether directly or indirectly.

15 Settlements for damages relating to loss of support were, as of 2018, in the process of finalisation as offers of compensation from the state were being considered by the families of the slain miners. Damages for pain and suffering and constitutional damages were not yet settled.

16 The Commission submitted its report on 31 March 2015. It was released to the public on 25 June 2015.

17 The president established a board of inquiry in terms of section 9(1) of the South African Police Service Act 68 of 1995 on 21 September 2015. The board was convened to investigate allegations of misconduct against the national commissioner, Ms Mangwashi Victoria Phiyega, and into her fitness to hold office and her capacity for executing her official duties efficiently and lawfully. In particular, the board had to make findings relating to whether she misled the Farlam Commission; she, in taking a decision to implement a tactical option, ought reasonably to have foreseen the tragic events of the Marikana massacre; whether a report prepared for the President by her and a media statement subsequently issued were deliberately amended to conceal material facts about the deaths of striking miners; and whether her overall testimony at the commission was in keeping with her office, among other things. Justice Neels Claassen was appointed as chair of the board, together with Adv Vusi Khuzwayo and Adv Anusha Rawjee.

18 In December 2016, the board found that Ms Riah Phiyega failed to exercise discretion judiciously when endorsing the decision to disarm, disperse and arrest the protesters and that her conduct in amending a media statement to conceal material facts constituted serious misconduct and a breach of her duty to manage and control the police in an honest and transparent manner. It recommended that she should be dismissed as unfit for the position of national commissioner of police. In January 2017, Riah Phiyega filed an application in the court to review and set aside the Claassen Inquiry's findings.

19 The Ginwala Commission was established following the suspension of Adv Vusi Pikoli from office as the national director of public prosecutions by President Thabo Mbeki on 23 September 2007. It was asked to investigate and determine the fitness of Adv Pikoli to hold office. Mr Simelane presented the government's submissions to the Ginwala Commission and gave evidence under oath before it. The Ginwala Commission's report strongly criticised the approach taken by Mr Simelane in making the government's submissions and also the credibility of his evidence. Following the Ginwala report, the Public Service Commission (PSC) investigated Mr Simelane's conduct during the commission and recommended disciplinary action against him arising from his conduct before the commission. The minister of justice rejected these recommendations and the president subsequently appointed Mr Simelane as head of the NPA.

NOTES: CHAPTER 24

20 *Democratic Alliance v President of South Africa and Others* [2012] ZACC 24; 2013 (1) SA 248 (CC); 2012 (12) BCLR 1297 (CC).

21 *Democratic Alliance v President of South Africa and Others* at para 49.

22 This was followed by a notice that President Zuma was considering suspending Mr Nxasana and requested him to give representations why he should not be suspended. Subsequent correspondence ensued parallel to the inquiry processes, which eventually led to a settlement agreement between the parties.

23 *Corruption Watch NPC and Others v President of the Republic of South Africa and Others; Nxasana v Corruption Watch NPC and Others* [2018] ZACC 23; 2018 (10) BCLR 1179 (CC); 2018 (2) SACR 442 (CC). The high court judgment preceding the judgment of the Constitutional Court is cited as *Corruption Watch (RF) NPC v President of the Republic of South Africa* [2017] ZAGPPHC 743; [2018] 1 All SA 471 (GP); 2018 (1) SACR 317 (GP).

24 *Corruption Watch NPC and Others v President of the Republic of South Africa and Others; Nxasana v Corruption Watch NPC and Others* (Constitutional Court judgment) at para 87.

25 *Corruption Watch NPC and Others v President of the Republic of South Africa and Others; Nxasana v Corruption Watch NPC and Others* (Constitutional Court judgment) at para 25.

26 *Corruption Watch NPC and Others v President of the Republic of South Africa and Others; Nxasana v Corruption Watch NPC and Others* (Constitutional Court judgment) at para 88.

27 *Corruption Watch NPC and Others v President of the Republic of South Africa and Others; Nxasana v Corruption Watch NPC and Others* (Constitutional Court judgment) at para 88.

28 The report compiled by the minister of police exonerated President Zuma from liability. The National Assembly set up two ad hoc committees to examine the public protector's report as well as other reports, including the one concluded by the police minister. The ad hoc committee dealing with the minister's report fully endorsed it. The National Assembly resolved to absolve President Zuma from liability.

29 *Economic Freedom Fighters v Speaker of the National Assembly and Others; Democratic Alliance v Speaker of the National Assembly and Others* [2016] ZACC 11; 2016 (3) SA 580 (CC); 2016 (5) BCLR 618 (CC)

30 *Allpay Consolidated Investment Holdings (Pty) Ltd and Others v Chief Executive Officer of the South African Social Security Agency and Others (No 1)* [2013] ZACC 42; 2014 (1) SA 604 (CC); 2014 (1) BCLR 1 (CC).

31 *Allpay Consolidated Investment Holdings (Pty) Ltd and Others v Chief Executive Officer of the South African Social Security Agency and Others (No 2)* [2014] ZACC 12; 2014 (4) SA 179 (CC); 2014 (6) BCLR 641 (CC).

32 *Allpay Consolidated Investment Holdings (Pty) Ltd and Others v Chief Executive Officer of the South African Social Security Agency and Others (No 3)* [2015] ZACC 7; 2015 (6) BCLR 653 (CC); *Black Sash Trust v Minister of Social Development and Others (Freedom Under Law NPC Intervening)* [2017] ZACC 8; 2017 (3) SA 335 (CC); 2017 (5) BCLR 543 (CC);

NOTES: CHAPTER 24

Black Sash Trust v Minister of Social Development and Others (Freedom Under Law NPC Intervening) [2017] ZACC 20; 2017 (9) BCLR 1089 (CC); *South African Social Security Agency and Another v Minister of Social Development and Others* [2018] ZACC 26; 2018 (10) BCLR 1291 (CC); and *Black Sash Trust v Minister of Social Development and Others (Freedom Under Law Intervening)* [2018] ZACC 36; 2018 (12) BCLR 1472 (CC).

33 *Zuma v Democratic Alliance and Others* [2014] ZASCA 101; [2014] All SA 35 (SCA)

34 *Democratic Alliance v Speaker of the National Assembly and Others* [2016] ZACC 8; 2016 (3) SA 487 (CC); 2016 (5) BCLR 577 (CC).

35 *Oriani-Ambrosini, MP v Sisulu, MP Speaker of the National Assembly* [2012] ZACC 27; 2012 (6) SA 588 (CC); 2013 (1) BCLR 14 (CC).

36 *Mazibuko v Sisulu and Another* [2013] ZACC 28; 2016 (6) SA 249 (CC); 2013 (11) BCLR 1297 (CC).

37 *Ramakatsa and Others v Magashule and Others* [2012] ZACC 31; 2013 (2) BCLR 202 (CC).

38 South Africa hosted the 25th African Union Summit in Johannesburg between 7 and 15 June 2015 under the theme '2015 Year of Women's Empowerment and Development towards Africa's Agenda 2063'.

39 Reasons for the order were provided on 24 June 2015 in *Southern Africa Litigation Centre v Minister of Justice and Constitutional Development and Others* [2015] ZAGPPHC 402; 2015 (5) SA 1 (GP).

40 The ICC held a hearing to make a decision concerning the non-compliance by South Africa with the request by the ICC for the arrest and surrender of al-Bashir. The majority decision of the ICC is recorded as ICC: Pre-Trial Chamber II, The Prosecutor v. Omar Hassan Ahmad al-Bashir, 'Decision under article 87(7) of the Rome Statute on the non-compliance by South Africa with the request by the Court for the arrest and surrender of Omar al-Bashir', 6 July 2017.

41 *Minister of Justice and Constitutional Development and Others v Southern African Litigation Centre and Others* [2016] ZASCA 17; 2016 (3) SA 317 (SCA).

42 *Democratic Alliance v Acting National Director of Public Prosecutions and Others* [2016] ZAGPPHC 255; 2016 (2) SACR 1 (GP).

43 *Zuma v Democratic Alliance and Others; Acting National Director of Public Prosecutions and Another v Democratic Alliance and Another* [2017] ZASCA 146; 2018 (1) SA 200 (SCA).

44 In January 2018, former President Jacob Zuma made fresh representations to the NPA on why he should not be indicted on criminal charges in connection with the controversial arms deal. The national director of public prosecutions decided in March 2018 that he will be prosecuted on sixteen charges of corruption, money laundering and racketeering. The case was set to commence in November that year, but it was postponed after Zuma's legal team applied for a permanent stay of prosecution. In May 2019, the high court in Pietermaritzburg, KwaZulu-Natal, heard arguments on whether it should grant the permanent stay of prosecution.

NOTES: CHAPTER 25

25 JURISPRUDENCE AMID EXECUTIVE HOSTILITIES

1 *Raduvha v Minister of Safety and Security and Another* [2016] ZACC 24; 2016 (2) SACR 540 (CC); 2016 (10) BCLR 1326 (CC); *Teddy Bear Clinic for Abused Children and Another v Minister of Justice and Constitutional Development and Another* [2013] ZACC 35; 2014 (2) SA 168 (CC); 2013 (12) BCLR 1429 (CC); *Children's Institute v Presiding Officer of the Children's Court, District of Krugersdorp and Others* [2012] ZACC 25; 2013 (2) SA 620 (CC); 2013 (1) BCLR 1 (CC); *Van der Burg and Another v National Director of Public Prosecutions* [2012] ZACC 12; 2012 (2) SACR 331 (CC); 2012 (8) BCLR 881 (CC); and *C and Others v Department of Health and Social Development, Gauteng and Others* [2012] ZACC 1; 2012 (2) SA 208 (CC); 2012 (4) BCLR 329 (CC).

2 *Rural Maintenance (Pty) Limited and Another v Maluti-A-Phofung Local Municipality* [2016] ZACC 37; 2017 (1) BCLR 64 (CC); (2017) 38 ILJ 295 (CC); *Solidarity and Others v Department of Correctional Services and Others* [2016] ZACC 18; 2016 (5) SA 594 (CC); 2016 (10) BCLR 1349 (CC); *Transport and Allied Workers Union of South Africa obo Ngedle and Others v Unitrans Fuel and Chemical (Pty) Ltd* [2016] ZACC 28; 2016 (11) BCLR 1140 (CC); (2016) 37 ILJ 2485 (CC); *Transport and Allied Workers Union of South Africa v PUTCO Limited* [2016] ZACC 7; (2016) 4 SA 39 (CC); 2016 (7) BCLR 858 (CC); *Steenkamp and Others v Edcon Limited* [2016] ZACC 1; 2016 (3) SA 251 (CC); 2016 (3) BCLR 311 (CC); *Toyota SA Motors (Pty) Ltd v CCMA and Others* [2015] ZACC 40; 2016 (3) BCLR 374 (CC); (2016) 37 ILJ 313 (CC); *F & J Electrical CC v MEWUSA obo E Mashatola and Others* [2015] ZACC 3; 2015 (4) BCLR; (2015) 36 ILJ 1189 (CC); *National Union of Metal Workers of South Africa v Intervalve (Pty) Ltd and Others* [2014] ZACC 35; 2015 (2) BCLR 182 (CC); (2015) 36 ILJ 363 (CC); *National Union of Public Service & Allied Workers obo Mani and Others v National Lotteries Board* [2014] ZACC 10; 2014 (3) SA 544 (CC); 2014 (6) BCLR 663 (CC); *Food and Allied Workers Union v Ngcobo N.O. and Another* [2013] ZACC 36; 2014 (1) SA 32 (CC); 2013 (12) BCLR 1343 (CC); *South African Transport and Allied Workers Union (SATAWU) and Others v Moloto NO and Another* [2012] ZACC 19; 2012 (6) SA 249 (CC); 2012 (11) BCLR 1177 (CC); and *South African Transport and Allied Workers Union and Another v Garvas and Others* [2012] ZACC 13; 2013 (1) SA 83 (CC); 2012 (8) BCLR 840 (CC).

3 *Federation of Governing Bodies for South African Schools (FEDSAS) v Minister of the Executive Council for Education, Gauteng and Another* [2016] ZACC 14; 2016 (4) SA 546 (CC); 2016 (8) BCLR 1050 (CC); *MEC for Education in Gauteng Province and Other v Governing Body of Rivonia Primary School and Others* [2013] ZACC 34; 2013 (6) SA 582 (CC); 2013 (12) BCLR 1365 (CC); and *Head of Department, Department of Education, Free State Province v Welkom High School and Another; Head of Department, Department of Education, Free State Province v Harmony High School and Another* [2013] ZACC 25; 2014 (2) SA 228 (CC); 2013 (9) BCLR 989 (CC).

4 *Competition Commission of South Africa v Pioneer Hi-Bred International Inc and Others* [2013] ZACC 50; 2014 (2) SA 480 (CC); 2014 (3) BCLR 251 (CC); *Competition Commission v Loungefoam (Pty) Ltd and Others* [2012] ZACC 15; 2012 (9) BCLR 907 (CC); *Competition Commission v Yara South Africa (Pty) Ltd and Others* [2012] ZACC

NOTES: CHAPTER 25

14; 2012 (9) BCLR 923 (CC); and *Competition Commission of South Africa v Senwes Ltd* [2012] ZACC 6; 2012 (7) BCLR 667 (CC).

5 *Turnbull-Jackson v Hibiscus Court Municipality and Others* [2014] ZACC 24; 2014 (6) SA 592 (CC); 2014 (11) BCLR 1310 (CC); *South African Informal Traders Forum and Others v City of Johannesburg and Others; South African National Traders Retail Association v City of Johannesburg and Others* [2014] ZACC 8; 2014 (4) SA 371 (CC); 2014 (6) BCLR 726 (CC); *Minister of Local Government, Environmental Affairs and Development Planning of the Western Cape v Lagoonbay Lifestyle Estate (Pty) Ltd and Others* [2013] ZACC 39; 2014 (1) SA 521 (CC); 2014 (2) BCLR 182 (CC); *Britannia Beach Estate (Pty) Ltd and Others v Saldanha Bay Municipality* [2013] ZACC 30; 2013 (11) BCLR 1217 (CC); *Rademan v Moqhaka Local Municipality and Others* [2013] ZACC 11; 2013 (4) SA 225 (CC); 2013 (7) BCLR 791 (CC); and *Camps Bay Ratepayers and Residents Association and Another v Harrison and Another* [2012] ZACC 17; 2012 (11) BCLR 1143 (CC).

6 *Provincial Minister for Local Government, Environmental Affairs and Development Planning, Western Cape v Municipal Council of the Oudtshoorn Municipality and Others* [2015] ZACC 24; 2015 (6) SA 115 (CC); 2015 (10) BCLR 1187 (CC); *Minister of Police and Others v Premier of the Western Cape and Others* [2013] ZACC 33; 2014 (1) SA 1 (CC); 2013 (12) BCLR 1365 (CC); *eThekwini Municipality v Ingonyama Trust* [2013] ZACC 7; 2014 (3) SA 240 (CC); 2013 (5) BCLR 497 (CC); *MEC for Local Government, Environmental Affairs and Development Planning, Western Cape Province: In re Minister for Mineral Resources and Swartland Municipality and Others and Maccsand (Pty) Ltd and The City of Cape Town and Others* [2012] ZACC 10; 2012 (9) BCLR 947 (CC); *Premier: Limpopo Province v Speaker of the Limpopo Provincial Legislature and Others* [2012] ZACC 3; 2012 (4) SA 58 (CC); 2012 (6) BCLR 583 (CC).

7 *Land Access Movement of South Africa and Others v Chairperson of the National Council of Provinces and Others* [2016] ZACC 22; 2016 (5) SA 635 (CC); 2016 (10) BCLR 1277 (CC); *Klaase and Another v Van der Merwe N.O. and Others* [2016] ZACC 17; 2016 (6) SA 131 (CC); 2016 (9) BCLR 1187 (CC); *Bakgatla-Ba-Kgafela Communal Property Association v Bakgatla-Ba-Kgafela Tribal Authority and Others* [2015] ZACC 25; 2015 (6) SA 32 (CC); 2015 (10) BCLR 1139 (CC); *Sarrahwitz v Marits N.O. and Another* [2015] ZACC 14; 2015 (4) SA 491 (CC); 2015 (8) BCLR 925 (CC); *Arun Property Development (Pty) Ltd v City of Cape Town* [2014] ZACC 37; 2015 (2) SA 584 (CC); 2015 (3) BCLR 243 (CC); *Country Cloud Trading CC v MEC, Department of Infrastructure Development, Gauteng* [2014] ZACC 28; 2015 (1) SA 1 (CC); 2014 (12) BCLR 1397 (CC); *Malan v City of Cape Town* [2014] ZACC 25; 2014 (6) SA 315 (CC); 2014 (11) BCLR 1265 (CC); *Florence v Government of the Republic of South Africa* [2014] ZACC 22; 2014 (6) SA 456 (CC); 2014 (10) BCLR 1137 (CC); *Kwalindile Community v King Sabata Dalindyebo Municipality and Others; Zimbane Community v King Sabata Dalindyebo Municipality and Others* [2013] ZACC 6; 2013 (6) SA 193 (CC); 2013 (5) BCLR 531 (CC); *Hattingh and Others v Juta* [2013] ZACC 5; 2013 (3) SA 275 (CC); 2013 (5) BCLR 509 (CC); *Motswagae and Others v Rustenburg Local Municipality and Another* [2013] ZACC 1; 2013 (2) SA 613 (CC); 2013 (3) BCLR 271 (CC); and *Occupiers of Saratoga Avenue v City of Johannesburg Metropolitan Municipality and*

NOTES: CHAPTER 25

Another [2012] ZACC 9; 2012 (9) BCLR 951 (CC).

8 *Absa Bank Limited v Moore and Another* [2016] ZACC 34; 2017 (1) SA 255 (CC); 2017 (2) BCLR 131 (CC); *Baliso v Firstrand Bank Limited t/a Westbank* [2016] ZACC 23; 2017 (1) SA 292 (CC); 2016 (10) BCLR 1253 (CC); *Nkata v Firstrand Bank Ltd and Others* [2016] ZACC 12; 2016 (4) SA 257 (CC); 2016 (6) BCLR 794 (CC); *South African Reserve Bank and Another v Shuttleworth and Another* [2015] ZACC 17; 2015 (5) SA 146 (CC); 2015 (8) BCLR 959 (CC); *Chevron SA (Pty) Limited v Wilson t/a Wilson's Transport and Others* [2015] ZACC 15; 2015 (10) BCLR 1158 (CC); *Paulsen and Another v Slip Knot Investments 777 (Pty) Limited* [2015] ZACC 5; 2015 (3) SA 479 (CC); 2015 (5) BCLR 509 (CC); *Stopforth Swanepoel & Brewis Incorporated v Royal Anthem Investments 129 (Pty) Ltd and Others* [2014] ZACC 39; 2015 (2) SA 539 (CC); 2014 (12) BCLR 1465 (CC); *Cool Ideas 1186 CC v Hubbard and Another* [2014] ZACC 16; 2014 (4) SA 474 (CC); 2014 (8) BCLR 869 (CC); *Kubyana v Standard Bank of South Africa Ltd* [2014] ZACC 1; 2014 (3) SA 56 (CC); 2014 (4) BCLR 400 (CC); *Ferris and Another v Firstrand Bank Limited and Another* [2013] ZACC 46; 2014 (3) SA 39 (CC); 2014 (3) BCLR 321 (CC); *National Credit Regulator v Opperman and Others* [2012] ZACC 29; 2013 (2) SA 1 (CC); 2013 (2) BCLR 170 (CC); *Sebola and Another v Standard Bank of South Africa Ltd and Another* [2012] ZACC 11; 2012 (5) SA 142 (CC); 2012 (8) BCLR 785 (CC); and *Wiese v Government Employees Pension Fund and Others* [2012] ZACC 5; 2012 (6) BCLR 599 (CC).

9 *Bapedi Marota Mamone v Commission on Traditional Leadership Disputes and Claims and Others* [2014] ZACC 36; 2015 (3) BCLR 268 (CC); *Nxumalo v President of the Republic of South Africa and Others* [2014] ZACC 27; 2014 (12) BCLR 1457 (CC); *Sigcau v President of the Republic of South Africa and Others* [2013] ZACC 18; 2013 (9) BCLR 1091 (CC); and *Pilane and Another v Pilane and Another* [2013] ZACC 3; 2013 (4) BCLR 431 (CC).

10 *Dengetenge Holdings (Pty) Ltd v Southern Sphere Mining and Development Company Ltd and Others* [2013] ZACC 48; 2014 (5) SA 138 (CC); 2014 (3) BCLR 265 (CC); *Minister of Mineral Resources and Others v Sishen Iron Ore Company (Pty) Ltd and Another* [2013] ZACC 45; 2014 (2) SA 603 (CC); 2014 (2) BCLR 212 (CC); *Agri South Africa v Minister for Minerals and Energy* [2013] ZACC 9; 2013 (4) SA 1 (CC); 2013 (7) BCLR 727 (CC); and *Minister for Mineral Resources v Swartland Municipality and Others* [2012] 2012 (7) BCLR 712 (CC).

11 *National Commissioner of the South African Police Service v Southern African Human Rights Litigation Centre and Another* [2014] ZACC 30; 2015 (1) SA 315 (CC); 2014 (12) BCLR 1428 (CC).

12 *Mighty Solutions CC t/a Orlando Service Station v Engen Petroleum Ltd and Another* [2015] ZACC 34; 2016 (1) SA 621 (CC); 2016 (1) BCLR 28 (CC); *Paulsen and Another v Slip Knot Investments 777 (Pty) Limited* [2015] ZACC 5; 2015 (3) SA 479 (CC); 2015 (5) BCLR 509 (CC); *Loureiro and Others v Imvula Quality Protection (Pty) Ltd* [2014] ZACC 4; 2014 (3) SA 394 (CC); 2014 (5) BCLR 511 (CC); and *Government of the Republic of Zimbabwe v Fick and Others* [2013] ZACC 22; 2013 (5) SA 325 (CC); 2013 (10) BCLR 1103 (CC).

13 *Solidarity and Others v Department of Correctional Services and Others* [2016] ZACC

NOTES: CHAPTER 25

18; 2016 (5) SA 594 (CC); 2016 (10) BCLR 1349 (CC); and *South African Police Service v Solidarity obo Barnard* [2014] ZACC 23; 2014 (6) SA 123 (CC); 2014 (10) BCLR 1195 (CC).

14 *National Treasury and Others v Opposition to Urban Tolling Alliance and Others* [2012] ZACC 18; 2012 (6) SA 223 (CC); 2012 (11) BCLR 1148 (CC).

15 On the main review application, the Supreme Court of Appeal held in *Opposition to Urban Tolling Alliance and Others v The South African National Roads Agency Ltd and Others* [2013] ZASCA 148; [2013] 4 All SA 639 (SCA), that the 180-day time limit provided by legislation to review an administrative decision could not be extended. The review was out of time and therefore failed.

16 28 of 2002.

17 *Agri South Africa v Minister for Minerals and Energy* [2013] ZACC 9; 2013 (4) SA 1 (CC); 2013 (7) BCLR 727 (CC) (*Agri South Africa*) at para 25.

18 *Agri South Africa* at para 2.

19 The narrow issue was whether the commencement of the Act resulted in deprivation or expropriation in terms of section 25 of the Constitution for a holder of an unused old-order right who failed to apply for a permit to mine during the specified one-year period after the statute came into effect. The majority held that the Act did have the effect of depriving the holder of mineral rights, but that deprivation did not rise to the level of expropriation.

20 *Lee v Minister of Correctional Services* [2012] ZACC 30; 2013 (2) SA 144 (CC); 2013 (2) BCLR 129 (CC); 2013 (1) SACR 213 (CC) at paras 6 and 8.

21 The majority judgment was penned by Justice Nkabinde and supported by Moseneke DCJ, Froneman J, Jafta J and Van der Westhuizen J, while Justice Cameron wrote the minority judgment, with Mogoeng CJ, Khampepe J and Skweyiya J concurring.

22 *Association of Regional Magistrates of Southern Africa v President of the Republic of South Africa and Others* [2013] ZACC 13; 2013 (7) BCLR 762 (CC).

23 *Mukaddam v Pioneer Foods (Pty) Ltd and Others* [2013] ZACC 23; 2013 (5) SA 89 (CC); 2013 (10) BCLR 1135 (CC).

24 The Treaty of the Southern African Development Community (1993) 32 ILM 116 (Treaty) was signed on 17 August 1992 in Namibia and came into force on 30 September 1993. Zimbabwe ratified the treaty on 17 November 1992 and South Africa became a member state to the treaty in August 1994. The tribunal was established by the treaty, and its composition, powers, functions and procedures were provided for in the Protocol on the Tribunal in the Southern African Development Community (Tribunal Protocol), which was adopted in August 2001. However, the tribunal did not become operational as the Tribunal Protocol did not receive the required number of ratifications to come into effect. Recognising the importance of the tribunal to achieve the objects of the treaty, the Summit of the Southern African Development Community – which has the power to amend the treaty if adopted by three-quarters of its member states – amended the treaty to remove the ratification requirement and incorporate the Tribunal Protocol into the treaty. The tribunal could therefore become functional in 2001.

25 *Government of the Republic of Zimbabwe v Fick and Others* [2013] ZACC 22; 2013 (5) SA 325 (CC); 2013 (10) BCLR 1103 (CC).

26 The Summit of Heads of State, the supreme organ of SADC, resolved to suspend the operations of the tribunal by failing to reappoint sitting members to the tribunal whose term of office had expired. This had the effect of incapacitating the tribunal as it no longer had enough members to form a quorum. In 2014, the government of South Africa, through its president, together with other member states, adopted the Protocol on the Tribunal in the Southern African Development Community, which had the effect of formally stripping the tribunal of its jurisdiction over disputes of individuals against member states. The Law Society and six other individuals who owned land in Zimbabwe approached the high court in South Africa to challenge the president's decision to suspend the operations of the tribunal and to sign the Protocol divesting the tribunal of jurisdiction over individuals' disputes. The actions were challenged on the grounds that they were unlawful, irrational and unconstitutional. On 11 December 2018, the Constitutional Court upheld the claim that the president's actions in representing South Africa were unconstitutional, unlawful and irrational. The president was directed to withdraw his signature from the 2014 Protocol (*Law Society of South Africa and Others v President of the Republic of South Africa and Other* [2018] ZACC 51; 2019 (3) SA 30 (CC); 2019 (3) BCLR 329 (CC)).

27 *Magidiwana and Others v President of the Republic of South Africa and Others* [2013] ZACC 27; 2013 (11) BCLR 1251 (CC) at para 3.

28 *Magidiwana and Others* at paras 15-6.

29 The review of Legal Aid's failure to provide the miners with state-funded legal representation later came before the Constitutional Court in *Legal Aid South Africa v Magidiwana and Others* [2015] ZACC 28; 2015 (6) SA 494 (CC); 2015 (11) BCLR 1346 (CC). The court dismissed the application for leave to appeal as the dispute was moot and it was not in the interests of justice to entertain the matter.

30 I believe in time Legal Aid South Africa reached a funding agreement with the representatives of the miners.

31 *Southern Africa Litigation Centre v Minister of Justice and Constitutional Development and Others* [2015] ZAGPPHC 402; 2015 (5) SA 1 (GP).

32 *Democratic Alliance and Others v Acting National Director of Public Prosecutions and Others* 2013 (3) SA 486 (SCA); *Democratic Alliance v Acting National Director of Public Prosecutions and Others* [2013] ZAGPPHC 242; [2013] 4 All SA 610 (GNP); and *Zuma v Democratic Alliance and Others* [2014] ZASCA 101; [2014] 4 All SA 35 (SCA).

26 FINAL SITTING

1 *Federation of Governing Bodies for South African Schools (FEDSAS) v Member of the Executive Council for Education, Gauteng and Another* [2016] ZACC 14; 2016 (4) SA 546 (CC); 2016 (8) BCLR 1050 (CC) at paras 1-4.

Index

Index arrangement is word by word.
DM indicates Dikgang Moseneke; and
CJ chief justice.

Abrahams, Shaun 245
access to information *see* rights, to information
Ackermann, Laurie 72, 79, 85
advocates (barristers) 12–13, 15, 43
Africa Cup of Nations (1996) 92
African Charter on Human and Peoples' Rights (Banjul Charter) 46, 311 n6.2
African National Congress (ANC) 116, 137, 145–46, 147, 249
African Peer Review Mechanism 47
African Union (AU) 45, 46–47, 52, 249, 312 n6.3–4
age of consent 186
Agri South Africa 255
Al-Bashir, Omar 249, 262, 323 n14.4, 343 n24.40
Alexkor 131
amnesty and reparation 111–14, 192, 211
Andrews, Penny 291
apartheid 11–12, 17, 62–63
appeal, right of *see* rights, to appeal or review
arbitration 189

arms deal 242, 339 n24.7–8, *see also* Zuma, Jacob, and arms deal corruption
Association of Regional Magistrates of Southern Africa 256–57
attorneys (solicitors) 12, 13–14, 43
Azanian People's Organisation 113

Bader Ginsburg, Ruth 293
bail 98
Basson, Wouter 133–34
Berrangé, Vernon 15
Bhagwati, Prafullachandra Natwarlal 84, 315 n11.1
Bizos, George 15, 57, 246
Black Administration Act 132–33
Black Lawyers Association (BLA) 31, 55, 56, 311 n4.4
Botha, *Mr* 39
Botha, Chris 35
bread producers 257
Breyer, Stephen 293
Browde, Jules 15
Buthelezi, Mangosuthu 73

Cameron, Edwin
as advocate 15
at Constitutional Court 194–95, 213, 233
and DM 211

INDEX

capital punishment *see* death penalty
Carling Black Label 130
Carruthers & Co. (legal firm) 14, 308 n2.6
Cash Paymaster Services 247
Cele, Bheki 242
Chaskalson, Arthur
  as advocate 15
  at Constitutional Court 71, 72, 73, 74, 80, 85, 93, 96, 105, 123, 125, 134, 138, 310 n3.4
  and DM 21, 22–23, 32, 56, 303
  and interim Constitution 94
  and Judicial Observer Mission to Zimbabwe 48
  memorial service 289
  and swearing-in of state president 65, 137
Chidyausiku, Godfrey 49
chief justice and deputy 31, 122–23, 138, 139, 204, 205–06, 214–15, 219–21, 224, 231–32, 235, 327 n16.5, 338 n23.3, 338 n23.5–6
Chigovera, Andrew Ranganayi 49
Chikane, Moses 99
children 7, 41, 131, 188, 192, 209, 253
Chinamasa, Patrick 49
Cillié, Petrus 4
Civil Co-operation Bureau (CCB) 133
Commission for Conciliation, Mediation and Arbitration (CCMA) 188–89, 333 n19.41
Commission of Inquiry into the Arms Deal (Seriti) 242, 339 n24.7–8
Commission of Inquiry into State Capture (Zondo) 214, 337 n21.58
commissions of inquiry 325 n15.11
common purpose 120–21
Commuter Corporation 132
compensation for expropriation 186, 212
Competition Commission 257
confessions 97–98
confiscation of property *see* forfeiture of assets
constituent assembly 103

Constitution
  final 103, 104–105, 323 n14.7
  interim 103, 112
  supremacy of 62, 64, 68
Constitutional Court
  appointments to and composition of 71–72, 73, 74–75, 79–80, 86, 127–28, 138–40, 207, 194–95, 206, 219
  attacks on 237, 251, 339 n23.8
  certification of Constitution 103–4, 316 n12.17, 317 n13.1
  culture of 83–86, 230–31, 233, 304–05
  digital access 88–90
  founding of and early years 71, 72–73, 93, 94, 115
  judgments 86, 87–88, 89, 120, 122–25, 127, 129, 199, 204, 230, 235
  jurisprudence 96, 115, 119, 129–30, 139–40, 180–81, 208
  law clerks and researchers 86–87, 227
  and leave to appeal applications 118, 127, 182–83, 235, 252
  name and powers of 64–65, 67–68, 94–96, 102, 103
  reputation and status 104, 250, 260
  site and buildings 78–79, 80–82, 93–94, 314 n10.3
  workload and routine 118–20
contracts 212, 247
Convention for a Democratic South Africa (CODESA) 61, 312 n8.1
convictions 41–42, 99
Corbett, Michael 19, 71, 73
corporal punishment 98
corruption 214, 242, 243
Cotler, *Professor* 293
courts
  apartheid 62–63
  appeal *see* Supreme Court of Appeal
  competition appeal 253
  constitutional *see* Constitutional Court
  district 313 n8.4–5
  divorce 41

high 66–67, 84, 95, 102, 128, 189,
    313 n8.6–7
labour 189, 253
magistrates' 66, 102, 311 n5.4
motion 40–41
and political cases 251–52, 261, *see also*
    judicial trespass
powers of 68
precedent system 206–7, 335 n21.5
quarterly roster 37–38, 42–43
regional 66, 313 n8.5
resources of 260–61
specialised 313 n8.8
Crawford-Browne, Terry 242
criminal justice *see* law, criminal

damages 184, 210, 282–84, 332 n19.15
death penalty 36, 39, 73, 92, 96–97, 104,
    181–82, 314 n9.3, 315 n12.4
debtors 98, 131, 191, 209, 210
deceased estates 22
defamation 211
Democratic Alliance (DA) 247–48, 262–63
detention without trial 99
Didcott, John Mowbray 72, 76
Directorate for Priority Crime
    Investigation (Hawks) 213–14
Directorate of Special Operations
    (Scorpions) 143, 203, 213

Economic Freedom Fighters (EFF) 243,
    247, 248, 340 n24.12
education 267–69, 291
elections 52–53, 54, *see also* South Africa,
    elections
Electoral Supervisory Commission
    (Zimbabwe) 49, 51, 312 n6.5
electricity 191–92
Eloff, Frederik (Frikkie) 18, 19, 24, 310 n3.2
essential services 211–12
extradition 253

fairness and the law 98–99, 102, 172, 182,
    187, 209, 210, 227
Farlam, Ian 15, 128, 243
#FeesMustFall 291
First, Ruth 290
Fischer, Bram Louis 289
floor-crossing 107
forfeiture of assets 187, 211
Froneman, Johan 206, 237, 238
fronting 211

Gaddafi, Muammar 198
gambling 187
Gauntlett, Jeremy 15
gender equality 130–31, 133, 190
Ghana 137, 327 n16.2
Ginwala Commission 244, 341 n24.19
Goldstone, Richard 72, 79, 123, 313 n9.1
Govender, Jay 237
Grobler, Lesley 232
Gumbi, Mojanku 23, 24, 138, 310 n3.6
Gware, P 49

habeas corpus 67
Hani, Thembisile Chris 92, 315 n12.3
Harms, Louis 150
Helen Suzman Foundation 214
Higginbotham, A Leon 76
HIV/AIDS 117, 195
Hlophe, Mandlakayise John 151–53, 154–55,
    157–58, 159–79
housing
    evictions 190–91, 211
    service charges 131–32
Hulley, Michael 143
human rights violations 111, 112, 114–15

immigration regulations 131
Independent Commission against
    Corruption (Mauritius) 144
Independent Commission for the
    Remuneration of Public Office
    Bearers 195–96
information *see* rights to information

INDEX

inheritance 184–86
insurance claims 126–27, 183–84
intelligence services 192–93, 237
International Criminal Court (ICC) 249, 293, 343 n24.40
International Defence and Aid Fund 14, 308 n2.5

Jafta, Chris
  at Constitutional Court 206, 257
  and Hlophe complaint 152, 153–54, 155, 157, 158, 159, 160–62, 164–65, 166, 167, 168–69, 170–74, 175, 178–79
Jordan, Pallo 19–20
judges
  acting 17–18, 27, 36
  African 288
  apartheid-era 6, 14–15, 17
  attacks on 145, 147, 199, 262, 263–65
  European 287, 324 n15.4
  misconduct complaints 40–41, 151–79
  national conference (2009) 196–97, 198
  partiality and recusal of 166, 210, 233–34, 261–62, 269–70, 286–87, 288, 310 n4.1, 338 n23.2
  post-apartheid 24–27, 29–31, 56, 63–64, 71
  retired and non-active 128, 273, 293–94, 325 n15.8
  status and conduct 55, 84, 101–02
  terms of office and remuneration 195, 314 n9.2, 325 n15.7, 334 n20.1, 338 n23.4
  United States 287–88, 324 n15.5–6
  workload 285–86
Judicial Conduct Committee (JCC) 40, 264, 311 n5.3, 330 n18.12
Judicial Observer Mission to Zimbabwe 48–52, 109, 139
Judicial Service Commission (JSC) 30–31, 32, 57, 138–39, 151, 152–53, 154–55, 163, 164, 167, 170, 179, 194, 203, 214, 219, 220, 221–24, 225, 231, 310 n4.2
judicial trespass 261, 265, 339 n23.8

jurisprudence 207

Kaunda, Lakela 227
Kentridge, Sydney 15, 95–96, 313 n9.1
Khampepe, Sisi 25, 48, 49, 52, 53, 139, 204, 206
Khoza, Bongani 38, 119
Kriegler, Johann Christiaan 15, 55, 72, 77–78, 79, 119
Kroon, Frank 152
Kruger, Stephanus Johannes Paulus (Paul) 310 n3.3
Kunene, Zoli 99
Kuny, Denis 15
KwaZulu-Natal 106–7

land
  development 209–10
  expropriation 131, 186
  rights 131, 209, 253
Langa, Beauty 196
Langa, Pius Nkonzo
  as CJ 134, 138, 139, 141, 147, 150, 229, 174, 181, 199–200
  at Constitutional Court 72, 73, 74, 85, 124, 127, 143, 180, 194
  and DM 139–140, 146, 198–99
  health, retirement and death 196, 200, 289
  and Hlophe complaint 152, 154, 155–67, 168, 169, 179, 199
  and National Association of Democratic Lawyers 327 n16.6
language policy 192
Laugh It Off Promotions 130
law
  commercial 7, 253
  common 6–7, 8, 65, 94, 104, 105, 183–88, 253
  constitutional 65, 94, 104–05
  criminal 97
  indigenous and customary 6, 65, 104, 132–33, 190

INDEX

labour 188–89, 209, 211–12, 253
purpose of 7
reports 44, 207
Roman-Dutch 5, 7
study and qualifications for 5, 7
Law Society of Zimbabwe 49
lawyers
  academic 75
  black 12, *see also* Black Lawyers
    Association
Lee, Dudley 255–56
Legal Aid South Africa 41, 259,
  348 n25.29–30
legal cases
  Alexkor 131
  Azanian People's Organisation 113–14
  Barkhuizen 126, 183–84
  Basson 133–34, 142
  *Bhe and Others v Khayelitsha Magistrate
    and Others* 132–33
  Chirwa 189
  De Reuck 131
  Du Toit v Minister of Transport 131, 186
  Eisenberg 131
  E-tolls 253–54
  Fourie 131, 184
  Geldenhuys 186
  Glenister 213–14
  Gory 185–86
  Gumede 185
  Hassam 184–85
  Hoërskool Ermelo 192
  J and Another 131
  Jaftha v Schoeman 131
  Joseph 191–92
  K 132
  Laugh It Off 130
  Liquor Bill 108
  Magajane 187
  Mazibuko 191
  Minister of Finance v Van Heerden 129
  Minister of Home Affairs v NICRO 132
  *Mkontwana v Nelson Mandela
    Metropolitan Municipality* 131–32
  Mohunram 187
  Njongi 191
  *President of the Republic of South Africa
    v Hugo* 108
  *President of the Republic of South Africa
    and Others v SA Rugby Football Union
    and Others* 166
  Rail Commuters Action Group 132
  Richter 187
  S v Sefatsa 121
  Satchwell 130–31
  Shilubana 190
  Sibiya 181–82
  Sidumo 188–89
  State v Makwanyane 73, 96–97, 104, 181,
    314 n9.3, 316 n12.16
  State v Mhlungu 95–96
  Steenkamp 184
  Thebus v S 120, 121–22, 123, 124
  Treatment Action Campaign 116–18, 142
  United Democratic Front 107
  Van der Merwe 185
  Volks v Robinson 133
legal costs and fees 13–14, 192, 212, 252
legal judgments 43–44, 88, 142, 207–8, *see
  also* Constitutional Court, judgments
legal privilege 153, 158, 159, 160, 165, 172, 177
legal representation 98
legal system digitisation 90
legislature 109–10, 247–49, 318 n13.20
Life Esidimeni Commission of Inquiry
  (Moseneke) 273–78, 279–82, 283–84
life partnerships 133
liquor licences 108
local government 130, 190–92, 211, 253
Local Organising Committee of the
  Commonwealth Magistrates and
  Judges Association 175
Lovell Banks, Taunya 291
Luyt, Louis 110

Mabiletsa, 'Sgoob' 15

INDEX

Machel, Graça 246
Madala, Tholakele Hope (Tholi)
  career 310 n3.1
  at Constitutional Court 72, 124–25, 194
  and DM 119
  and Hlophe complaint 152, 173, 174
  as Transkei judge 17
Madlanga, Mbuyiseli 245
Madonsela, Thuli 246, 250
Maduna, Penuell 57
Magidiwana, Mzoxolo 259–60
magisterial districts 313 n8.4
magistrates 256–57
Mahlangu, Qedani 277, 278, 279, 280
Mahlangu-Nkabinde, Gwen 253
Mahlmann, Matthias 292
Mahomed, Ismail
  as advocate 15
  career 309 n2.8
  at Constitutional Court 72, 73, 113–14
  and DM 23
  as judge 17, 19
  at Supreme Court of Appeal 75, 314 n9.4
  swearing-in of president 65
Mailula, Lucy 25
Maisels, Issy 15
Makgoba, Malegapuru 275
Makhura, David 273
Malachi, Tatiana 210–11
Malema, Julius 243, 247, 340 n24.11
Maleka, Vincent 22
Maluleke, Seriti & Moseneke (legal firm) 24
Manamela, Makgabo 277
Mandela, Nelson
  death 246
  and DM 20, 23, 290, 303
  on education 268
  and judiciary 72, 93–94
  as president 45, 69–70, 71, 91, 92, 110, 116
Mantashe, Gwede 148
Marathon Project *see* mental health care

Marikana Commission of Inquiry (Farlam) 243–44, 259–60, 340 n24.14, 341 n24.15–16, 348 n25.29–30
Marikana massacre (2012) 243, 259, 340 n24.13
Marivate, CTD 57
marriage *see also* life partnerships
  African indigenous 6–7
  in community of property 185
  customary 6–7, 185
  Hindu and Muslim 6–7, 184–85
  same-sex 131, 184, 185–86
Martin Gibbs (photography) 35
Masemola, Jafta Kgalabi 290
Mashikwane, Rrakgadi (DM's aunt) 3
Masipa, Thokozile 25
Maya, Mandisa 25
Mazibuko, Lindiwe 248–49
Mbeki, Govan 290
Mbeki, Thabo
  and DM 20, 21, 34, 77, 139, 196, 303
  and HIV/AIDS 117
  and Jacob Zuma 141, 148, 149
  and judiciary 24, 81
  as president 45, 46, 65, 116, 137, 138, 141, 142, 146, 148, 149
  and Zimbabwe 48, 49
McDougall, Gay J. 291, 309 n2.7
McKenzie, Karen 294
Mdluli, Richard 241, 339 n24.2–3
mental health care 275–81, 283
Metrorail 132
Mhlantla, Nonkosi 25
Michelman, Frank 291
Mineral and Petroleum Resources Development Act (2008) 254, 255, 347 n25.19
mining 211, 253, 254–55
miscarriage of justice 99–101
Mkhwebane, Busisiwe 250
Mlambo, Dunstan 249, 262, 291
Mlambo-Ngcuka, Phumzile 142
Moerane, Marumo 23, 32

INDEX

Mogoba, Stanley Mmutlanyane 290
Mogoeng, Mogoeng
 as CJ 214, 221–23, 225–26, 227–28,
  229–30, 232–33, 234, 235, 236–37, 248,
  251, 304
 at Constitutional Court 206
 lectures 262
Mojapelo, Phineas 32
Mokgokong, Anna 195
Mokgoro, Yvonne
 at Constitutional Court 72, 75, 127, 129,
  196, 200
 and DM 204
 and Hlophe complaint 152, 157, 158, 159,
  160
Molaudzi, Thembekile 100, 101, 317 n12.29
Moroka, Kgomotso 32
Moseneke, Botshelo (DM's son) 92–93, 303
Moseneke, Dikgang Ernest
Early life
 career ambitions 3, 5
 on Robben Island 3, 5, 8, 197, 301–02
 as a Scout 57
 studies 5, 8
 trial of 4–5, 11, 18, 121
Lawyer
 admission as attorney 9, 23–24, 43, 302
 as advocate *see* at Pretoria Bar
 before Constitutional Court 73–74
 and fees 14
 and lawyers' associations 31, 327 n16.6
 political cases 14, 76, 302
 at Pretoria Bar 9, 10, 11, 12, 18, 24, 37, 111,
  302–03
 as senior counsel *see* at Pretoria Bar
Business person
 at Nail and Metropolitan Life 20, 23
 as Telkom chair 19–20, 23, 92
Judicial career
 acting CJ 236
 acting judge 18–19, 22–23, 24, 27–28
 at Constitutional Court 19, 55–57, 77,
  79, 119, 120, 121, 124, 126–27, 128–29,
  198–99, 213, 227, 266, 303
 deputy CJ 138–40, 141, 204–05, 219,
  220–25, 226–28, 229, 232, 235–36
 and Hlophe complaint 152, 158, 159, 161,
  162, 163, 164, 165, 168, 169, 174, 179, 199
 and Independent Commission for
  the Remuneration of Public Office
  Bearers 195
 and intelligence report 237–39
 as judge 21, 31–33, 34–36, 37–38, 55, 146,
  289
 and Judicial Observer Mission to
  Zimbabwe 48–52, 53, 109, 139
 and Lesotho facilitation team 294
 and Life Esidimeni Commission of
  Inquiry 270, 273–74, 279, 281, 283–84,
  294
 retirement 87, 266–70, 299–305
 and Sri Lanka constitutional reform 294
Public and community work
 and Independent Electoral Commission
  (IEC) 78
 and interim Constitution 21, 24, 94
 and Nelson Mandela Children's Fund 78
 and Project Literacy 78
General
 awards and honours 295
 family life 304
 and golf 286
 and Jacob Zuma 197–98, 220, 226,
  227–28
 and law schools 290–91
 Morogoro pilgrimage xiii–xvi
 sixtieth birthday 146, 303
 speeches, lectures and publications 200,
  262, 289–93, 299–305
 travel 291–93, 294
Moseneke, Kabonina Naomi (née
 Mashianoke, DM's wife) 23, 36, 92, 197,
 292, 294, 295
Moseneke, Karabo Mabel (née Makhaza,
 DM's mother) 303
Moseneke, Malatsi (DM's brother) 99

INDEX

Moseneke, Samuel John Sedise (DM's father) 21–22
Moseneke, Sedise (DM's son) 92–93
Moseneke, Tiego (DM's brother) 99
Motlana, Nthato 20
Motlanthe, Kgalema 146, 149, 194, 195, 196
Motsuenyane, Samuel 48
Movement for Democratic Change (MDC) 47, 49, 50, 53–54
Mpshe, Mokotedi Joseph 148, 150
Msimang, Herbert 144
Mudede, Tobaiwa 49
Mukaddam, Imraahn Ismail 258
municipalities *see* local government
Mxenge, Griffiths and Victoria 197, 289

Naidoo, Jay 20
National Assembly *see* legislature
National Association of Democratic Lawyers 74
National Prosecuting Authority (NPA) 115, 203, 241, 244–45, 247, 249–50
national security 193
Ndlovu, Lot 290
Neethling, Johann 32
Netshitenzhe, Joel 291
Nevirapine 117
New Africa Investment Limited (Nail) 20–21
New Partnership for Africa's Development (NEPAD) 47, 48
Ngcobo, Sandile
  as CJ 199, 204–05, 214–15, 227–28
  at Constitutional Court 76, 129, 143, 213
  and DM 79, 80, 119, 126, 127
  and Hlophe complaint 152, 173–74, 175
Ngcuka, Bulelani 142
Ngoepe, Bernard Makgabo 23–24, 32, 34, 48, 56, 94, 143
Nhleko, Nathi 246
Nicholson, Chris 148, 149–50
Nkabinde, Bess
  career as judge 25
  at Constitutional Court 233, 255–56
  and Hlophe complaint 152, 153–54, 155, 157–59, 160, 161, 162, 164–65, 166, 167, 168–69, 170, 174, 175–79
Nkandla 246–47, 342 n24.28
Nokwe, Philemon Pearce Dumasile (Duma) 15, 309 n2.9
notices of motion 38–39, 40
Nxasana, Mxolisi 244–45, 342 n24.22
Nxasana, Sizwe 20

Obama, Barack and Michelle 292
occupational injury 210
Old Fort Prison (Johannesburg) 80–81
Old Synagogue (Pretoria) 307 n1.1
Olympic Games (Atlanta, 1996) 92–93
Omar, Dullah 73, 80
Opposition to Urban Tolling Alliance (OUTA) 253
O'Regan, Kate
  at Constitutional Court 72, 75, 127, 196, 200
  and Hlophe complaint 152, 158, 159, 165, 168, 172
  at Oxford University 292
Organisation of African Unity (OAU) 45–46
overseas voters 187

Palace of Justice (Pretoria) 18, 24
Palacia, Pilar 293
Pan Africanist Congress of Azania (PAC) xv, 4, 92
pardon and reprieve 108
parliament *see* legislature
parody 130
parole 209
pensions 129
Phiyega, Mangwashi Victoria (Riah) 244, 341 n24.17–18
Phosa, Mathews 146–47
Pikoli, Vusi 142, 148, 341 n24.19
Pillay, Navanethem (Navi) 25

356

INDEX

Pistorius, Oscar 291
Pitje, Godfrey Mokgonane 289
political parties 252
Pollsmoor prison 255–56
pornography 73–74, 131
positivism 63
prescription 191, 210, 336 n21.27
Pretoria Bar 9, 12, 13, 15–16, 24, 79, 111
prisoners
    awaiting trial 188, 255
    convicted 132
privacy *see* rights, to privacy
proportionality 189–90, 292, 316 n12.16
prospecting licences 211
provinces 106–08, 192, 209, 212, 318 n13.9, 318 n13.11
Public Protector 246–47, 250
public service 278–80

race 253
Radebe, Faith 237, 239
Radebe, Jeff 203, 215, 236
rail passenger safety 132
Ramaphosa, Matamela Cyril xiii, xiv, 20, 240, 245, 294
rape 132, 143–44, 187–88, 212
Rawulinga, Joe 175
res judicata 100–01
restraint orders 212
Richtersveld 131
rights
    to appeal or review 102, 118, 182, 187
    of children 7, 188, 209, 253
    to information 212
    land *see* land, rights
    to privacy 187
    to religious and cultural practice 189–90
    to remain silent 122
    socio-economic 190–92, 303
Road Accident Fund 185
road tolls 253–54
Roberts, *Chief Justice* (USA) 293

Rugby World Cup (1995) 92
Rwanda 91, 315 n12.2

Sachs, Albie 72, 127, 129, 130, 152, 196, 200
Sandler, Jonty 20
Sangoni, Themba 246
Satchwell, Kathy 25
schools 189–90, 192, 211, 253, 269
Schreiner, Oliver Deneys 289
Schrider, Geraldine 175
search and seizure 143, 151, 153, 156, 187
Selebano, Tiego Ephraim 277, 278, 280
Selebi, Jackie 242
Seligson, Milton 32
senior counsel 10–11, 14, 29
sentences 209
separation of powers 109, 110
Seriti, Legoabe Willie 175, 242
Seriti Commission *see* Commission of Inquiry into the Arms Deal
Shaik, Schabir 128, 141–42, 144–45
Sharpeville massacre (1960) 243, 315 n10.5
Sharpeville Six 121, 323 n14.14–15
Shiceka, Sicelo 243
Sifuba, Theo 175
Simelane, Menzi 244, 341 n24.19
Sisulu, Zwelakhe 20, 99, 302
Skweyiya, Sayo 197
Skweyiya, Thembile Lewis
    as advocate 15, 76
    career 309 n2.10
    at Constitutional Court 79, 80, 233
    and DM 197, 204, 289
    and Hlophe complaint 152
Sobukwe, Robert Mangaliso 289–90
social grants 191, 247
Solomon Mahlangu Freedom College (SOMAFCO, Mazimbu, Tanzania) xiii, xv
South Africa
    elections 116, 150, 187, 211
    federalism and centralisation 105–06
    socio-economic conditions 70–71

South African Council of Churches 14, 308 n2.4
South African National Roads Agency Limited (SANRAL) 253–54
South African Observer Mission to Zimbabwe Elections 48, 49
South African Police Service (SAPS) 132, 188, 212, 213, 241, 242, 247–48
South African Rugby Football Union (SARFU) 110
South African Social Security Agency (SASSA) 247
Southern Africa Project of the Lawyers' Committee for Civil Rights under Law 14, 309 n2.7
Southern African Catholic Bishops' Conference 14, 308 n2.3
Southern African Development Community (SADC) 258–59, 294, 347 n25.24, 348 n25.26
Southern African Legal Information Institute (SAFLII) 208
spy tapes 247, 262–63
Squires, Hillary 128, 141
Sri Lanka 294
stare decisis see courts, precedent system
state of the nation address (SONA) 247
state president
 motion of no confidence 248–49
 and pardons 209
 powers 108–09, 110–11
 recall of 148–49
 swearing in 69–70, 137–38, 150
 terms of office 146
Storey, Peter 290
Supreme Court of Appeal 31, 65, 67, 95, 102, 128, 149–50, 205–06, 247, 262
Surty, Enver 203, 334 n21.1
Suzman, Helen 290

Tambo, Oliver Reginald xv, 290
Telkom 20
Thales International Africa Ltd 144

Theron, Leona 25
Thint (company) 143, 144, 153, 156, 157, 158, 159, 160, 161, 172, 173, 177
Thugwane, Josia 92, 93
trademarks 130
traditional leadership 190, 253
Transkei 209
Treatment Action Campaign (TAC) 116–17, 323 n14.9
Truth and Reconciliation Commission (TRC) 112–13, 115, 192
Tshabalala-Msimang, Manto 117
Tshwane High Court 35–36
tuberculosis (TB) 255–56

Ubuntu 281
Unterhalter, Jack 15
urban development and planning 211, 253

Van der Walt, Piet 24
Van der Westhuizen, Johann
 as judge 25–26
 at Constitutional Court 79, 80, 233
 and DM 204, 211
 and Hlophe complaint 152
 and intelligence report 237, 238, 239
Van Dijkhorst, Kees 44
Variawa, Joe 99
vicarious liability 183, 212
Vodacom 20
Vundla, Mfundi 137
Vundla, Peter 137, 146

water 191
Western Cape 107, 109, 317 n13.6, 318 n13.11–12
Wilson, Andrew 15

Yacoob, Zakeria Mohammed (Zak)
 as advocate 15, 309 n2.11
 at Constitutional Court 75, 80, 233, 234–35, 244
 and DM 75–76, 79, 119, 204, 211

INDEX

and Hlophe complaint 152

Zimbabwe 47–52, 53–54, 109, 253, 258
Zimbabwe African National Union-
    Patriotic Front (ZANU-PF) 47–48,
    49, 50, 53
Zondo Commission *see* Commission of
    Inquiry into State Capture
Zuma, Jacob
    and arms deal corruption 141–43, 144,
        148, 149, 150, 151, 152, 153, 156, 157,
        158, 159–60, 161, 165, 172, 173, 177, 178,
        247, 249–50, 263, 343 n24.44, *see also*
        Shaik, Schabir; spy tapes
    as deputy state president 116, 138
    and DM 197–98, 220, 226, 227–28
    elected ANC president 145–46
    and judiciary 196, 206, 214–15, 221, 222,
        229, 236, 237, 256–57, 262, 263
    and Nkandla 246–47
    and rape charge 143–44
    as state president 150, 203, 240, 241,
        242–43, 244–45